Baedeker

GW00746333

Florida

www.baedeker.com

Verlag Karl Baedeker

SIGHTSEEING HIGHLIGHTS ✶✶

»Fun in the Sun« - one of the many slogans used by advertisers to attract attention to the »Sunshine State«. And it's true: Nowhere in the USA does the sun shine more than in St. Petersburg, nowhere in the USA are there as many beautiful beaches as in Florida and nowhere in the USA are there as many amusement parks as in Florida. And Florida also has the oldest city in the USA!

Eldorado for shell collectors
the beaches of Sanibel & Captiva

Pulsating nightlife
on Ocean Drive in Miami Beach

16 Pensacola

©Baedeker

15 Tallahassee

14 Amelia Island

13 St Augustine

12 Cape Canaveral
• Kennedy Space Center

10 Walt Disney World   11 Orlando

9 Tampa

8 St Petersburg

7 Sarasota

6 Palm Beach

5 Sanibel & Captiva Islands

2 Miami Beach
1 Miami
3 Everglades Nat. Park

4 Key West

8 ✳✳ St. Petersburg
America's sunniest city is now appreciated by young people, as it has been for decades by pensioners. ▶ page 314

9 ✳✳ Tampa
The port city on Tampa Bay with the charmingly restored Ybor City presents itself as young, dynamic, but also tradition conscious. ▶ page 342

10 ✳✳ Walt Disney World
Mickey Mouse and friends, as well as the latest high-tech attractions, have both young and old spellbound. ▶ page 351

11 ✳✳ Orlando
Mega-parks like Universal Studios, Sea-World etc. attract guests from all over the world. ▶ page 273

12 ✳✳ Cape Canaveral Kennedy Space Center
Do not miss the US space port! ▶ page 141

13 ✳✳ St. Augustine
The oldest city in the USA is proud of its colonial heritage. ▶ page 305

14 ✳✳ Amelia Island
The island has beautiful beaches and an interesting history. ▶ page 132

15 ✳✳ Tallahassee
Florida's capital has the atmosphere of the Deep South. ▶ page 335

16 ✳✳ Pensacola
The attraction here is a restored old town and great beaches. ▶ page 298

BAEDEKER'S BEST TIPS

We've collected the most interesting of the numerous Baedeker tips in this book, so that you can enjoy what Florida and its peninsula have to offer!

🔣 For mystery buffs
Experience Agatha Christie's *Murder on the Orient Express* in Florida on the Murder Mystery Train. Anyone who would like a train ride guaranteed to make the spine tingle should contact the Seminole Gulf railway. ▶ **page 105**

🔣 Cheap bus rides
Florida is easy to explore on a Greyhound bus. The Greyhound AmeriPass is especially good value. ▶ **page 120**

🔣 Riding the waves
Learn how to use a surfboard in Cocoa Beach, not far from the US space port Cape Canaveral. ▶ **page 149**

🔣 Easy Rider ...
In Daytona, the city of the whining motors, there are not only fast cars but also one of the largest Harley-Davidson shops in the world. The bikes are always available for a test ride. ▶ **page 158**

🔣 Sleep under water ...
... on the Florida Keys, in the Jules' Undersea Lodge, a former underwater research station. ▶ **page 172**

🔣 Attention nighthawks!
Great live jazz every night in Fort Lauderdale at O'Hara's Pub, where you can show up in worn-out jeans.
▶ **page 180**

🔣 Bargain hunters
Designer labels (Nike, Reebok, Tommy Hilfiger etc.) at a bargain near Fort Walton Beach. ▶ **page 193**

Easy Rider
in Daytona Beach

Bird's-eye view
from a flight over Florida in a bi-plane

❚ A brilliant sunset
on the high seas on a boat chartered from
Key West.   ► page 213

❚ Fall guys
will get their money's worth at Lake
Okeechobee. Try out a tandem jump with a
professional skydiver.
► page 222

❚ Adventurous canoe trips
– maybe even with a close-up look at an
alligator – are available on the Chipola
River, which winds through the karst
landscape of northern Florida.
► page 223

❚ Tasty stone crabs
are on the menu from October to March in
the fish restaurant Joe's Stone Crab in
Miami Beach.   ► page 255

❚ Swinging from tree to tree
– like Tarzan and Jane; try it out at Juniper
Springs in the jungle-like Ocala National
Forest.   ► page 271

❚ Very good wine
is available a half hour's drive west of
Orlando at Lakeridge Winery, one of the
best of the ever-increasing number of
wineries in Florida.   ► page 284

❚ Mantas and dolphins
show up off the pier of Pensacola Beach
every evening.   ► page 302

❚ Bike along the Gulf Coast
A former railway track along the sun coast
of St Petersburg was recently converted
into a pleasant bicycle path.
► page 319

❚ Airboat into the jungle
Adventures including alligators up close
are available in Myakka River State Park
near Sarasota.   ► page 331

Tasty seafood
as served in Miami Beach

Meet an alligator
in the jungle along the Myaka River

Postmodern architecture
in Miami
► **page 57**

BACKGROUND

Sun, sand, sea ...
Holiday at Miami South Beach
► **page 75**

PRACTICALITIES

Will Spiderman get away?
Find out at Universal in Orlando
▶ **page 272**

See you later ...
... alligator!
▶ **page 166**

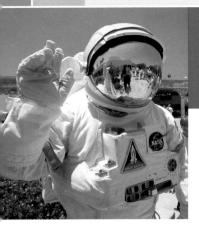

Look, look ...
*... an astronaut in
Cape Canaveral*
► **page 141**

SIGHTS FROM A to Z

Travelling by air taxi ...
... to the Florida Keys
► **page 168**

Pastel »eyebrows«
Art deco in Miami Beach
► **page 260**

Price categories

Hotels:
Luxury: from $150
Mid-range: from $80
Budget: from $30
(double room per night)

Restaurants:
Expensive: from $30
Moderate: from $15
Inexpensive: from $7
(main dish without drinks)

That's fun!
Walking through the Magic Kingdom with Mickey Mouse
► **page 351**

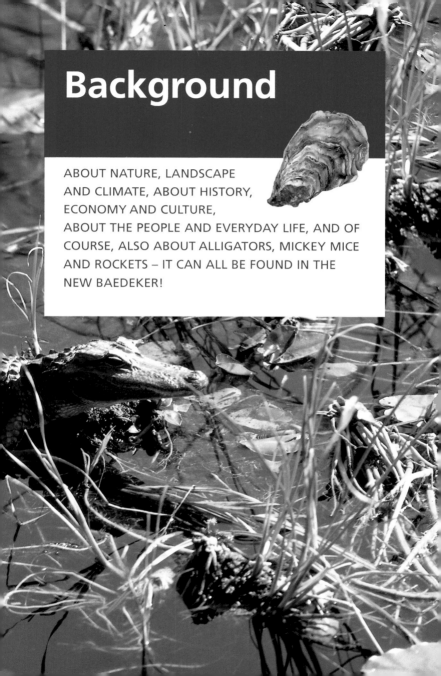

Background

ABOUT NATURE, LANDSCAPE
AND CLIMATE, ABOUT HISTORY,
ECONOMY AND CULTURE,
ABOUT THE PEOPLE AND EVERYDAY LIFE, AND OF
COURSE, ALSO ABOUT ALLIGATORS, MICKEY MICE
AND ROCKETS – IT CAN ALL BE FOUND IN THE
NEW BAEDEKER!

FUN IN THE SUN

So much to do – so little time: this phrase can be heard again and again, sighed out loud by visitors to Florida. Rightly so, as the variety of activities and entertainment on offer is overwhelming. It's impossible to see everything within a single visit! And to spend the entire holiday at the beach or in theme parks is not recommended. Florida is – of course – more than just sun, sand and Mickey Mouse.

First there was the disputed evaluation of the ballots cast during the US presidential election of 2000. Then came the terror attacks of 11 September 2001, the shock waves of which led to a fall in tourism even in Florida, which is consistently well-visited. And just when the

most important branch of the state's economy had recovered from these record-breaking losses, the summer of 2004 brought a quartet of hurricanes, Charley, Frances, Ivan and Jeanne, spreading death and destruction throughout the entire Caribbean, once again reducing the number of bookings to Florida to the levels seen after September 11th. Florida sure didn't have it easy! But despite damage running into billions – the tourist areas along the west coast were worst affected – the Sunshine State declared »business as usual« within the same year: most holiday areas, including Miami and the Florida Keys, re-

See and be seen
There's always a lot happening on the beach at Miami Beach.

mained largely untouched by the tropical storms, and in Orlando, Disney World and the others opened their doors the very next day as if nothing had happened.

True Lies

Nobody worried that the guests would stay away permanently. Who first thinks of hurricanes when Florida is mentioned? First and foremost, what comes to mind are lazy holidays beneath the palms, expeditions to see alligators in the Everglades, pink flamingos and cocktails on the beach. Ever since the cult crime series *Miami Vice*, Miami has been synonymous with suntanned bodies and pastel sunsets, and means hot nights and beautiful people at MTV awards parties. Flori-

Oranges galore
Oranges flourish in Florida thanks to the long hours of sunshine.

Southern Belles
is the only possible name for the pretty ladies in the wonderful Cypress Gardens at Lake Wales.

Spaceship Earth
is one of the trademarks of Disney World near Orlando.

Alligators ...
... even little ones are a frequent sight in Florida.

Traditional crafts
*can be seen where the Miccosukee Indians
live in the Everglades.*

Art deco architecture
in all forms is best seen in Miami Beach.

da means swimming with the dolphins just like Bud and Sandy Ricks did with Flipper, hanging out at breezy beach bars like »Papa« Hemingway, America's most famous drinker, who threw wild parties and caught swordfish in Key West, and while at it, wrote some of his best novels. And no string of clichés would be complete without mentioning Florida's – no exaggeration – gigantic theme parks, from Disney World in Orlando to the Kennedy Space Center in Cape Canaveral. Put bluntly, everyone thinks of enjoyment in tropical temperatures. The variety of amusement on offer in Florida is as massive as the cumulus clouds floating above the Keys.

Relaxed in the Here and Now

Those staying for longer will, most of all, learn to appreciate Florida's carefree lifestyle. Nowhere else on the continent does the sky seem to be so blue, the sand so soft and the heat so pleasant as it does here. It provides the best possible conditions for a tropical version of the »American way of life«, mixing freedom and free time, sand and sun, candour and optimism into a very tempting cocktail. Inevitably, it's impossible to be completely alone on the palm-fringed beaches, on the hot sand and the tropical islands. Meanwhile, 75 million visitors come to Florida each year. But the »Sunshine State« is more than just a tourists' paradise. Those in the know argue that Florida is one of the least understood areas in the USA. With up to 1,000 immigrants per day, it is still a long way away, politically and socially, from being a »complete« state.

The metropolis is growing
Hardly any other city in the USA had developed as dramatically and as dynamically as Miami Beach.

Boredom? No thanks!

It is indeed often just a frisbee-throw from the rows of bronzed sun-worshippers to an idyllic beach known only to nature lovers. Islands that are otherwise the preserve of bird watchers offer great coral reefs for snorkelling. And untouched forests, lakes and huge swamps with alligators and other primitive creatures can be found at the borders of modern cities. Anyone who gets bored in Florida, an American newspaper wrote recently, should be locked up.

Facts

What are the Everglades? Where are the mountains in Florida, and where are the coral reefs? What are the main sectors of the economy and in which regions do the most people live?

Nature

Flat Peninsula

Located on a **peninsula** between the Atlantic Ocean and the Gulf of Mexico, on the same latitude as North Africa, the »Sunshine State«« of Florida is the southernmost state in the continental USA and its south-eastern extremity. The southern tip of the peninsula **reaches all the way to the tropical belt**. It is only 145km/90 mi from Key West to Havana on the Caribbean island of Cuba, and only 100km/60 mi from Miami Beach to the Bahamas in the Atlantic. The greatest distance between north and south – from Pensacola to Key West – is 834 mi/1342km. To the north, Florida shares a border with Georgia. In the north-west, the flagpole-like extension known as the Panhandle borders the state of Alabama.

◄ Location and size

Encompassing 58,560 sq mi/151,670 sq km – about 10% larger than England– Florida ranks as the 22nd largest state in the US. The coast is 1900mi/3000km long (800mi/1280km of which is beach), and even inland, the sea is never further than 60mi/100km away.

◄ Area

The Florida Peninsula is largely flat. The highest »mountains« are the merely 100m/330ft-high **Iron Mountain near Lake Wales** and, at 113m/371ft above sea level, **Lakewood, near DeFuniak Springs** in the north-west. Only the **Panhandle** in the north-west is a gently rolling hill landscape, with a **Gulf coast** interspersed with extensive swamp areas. The **Atlantic coast**, with its shallow bayous and lagoons, is mainly protected by offshore sand banks and islands, known as the Barrier Islands. Inland, the peninsula is dotted with around 7,800 lakes.

◄ Elevation

Around 250 million years ago, at the end of the Palaeozoic Era, after the super-continent of Pangaea broke up, Florida was still a small part of Gondwana, the huge continent in the southern hemisphere. The dissolution of Gondwana, accompanied by intense volcanic activity, took place during the Mesozoic era, from 230 to 65 million years ago. Similarities in the rock structure show that the present-day south-eastern corner of the USA was once joined to West Africa. Along with the present-day Caribbean islands, Florida and the eastward-lying Bahamas were once a group of volcanic islands.

Geology at a glance

With the Tertiary period, which began around 65 million years ago, the land sank gradually into the ocean. Over this time, rivers displaced huge masses of quartz sand, marl and clay from the Appalachians to the sea, creating enormous deltas in what is now the north of Florida. To the south, the **Florida Platform** (Florida Plateau) was formed. This layer of limestone and dolomite, 3,800–5,400m/12,500–17,700ft thick, pushed the bedrock even deeper into the

◄ Tertiary period

← *Florida's swamps are best explored in an airboat.*

earth. Only in the late Tertiary period, around 20 million years ago, did an opposing force take effect: Florida was the last area of the continental USA to be pushed up above sea level.

Ice Ages ▶ During the Ice Ages, which began around two million years ago, enormous masses of water were frozen. This led to a sinking of sea levels by up to 120m/400ft. The receding of the oceans exposed the ground near to the coasts. For a time the Florida Peninsula – measured by its surface area – was twice the size it is today. Rivers and wind transported tremendous amounts of sand onto the exposed shelf. Between the Ice Ages the sea levels rose again, in places to above the present-day levels, as terraces and previous beach-lines show.

From the end of the Ice Ages to today ▶ At the end of the last Ice Age, around 12,000–10,000 years ago, waves and currents distributed the sand-masses along the coasts. Huge sand banks and rows of dunes were formed. Expansive islands of sand arose, separated by lagoons of varying width, some of which exist to this day. Thick layers of chalk formed in the warm, salty water. Coral created reefs in the clear, oxygen-rich water. Along the shallow coasts off the estuaries of North Florida, wetlands with mudflats, salt marshes and swamps were created. Since then, belts of mangrove have surrounded the southern tip of Florida, with their network of roots protecting the low-lying areas from flooding during storms.

Erosion, karst formation ▶ Groundwater is pressed into the porous layers of limestone on the mainland. The carbonic acid dissolved in the water leads to the corrosion of the stone. Fissures and cracks in the rock spread to form crevices and caves, even entire systems of caves.. And when advanced erosion leads to the collapse of the cave roofs, funnels are formed, which are then suddenly filled with water. The groundwater, which is under pressure in many places, comes to the surface in rapidly-flowing springs.. The present-day appearance of the Florida Peninsula is largely a result of the erosive power of water. The karst formation of the limestone shelf, which is often only a few metres above sea level, has led to widely differing landscapes.

North Florida

Almost half of Florida, particularly the area north of the Tampa–Orlando line, **is covered with forests and swamps** and is sparsely populated. In the shadow of the mega-sized theme parks in and around Orlando, Florida's four national forests – Apalachicola, Choctawhatchee, Ocala and Osceola –offer a quite different experience. Canoe tours through cypress swamps, walking tours through largely unspoiled subtropical forests, swimming in crystal-clear spring waters and nights spent in rustic huts or magnificently-situated campgrounds can put sandy beaches and Mickey Mouse far from the mind. This is also where the most important of Florida's 34 rivers flow. Some of the estuaries on the Gulf Coast are the last refuge of the endangered manatee (sea-cow): they are particularly at home in the swampy delta of the Crystal River. In North Florida's hinterland, all roads lead to Gainesville. Half of the 80,000 residents are students at the local University of Florida, which guarantees lively nightlife. But the nearby Paynes Prairie Preserve State Park is much more worth visiting. Its diverse forests in swampy marshes are a reminder of how large parts of the inland once looked before they were drained. »The Ridge«, which runs from Lee in the north, through central Florida, down to Sebring in the south, with rows of hills rising up to 100m/330 feet, is used for agriculture: to this day it is the largest citrus-growing area in the world. That progress and entertainment can coexist is demonstrated by North Florida's Atlantic coast: the **Canaveral Peninsula** is not only where rockets are launched into space. It is also a place where migratory and marsh birds, as well as wildcats, sea turtles and other rare species live in the nature reserves of Canaveral National Seashore and Merritt Island National Wildlife Refuge.

Picturesque spring ponds are typical of Florida, especially the north.

South Florida

South of this line Florida really lives up to its cliché. The **Coastal Lowlands**, reaching up to 90km/55mi inland, make dreams of a holiday spent lazing in a hammock come true. While the expansive northern areas are used for farming and grazing, it seems the only reason for the existence of the populated places along the coast is tourism: every town has a pier, a restaurant with a view, and at least one motel. Where the dry coastal areas were too narrow, such as in Naples, swamp areas were drained. Within a few decades, this former fishing village grew into the tourist centre of the south-west coast. The most densely populated area is the south-east coast. Miami and Fort Lauderdale have merged into a metropolitan area with over four million inhabitants. Nevertheless, the south-east coast more than makes up for all the urban bustle with its fabulous beaches and an exceptional array of culture.

Just how much life in Florida is concentrated on the coasts can be seen in Naples. Directly beyond the city limits begins the expansive swamp areas of **Big Cypress Swamp** and the **Everglades**. There are no settlements to be found in this primeval landscape at the peninsula's southern corner. Lying just a foot or two above sea level, the

A bird's-eye view of the Gulf coast of southern Florida with its brilliant white beaches

Everglades are a succession of freshwater marshes, swamp areas and grasslands occasionally interspersed with hammocks (hardwood groves). The fact that this is actually a river, 50mi/80km wide but only 6in/15cm deep, is not visible to the naked eye. This »river of grass« is the largest subtropical wetland in North America, the habitat for hundreds of animal species, including in particular the famous alligator, the »mascot of the Everglades«, and pelicans, herons and ibises. Their future is far from secure. The highly sensitive ecosystem is subject to many threats, among them are dry spells and tropical storms. But the biggest threat is from people. Ever-increasing areas are drained to create farmland, or water is diverted for irrigation. Whether or not the conservation projects initiated by the government and private groups will be effective remains to be seen. For now, the remains of this unique landscape are protected at Everglades National Park and Big Cypress National Preserve, which was devised as a buffer between the inhabitants and the swamps.

? DID YOU KNOW ...?

■ The world's third-largest coral reef extends offshore of the island chain known as the Florida Keys

Last but no least: the **Florida Keys**. This chain of islands, which on the map reaches out into the Caribbean like a hook, is a 137mi/220km -long arc, beginning half an hour's drive south of Miami and ending where the Dry Tortugas disappear into the Gulf of Mexico. The islands – some smaller than a football field – are ridges of a coral reef formed over the last 150,000 years. Today, it is a brightly coloured stage for dolphins, sharks and stingrays, attracting divers from around the world.

Climate

The most south-eastern state of the United States of America is influenced by two climate zones. While the north of Florida lies in the subtropical to temperate zone, the southern part of the peninsula is entirely subtropical. To the extreme south, the periodically wet tropical climate of the Caribbean is noticeable.

Climate zones

The four seasons of the year are clearly definable in the north of Florida. Rainfall can also be expected practically all year round. In southern Florida, by contrast, there are practically only two seasons. The warm water, high humidity and high evaporation rates contribute to sweltering summers, which can be oppressive between May and October. However, the season from November to April is constantly cool and characterized by three to five months of little precipitation.

Seasons

From June to September it is rather hot throughout the entire peninsula. The highest temperatures are found around the Florida Keys as

Temperatures and rainfall

THE NIGHT WHEN ANDREW CAME

It will take a long time for the people of south Florida to forget the night of 24 August 1992, when Hurricane Andrew swept across the southern tip of the peninsula, leaving a trail of devastation. Gusts of this tropical cyclone reached peak speeds of 240kmh/150mph, making Andrew one of the severest hurricanes ever recorded in the south-east of the USA.

Everything that had not been battened down was blown away: palm fronds, fences, the roofs of whole houses. Powerful breakers crashed onto the coast and sank countless boats. Over an area of 300 sq km/120 sq mi the hurricane flattened everything that stood in its path. Tens of thousands of houses and apartments were destroyed, leaving **over 300,000 people homeless**. Thanks to the timely warnings issued by the authorities »only« **55 people lost their lives** in the catastrophe.

Damage in Billions

Hurricane Andrew caused about US-$ 27 billion of damage, which made it one of the most destructive storms ever. However, the insurance companies came off almost lightly: if the centre of the storm had passed just a few miles further north over the densely populated conurbation of Miami–Fort Lauderdale, the destruc-

tion and insurance claims would have been much higher. As it was, the devastation that Andrew left in its wake meant bankruptcy for many small companies.

Climate Change

Andrew was not the first or the last hurricane that brought deluge-like rainfall. **Within the space of just six weeks in the late summer of a single year, 2004, four hurricanes passed over the Sunshine State**. The worst of them was called Ivan. And in July 2005 Hurricane Dennis inundated the Gulf coast and the Florida Keys. This has made the insurance companies think. The ever more frequent occurrence of storms is being attributed to climate change, for which humankind is partly responsible. The insurance business had long regarded Florida as a land of milk and honey. Little attention was paid to risks that had been known for a long time. How-

Chaotic conditions after Hurricane Andrew swept through

ever, the industry has now become more circumspect. The actuaries receive support from climate researchers who forecast that **the destructive potential of the hurricanes will increase**.

Hurricane Season

Hurricanes originate in the months from June to November over water surfaces of the Atlantic Ocean near to the equator that have a temperature of at least 26°C, where thunder clouds rise to a great height. Every year several tropical cyclones pass over the Caribbean Sea or Gulf of Mexico towards Florida with a wind force of 12 (118kmh/73mph) or more on the Beaufort scale. The core area of the storms can attain a diameter of between 100 and 200 kilometres (60 to 125 miles).

The whole area of a storm (wind force 8) can extend as much as 500 kilometres (300 miles). However, a hurricane moves relatively slowly, at about 30kmh/20mph. At the eye of the storm (about 20 kilometres/12 miles in diameter) the atmospheric pressure can fall below 950 millibars. This pressure gradient can lead to extremely strong winds, and even cause tornadoes and form vortices of cloud with gigantic dimensions.

Hurricane Diagram

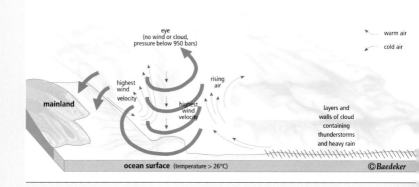

eye
(no wind or cloud, pressure below 950 bars)

warm air

cold air

highest wind velocity

rising air

highest wind velocity

mainland

layers and walls of cloud containing thunderstorms and heavy rain

ocean surface (temperature > 26°C)

©*Baedeker*

well as in the drier inland areas. Several weeks of hot spells with day-time temperatures of up to 40°C or even more are not uncommon. In the south-eastern USA, temperatures of up to 35°C are considered normal.During summer, heavy storms can be expected practically every day, bringing not only hail , but also dangerous tornados.

The months of March, April and May, as well as October and November are very pleasant. Temperatures rise to summer levels, mostly with plenty of bright sunshine.

From December to February, it can get noticeably cool in northern and central Florida.Heavy gusts of cold air from the north can also bring frosts, which do enormous damage to the citrus and vegetable crops. The southern tip of Florida is free of frost. Average winter temperatures here rarely sink below +6°C.

The highest rates of precipitation are measured in the north of the state in the area of the Florida Panhandle, where sometimes well over 1500mm/60in of rain fall annually. It is drier in the Keys, with 1000mm/40in, only two thirds of the rainfall levels in the north.

Hurricane season

Every year, Florida can expect several tropical storms to pass through or pass by, usually occurring in the time from June to September. Hurricanes can not only reach enormous magnitudes, they can also develop a **tremendous potential for destruction.** No-one has forgotten Hurricane »Andrew«, which blew through southern Florida in August 1992, leaving a trail of destruction, primarily in the southern perimeter of Miami.

Gulf stream

The Gulf Stream, an important component of the circumplanetary weather system, has a major influence on the weather conditions in western and central Europe. As the Florida Stream, warm surface waters flow from the Gulf of Mexico through the Florida Strait where, off Florida's east coast, they meet the equally warm Antilles Stream, from the area of the West Indies. 30mi/50km wide on average and up to 1000m/3,300ft deep, the Gulf Stream continues up along the American east coast, before flowing north-east towards western Europe. Up to 55 million cubic metres of water per second are transported north-eastwards.

? DID YOU KNOW ...?

■ The phenomenon of the Gulf Stream was first described by Ponce de León in 1513.
The Spanish made use of the current on their homeward journey from the West Indies.

Flora

Forests

The transition from the pine forests of the temperate zone to the lush vegetation of the subtropical and fringe of the tropical zone is typical of Florida. Many varieties of pine thrive in northern and central Florida, and **Sabal palms** make up the underwood of the **pine forests**, which are not dense. From north to south, the number of palms palms increases, particularly coconut, date and dwarf palms. Majestic king palms also grow here and there in large numbers. Among the most impressive trees are the evergreen **live oaks**, which have dense underwood and branches hung with whole beards of the bromeliad known as **Spanish moss**. In the wetlands, **cypresses** are the typical tree.

Grasslands and swamps

To the south, the forests give way to grasslands and wetlands, in which numerous tropical plants thrive. The characteristic plants of these zones are **swamp cypresses**, a large variety of grasses, **epiphytes, ferns, lianas**, as well as all kinds of **orchids**. Numerous **vines and bromeliads** can also be found. In the actual swamp areas, many **reeds, sedges, rushes, water lilies, and especially water hyacinths** can be spotted. Those who know where to look can also find many varieties of orchid.

Florida's wetlands feature a large number of **hammocks**, or hardwood groves, with palm, mahogany, oak and magnolia trees. Sabal palms, palmettos and many climbing plants make up the impenetrable underbrush.

Southern Florida, where the mainland gradually sinks to below sea level, is also home to extensive **mangrove coasts**. Due to their highly specialized nature, these mangrove forests are home to only a few varieties. The predominant species is the **red mangrove**, the tannin of which lends the water a reddish shimmer. In addition, there are **white and black mangroves**. These salt-loving plants with their thick, evergreen leaves live in the amphibious bush forests. Stilt roots and pneumatophoric roots hold the plants up.

Florida is famous for its **citrus fruit farming**. Extensive citrus plantations along the Indian River, in

Ripe grapefruit

central Florida and on the Gulf Coast primarily grow oranges and grapefruits, but also tangerines and lemons. These fruits are mainly processed into juices and juice concentrates. Florida also has its own characteristic citrus fruit: the Key lime, a green to yellowish, thin-skinned fruit, the acidic juice of which is used for cooking. Essential oils are produced from the citrus rinds.

Fauna

Diversity of species
Despite the massive impact of humans upon the natural habitat of the Florida Peninsula, a number of protected areas give an idea of just how diverse the region's fauna once must have been. This impression is confirmed when reading descriptions by naturalists such as Muir or Audubon.

Bird life
A colourful variety of bird life can be found in Florida, especially in the area of Merritt Island (near Cape Canaveral) on the Atlantic coast, and in the mangrove coasts of south-western and southern Florida, where hundreds of species mate and nest in the largely unspoiled marshes as well as in the swamp areas. Among them are grey herons, little blue herons, egrets, little egrets, green-backed herons, as well as white and brown pelicans. Wood storks, darters (anhingas), roseate spoonbills, various woodpeckers and vultures can also be seen. Very often it is possible to spot ospreys, also known colloquially as fish eagles or seahawks, which are common in South Florida. The American national emblem, the bald eagle, soars among them over bays and swamps. Keen ornithologists will also spot limpkins, cormorants, glossy ibises, skimmers and little owls. A number of flamingos still live in the wild.

Reptiles
Around one million **alligators** have their home in Florida's waterways and swamp areas. They can be found in the Everglades and in the canals surrounding the space station at Cape Canaveral. They turn up in the greenery around big shopping malls, on golf courses, in gardens, and at night it's not an uncommon occurrence to see a »gator« crawling across the highway.

The **American crocodile** is a far rarer sight. This reptile is in danger of extinction as a result of extensive hunting and poaching. The important sanctuaries for these reptiles are the Everglades as well as the swamp areas along Florida Bay, where a few dozen crocodiles still live.

Turtles ►
Several species of turtle are also in danger of extinction. They include the Florida softshell turtle, the slider turtle and a variety of sea turtles, whose sandy nests are sometimes discovered by hungry alligators or destroyed by careless tourists.

Snakes ►
The palmetto undergrowth of hammocks and other dry biotopes is a refuge for poisonous and often highly aggressive **diamond snakes** and **ground rattlers**. The **cottonmouth**, the **coral snake** and the

North Florida native **copperhead** are life-threatening to humans. Alongside these dangerous reptiles, Florida is home to numerous less poisonous snakes, as well as various colubrid snakes, including the **garter snake** and the yellow rat snake.

Numerous mammals live in Florida, including some endangered species. Raccoons are often spotted, as are bobcats, white-tailed deer and other deer species. Coyotes, foxes, wild boars, minks and armadillo can also be seen, and **opossums**, marsupials resembling rats, are quite common.

Mammals

Very few of these lithe big cats live reclusively in southern Florida's Everglades National Park and Big Cypress Preserve. Despite strict protective measures, the Florida panther's chances of survival are decreasing.

◄ Florida panther

Manatees (sea cows) are also in danger of extinction. These bulky yet cute animals live in shallow coastal waters and feed on the water plants that thrive there. During the colder times of year they leave the cooler waters and head inland towards the relatively warm waters emerging from springs, or canals heated with effluent water from power plants and factories. Their worst enemies are careless recreational motorboat captains, who kill dozens of manatees each year.

◄ Manatees

A large sea turtle comes ashore to lay eggs.

SAVE THE MANATEES

They look so benign – and yet they face extinction. The population of the plump, appealing creatures known as sea cows or manatees, from the Spanish word manatis, has now fallen to only a few hundred.

There must once have been large numbers of manatees. What other explanation could there possibly be for all the seamen's yarns about mermaids?

The creatures, which have a considerable body mass but nevertheless a cute appearance, live in both salt water and fresh water, but seem to prefer fresh-water habitats. They can be found on the Florida Peninsula in **shallow coastal waters, fresh-water lakes close to the ocean, watercourses and canals** – and even in harbours and the cooling water effluent of power stations.

The best chance of getting a glimpse of one of the Florida manatees is on the bays and estuaries of the Gulf coast, in certain spring pools and in some of the rivers.

Torpid Vegetarians

Manatees are vegetarians that graze on water plants. They are between three and five metres (ten to sixteen feet) long and often weigh more than half a ton. They can eat up to 50kg/110lb of food per day, an activity which takes them up to eight hours. Every ten or fifteen minutes, when they come to the surface for air, onlookers have a chance of seeing the whiskered snout or even the whole head of a manatee.

Playful manatees in the
warm waters of Tampa Bay

They are very slow to reproduce. Females do not give birth before the age of seven years, and they remain pregnant for thirteen months. The young stay with their mother for two years before going their own way. It then takes three to five years after the birth for the mother to conceive again. Manatees can live for up to **50 years** – so long as they do not fall prey to sharks or alligators.

Keen Travellers, Sensitive to Cold

Manatees are extremely sensitive to cold and die if they cannot find a warm place. The water temperature

York area. However, in normal circumstances they **keep contact to other manatees**, which live further south in the warm waters of the Caribbean.

Endangered Species

Many owners of motor-boats and sailing boats know that manatees help to keep waterways from being clogged by thick vegetation and are thus a help to boat traffic. However, it is leisure boating – especially the motor boats that churn up the beds of waterways with their propellers – that have fateful consequences for the manatees.

Hard to believe but true: During the winter month's manatees even play in the cooling water of the power station on the edge of Tampa.

has to be at least 20°C. For this reason many manatees move inland in winter to the warm spring pools or look for warmed water near to power stations or factories.

The fact that they like to travel has been known for certain since the summer of 1995. In that year the media reported on an animal that had made its way north along the east coast of the USA as far as the New

Each year careless **boat skippers and drivers of water scooters injure dozens of the animals**, which then suffer an unpleasant death. Although the media in Florida again and again show pictures of horribly mutilated manatees, this seems to have no effect. Only on a few waterways such as the Orange River and the Caloosahatche River do members of the boating community seem to take more care.

The dolphins in Florida's waters are usually in a good mood.

Dolphins ▶ In Florida it is not only possible to see dolphins in captivity, but above all, in the wild. They are often spotted in the coastal waters off of south and south-western Florida. Dolphins often accompany boating excursions, and can be encouraged to perform photogenic jumps in the air.

Fish The waters around the Florida Peninsula are home to a large number of **sharks** of various species, among them tiger sharks and hammerhead sharks as well as gigantic whale sharks. **Stingrays** are a danger to beachgoers and swimmers. Particularly in summer, these fish venture into the shallow waters of beaches and swimming areas to reproduce. They bury themselves in the sand and mud with only their eyes and tails exposed. Anyone stepping on such a fish usually comes away with a serious injury as a result of the ray's poisonous stinger.

Insects During the hot, humid summers, time spent in the open air can be torturous. Myriads of **mosquitoes** and flies, which can transmit dangerous diseases such as meningitis, are a plague for people and animals alike in many areas of the Florida Peninsula. Ticks, as well as fleas and **spiders** represent a further nuisance. It is also advisable to beware of poisonous **scorpions**.

Environmental Issues and Ecology

Effects of climate change Protection of the environmental is no longer a low priority in the US. It is not just the increase in fuel prices that has led Americans to use their cars less. The greenhouse effect,, the hole in the ozone layer, destruction of coral reefs and ecology are common themes in the US media. The biggest cause for concern is global warming. The predicted rise in sea levels threatens Florida as much as the increase in **tropical storms (hurricanes)**.

Water pollution is not the only problem along the coast. In addition, the increased temperature of coastal waters has led to a dramatic decrease in the diversity of marine flora and fauna. The worst-affected areas are the coral banks of the Florida Keys, which react to the slightest of temperature changes in their ecosystem. Studies have shown that as much as 10% of the coral dies each year: ifcoral destruction continues at this pace, most of Florida's reefs will have vanished within a short time. The immense water consumption of the cities and the fruit and vegetable plantations has led to a dramatic sinking of groundwater levels in many areas. This has a negative effect upon the remaining swamp areas: they are gradually drying up. Yet another environmental issue is the contamination of plants and animals by fertilizers and insecticides.

Water pollution

The State of Florida reacts to these threats to its nature with laws, regulations, public awareness campaigns. Environmentalists hand out bumper stickers reading »Save the Manatees«. The environmental awareness of Florida's citizens has never been higher. At two national parks, four national forests and at over 100 state parks, Florida's nature is protected or its use is restricted. These protected areas have their own management, with rules that are strictly enforced by park rangers. Visitor centres serve as points of reference and provide information to the public.

Laws and regulations

At the same time, many good programmes have fallen victim to political wheeling and dealing. In the last four years alone, the federal government in Washington has cut funding for wastewater reclamation programs; the »Clean Water Act« to limit pollution from industrial farming has been weakened by making exceptions; and an end has been imposed upon the protection of 300,000 acres of wetlands. With Washington's approval, Florida's powerful sugar industry has delayed the long-agreed timetable to stop the disposal of waste in the Everglades. And the federal government has made an inventory of all potential offshore oil and gas reserves – an act that not only environmentalists suspect will inevitably lead to drilling in the Gulf of Mexico, with incalculable consequences for flora, fauna and people.

Population · Politics · Economy

Population

The favourable climate and economic opportunities have led to extraordinary population growth in America's south-eastern peninsula.

Dynamic growth

In 1830, only around 35,000 people lived in the then undeveloped area. Today the figure is 18 million – with hundreds more arriving each day.

The development after the end of World War II, when only 2.7 million people lived in Florida, was particularly dramatic. Strong impulses for growth came from the tourist industry, as well as the space programme and the relocation of related high-tech industries. In the 1960s and 1970s came the huge amusement parks, which brought further tourists and migrants to the state. Florida is also a magnet for retired persons and pensioners wishing to live out their twilight years in leisure, and for sun-hungry residents from the cooler northern regions, who spend their winters here.

Conurbations ► Florida is growing, especially in the south. Whereas one hundred years ago only five per cent of Florida residents lived in the south, it is now home to forty per cent of the population. The most densely populated area is the megalopolis on the south coast, a continuously settled area of well over five million people, spanning from Miami all the way to West Palm Beach. Miami itself is today the hotspot of one of the most financially powerful areas of the USA, as well as an important trade and transport hub between North and South America on the one side, and Europe on the other. The second large conurbation is Tampa, combined with St Petersburg and Clearwater. 2.5 million people live here. Further important, densely populated areas are Orlando, with 1.7 million inhabitants, and Jacksonville, with 1.2 million.

Multicultural Florida When it comes to the make-up of the population, Florida's proximity to the Caribbean and to Latin America is unmistakable. Nearly a third of the residents are of African-American or Hispanic origin, and nearly one quarter speak a language other than English at home. In greater Miami alone, Hispanics, or Latinos, many of them Cuban exiles, make up over sixty per cent of the population. Other numerically strong ethnic minorities are Filipinos, Vietnamese, Chinese and Thais. The daily influx of several hundreds of mostly young, qualified professionals is at odds with Florida's image as America's favourite refuge for seniors and retired persons. At the same time, this hardly decreasing flow of immigrants from the south is a reminder of Florida's historic relationship with the Caribbean and Latin America. Today in Miami, Spanish is heard more commonly than English, the Cuban community exerts considerable political influence, and the Creole-speaking districts of Miami often make their voices heard.

Problems in the melting pot ► Florida, where English, Spanish and Creole is spoken, is a prime example of the American melting pot. But not all is well. There is a shortage of housing, there are too few schools, and poverty is on the increase. The low rate of taxation in Florida, intended to stimulate growth, also leads to difficulties in funding public services. A high rate of infant mortality among the very poorest and street crime are the consequences. Under such conditions, it doesn't take much for

Multicultural Sunshine State

the ethnic tensions bubbling beneath the surface of this multicultural society to boil over.

African-Americans
Around a sixth of the population are black. In addition, there are many black immigrants from the Caribbean region (boat refugees). As a result of years of institutionalized racism and a continuing lack of employment opportunities and education, a disproportionate percentage of the black population remains in extreme poverty.

Native Americans
After reaching a low in the 1950s, the Native American (Indian) population is growing once again, and is currently at around 40,000. This is due to the influx of Native Americans from other parts of the USA, who come seeking economic opportunities in Florida. The approximately 3,000 descendents of the Seminole and Miccosukee live not only on the reservations in the Everglades and in Big Cypress Reserve: many of them have adopted the mainstream American way of life and live inconspicuously in various cities in Florida.

Religion
The six largest religious groups in Florida are Roman Catholic Christians (around 30%), Baptists (around 30%), Methodists (around 15%), Jews (around 12%), Presbyterians (about 7%) und Anglicans (around 5%). There has been a recent increase in Muslims and followers of various natural religions.

State and Society

The State of Florida

Florida joined the union of the United States of America in 1845. The state government is headed by a governor. As at federal level, there is a congress comprised of a senate and a house of representatives. Both houses of congress hold session at the Capitol in the capital city of Tallahassee. The governor is politically important, though the holder of the office remains subject to the resolutions of Congress. A veto of a congressional resolution by the governor can be overturned by a simple majority vote of congress. The authority of the governor to reinforce the state police with units of the National Guard in the case of civil disturbance is a significant power.

Anyone travelling through Florida will come across striking examples of the state's independence in everyday life: the state regulates the traffic code (i.e. speed limits, blood alcohol limits) and licensing laws for the sale of alcoholic beverages, and determines police policy, voting regulations and the school system.

Florida has its own constitution, written in 1885 and revised in 1968. The judicial system is organized on four levels. The basis is a system of county courts. Above these are the circuit courts and the district court. The highest instance is the supreme court, with judges appointed by the governor. At the US Capitol in Washington D.C., Florida is represented by two senators and fifteen representatives.

Local government

Florida is divided into 67 counties, each with its own county seat or centre of county administration. The Indian Reservations are governed by the residents themselves, and are not liable to taxation.

Economy

Economic history

Florida's economy has developed very dynamically since the end of the 19th century. The decisive impulse was the construction of railways. On the one hand, Florida's tourist potential was unlocked; on the other, agricultural products could be transported faster to key markets in the north. The role of the military in the development of the state should not be underestimated. Thousands of Americans went through training camps before and during the two world wars, or worked in the factories of the armaments industry. They spread the reputation of the »Sunshine State«, and so encouraged tourism from north to south.

The economy has boomed particularly since the end of World War II. A strong impulse came from the US space station at Cape Canaveral. The rocket builders jump-started the establishment of new industrial and service enterprises. Additionally, in the more recent past, mega-amusement parks such as SeaWorld, Walt Disney World, EPCOT, Universal Studios etc. have shot up, contributing not only to an increase in the flow of tourism, but also to the creation of many new jobs.

Facts and Figures Florida

Florida

Location
► south-eastern USA

Area
► 140,256 sq km/54,109 sq mi
  (cf UK 95,000 sq mi)

Population
► 18 million residents
  (about 6% of the population of
  the USA)
► population density: 123 per sq km
  (319 per sq mi)
► largest conurbations:
  Miami/Ft. Lauderdale/Palm Beach
  over 5 million
  Tampa/St Petersburg/Clearwater
  2.5 million
  Orlando area 1.7 million
  Jacksonville area 1.2 million

Languages
► English and Spanish

Religion
► Catholics: 30%
► Protestants: 57%
► Jews: 12%
► others: (e.g. Muslims) 1%

Government
► capital: Tallahassee
► 67 counties
► several Indian reservations

Economy
► income per capita:
  about 42,000 US-$
  (UK 37,000 US-$)
► poverty rate: 12.5%
► agriculture:
  citrus fruit, vegetables, sugar, cattle
  rearing, horse breeding, dairy farms
► industry:
  food, aerospace, electronics,
  electro-technology, printing, media,
  engineering
► services:
  tourism, banking and insurance,
  transport
► tourism:
  84 million visitors annually (2006),
  4.1 million from overseas

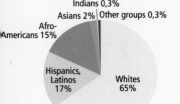

Indians 0,3%
Asians 2% | Other groups 0,3%
Afro-Americans 15%
Hispanics, Latinos 17%
Whites 65%

Mining Florida is the source of a number of mineral resources, including the metals titanium and zirconium. When it comes to non-metallic resources, Florida produces huge quantities of chalk, phosphate (around a third of world production) and high-quality clay. Large amounts of phosphates are mined in western Florida. The chalk deposits gave rise to a significant cement industry. Off the south-west coast of Florida oil and gas reserves have been tapped through offshore drilling in recent years.

Fishing An important role is played by oyster beds (especially in Apalachicola Bay) as well as the shrimp and prawn catch (in the area of Amelia Island, amongst others). In addition, each year a great quantity fish for everyday consumption is brought ashore. Sponge diving, too, is a source of income. It was immigrants from Greece who first recognized the wealth of natural sponges off the coast of Florida. Freshwater fishing in Florida's inland waters is also worth mentioning. The main catches are catfish, carp, eel and various sunfish.

Forestry Some regions in the north of Florida are known for their wealth of forests. Over 7 million ha/17 million acres of land are used for forestry operations. The wood is mainly processed for the paper and cellulose industry. For many years, turpentine has been extracted from the pine forests. The original profusion of hardwoods has been vastly diminished. In order to meet the demand from the timber processing industry and the construction industry, reforestation programmes were implemented as early as the 1920s.

Agriculture The most important branch of agriculture by far is the extensive citrus production. Primarily in central and eastern Florida (along the Indian River), each year around five million tons of oranges, two million tons of grapefruits, as well as large quantities of tangerines and lemons are harvested. Despite the costly heating of fruit crops, cold winter spells regularly lead to considerable crop failure. The vegetable crop is also significant. The most commonly planted vegetables are potatoes, cucumber, tomatoes, onions, celery, radishes, cabbage, green beans, melons, pumpkins, eggplant and avocados. These crops also regularly suffer from frosts. After Hawaii and Louisiana, Florida now takes third place in the USA when it comes to the cultivation of sugar cane. The crops now cover around 100,000 ha/25,000 acres of land. Huge sugar cane fieldscan be found in the Clewiston-Belle Glade area, created by the dyking of Lake Okeechobee and the draining of swamp and reed areas. More recently, cultivation of flowers and tree nurseries have been established as new branches of agriculture. All kinds of cut flowers, palms and decorative trees are grown, mainly in subtropical southern Florida.

Cattle farming ▶ Large amounts of land are taken up by cattle grazing. Currently, around two million head of cattle are kept, around 10% of which are milk cows. The successful crossing of robust European cattle breeds

Citrus harvest

with Indian zebus has contributed to this development. Only relatively recently established in Florida, horse breeding is also successful. Numerous studs have proven highly effective at breeding full-blooded Arabians.

In the past, industry played a secondary role in Florida. At most, only the food industry and tobacco manufacture were of note. At the beginning of the 20th century there were more than a hundred cigar factories in Tampa alone, whereas today there are only around two dozen in all of Florida. In contrast, the so-called citrus industry, the raw materials of which come from orange and grapefruit plantations, has prospered. There are companies that produce juices and juice concentrates , as well as those that pack and preserve fruit, juices, concentrates etc.This sector also includes companies that specialize in the processing of citrus rinds for the production of oils, preservatives, cosmetics and cleaning solutions. **Industry**

A conspicuous feature of northern Florida are the hugepaper and cellulose factories that process the local softwood. Here and there sawmills, where hardwoods are cut to size for the construction industry and for building boats, can be seen.

The chemicals industry has arisen from the lumber industry. One of its most important raw materials is the turpentine that has been extracted from Florida's forests for many years. The fertilizer industry processes local raw materials such as chalk and phosphate.

A further important sector of the economy of Florida is the construction industry, which profits highly from booming tourism. New holiday complexes, retirement settlements, shopping centres and the likes are being built on every reasonably attractive stretch of coastline. These are followed by amusement parks, marinas, roads, sewage plants and other infrastructure building. Annually, Florida sees well over twenty billion dollars worth of new construction.

With the building of the space station at Cape Canaveral, many companies related to the aerospace industry as well as electronics and technology have emerged. All of the well known American aircraft manufacturers, machinery firms and computer giants have offices in the »Sunshine State«. As a result of the aerospace boom, many highly specialized service industries have also been established.

Tourism »They came with a twenty-dollar bill and a t-shirt and never changed either of them ...« This cutting remark refers to the tourists of by-gone days, who came with a healthy sense of adventure in rickety automobiles to spend the winter in the largely unexplored, still provincial Florida. Today, tourism is a pillar of the economy. Not without pride, an official study noted that well over 90% of holidaymakers from the US and Canada would like to return to Florida. Each year, over 75 million people spend their holidays in the »Sunshine State«. One in five visitors to the US from overseas spend at least part of their stay in Florida. In good years, around six million tourists from overseas come to Florida. Highlights such as the fabulous beaches on the Atlantic and Gulf coasts, the mega-amusement parks of the Orlando area, the US Space Station at Cape Canaveral, Miami and Miami Beach as well as the Everglades and the Keys are magnets for an

Florida's airplane and spacecraft builders have lots to do.

endless flow of visitors. In the meantime, over two million jobs in the »Sunshine State« are directly or indirectly related to tourism. This so-called »white industry« brought in revenues of around 65 billion dollars in 2006 alone.

Each year, over four million cruise passengers dock in Florida's harbours. Most cruise passengers board in Miami. Further north, near Fort Lauderdale, the ultramodern Port Everglades takes second place in terms of passenger numbers. In addition, Port Canaveral, not far from the US Space Station, is enjoying increasing popularity. Other important cruise-liner ports include Tampa and Key West.

◄ Cruise tourism

Florida's appeal as a winter domicile for the wealthy, its industrial growth, and its proximity to attractive tax havens (i.e. the Bahamas) has led to more and more financial services opening branches here. Miami, the hub between North, Central and South America, is today one of the world's leading financial centres. The glittering facades of the banking palaces along Miami's Brickell Avenue emphasize this in a most impressive manner.

Financial markets

Other sectors of the economy are currently enjoying rapid growth in Florida: the software industry, biotechnology and medical technology, research as well as highly qualified services (health, trade, finance and law). Florida's research centres alone see an annual investment of over 500 million dollars.

Future technologies

History

For some, Florida's history begins with Mickey Mouse and Walt Disney. But on the sunny peninsula in the south-eastern USA, humans can be traced back for at least 12,000 years.

Original Inhabitants

12th–10th century BC	Fishermen, hunter-gatherers come to the peninsula of Florida.
7th century BC	First settlements are established.
1492	Christopher Columbus discovers America.
16th century AD	About 100,000 Native Americans live on the Florida Peninsula.

Paleo-Indian settlements

It is believed that about 30,000 to 10,000 years ago – at the end of the last Ice Age – the Native Americans of North America crossed from North Asia into North America over the Bering Strait. Groups of different ethnic backgrounds immigrated in several waves and developed their own cultures. About 12,000 to 10,000 years ago, the first **nomadic fishermen and hunter-gatherers appeared** on the Florida Peninsula. Numerous springs, lakes and rivers full of fish, shallow lagoons, bays full of shellfish and other marine life, lush vegetation and a rich game population provided favourable living conditions all year round.

Advances in several waves

The oldest human traces were discovered south of Sarasota, near Warm Mineral Springs, and can be dated to an age of 10,000 years. Close to Titusville is evidence of an approximately 8,000-year-old camp. In the 7th millennium BC, Paleo-Indian founded first settlements near springs and streams. Findings such as potsherds, copper, iron ore and maize seeds suggest trade relations with the peoples along the Mississippi and in Mexico. Villages with fortified palisade walls were established. The tribal communities were hierarchically organized. The dead of a higher status were buried in hills of earth up to 30m/100ft in height, or **mounds**.

Oldest finds

? DID YOU KNOW ...?

■ So far, archaeologists have found evidence of around 12,000 mounds on the entire Florida Peninsula.

Arrival of the first Europeans

In the early 16th century, when the first explorers from Europe came to the peninsula, around 100,000 Native Americans lived here. They were divided into several peoples. In North Florida, the **Apalachee** and the **Timuacan** lived as farmers. The south-west coast was the territory of the martial **Calusa**, who lived mainly from fishing and

Native Americans

← *Relic of Spanish colonial times in St Augustine*

Indian settlement surrounded by palisades at the time of the first white settlers

hunting. They managed to get as far as Cuba in their canoes. The south-east coast was settled by a number of smaller tribes, among them the **Tequesta, Mayaimi and Jeagas**. They lived by fishing in the Atlantic Ocean and hunting in the swamps.

Demise of the Native Americans During the 16th and 17th centuries, the Native American population was largely decimated by the Spanish, French and English, who were advancing into the New World. Many Native Americans fell prey to the illnesses (especially influenza) brought over by the Europeans. In the 18th century the last sizeable groups of Timucuans and Apalachee left Florida when the Spanish retreated to Cuba.

Spanish, French and British

1492	Columbus discovers America.
1513	Ponce de León claims the peninsula, which he names »La Florida«.
1563–64	French colonists attempt to settle without success.
1586	Sir Francis Drake completely destroys St Augustine.
1763	The Treaty of Versailles returns Florida to Spain.
1817/1818	First Seminole War
1821	Spain cedes Florida to the USA.

During the Civil War, Union and Confederate troops paid a high price in life and limb.

After the war ended, towns were filled with investors from the north. They boosted Florida's economy, but also instigated a reorganization of the structures of ownership, which to this day is still a sore point. In 1881, **Hamilton Disston**, a rich manufacturer from Philadelphia, set the course for the future: with the so-called **Disston Purchase** he acquired four million acres of land between the Kissimee Basin, the Gulf Coast and the Everglades, drained the swap and sold it in parcels to farmers, investors and wealthy east coast notables. Practically overnight, new towns and agricultural regions appeared, among them the citrus-growing areas. Already in 1884, several hundred tourists, among them the inventor **Thomas A. Edison**, spent their winter on the Gulf Coast.

The »Disston Purchase« put Florida in the sights of the railway barons. **William D. Chipley**, with his **Pensacola & Atlantic Railroad**, connected the timber industry of the Panhandle with the markets in the north. The South Florida Railroad of **Henry B. Plant** connected Sanford, on the St John's River, with the Gulf Coast, turning this unimportant fishing town into a port overnight. Convinced of Florida's potential for tourism, Plant built hotels, notably the fine Tampa Bay Hotel, with rooms that already cost 100 dollars per night 120 years ago. **Henry M. Flagler**, the most dazzling of these »railway barons«, connected New York and St Augustine with his **Eastcoast Railroad** in 1886. St Augustine was thereby transformed into a winter destination for tourists, so Flagler extended his railway even further south. It reached Palm Beach in 1894, and Miami in 1896. From 1904 to 1912, he built his railway over the Keys and the open sea all the way down to Key West.

Florida in the 20th Century

From 1868	Cuban War of Independence: numerous refugees come to Florida.
1914–18	World War I: Florida's dockyards flourish.
After 1920	Florida land boom. Famous architects follow their visions.
1930s	Florida suffers from the consequences of the stock market crash of 1929.
1939–45	World War II: Florida is a training and recreation area for the US army.
1950	Begin of the rocket testing programme in Cape Canaveral
1959	Castro takes power in Cuba. Many thousands of Cubans escape to Florida.
1961	Launch of the first US manned space flight
1969	Apollo 11 lifts off to the moon.
1971	Walt Disney World opens its gates.
1981	The first space shuttle, *Columbia*, takes off into space.

From Land Boom to Land Bust

Tobacco and tourism
Cuba had been suffering unrest since the breakout of its war for independence in 1868. Many Cuban refugees had settled in Tampa, bringing with them the manufacture of tobacco as a profitable economic activity. More and more celebrities built luxurious villas in places such as Fort Myers, St Petersburg and Palm Beach. The first automotive tourists rolled in on brand-new highways. World War I made Florida's dockyards flourish.

Unparalleled building boom
From 1920, the sunny state experienced the »Florida land boom«: hundreds of thousands came, saw and purchased.Famous architects, above all Addison Mizner, created dreams in pink that sprang up out of the dunes. Visionaries created islands and towns: George Merrick built Coral Gables, Carl Fisher constructed a dikefacing the offshore dune. Shortly thereafter, Miami Beach became »the« seaside resort of America. Less wealthy Americans became a new type of tourist, the so-called »tin canner«. These early motorized tourists camped in tent camps on the outskirts of the resorts to enjoy the sand, beach and sun.

Economic crisis and the World War II
In 1926, Florida's overstretched real estate market had a massive meltdown. The stock market crash of 1929 and the disastrous hurricane of 1935, which destroyed Flagler's railway over the Keys, wors-

ened the economic chaos in Florida. Not until the reforms of the New Deal was the state revived. Then World War II pushed Florida's war industry forward. Huge training camps were established, particularly for the US Air Force. The invasions of Italy and France were rehearsed on the beaches of St Petersburg and Daytona.

Rockets, Amusement Parks and Refugees

After 1945, decades of unfettered growth began. The development of **The Fifties ...** juice concentrates led to the expansion of acreage for oranges and grapefruits. In 1950, the beginning of the rocket development programme on Cape Canaveral signalled the birth of Florida's aerospace industry and related futuristic sectors. And, of course, tourism! The introduction of the two-week paid holiday from now on brought millions of people to the south each year. Most of all, the south-east coast experienced an unparalleled building boom. Up until the middle of the 1950s, in Greater Miami alone, more hotels were built than in all the other states combined. Gigantic highway projects, among them the Sunshine Skyway over Tampa Bay and the Florida Turnpike, helped bring together the different regions of Florida. By 1959, the Sunshine State already boasted 5 million inhabitants.

In 1959, Fidel Castro came to power in Cuba. Thousands of Cubans **Cuban missile** left their homeland and settled in Florida. In Miami, **Little Havana crisis** emerged. In 1961, the so-called Sugar War broke out between the USA and Cuba, culminating in the breakdown of diplomatic relations between the two countries. In a new wave, thousands of Cubans once again came to Florida. The Cuban missile crisis (1962) nearly caused a Third World War. The USSR, at that time allied with Cuba, began to build a marine and air force base and a missile launching site on the Island. The USA perceived this as a direct threat and imposed an air and naval blockade against Cuba. Finally the Soviets backed down. But to this day, massive sanctions are imposed by the USA against the Caribbean island-state. From 1965 to 1973, as part of the Freedom Flights, thousands of Cubans were flown out of their home and into Florida. During the 1980s, the Cuban government allowed more than 120,000 people to emigrate to the USA. Most of them chose Greater Miami as their new home. By 1990, the number of Cubans living in Florida had increased to well over 650,000.

As early as 1961, the first manned American space mission was **Highlights of** launched from Cape Canaveral. In following years, Cape Canaveral **space travel** was to become the American space base. From here, the successful Mercury, Gemini, Apollo and Skylab missions were launched. In 1966, the first »soft« moon-landing was launched from Cape Kennedy. US space travel suffered a major setback in 1967, when three astronauts lost their lives due to a fire that broke out aboard Apollo

1969: Neil Armstrong and Edwin Aldrin on the moon

I. On 21 July 1969, the **Apollo 11** astronauts Neil Armstrong and Edwin Aldrin became the first human beings to set foot on the moon. 1986 was year of the **Challenger catastrophe**: all seven astronauts died aboard the space shuttle Challenger. All manned space travel was cancelled for the period of around two and a half years. In 1988, the Kennedy Space Center prepared for a new series of manned space flight. The space shuttle Discovery was launched into the earth's orbit.

In 1971, a new era began in Florida with the **opening of Walt Disney World in Orlando**. This mega-amusement park set new standards in entertainment and tourism. Other similarly designed attractions followed.

In the shadow of the tourist industry, Florida's traditional economic sectors such as phosphate mining, fishing, vegetable and citrus plantation also blossomed. New economic sectors such as technology for space travel and the military, biotechnology and software development led to constant structural change in the economy. More and more pensioners chose Florida as a place to enjoy retirement.

Its proximity to the Caribbean and Latin America also happened to make Florida the promised land for refugees arriving by boat from the Caribbean. Cohabitation between the most varied of ethnic groups is not always peaceful: more than once social tensions have been aired violently. The gang warfare in Miami, drug-related crime – Miami was a key hub of drug trafficking in the 1980s and 1990s – and the armed robbery of tourists, including even the murder of some visitors, has to seen within this context.

Florida in the Early 21st Century

Turbulent times

7 November 2000	Irregularities during the election of the new US President
11 September 2001	Terrorist attacks in New York and Washington affect Florida's tourism.
2003	After many successful missions, *Columbia* burns up while re-entering earth's atmosphere on its last flight.
Late summer 2004	An entire series of hurricanes leaves enormous damage.

Two issues polarized Florida at the same time in 2000: thefate of the young Elian Gonzales, who was separated from his relatives and forcibly repatriated to Cuba, and the strange procedures during the election of the new US president. Protest against the election result was loudest of all in Greater Miami. Prior to that, Secretary of State Katherine Harris had halted the counting of all cast votes, declaring her Republican colleague George W. Bush the winner in Florida. At this point, Bush was ahead of his Democratic opponent Al Gore by less than 1,000 votes. This and the allegation that roadblocks, which were illegally installed by police, had kept potential Gore-voters – above all African Americans – away from the ballot box, threw light on questionable practices in US politics.

Elian and the election scandal

President Bush was visiting a school in Sarasota, Florida, when he heard the news about the terrorist attacks in New York and Washington. The consequences of those terrible events were soon noticeable in the Sunshine State. The tourist sector, which had to cope with a steep decline in tourism, was drastically affected. However, visitor numbers are on the increase once again.

11 September 2001

Over the course of its history, the Florida Peninsula has been visited again and again by disastrous tropical storms, which cause immense damage. Hurricane Andrew alone took 55 human lives and made more than 300,000 people homeless when it raged through Florida in 1992. In the late summer of 2004, no less than four hurricanes within six weeks caused massive damage. In total they destroyed property with insurance values of at least 30 billion dollars. Not only insurance companies, but also the state government now faces the question as to whether these extreme weather events might be consequences of global warming.

More and more hurricanes

Art and Culture

Florida not only brings comic figures to life, it also has some of the best art museums and galleries in the USA. The way to get to know Florida's special architectural style is beneath the open sky – at best in the late afternoon, when the sun begins to work its magic.

Visual Arts

Miami Vice and Universal Studios, Kennedy Space Center and Disney World are what first spring to mind when Florida is mentioned. But the Sunshine State not only has »fun & sun«: it also has »real« culture. Aside from the art of the Native Americans –the patchworks and weavings of the Miccosukee are famous – it has been painters and photographers who have taken Florida as their theme since the 16th century.

The earliest pictures originate from the Frenchman **Jacques le Moyne de Morgues** (1533–88), who accompanied the French Expedition Laudonnière as an illustrator and painter in 1564. Whereas his interests were more of scientific nature, a romantic enthusiasm for the landscape and its hidden allure was the main emphasis of the painters and photographers of the 19th and early 20th centuries. There are a number of impressive landscape paintings by the Bostonian painter **Homer Winslow** (1836–1910). The photographer **Walker Evans** (1903–75) also worked in Florida from time to time, especially in the years from 1928 to 1941. The natural beauty of the Everglades and the views of St Augustine, the oldest town of continental USA, were popular motifs for painters and photographers. Views of St Augustine, alongside those of Niagara Falls, were the most common decoration in American living rooms for quite some time.

The activity of rich collectors was what finally gave Florida a real taste for the arts: the Gallery of Fine Arts, established by **Ralph Hubbard Norton** (1875–1953) in West Palm Beach, and the Museum of Art, founded by **John & Mable Ringling** in Sarasota laid the foundations. **A. E. »Bean« Backus** (1906–90) of Fort Pierce made a name for himself with naturalistic landscape pictures. **Hiram D. Williams** (1917–2003) from Gainesville painted his way to an established position among the American Impressionists, and the painter **Doris Leeper** (1929–2000) from New Smyrna Beach was, as an environmentalist, instrumental in the founding of the Canaveral National Seashore. In the 1970s, Floridan artistic activities received some support from the state's highest-ranking guardian of culture: Secretary of the Interior **George Firestone** (born in 1931), who endeavoured to turn Florida into a »State of the Arts«, raised financial support for young artists by an unbelievable 3200 per cent during his term in office. In addition, established modern artists such as **Robert Rauschenberg** (born in 1925) in Captiva, and in Aripeka, the pop-artist **James Rosenquist** (born in 1933) each took new talent under their wings. »Beanie« Backus was a mentor to the **»Highwaymen«**, a group of African-American painters around **Alfred Hair** (1941–70) who sold nearly 200,000 pictures with tropical motifs for American living

Painting and photography

← *Nowhere else as conspicuous: art deco in Miami Beach*

rooms in the 1960s and are currently experiencing a renaissance nationwide. Photographers also fell for the same tropical landscapes. Two excellent contemporary photographers document this: the detail-obsessed **Clyde Butcher** (born in 1942) from Ochopee records threatened nature for generations to come, and the Gainesville-based **Jerry N. Uelsmann** (born in 1934) captivates his audience with abstract, dreamlike montages.

Contemporary sculpture In many public spaces, parks, transportation buildings and cultural facilities, sculptures by contemporary artists have been displayed to an increased extent since the 1970s. Among them are works by **Claes Oldenbourg, Isamu Noguchi, Nam June Paik, Edward Ruscha** and many others. The intention is to upgrade the quality of life and to emphasize the identity of the community. In front of the Center for the Performing Arts in Miami Beach, for example, the sculpture *Mermaid* by **Roy Lichtenstein** catches the eye. The artist quotes the local art deco style in this work. In collaboration with his wife **Coosje van Bruggen**, **Claes Oldenbourg** designed a fountain at the hypermodern Metro-Dade Government Center. The work is entitled *Dropped Bowl with Scattered Slices and Peels* and is meant to symbolize the multicultural diversity of Florida's metropolis, a city which, according to Claes Oldenbourg, is »in a state of constant development and whose system of organization is based upon the disorder of its urban development, which doesn't go according to plan ...«.

Architecture

Mediterranean influences Over 200 years of Spanish colonialism did not fail to leave its mark on Florida's buildings. Combining Spanish and Italian influences, the Mediterranean style emerged at the end of the 19th century as an increasingly popular architectural style alongside the strict Victorian and the symmetrically-orientated Colonial style. Today – much simplified – it is the predominant form for domestic building in Florida.

The characteristics of the Mediterranean style are curved arches, terracotta-tiled roofs and sand-coloured stucco walls with adornments painted in pastel colours, emulating the light so typical to Florida. Italian and Spanish influences are often clearly recognizable on expensive villas and buildings designed to impress. While Italian-inspired buildings, in their love of detail – balustrades, doors and windows are elegantly decorated – appear more feminine and commonly make use of brick walls, Spanish-inspired houses abstain from too much ornamentation and seem therefore more masculine. This style,

An example of Italian-inspired Mediterranean style: →
the luxury hotel The Breakers in Palm Beach

also known as the **Mizner style**, had its heyday during the 1920s. Impressive examples of »Mediterranean« architecture can be found not only in the area around Miami (above all in Coral Gables, Coconut Grove, Miami Beach), but also in Palm Beach, Naples and Tampa. Miami Beach even developed the architectural style known as **Mediterranean Revival**, a southern variation of the »Colonial Revival« in New England. Pretty details with the appeal of Spanish, Italian and Moorish forms adorn the buildings of the Mediterranean Revival style. The local **coquina limestone** was often chosen as a construction material.

Art deco When visiting Miami Beach, it is impossible to miss the **Art Deco Historic District** (► Baedeker Special p.256). Nowhere else are there so many different examples of this eclectic architectural style, which unites streamlined forms and motives from all epochs und cultures. Since the 1970s, many famous citizens have mobilized for the conservation of the approximately 600 art deco buildings in Miami Beach. Beautifully renovated houses can mainly be seen along promenades such as Ocean Drive, Collins Avenue and Española Way.

Conch houses Another specialty awaits travellers to the Florida Keys: **Conch houses**, which are suited to the tropical climate. Built on stilts for better ventilation, their tilted metal roofs reflect the heat and conduct rainwater into water butts. Blind-like shutters keep out the heat and provide protection from hurricanes. Balconies and surrounding verandas offer shade and protect from too much heat. Some particularly attractive old Conch houses can be admired in Key West.

Architecture after 1945 During the booming years after the World War II, especially along the Atlantic coast between Miami Beach and Palm Beach, skyscraper hotels and apartments sprung up like mushrooms. In Miami Beach, these huge tourist hotels threatened to overpower the art deco architecture that been built since the 1930s. Along with a lot of unattractive »boxes«, a few architecturally interesting new buildings were designed. One of them is the **Fontainebleau Hilton** in Miami Beach, a hotel complex and typical example of the flamboyant architecture of the 1960s. In recent years, huge postmodern skyscrapers have been constructed around Miami. On the one hand they put all previous buildings in the shade, and on the other hand, they quote the architectural forms and design elements of art deco. During the 1970s and 1990s, Downtown Miami developed at a breathtaking pace along Biscayne Bay. The new skyline and above all the flashy banking palaces on Brickell Avenue show very impressively how the city is the second most important financial and service industries centre in the

Spectacular Miami: the 20-storey apartment building Atlantis with a hole in the façade

USA. A prime example is the **Centrust Tower**, completed in 1987 and designed by America's most famous contemporary architect, I. M. Pei in collaboration with Spillis Candela & Partners. **Atlantis** (see above) is a creation of the architectural group Arquitectonica and caused a furore with the hole in its facade containing a red staircase, a palm tree and a swimming pool.

In recent times there an increased orientation towards tradition, by using construction methods of the Native Americans and quoting stylistic elements of the colonial period. Architectural forms that are spread throughout the Caribbean area, as well as those of Anglo-American monumental architecture are apparent. The impact of the huge skyscrapers of banks, insurance companies and other big enterprises is alleviated by the influence of postmodernism. Nowadays successful contemporary architecture can be seen everywhere in Florida.

Contemporary architecture

Hotels like pyramids and shopping malls like oriental towns, houses like medieval castles, statues and fountains: in the theme parks of Florida, America's architects are allowed to let off steam. **»Entertainment architecture«** is intended to inspire, stimulate the imagination and, quite simply, just amuse. A classical example is the Swan & Dolphin Hotel at Walt Disney World. The roofs of the 2500-room hotel are decorated with statues; playful fish and swan sculptures suggest buoyancy and a sense of humour. Wall paintings with tropical motifs and postmodern-style pastel interiors provide relaxation.

The new holiday-home settlements of Seaside, Grayton Beach and Seagrove Beach along the Gulf coast are also remarkable. The completely new holiday resorts which are appearing here represent a step away from massive and bulky concrete architecture toward a filigree, individualized architecture quoting all kinds of styles.

Famous People

Who can we thank for not having to sweat in Florida's buildings, even on the hottest of days? Why have the Everglades not long since disappeared? And why is Miami called Miami? Here are brief biographies of some of those who shaped Florida.

Neil Alden Armstrong (born 1930)

As a member of the Apollo 11 mission, launched from Cape Canav-   **Astronaut**
eral, the astronaut Neil Armstrong, a native of Wapakoneta, Ohio,
became **the first man to set foot on the moon on 21 July 1969.** Armstrong was a US-Navy pilot during the Korean War. Later he studied
aircraft engineering, then worked as a test pilot for NASA before becoming an astronaut in 1962. He made his first flight into space in
1966, as part of the Gemini 8 mission. As a commander, he was in
charge of the first coupling manoeuvre between two spacecraft. From
1971 he worked as a lecturer In aerospace engineering.

John James Audubon (1785–1851)

The son of a tradesman, the illustrator and ornithologist Audubon   **Ornithologist**
was born in Les Cayes (Haïti). He came to the USA in 1805, settling   **and painter**
near Philadelphia. At first he attempted diverse business enterprises
with limited success, but Audubon was an exceptionally gifted illustrator. His copper engravings and drawings displaying flora and fauna made him famous. Between 1827 and 1838 he produced the *Birds
of America* atlas. Many of his impressions were collected during his
expeditions to Florida, which also led him to the Keys. Beside his
drawing activities, he also authored articles introducing Florida's
birds. America's oldest nature conservation organization, the National Audubon Society (NAS), founded in 1905, bears the name of this
great illustrator.

Jimmy Buffett (born 1946)

The Grateful Dead have the »Deadheads«; Jimmy Buffett has the   **Musician**
»Parrot Heads«: His fans, who always appear in colourful Hawaiian
shirts and wearing fanciful headgear, turn every Buffet concert into a
happy beach party. The well-fed bard has been singing about nothing
other than the lightness of being under Florida's palm trees for 30
years – becoming one of the state's cultural assets. Hits like *Why
Don't We Get Drunk, Margaritaville* and *Come Monday* have made
Key West's best-known son famous. Today Jimmy Buffett is to Florida what the Beach Boys are to California.

Al(fonso) Capone (1899–1947)

Alfonso Capone, originally from the southern Italian city of Naples,   **Gangster boss**
grew up in Brooklyn, New York. In 1920 he moved to Chicago,
where he became a redoubtable underworld legend. As the boss of
the local mafia syndicate, he controlled gambling, alcohol smuggling
and prostitution, among other things. Furthermore, he exerted con-

← *Andrew Jackson, seventh president of the USA, on the 20 dollar bill*

siderable influence on the work of the police. He became enormously wealthy. Although he was suspected of initiating many brutal murders and robberies, no one dared to bring him to trial, for fear of reprisals. Finally, in 1931, he was sentenced to eleven years in prison for tax evasion. He served part of his sentence on the notorious prison island of Alcatraz, near San Francisco. He was released early due to ill health. In 1939 he moved to Florida (Deerfield Beach) and died in Miami in 1947.

Ray Charles (1930–2004)

Musician On his death, a newspaper adoringly wrote: »Heaven gets some blues«. Ray Charles, who was also at home with soul and pop, spent the first 18 years of his life in Florida. He went blind at the age of seven, and first attended the Florida School of the Deaf and Blind in St Augustine. Here he learned Braille – and to play the piano. At the age of 15 he earned his first money in the bars of Jacksonville, Tampa and Orlando. At the age of 18 he moved to Seattle, and the rest is history. With songs like *Georgia On My Mind* and *What I'd Say* he captured hearts of a worldwide following.

Thomas A. Edison (1847–1931)

Inventor When, on the advice of his doctor, Edison began to spend the winter in Florida, he was already a famous man and had invented the electric light bulb. From 1901 on, he came every winter to Fort Myers to recuperate. He did not come up with any epoch-making inventions there, but the reputation of this genius resident attracted further prominent figures, above all the automobile manufacturer Henry Ford. In order to thank the native Floridans for their hospitality, he planted 200 Cuban palm trees along the streets of Fort Myers.

Gloria Estefan (born 1957)

For over two decades – and she still has plenty of rhythm in her blood – **the Latino icon** Gloria Estefan has had international success in the music business. She eventually gained recognition with her English speaking album *Unwrapped*. Born in Havana and raised in Miami, the future singer of Miami Sound Machine became famous for songs in Spanish. Her two albums *Mi Tierra* and *Alma Caribena* are unforgotten. Hardly any other star of the music scene has her ability to combine catchy pop with

Latino icon Gloria Estefan

salsa rhythms and elements of soul. She came to worldwide fame when the song *Reach* from her 1996 album *Destiny* was chosen as the official song of the Olympic Games in Atlanta. That Gloria Estefan still has very strong charisma is proven by the success of much younger colleagues such as Jennifer Lopez and Shakira, who have adopted her as a role model and learned much from her.

Henry Morrison Flagler (1830–1913)

In the »Sunshine State« the co-founder of Standard Oil made the impossible possible. In 1878, due to the illness of his wife, Flagler came to the peninsula and recognized its tourist potential. By merging the railway companies of Florida into Eastcoast Railroad, he linked the East Coast towns of the North with Miami, and finally with the Keys. In 1912 his railway reached the treacherous bridges of Key West. Flagler was also prominent in the hotel sector: In St. Augustine he built the Ponce de Léon Hotel, and in Palm Beach the Royal Poinciana Hotel. However, he rejected the request of the people in Biscayne Bay to name their town Flagler. Instead, he suggested Miami.

Railway magnate

John Gorrie (1803–55)

Doctor Scientist, humanist, politician, doctor: Gorrie, born in the Caribbean, had many talents. But his monument at the National Statuary Hall in Washington D.C. is in honour of his study of tropical diseases. Shortly after his arrival in Apalachicola, he recognized that his patients recovered from yellow fever more quickly in chilled rooms, and invented – with a machine producing artificial ice, thereby effectively lowering the temperature in the hospital wards – the prototype of the air conditioner.

Ernest Hemmingway

Ernest Hemingway (1899–1961)

When Hemingway settled in Florida in 1928, he was already well known as a writer. Key West, at that time still a backwater town of smugglers and adventurers, inspired him to write some of his best works, including *Death in the Afternoon* and *The Snows of Kilimanjaro*. For twelve years, he lived in his house at 907 Whitehead Street. He worked in the mornings, spent the afternoons deep sea fishing and he frequented the bars in the evenings. Today Ernest Hemingway is as much a part of Key West as the sunsets on Mallory Square, and his face smiles from the T-Shirts at Sloppy Joe's, his favourite bar.

Zora Neale Hurston (1903–60)

Writer Her most important novel angered both sides: blacks, who accused her of accepting financial support from whites, and whites, because she challenged the stereotypes of black Americans that was accepted at the time. In *Their Eyes Were Watching God* (1937), Hurston, **one of the most important African-American authors**, portrayed her black fellow-citizens simply as normal people. In doing so, she was far ahead of her contemporaries. Raised in Eatonville, near Orlando, she first studied ethnology. In New York she joined a group of African-American artists who became known as the Harlem Renaissance. Later she travelled back and forth across Florida and Mississippi, collecting old African-American stories. Following her death, her work faded into obscurity. She was rediscovered in the 1980s and since then her books have become required reading at American universities.

Andrew Jackson (1767–1845)

Jackson, a lawyer and plantation owner from Waxhaw, South Carolina became a judge at the Supreme Court of the State of Tennessee in 1798, but he gained fame for his service as a major general. In January 1815 he defended New Orleans against the British. Afterwards he participated in military campaigns against the Seminole and against Florida, which was still under Spanish control. In 1817–18 he took the town of Pensacola. His bold course of action led to tensions between Spain and England. The Seminole even called him »Devil«. Nevertheless he found support within the American government. In 1821 Jackson became **the first governor of both of the territories of West and East Florida.** Three years later he ran for office as a presidential candidate, but was defeated. However, he went on to win the elections of 1828, and then 1832. As **US president** he represented the interests of common citizens and was known as liberal and anti-monopolistic. Although he caused a serious financial crisis with the divestiture of the National Bank, and despite his controversial resettlement of Native Americans, he enjoyed a high reputation throughout his life.

General, 7th President of the USA (see picture on page 58)

George Edgar Merrick (1886–1942)

As a small boy, Merrick dreamed of castles in Spain. He came to Florida with his parents in 1898. In 1922, now grown-up and a lawyer, Miami real estate agent, businessman and aesthete, he began to make his dreams of Spain a reality. In 1924 he built his »City Beautiful«, a romantic, aesthetic ensemble of wide, palm-fringed streets, hacienda-like villas, peaceful golf courses and fanciful swimming pools. That same year, Coral Gables was declared the most beautiful suburb in America. Merrick stayed in the real estate business until 1940.

Businessman and town planner

Addison Mizner (1872–1933)

Mizner was Florida's leading architect during the 1920s and a darling of high society. Influenced by Spanish and Mediterranean architecture, in Palm Beach alone he designed over 50 exclusive residences with playful ornamentation for the likes of Irving Berlin, Oscar Hammerstein and the Vanderbilts – even though he never studied architecture and could not draw plans. Even his first house in Palm Beach, El Mirasol, had 37 rooms, an illuminated pool and an underground garage for 40 cars. There was nothing he liked less than soulless houses. His credo was that a house has to look as if it had fought its way from ugly duckling to beautiful swan, and to this end he encouraged his workers to break roof tiles to make them look older. The Depression thwarted his ambitious plans for Boca Raton and ruined him. Mizner died in poverty, but the unconventional »Mizner Style« had already made its mark on Florida's architecture.

Architect

Osceola (about 1800–1838)

Leader of the Seminole

The son of a white settler and a Native American, Osceola Nickano-chee was born in the north of Georgia. When he was four years old his mother left Georgia with him in order to escape discrimination by the whites, taking refuge in Florida. Osceola became a leading fig-ure among the Seminole. In 1812 and 1818 he fought against Gener-al Andrew Jackson and declined to sign any treaties with white peo-ple. His attacks against white settlers and army patrols were among the reasons for the outbreak of the second Seminole War. The Amer-ican Army was unable to achieve any victory against the guerrillas of the Seminole. There were attempts to negotiate. In 1837 Osceola, his family and a few of his adherents were arrested during peace talks, although he had been promised free passage beforehand. He died of malaria one year later in Fort Moultrie, South Carolina. Afterwards, his head was exhibited as a circus attraction.

Juan Ponce de León (1460–1521)

Ponce de León was **the first Spanish conquistador to set foot upon North American soil.** This took place on Easter Monday (Spanish: »Pasqua de Flores«) in 1513. On behalf of the Spanish crown he founded the colony La Florida, which reached from the swamps of the Gulf of Mexico to Labrador. In addition, it was Ponce de León who first recognized the phenomenon of the Gulf Stream. The Span-iard accompanied Columbus on his second trip to America in 1493. From 1502 to 1504 he took part in the conquest of Higüey on the An-tilles island of Hispaniola. From 1509 to 1512 he was governor of the neighbouring island of Puerto Rico. In 1513 he left for the first recorded expedition to present-day Florida. He landed in the area now known as Ponte Vedra Beach, be-lieving he had discovered another large island. In 1521 he made an-other expedition to Florida, deeply driven by the wish to find the fountain of youth. As he examined one of the many springs he was hit by the poisoned arrow of a Native American. He died on his way back to the Caribbean. Ponce de León was buried in the Cathedral of San Juan on the Caribbean island of Puerto Rico.

Ponce de León

Hernando de Soto (about 1500–42)

After studying at the University of Salamanca, Hernando de Soto **Spanish** served in Central America from 1519 to 1532. In 1532–33 he took **Conquistador** part in the conquest of Peru and the capture of Atahualpa, the last ruler of the Inca. After disputes with Pizarro, he returned to Spain a wealthy man in 1535. In 1537, he was appointed governor of Cuba and the royal representative in Florida. On 25 May 1539 he landed near the present-day harbour of Charlotte. He spent the next month on an unsuccessful search for the riches of Florida. During his march through the swamps he met the Spaniard Ortíz, a survivor of the failed Narvaez expedition, who from then served as an interpreter. With his help, De Soto gathered valuable knowledge about the south of the USA. His scouts reached as far as Carolina and Tennessee. He himself headed south in Alabama, where he again reached the Gulf of Mexico near Mobile. Here he waited in vain for supply ships. In 1541, during his westward march, he crossed the Mississippi, and spent the winter of 1541–42 in the present-day Arkansas. In April 1542 he returned to Florida. Constant attacks by Native Americans, fever and the disappointment of not finding any treasure demoralized De Soto. He died the same year.

Marjorie Stoneman Douglas (1890–1998)

»There are no other Everglades in the world«: the first sentence of **Writer and** her classic *The Everglades: River of Grass*, published in 1947, re- **environmental** mained her motto for the rest of her life. Stoneman fought until her **activist** death at the age of 108 years for the preservation of the Everglades in South Florida – and thus against speculators, factories and the drainage plans of the army. In 1915, as a reporter for the *Miami Herald*, she began to campaign against racial segregation and for women's rights. Long before scientists, she recognized the threat to the Everglades caused by human beings. In 1970 Florida's grande dame of environmentalism founded the society Friends of the Everglades, who continue their campaign to this day.

Practicalities

WHERE ARE THE MOST BEAUTIFUL BEACHES? WHAT IS A KEY LIME PIE AND WHAT IS A MOJITO? AND WHAT IN THE WORLD IS A »GATOR XING«? LOOK IT UP HERE – PREFERABLY BEFORE THE TRIP!

Accommodation

Huge selection of rooms

The selection of accommodation in Florida is huge. The centres of tourism have **hotels** for every taste. Many hotels also have a lounge or bar, a coffee shop and a restaurant. Swimming pools are standard, as are fitness or health centres. Many houses have a shuttle service to the airport free of charge and often also a travel and car rental agency, a cosmetic salon and a souvenir shop on site. Luxurious and often quite expensive holiday sites with all sorts of sports and entertainment offers, often like a vacation club, are called **resorts**.

Don't let the name deceive you: **bed & breakfast** costs money in Florida. But it usually means a high-class establishment (often in houses that are protected monuments) with tastefully furnished rooms. **Motels** are designed for tourists travelling in cars. These are often located at the junction of main highways and in the tourist centres. They have parking near the rooms and depending on the price level, they might have swimming pools, fitness rooms etc. The number of **villas, holiday flats, apartments and condominiums** (condos) is beyond measure. They range from luxurious villas with their own pier to a simple high-rise flat with an ocean view.

Baedeker TIP

Dorms

During the school holidays the rooms in the university dormitories in Florida's university towns (including Miami, Tampa, Gainesville) are rented out for quite affordable rates. The local tourist offices and university administrations have information.

Categories, furnishing and prices ▶

American inns can roughly be divided into the categories »simple«, »comfortable« and »luxurious« with sub-categories in between. Simple hotels and motels are furnished functionally but without great comfort. Mid-range establishments have a better level of comfort and service. Many of these houses, including most bed & breakfasts, can satisfy higher demands for service and amenities. First-class and luxury hotels or resorts offer a high standard of furnishings, amenities and service.

Amenities ▶

Even in simple accommodation a double bed, bath (shower or bathtub), air conditioning, radio, colour TV and telephone are standard. The size of the room and the furnishings depend on the category of accommodation.

Prices ▶

In the USA there is a price per room, which usually applies no matter if one, two, three or even four people are staying in it. **A rough rule of thumb** for the price of a room for one night would be: first-class, luxury more than $150; comfortable, middle class $80 to $150; good and budget $30 to $80.

Breakfast ▶

Most hotels and motels, unlike B & Bs, do not include breakfast in the price of the room. If a complimentary breakfast is offered, it is usually quite frugal. But the breakfast in a B & B is usually generous.

Attractive modern holiday architecture on the Gulf coast

Taxes and local charges will be added to the price of the room and can amount to 15% of the net rate. Many hotels charge extra for parking and the use of the safe.

◀ Additional charges

Many hotels and accommodation away from the tourist centres offer reduced weekend rates.

◀ Weekend rates

Reserving a room in advance by telephone or e-mail is especially recommended during the main travel times. Accommodation guides are available at the local tourist office and also on the internet.

◀ Reserving a room

The US youth hostel organization Hostelling International – American Youth Hostels (HI-AYH) is a member of the International Youth Hostel Association and its houses are furnished according to their standards. The prices run from $15 to 40 per night.
Caution! Among the youth hostel operators there are some black sheep who do not meet HI-AYH standards and are not members of this association. The authentic youth hostels have the triangle-shaped HI logo with the usual house-and-tree symbol.

Youth hostels

Young people can stay at the YMCA (Young Men's Christian Association) and YWCA (Young Women's Christian Association) in larger cities.

YMCA YWCA

Florida has many campgrounds and trailer parks. A plot with campsite, table, benches and fireplace is standard. Private camp grounds also have clean sanitary facilities. Often there are also additional fa-

Camping

ACCOMMODATION

HOTEL CHAINS

▶ **Best Western**
Tel. 1-800-528-1234
www.bestwestern.com

▶ **Choice Hotels**
Tel. 1-800-221-2222
www.choicehotels.com

▶ **Days Inn**
Tel. 1-800-DAYS-INN
www.daysinn.com

▶ **Hilton**
Tel. 1-800-HILTONS
www.hilton.com

▶ **Holiday Inn**
Tel. 1-800-HOLIDAY
www.ichotelsgroup.com

▶ **Howard Johnson**
Tel. 1-800-I-GO-HOJO
www.hojo.com

▶ **Hyatt**
Tel. 1-800-233-1234
www.hyatt.com

▶ **Marriott**
Tel. 1-800-228-9290
www.marriott.com

▶ **Motel 6**
Tel. 1-800-4-MOTEL-6
www.motel6.com

▶ **Quality Inn**
Tel. 1-800-228-5151
www.choicehotels.com

▶ **Radisson**
Tel. 1-800-333-3333
www.radisson.com

▶ **Ramada**
Tel. 1-800-2RAMADA
www.ramada.com

▶ **Sleep Inn**
Tel. 1-800-SLEEP-INN
www.choicehotels.com

▶ **Super 8**
Tel. 1-800-8000
www.super8.com

▶ **Travelodge**
Tel. 1-800-578-7878
www.travelodge.com

BED & BREAKFAST

▶ **Florida Bed & Breakfast Inns**
Tel. 1-800-524-1880
www.florida-inns.com

▶ **American Historic Inns**
Tel. (949) 497-2232
www.bnbinns.com

YOUTH ACCOMMODATION

▶ **Hostelling International USA Florida Council**
Tel. 1-888-520-0568
www.hiflorida.org

▶ **YMCA/YWCA**
Tel. 1-888-477-9622
www.ymcainternational.org

CAMPING

▶ **Florida Association of RV Parks & Campgrounds**
Tel. (850) 562-7151
www.floridacamping.com

▶ **Kampground of America (KOA)**
Tel. (406) 248-7444
www.koakampgrounds.com

cilities like grocery stores, snack bars, washrooms and swimming pools. State camp grounds in national parks and state parks are often beautifully situated, but might lack the comfort and equipment of private campgrounds.

Campgrounds are especially busy during the summer holidays and on long weekends. Reserving well in advance is highly recommended. ◄ Reservations

Camping outside of campgrounds is prohibited in the USA. Permission for exceptions must be obtained from the local authorities. ◄ Camping in the wild

Arrival · Before the Journey

The popularity of Florida as a holiday destination means that there are daily scheduled and charter flights from major airports in Britain and other European countries Florida. The domestic flights from other parts of the USA are numerous. The most important airports for non-stop and direct flights to Florida are Miami, Orlando, Fort Lauderdale, Fort Myers, Daytona and Tampa. Non-stop flights from Europe to Florida take about eight or nine hours. Refer to the address list opposite for affordable non-stop, direct and transfer connections. *By air*

Some cruise ships that operate between Europe and America stop regularly in Miami, the busiest cruise ship port in the world. Many tourists begin and end their ocean trip here. Other cruises destinations in Florida are Port Everglades (Fort Lauderdale), Port Canaveral (near the space centre) and Tampa on the Gulf of Mexico. *By cruise ship*

A trans-Atlantic crossing by freighter with private cabins for passengers and the appropriate service is becoming more and more popular, for example to the American ports Miami, Savannah (Georgia) and New Orleans. Contact a travel agent for further information. *By freighter*

There are limited train services to Florida from other parts of the USA. Express trains run daily from New York via Washington D.C. to Orlando, Miami or Tampa. The »Sunset Limited« runs three times a week from Los Angeles via Tucson AZ, Houston TX and New Orleans to Florida (Pensacola, Tallahassee and Orlando). *By train*

Florida is of course included in the US network of **Greyhound buses**, which are useful for reaching Florida from other states and for travelling within Florida (details: p.105–106). Depending on the distance involved and the special offers available, this is not necessarily cheaper than flying or renting a car. Reserve in advance to get cheaper tickets. *By bus*

⏵ ARRIVAL INFORMATION

EUROPEAN AIRLINES

▶ **Air France**
Tel. (0870) 142 43 43 (GB)
Tel. 1-800-237-2747 (USA)
www.airfrance.com

▶ **Alitalia**
Tel. (0870) 544 82 59 (GB)
Tel. 1-800-223-5730 (USA)
www.alitalia.it

▶ **British Airways**
Tel. (0870) 850 98 50 (GB)
Tel. 1-800-AIRWAYS (USA)
www.britishairways.com

▶ **Deutsche Lufthansa**
Tel. (0845) 773 77 47 (GB)
Tel. 1-800-399-5838 (USA)
www.lufthansa.com

▶ **Iberia**
Tel. (0845) 601 28 54 (GB)
Tel. 1-800-772-4642 (USA)
www.iberia.com

▶ **KLM/NWA**
Tel. (0870) 507 40 74 (GB)
Tel. 1-800-225-2525 (USA)
www.klm.com
www.nwa.com

▶ **Virgin Atlantic**
Tel. (0870) 574 77 47 (GB)
Tel. 1-800-862-8621 (USA)
www.virginatlantic.com

US AND OTHER AIRLINES

▶ **Air New Zealand**
Tel. (0800) 028 41 49 (GB)
Tel. 1-800-262-1234 (USA)
www.airnz.co.nz

▶ **American Airlines**
Tel. (0845) 778 9789 (GB)
Tel. 1-800-433-7300 (USA)
www.aa.com

▶ **Continental**
Tel. (0800) 77 64 64 (GB)
Tel. 1-800-231-0856 (USA)
www.continental.com

▶ **Delta Air Lines**
Tel. (0800) 41 47 67 (GB)
Tel. 1-800-241-4141 (USA)
www.delta.com

▶ **Qantas**
Tel. (0845) 774 7767 (GB)
Tel. 1-800-227-4500 (USA)
www.qantasusa.com.au

▶ **United**
Tel. (0845) 844 47 77 (GB)
Tel. 1-800-538-2929 (USA)
www.united.com

BY TRAIN

▶ **Amtrak**
Tel. 1-800-USA-RAIL (USA)
Tel. 1-800-872-7245 (USA)
www.amtrak.com

Arrival and Departure Regulations

Pre-Information Anyone planning a trip to the USA should absolutely get up-to-date information from the US embassy at home (▶ Information, embassies).

A passport and, for the citizens of most countries, a visa are necessary to travel to the USA. By the terms of the **Visa Waiver Program (VWP)** citizens of the United Kingdom, Ireland and many other EU countries, as well as Australians and New Zealanders, can normally enter without a visa for a 90-day stay for business or holiday, provided they arrive with a recognized airline or shipping company and have a return or onward ticket that is valid for the period of 90 days after the date of entering the USA. If you are unsure of your eligibility for the VWP, refer to the website www.travel.state.gov. it is advisable to take care on this point, as the regulations are liable to change. All travellers must have their own machine-readable passport when entering the USA. This applies to children as well.

Travel documents

Upon entering a digital fingerprint of the index finger and a digital photo will be taken of everyone. Upon leaving the same procedure is followed in order to compare and make sure that the same person is leaving.

◄ Fingerprint and photo

The actual length of stay will be determined individually and should be appropriate to the purpose of the trip. Only people who have entered with a visa can extend their stay. The latest possible departure date will be stamped into the passport upon arrival.

◄ Length of stay

In many cases a visa will be required to enter the USA for people from countries where a visa is not normally required for a tourist trip. This includes: people who do not enter with a regular means of transportation, people who want to study, exchange students, people who want to work in the USA (even if only temporarily; this includes journalists and au-pairs!), people who want to conduct research, people who want to get married in the USA and to stay there.

Visas required

Adequate finances must be proven when entering. They must be enough to cover the cost of the stay and a return or continuing ticket.

Adequate finances

A vaccination record will only be requested from persons who arrive from an endangered area. It is advisable in any case to get information on the latest requirements from the nearest consulate.

Vaccinations

Anyone who wants to take his dog along to the USA has to show a veterinary health and rabies vaccination record, which was produced at least one month and no more than twelve months before travelling and that is valid for no more than one year. All other pets require a veterinary health record. US embassies have the details.

Pets

Anyone who wants to drive in the United States has to have a valid national driving licence. An international driving licence is not necessary and only recognized in connection with a valid national driving licence.

National driving licence

Duty Regulations

Arriving in the USA   When arriving fill out the immigration card as well as a customs declaration. Duty free goods include personal belongings (including clothing, toilet articles), jewellery, cameras and video cameras, film, binoculars, portable typewriter, portable radio, tape recorder or TV, sporting goods, car (up to 1 year); for adults over 21 years old 1 quart (1.1 litres) of alcoholic beverages, 200 cigarettes or 50 cigars or 3 US pounds (lbs; about 1350 g) of tobacco. In addition gifts worth US$ 100 (excluding alcohol and cigarettes) per person may be brought in. Groceries, plants, sweets or fruit are strictly forbidden.

Departure ▶   In general the customs regulations of the country of destination apply. As a member of the EU, the following may be brought into the UK (from the age of 17 upwards): tobacco (200 cigarettes, 100 cigarillos, 50 cigars, 250g of loose tobacco), alcohol (1 litre of high-proof spirits), coffee (500g of coffee and 200g of instant coffee), scent (60g of perfume and 250g of eau de toilette), medicines for personal use and all other goods up to a value of £ 145 or approx. US$ 290, excluding articles for personal use.

Travel Warnings

Danger of terrorist attacks   The danger of terrorist attacks continues to exist worldwide. Primary targets are especially places of symbolic character, government buildings, airports, railway stations as well as crowded places. The US Department of Homeland Security warns against attacks and calls on travellers to be especially cautious. There are meticulous security checks for air and ocean travel. For this reason plan enough time for the security checks when travelling.

Travel Insurance

Medical and accident insurance   The cost of medical treatment can be a problem for tourists. A stay in hospital can be extremely expensive. Treatments must be paid for in advance or in cash on the spot. Medical insurance that includes coverage in the USA is strongly recommended, as is a credit card with an adequate line of credit. In many cases it is even cheaper to go back home and to be treated there. Before travelling to the USA it is absolutely necessary to consult your medical and accident insurance company to see to what extent you are covered. In most cases it will be necessary to buy additional travel medical insurance.

Third party auto insurance   In the USA auto insurance is compulsory. However, auto insurance from the UK is not valid in the USA. Before travelling to the USA it is advisable to make sure that you are covered by an auto insurance that is valid in the USA. Travel agents, insurance agents and auto clubs will have more information.

Beaches

The clean water and the mostly sandy beaches and bays both on Florida's Atlantic coast and on the Gulf coast enjoy an excellent reputation. Near larger cities and on beaches that happen to be »in« the crowds of bathers can be pretty big, especially on long weekends (like Memorial Day Weekend) and during the school holidays. But it is never more than a few miles to less crowded beaches away from the more popular ones.

Beach paradise

On the northern section of the Atlantic coast there are still miles of high sand dunes; along with longer shell beaches there are also some with relatively soft and fine sand. In other areas the beaches are mainly broad, with sand that is firm or even quite hard. It is still possible at some beaches, for instance at **Daytona Beach**, to drive onto the beach and right up to the water. The beaches between Palm Beach and Miami have changed greatly in the last years due to erosion. Considerable efforts are being made to preserve what remains in Palm Beach, Fort Lauderdale and Miami Beach.

Beaches on the Atlantic coast

On the south-western Gulf coast, specifically around Fort Myers – Naples, the beaches on **Sanibel** Island and **Captiva** Island as well as Bonita Beach and Naples Beach deserve mention. There are top beaches at **Pinellas Suncoast** near **St Petersburg**. Here **Clearwater Beach** as well as the beaches on **Caladesi Island** and **Honeymoon Island** are among the best. The superb beaches at **St George Island** and **Cape San Blas** or St Joseph's Point on the north-western Gold coast are still considered to be hot tips; they can be reached best via US 98 or via Apalachicola. There are beautiful quartz sand beaches between **Panama City** and **Pensacola**, especially on the Gulf Islands. Others worth mentioning are **St Andrew's Beach**, **Panama City Beach**, the beach at **Destin** and the beach on **Perdido Key** off the coast of Pensacola. The beaches of the planned holiday village of **Seaside** as well as **Grayton Beach**, which border the popular Panama City Beach on the north-west, are some of the most beautiful in North America.

Beaches on the Gulf coast

On Florida's beaches **nude bathing is frowned on,** even though the swimwear is sometimes quite daring. Topless bathing is tolerated at a growing number of beaches – like South Beach at Miami Beach, Daytona Beach, Key West and Panama City Beach as well as private beaches at exclusive resorts. Outside these places, nude bathers can count on heavy fines.

Nude sunbathing

Florida's coastlines generally have high waves and dangerous currents. Every year swimmers on Florida's beaches lose their lives because of their foolhardy behaviour. Thus it is advised only to make use of beaches with life guards or bay watch.

Danger on the beach and in the water

Lifeguards on Florida's Atlantic coast

Sunburn ▶ It is easy to forget that sea water and sun can quickly cause sunburns. Experience has shown that it helps to wear a cotton shirt or t-shirt, especially when snorkelling.

All sorts of wild life ▶ Occasionally snakes and alligators hunting for turtles or bird's eggs in the brush cause some excitement. Mosquitoes and sand fleas can also be a nuisance.

Danger under water ▶ Florida's warm waters are the home of many kinds of poisonous sea life. Fire coral, sea anemones and jelly fish (including the »Portuguese man o'war«, which is not a true jellyfish) have strong neurotoxins; pencil and diadema sea urchins have poisonous thorns which can easily break off; various kinds of scorpion fish like the red lion fish and the stone fish are equipped with poisonous fins; there is also danger from moray eels, stingrays, barracudas and sharks.

Florida Keys There are only a few and then quite small beaches in the Florida Keys, but they nevertheless offer outstanding snorkelling.

Snorkelling, diving Read more on this topic under ▶Sport and Outdoors (see p.99).

Children in Florida

Are we nearly there? Long cars trips, little to see and less to do: in the USA the unusually great distances are more of a challenge to parents with whining children in the back seat than in the densely populated European countries with comparatively short distances. But the situation is bearable in large parts of Florida, where the distances between attractions for children are acceptable.

Child-friendly infrastructure

Children under 2 years generally fly free as long as they don't need a seat of their own – which is less the case on transatlantic flights, but is tolerable on USA inland flights. Ask about children's discounts.

In airplanes

All car rental agencies have children's seats. They should be reserved with the car, since they might run out during the high season.

In rental cars

In hotels and motels children can stay in their parents' room at no charge. Extra beds can be provided. But ask about the age limit (mostly 12 years) and other conditions.

Accommodation

Going out to eat with children is no problem in Florida. It doesn't always have to be fast food either. Family restaurants like Denny's, Wendy's etc. have kids' menus at reasonable prices. Steakhouses and Chinese restaurants are also often affordable. High-class restaurants are less able to accommodate children. There are all you can eat spe-

Restaurants

Kids have lots of fun in the world of Walt Disney.

cials for anyone on a budget. When plates aren't finished off in a family restaurant doggie bags are available. Apart from hamburgers, French fries and ketchup, children love the pancakes and sundaes that are served up everywhere.

Roller Coasters, Rockets and Dolphins

Like heaven · Those who like to travel with children to children's amusements will think Florida is heaven. Some of the largest amusement parks in the world are here; they are described in the section Sights from A to Z. **Walt Disney World, Universal Studios Escape** and **SeaWorld** near ▶Orlando head the list. **Busch Gardens** in ▶Tampa and **Cypress Gardens** near Winter Haven are also popular. Kids love the many water parks. One of the best-known is **Wet 'n Wild** in Orlando. Apart from the large parks there are also animal parks, dolphinariums, aquariums etc. mostly near tourist centres. **Miami Metrozoo, Marineland of Florida** near St Augustine and **Gulfarium** near Fort Walton Beach are worth mentioning. Youngsters also enjoy the national and state parks, especially those where water plays a large role and where alligators, manatee, sea eagles etc. can be seen in the wild.

Rockets, airpla- · An absolute highlight for every young Florida visitor is **Kennedy**
nes and fast cars **Space Center** at the US space centre. There are also airplane museums scattered throughout the entire Sunshine State, the most attractive being the **Naval Air Museum** in Pensacola. The multi-media show **Daytona USA** at the world-famous racetrack is a highlight for both young and old car freaks.

Child- · The museum organizers in the USA are excellent at keeping the »lit-
friendly · tle ones« in mind. Many of Florida's museums have **»hands on« or**
museums **»please touch« departments**, where young and old can try out experiments and technical tricks from many branches of the sciences. This applies especially to the larger museums of natural science and technology like the Museum of Science & Industry in Tampa, or the Museum of Science & History in Jacksonville.

Cruises

Cruises · Many visitors to Florida do not want to miss out on a cruise to the Bahamas or to Key West, or a longer one through the Caribbean. Boating excursions for several hours start from many places along the coast as well. They offer sumptuous meals, duty-free shopping and sometimes gambling.

The main cruise · The port of **Miami** rightly deserves the title of »Cruise Capital of the
ports ▶ World«: About 4 million cruise ship passengers pass through here every year. It is also the home port of several large cruise ship lines.

CRUISES

CRUISE PORTS

► **Port of Miami**
Tel. (305) 371-7678
www.miamidade.gov

► **Port Canaveral**
Tel. (321) 783-7831
www.portcanaveral.org

► **Port Everglades**
Tel. (954) 523-3404
www.porteverglades.org

► **Port of Key West**
Tel. (305) 294-37 21
www.keywestcity.com

► **Port of Palm Beach**
Tel. (561) 842-42 01
www.portofpalmbeach.com

► **Port of Tampa**
Tel. (813) 905-7678
www.tampaport.com

CRUISE SHIP LINES

► **Carnival Cruise Line**
Tel. 1-888-CARNIVAL
www.carnival.com

► **Celebrity**
Tel. 1-800-647-2251
www.celebrity.com

► **Cunard**
Tel. 1-800-7-CUNARD
www.cunard.com

► **Norwegian**
Tel. 1-800-327-7030
www.ncl.com

► **Princess**
Tel. 1-800-PRINCESS
www.princess.com

► **Royal Caribbean**
Tel. 1-800-398-9819
www.royalcaribbean.com

Cruise ships head for the Caribbean from Miami.

Port Everglades outside of Fort Lauderdale is also a busy port. The third-largest port for cruise ships is **Port Canaveral** near the space centre Cape Canaveral. Cruises leave for the Bahamas from **Palm Beach**. From **Tampa** on the Gulf coast luxury liners leave for Key West or Mexico and the Caribbean. **Key West**, the southernmost port in mainland USA, has an almost Caribbean atmosphere, and a growing number of cruise ships stop there.

Electricity

110 Volts AC
The mains supply is 110 Volts AC. Those bringing European norm (set switch to 110!) electrical appliances need an adaptor which can be purchased at the airport or department stores.

Emergency

● IMPORTANT TELEPHONE NUMBERS

EMERGENCY TELEPHONES

There are emergency telephones along many of the interstate highways.

EMEREGENCY NUMBERS IN FLORIDA

► **Police, ambulance, fire department**
Tel. 911 (if no one answers dial 0 for the telephone operator.

► **Florida Highway Patrol**
Tel. FHP

► **Tourist emergency number**
Tel. 1-800-656-8777

► **US Auto Club AAA**
Tel. 1-800-AAA-HELP

► **ADAC emergency centre Orlando**
Tel. 1-888-222-1373

Etiquette and Customs

Strict rules for alcohol consumption
The laws and standards on the consumption of alcohol are regulated at the state level in the USA (sometimes even in individual counties) and thus vary greatly. The legal drinking age in Florida is 21 years; that means that anyone younger can neither buy alcohol nor get it in restaurants. Wine, beer and spirits are only available in liquor stores. On Sundays alcoholic products can only be bought after 1pm.

The consumption of alcohol is prohibited in public areas (administrative buildings, railway stations, beaches). The consumption of alcohol is even prohibited in parked cars. Driving under the influence of alcohol is prosecuted severely. The allowed **blood alcohol level is 0.0**. Moreover the transport of opened bottles or cans of alcoholic beverages is prohibited in cars (not even in the boot!).

The tolerance of smoking has been low for some time in the USA. None of the airlines allow smoking, nor is it allowed in public buildings. Restaurants only have small smoking areas. Meanwhile anyone smoking around children risks a public confrontation.

Smoking not tolerated

Greetings in Florida are informal. First names are used commonly, although older people are often alert to whether they are addressed as »Mr« or »Mrs«. By the way, using first names does not imply familiarity. Americans do keep strangers at a distance, but they are usually polite.

Greetings

»It's a fine day, isn't it?« No matter whether they are in an elevator or a queue: when Americans are present for anything more than a short time, they often make small talk. This does not mean that they want to start a conversation, but only that this is polite. Not speaking or turning away is considered to be rude.

Smalltalk

»Come and see us some time!« After a meeting and an animated conversation, friendly Americans often leave with this phrase. Do not take this invitation literally; it's only a polite expression. Americans would be very surprised if someone actually did turn up without first reconfirming the invitation by telephone.

Invitation

The belief that Americans are naïve and uneducated persists because of cliché Americans who appear in public regularly. Most US citizens do know something about the rest of the world and also that they do not live in paradise. Visitors from »old Europe« who criticize American problems like racial issues, immigration policies, the school system, arms control and foreign affairs could be seen as rude. It's better to wait until your opinion is asked for. Then you will notice that Americans are also interested and expressive conversationalists.

Discussions

In the USA tips are not included in the bill and are thus given separately. This is not required, but the personnel in restaurants and hotels are not paid well and genuinely depend on their tips. 15% of the bill before tax is usual. Leave the tip in the restaurant on the table. Hotel pages expect $1 per bag.
Maids get $2 per day. It's OK to leave the tip in the room in an envelope when checking out. If a hotel or restaurant offers valet parking, the valet gets $1 (when taking the car away and when returning it).

Tipping

Festivals · Holidays · Events

▶ HOLIDAYS

NATIONAL HOLIDAYS

▶ **New Year**
1 January

▶ **Martin Luther King Jr. Day**
3rd Monday in January

▶ **President's Day**
3rd Monday in February

▶ **Good Friday**
(only regional)

▶ **Memorial Day**
Last Monday in May

▶ **Independence Day**
4 July

▶ **Labor Day**
1st Monday in September

▶ **Columbus Day**
2nd Monday in October

▶ **Election Day**
1st Tuesday in November
(only in election year!)

▶ **Veteran's Day**
11 November

▶ **Thanksgiving Day**
4th Thursday in November

▶ **Christmas Day**
25 December

HOLIDAYS ONLY IN FLORIDA

▶ **Mardi Gras**
Shrove Tuesday (regional mainly in the panhandle and in Miami, Little Havana)

▶ **Confederate Memorial Day**
Memorial Day for the Confederate states, 26 April

▶ **Halloween**
31 October
(only in some areas)

Few holidays In the USA there are a few official holidays (public holidays). And even then, except for on Thanksgiving Day, Easter, Christmas Day and New Year's Day, many shops are open. Banks, government offices and schools are closed on public holidays.

The more important Christian holidays, Easter, Pentecost, Christmas, are celebrated on only one day. If a holiday falls on Sunday the following Monday is also a holiday. Most of the official holidays shift every year to the Monday before or after the actual date in order to create long weekends.

▶ CALENDER OF EVENTS

▶ **Key West**
Key West Literary Festival
(early January)
Literature event lasting several
days with a party in honour of the
authors Ernest Hemingway,
Thornton Wilder and Tennessee
Williams

▶ **Miami**
Miami Jazz Festival
(early January).
The world's best jazz musicians
meet in downtown Miami

▶ **Miami Beach**
Art Deco Weekend
(mid-January).
Events in the Art Deco
District in South Beach

▶ **Tarpon Springs**
Greek Epiphany
(6 January).

▶ **Daytona Beach**
Speed Weeks
(1st and 2nd weeks in February)
Auto and motorbike racing freaks
meet at the Daytona Speedway.

▶ **Fort Myers**
Edison Festival of Lights
(3rd week in February)
Festival of lights with parades
through the illuminated centre of
town in honour of the great
inventor.

▶ **Miami**
Miami Film Festival
(1st and 2nd week in February)
Latest American and international
productions

▶ **Miami,
Coconut Grove**
Coconut Grove Arts Festival
(mid-February)
Young artistic talents exhibit in
Peacock Park.

▶ **Palm Beach**
ArtiGras
Mixture of art festival and carnival
with horse racing and birthday
party for Henry Flagler.

▶ **Tampa**
Fiesta Day
Street festival for exiled Cubans in
historic Ybor City

Gasparilla Pirate Invasion Festival
In Hillsborough Bay sailboats
accompany the notorious pirate
ship; street festivals and parades
on land.

▶ **Daytona Beach**
Bike Week
In the 1st and 2nd weekend in
March motor bikers from all over
the USA and also from overseas
meet here.

▶ **Miami Downtown**
Carnival Miami
(1st week in March)
Exuberant street festival
with carnival background

▶ **Miami,
Calle Ocho**
Calle Ocho Festival
(2nd week in March
SW 8th Street)
Folk festival of the exiled Cubans
in Little Havana

APRIL

► **Key West**
Conch Republic Independence
Celebration
(4th week in April)
Party on Mallory Square to commemorate the Keys' declaration of
independence in 1982 (not to be
taken seriously)

MAY

► **Destin**
MayFest (3rd week in May)
Dixieland, blues and jazz festival

JUNE

► **Fort Walton Beach**
Billy Bowlegs Festival
(1st week in June)
Re-enactment of the conquest of
the city by pirates (1779).

► **Miami, Coconut Grove**
Goombay Festival
(1st week in June)
Carnival-like parties with lots of
music by Bahaman immigrants

JULY

► **Daytona Beach**
Pepsi 400 (1st week in July)
Highly respected NASCAR race

► **Key West**
Hemingway Days
(2nd and 3rd week in July)
Readings and live music in honour
of the great writer

► **Miami Downtown**
America's Birthday Bash (4th July)
Street festivals with music and
fireworks celebrate Independence
Day

Fiesta Day on Tampa's streets can get noisy.

AUGUST

► **Miami**
Miami Reggae Festival
(1st week in August)
Musical event celebrating Jamaican Independence Day

SEPTEMBER

► **Jacksonville**
Riverside Art Festival
(2nd week in September)
About 200 artists, mostly young, exhibit their work in Riverside Park; lots of music and even wine tasting.

OCTOBER

► **Clearwater**
Jazz Holidays
(3rd week in October)
American Top Acts

► **Crystal River**
Florida Manatee Festival
(early/mid-October)
Various entertaining events on the theme of the sea cows on both river banks

► **Daytona Beach**
Biketoberfest
(3rd week in October)
Biker and motorbike Octoberfest

► **Fort Lauderdale**
International Boat Show
(4th week in October)
One of the largest boat fairs in the world.

► **Miami**
Columbus Day Regatta
(2nd week in October)
Florida's largest sailing regatta

NOVEMBER

► **Pensacola**
Gulf Coast Art Festival
Event with local artists in downtown Pensacola.

Blue Angels Air Show
(mid-November)
Acrobatic feats of the world-famous flying troupe

► **St Petersburg**
Fall Boat Show
(3rd week in November)
Boat fair for the super-rich

DECEMBER

► **Miami**
Orange Bowl Parade
(late December)
Year-end and New Year's festival with colourful parades and the crowning of the Orange Bowl Queen

Food and Drink

Restaurants

For Europeans American cooking can take some getting used to. This starts with the hearty American breakfast with bacon, eggs, hash brown potatoes and pancakes. But hamburgers, ketchup, hot dogs and crisps are not the only originally American foods – on the contrary: many American restaurants now serve light and healthy meals.

From hearty to exotic

There are regional specialties like **Cajun cuisine** from the neighbouring state of Louisiana or **Tex-Mex**, and in good bars or pubs even the **burger** is served on a thick bed of lettuce, cucumber and tomato. As a classic land of immigrants, the USA also has **countless ethnic restaurants** to choose from. Cuban, Mexican, Brazilian, Thai, Indian, Arab, Italian, French: in Florida you can eat your way around the world. There are also kosher and vegetarian restaurants. The numerous **fish and seafood** restaurants, which offer many specialties, are also worth trying. Don't miss the chance to try the extremely palatable Florida wines, and for dessert a **Key lime pie**.

Prices
The many fast food restaurants (like Burger King, Kentucky Fried Chicken, McDonald's, Pizza Hut, Taco Bell) are cheap but not necessarily good. There are better restaurants, including the family restaurant Denny's, in all of the larger tourist locations. The spruced-up historical town centres, marinas and the areas around the luxury hotels often have very good but also very expensive restaurants.

Mealtimes

Breakfast
Breakfast is best eaten in a coffee shop or a fast food restaurant near the hotel or motel. American breakfast includes a glass of grapefruit or orange juice, coffee, eggs (poached, fried sunny side up or scrambled or an omelette), fried bacon or sausages, hash browns, pancakes with maple syrup and of coarse toast with butter and jam. Many breakfast buffets have cornflakes and milk, fresh muesli, fruit and flavoured yogurts.

Brunch ▶
Brunches are very popular on Sundays and holidays (combination of breakfast and lunch), when generous buffets await hungry guests from 11am to 3pm.

Lunch
A light meal is usually eaten at noon (lunch), for example a salad, chicken sandwich or grilled meat and vegetables.

Dinner
The main daily meal is eaten in the evening (dinner). It consists of meat or fish with all sorts of accompaniments and side dishes. An appetizer and dessert is usually included. In some restaurants dinner shows entertain the guests.

Typical Dishes and Drinks

Meat dishes
T-bone steaks, Porterhouse steaks and sirloin steaks are the main meat dishes in Florida as well, along with the ubiquitous burgers. A barbecue (BBQ) practically has a ritual of its own, where all sorts of meat are grilled on a charcoal grill. But chicken (chicken fingers are baked fingers of chicken breast) and pork (prime rib) are also popular. They are served with a baked potato with sour cream or French fries. The traditional food on Thanksgiving Day is turkey.

Florida is known for its tasty seafood.

There is not only seafood from the Atlantic and the Gulf of Mexico, but also fresh-water fish from rivers and lakes. Crab, shrimps, clams, lobster, crawfish, bass and snappers are popular. The native stone crabs, conches from the Keys and oysters from the oyster banks near Apalachicola are also valued as delicacies.

Excellent fish dishes

Along with these, many tasty dishes typical of the various immigrant groups can be sampled. The range of specialties covers everything from Italian pasta to Greek gyros and Spanish paella to delicious Caribbean, Mexican and Oriental cuisine, not to mention kosher food.

Immigrant cooking

Cheese cake and above all Key lime pie made with juicy limes and cream are popular desserts.

Desserts

Fresh fruits and vegetables are available all year in Florida. This applies especially to citrus fruits and vegetables that are easy to prepare, like cucumbers, tomatoes and avocados.

Fruit, vegetables

American coffee is not as weak as it used to be. New chains like Starbuck's have taken care of that and have popularized cappuccino, caffè latte etc. In areas where many exiled Cubans and immigrants live, coffee is usually drunk as a strong espresso or cafe Cubano from little cups. In the tourist areas the number of street cafés in the southern European style is growing.

Coffee

Wine is grown in some parts of Florida, as around St Augustine, but the restaurants mostly serve Californian and imported wines, generally chilled.

Wine

Beer   Beer in the USA is always chilled and frequently has noticeably less alcohol than European beer. Bars generally have a variety of bottled and draft beer on hand. In Florida US brands (Budweiser) are preferred. Import beers (like the Mexican Corona) are also popular, but considerably more expensive.

In the past few years an increasing number of small or local breweries have been able to prevail against the established large breweries. The »local brews« generally use traditional brewing methods and have already gained a good share of the market.

i The best local breweries

- Fernandina Beach: Williamsville Brewery
- Orlando: Beach Brewing
- Tampa: Ybor City Brewing
- Key West: Hammerhead's Sharkbite Brewery

Juices, soft drinks   Fruit juices made from local oranges, grapefruits or pineapples are available everywhere. Soft drinks and root beer, which is made from water, sugar, colouring and spices, as well as iced tea are popular thirst quenchers.

Water   A glass of water is served with every meal, but be warned: it is usually tap water with crushed ice. Anyone who wants real table water should order »sparkling water« (carbonated table or mineral water) or »mineral water« (often uncarbonated mineral water).

Spirits (Liquor)   Popular alcoholic drinks, which can only be bought in liquor stores and in bars only at certain times, include whiskey (Bourbon, Scotch, Canadian, rye, Irish, blended), gin, vodka, brandy, rum, vermouth and cordials.

Alcoholic drinks ▶   Drinks based on rum, whiskey or tequila are often mixed in bars. The favourites are mojito, daiquiri, planter's punch and caipirinha, mixed drinks that are made with rum or sugar cane liquor imported from the Caribbean or Brazil.

Health

Drugstore, pharmacy   In the USA a distinction is made between drugstores and pharmacies. Prescription medicines are available at the latter. In Florida there are numerous branches of Eckerd's drugstores. Every Winn-Dixie supermarket also has a drugstore.

Hours ▶   Drugstores or pharmacies are mostly open from 9am to 6pm. Some are even open until 9pm. The pharmacies in 24-hour supermarkets are open around the clock.

Emergencies ▶   There are no special emergency services outside of the regular opening hours. It might be necessary to go to the closest emergency room, ER, in a hospital. Hospitals are also open around the clock and have their own pharmacies.

Medical care is good. This applies not only to doctors in private practice and dentists, but also to the hospitals. Tourists who take medications regularly should take along a copy of the prescription in case an American doctor needs to write a new one.

◄ Medical care

A hospital stay or even just a visit to the emergency room can break the holiday budget. So it is advisable to get travel insurance for the USA before travelling.

◄ Medical care is expensive

Doctors in private practice and hospitals are listed in the Yellow Pages of local telephone books. In case of emergency dial 911 or 0 for the operator, who can connect you to the nearest emergency room.

◄ Medical emergency service

Personal negligence is the greatest health risk factor. It is easy to underestimate Florida's sun and heat and forget head covering and water bottles when going out, which can have disastrous consequences. The sun is at its most intense between 11am and 3pm. People with sensitive skin should stay out of the sun during this time. Along with a good sunscreen, a very good insect repellent is indispensable since mosquitoes are always present near water – which makes them all the more common in the swamps and wetlands of Florida. Mosquito season is from June to November. At this time long sleeves and long trousers are recommended (risks on the beach ►bathing holiday).

Health risks

Information

The U.S. no longer operates national tourist offices in other countries, and the U.S. Travel & Tourism Administration in Washington has also ceased to exist. In a number of countries the Visit USA Association provides information and literature (see addresses below). A number of American tourist destinations have representation abroad: see below for phone numbers in the UK. For visa information refer to US embassies and their websites.

● TOURIST INFORMATION

IN FLORIDA

► **Visit Florida**
661 E. Jefferson Street
Tallahassee, FL 32301
Tel. (850) 488-5607
www.visitflorida.com

VISIT AMERICA

► **Australia**
www.visitusa.org.au

► **Canada**
6519B Mississauga Road
Mississauga, ON L5N 1A6
Tel/fax (416) 352-5567
www.seeamerica.ca

► **Ireland**
60 Merrion Square, Dublin 2
Tel. 01-890 29 63
www.visitusa.ie

► **New Zealand**
www.visitusa.co.nz

► **UK**
US Embassy, 24 Grosvenor Square,
London, W1A 1AE
Tel. 0870 777 2213
Fax: 0207 495 4851
www.visitusa.org.uk

**FLORIDA DESTINATIONS:
UK CONTACT**

UK representations of cities and
areas in Florida
Central Florida: tel. 01373-466707
Daytona Beach: tel. 020-7932 2471
Florida: tel. 020-7932 2406
Keys & Key West: tel. 01564-794555
Space Coast: tel. 01293-449145
Fort Lauderdale: tel. 01628-778863
Kissimmee-St. Cloud
Tel. 01732-875722
Miami: tel. 01444-443355
Sarasota: tel. 020-7257 8858
St Petersburg/Clearwater:
Tel. 020-8339 6121

US EMBASSIES

► **In Australia**
Moonah Place,
Yarralumla, ACT 2600
Tel. (02) 6214-5600,
Fax (02) 6214-5970
http://canberra.usembassy.gov

► **In Canada**
490 Sussex Drive,
Ottawa, Ontario K1N 1G8
Tel. 613-688-5335
Fax 613.688.3082
http://canada.usembassy.gov

► **In Republic of Ireland**
42 Elgin Road,
Ballsbridge, Dublin 4
Tel. +353 1 668-8777
Fax +353 1 668-9946
http://dublin.usembassy.gov

► **In UK**
24 Grosvenor Square,
London, W1A 1AE
Tel. (0)20 7499-9000
http://london.usembassy.gov
US Consulates General in Cardiff,
Edinburgh and Belfast.

EMBASSIES IN USA

► **Australia**
1601 Massachusetts Ave, N.W.
Washington DC 20036
Tel. (202) 797 3000
www.austemb.org

► **Canada**
501 Pennsylvania Avenue, N.W.
Washington, D.C. 20001
Tel. (202) 682-1740, fax: 682-7619
www.canadianembassy.org

► **Ireland**
2234 Massachusetts Ave NW
Washington DC 20008
Tel. (202) 462-3939, 232-5993
www.irelandemb.org

► **New Zealand**
37 Observatory Cir NW
Washington, DC 20008
Tel. (202) 328-4800, 667 5227
www.nzembassy.com

► **UK**
3100 Massachusetts Avenue,
Washington DC, 20008
Tel. (202) 588 7800, fax 588 7850
Emergency tel.: (202) 588 6500
www.britainusa.com

CONSULATES IN FLORIDA

► **Australia**
Contact British or Canadian
consulate

► **Canada**
200 S. Biscayne Boulevard
Suite 1600, Miami

Tel. (305) 579-1600
http://geo.international.gc.ca/
can-am/miami

▶ **New Zealand**
Contact British or
Canadian consulate

▶ **UK**
1001 Brickell Bay Drive
Suite 2800, Miami, FL 33131
Tel. (305) 374-1522
www.britainusa.com/miami

▶ **US Government
Official Website**
http://www.firstgov.gov

▶ **USA Weather Information**
http://www.weather.com/

▶ **Recreation Services**
http://www.recreation.gov/

Literature

Max A. Collins: *CSI: Miami, Heat Wave.* Simon & Schuster, 2004.   Novels, prose
Florida's »Crime Scene Investigation« (CSI) dominates the TV channels around the world. Now also in book form.

Ernest Hemingway: *Islands in the Stream.* The Florida classic – not just for deep sea fishermen.

Ernest Hemingway: *To Have and Have Not.* A turbulent story about a boat owner with a dubious reputation who is killed in a battle with Cuban bank robbers.

Carl Hiaasen: *Stormy Weather.* The Miami Herald columnist's novel on profiteers who tried to take advantage of the chaos caused by Hurricane Andrew.

Zora Neale Hurston: *Their Eyes Were Watching God.* About a black woman in rural Florida.

Marjorie Kinnan Rawlings: *Cross Creek. My Planting Experiences in Florida.* The author is famous for her beautiful accounts of rural life.

Peter Matthiessen: *Killing Mister Watson.* Historical novel about Ed Watson, an Everglades pioneer.

Marjorie Stoneman Douglas: *The Everglades – River of Grass.* Sarasota: Pineapple Press, 1988. One of the most sensitive books on the fragile landscape of the American south-east.

Tennessee Williams: *Memoirs.* There is a generous chapter on his time in Key West in his memoirs.

Non-fiction **Michael Gannon:** *The New History of Florida*, 1996. A weighty and scholarly but readable work.

Laura Cerwinske and David Kaminsky: *Tropical Deco: The Architecture and Design of Old Miami Beach*, 1991. An informative and well-illustrated survey.

Stuart McIver: *Dreamers, Schemers and Scalawags: The Florida Chronicles.* About the gangsters and millionaires who shaped the Sunshine State.

Diane Roberts: *Dream State.* The author is a native of Florida and radio journalist who knows her subject well and can write interestingly about politicians, money-makers and rogues past and present

John Rothchild: *Up for Grabs.* An entertaining journey around Florida that takes a look at the deal-making in the history of the state.

Cookbook **Jeanne Voltz and Caroline Stuart:** *The Florida Cookbook: From Gulf Coast Gumbo to Key Lime Pie.* Traditional and modern recipes.

Nature **Herbert W. Kale, David S. Maehr and Karl Karalus:** *Florida's Birds: A Handbook and Reference.* The ideal companion for bird-watchers.

Kevin McCarthy: *Alligator Tales.* Lots of stories by alligator hunters, but also the arguments for protecting the animals.

Media

TV There is a television in every hotel room. The main television channels are free. Beyond thatthere are many TV programmes on private channels that sometimes charge quite steep fees (pay TV).

Radio American radio stations can be heard on medium wave (AM). They give the most up-to-date information on weather, traffic, events etc. FM carries stations with local information from individual towns, national parks etc. In sparsely populated areas fewer radio stations can be heard and more in more populated areas.

Newspapers and magazines A broad palette of daily newspapers and periodicals to suit every taste is available. Florida's leading daily is the **Miami Herald**. There are also several regionally important newspapers.

UK and Irish newspapers Newsstands sell papers from the UK and Republic of Ireland, but they are normally a day old. Some publications, such as the UK paper *The Times*, are available in a US edition the same day.

Money

The US monetary unit is the **dollar** (US$), colloquially called the »buck«. Apart from notes, or bills, worth $1, 2, 5, 10, 20, 50 and 100 (there are also larger notes for bank business), there are coins worth 1 (penny), 5 (nickel), 10 (dime), 25 (quarter) cents, and more rarely 50 cents (half-dollar) and 1 dollar in circulation. It is better to exchange money in your home country – part of it into traveller's cheques, which are accepted almost everywhere. Up to $10,000 may be brought into or taken out of the country freely. Larger amounts must be declared in the customs declaration form which non-residents are required to complete on the plane.

Currency

Traveller's cheques and major foreign currencies can be exchanged without difficulty in banks or in branches of Thomas Cook or American Express. It is much more convenient when changing to have traveller's cheques that were issued in dollars.

Traveller's cheques and foreign currency

Opening times of banks: Mon–Thu 9am–3.30pm, Fri until 4.30pm

The most common method of payment is the **credit card**; Euro/MasterCard and Visa are the most common. When renting a car, a credit card is required for the deposit; most hotels require them as well.

Credit cards

ATMs (automatic teller machines) are available at many locations around the clock. **UK bank cards** Most international bank cards enable the holder to withdraw money from ATMs in the USA, though there will probably be a charge incurred and the exchange rate is likely to be less advantageous than offered by banks and bureaux de change at home. Of course, the PIN is necessary for withdrawals.

◄ *Debit cards*

ALL ABOUT MONEY

EXCHANGE RATE

1 US$ = 0.51 GBP
1 GBP = 1.98 US$
1 US$ = 0.65 €
1 € = 1.54 US$
Current exchange rates:
www.oanda.com

LOST CREDIT CARD

► **Telephone numbers**
There is a number on the back of every credit card which should be called in the case of the card being lost or stolen – it's a good idea to make a note of this number as well

as those given by your bank. For Visa cards, the Visa Global Card Assistance Service will arrange for lost cards to be cancelled. In the USA, the number for this free and multi-lingual service is 1-800-847-2911.

 Telephone numbers

- American Express:
  Tel. 1-800-297-7672
- MasterCard:
  Tel. 1-800-627-8372
- Visa: tel. 1-800-847-2911

Museums

The most important museums are described in Sights from A to Z under the town in which they are located. For opening hours and admission ask the local tourist office or refer to the internet site www.flamuseums.org (see Tip). Many museums are closed Mondays. Admission fees can be quite high. Some museums offer generous discounts to children, students and seniors. Most museums have information centres and visitor services. Guided tours on specific highpoints are offered. Almost every museum has a shop where souvenirs, books, postcards etc. can be bought.

National Parks · State Parks

Protected areas Many parts of Florida are under nature protection. These are divided into **national** and state parks, national and state forests, national and state wildlife refuges or preserves, national seashore etc., **national state monuments, historic sites, archaeological sites** and **national and state recreational areas**. The use of this land is regulated and visitors need to follow strict rules. The reserves are controlled by specially trained supervisors (park rangers). Anyone who wants to explore these areas unsupervised can only do so with special permission from the park rangers. Most of the reserves charge admission (5 – 25 $ per person or vehicle!).

Accommodation Many of the national or state parks have accommodation in motels, lodges and cabins. Advanced reservations are recommended.

Behaviour in nature preserves Stay on the marked roads and trails in nature preserves. Camping and campfires are only allowed in specially marked areas. Do not litter or feed wild animals. Hunting is not allowed, fishing only with a permit. Of course, do not take any plants or animals along.

IMPORTANT ADDRESSES NATURE PRESERVES

NATIONAL PARKS

► **National Park Service**
Headquarters
1849 C Street NW
Washington, DC 20240
Tel. (202) 208-6843
www.nps.gov

► **National Park Service Southeast Region**
100 Alabama St. SW
1924 Building
Atlanta, GA 30303
Tel. (404) 562-3100
www.nps.gov

► **Biscayne National Park**
9700 SW 328 Street
Homestead, FL 33033-5634
Tel. (305) 230-7275
www.nps.gov./bisc/

► **Everglades National Park**
40001 State Road
Homestead, FL 33034-6733
Tel. (305) 242-7700
www.nps.gov/ever/

► **Canaveral National Seahore**
7611 S. Atlantic Ave.
New Smyrna Beach
FL 32169
Tel. (321) 867-0677
308 Julia Street
Titusville, FL 32796-3521
Tel. (321) 267-1110
www.nps.gov/cana/

► **Gulf Islands National Seashore**
1801 Gulf Breeze Pkwy.
Gulf Breeze, FL 32563-5000
Tel. (850) 934-2600
www.nps.gov/guis/

STATE PARKS, WILDLIFE REFUGES

► **Florida Department of Environmental Protection**
3900 Commonwealth Blvd.
Tallahassee, FL
Tel. (850) 245-2118
Fax (850) 245-2128
www.dep.state.fl.us

► **US Forest Service**
325 John Knox Road
Tallahassee, FL 32308
Tel. (850) 942-9300
www.fs.fed.us

Personal Safety

Thanks to Al Capone, Miami Vice and a few spectacular murders in the 1990s Florida has been considered to be the backyard of thieves. This applies especially to the metropolitan Miami – Fort Lauderdale – Palm Beach area. The social gap is very large here. Crimes involving drugs cause the police problems. The relatively long coastline and the proximity of the Central and South American drug production have turned Miami into a dangerous drug transhipment centre.

Crime

Even thought the situation has calmed down since the tourist murders of the 1990s, be careful in the Sunshine State. A good rule is to apply common sense. Avoid parks, unlit areas, dark streets etc. after dark and do not go out alone. If you become involved in an accident that took place under strange circumstances, stay in the car and wait before getting out until the circumstances are clearer. Keep valuables and large amounts of money in the hotel safe. When travelling keep everything that might look attractive to thieves in the boot. But if something does happen, do not resist the thieves. Heroism has had a high price before now in a number of cases. In case of an emergency contact the police immediately: **Emergency number 911**.

Be careful

Post · Telecommunications

U. S. Mail | The U. S. Mail is only responsible for mailing letters and packages (also for wiring money). Telephone and telegram services are in private hands.

---

i Postage

- Letter/postcard within the USA: 32 cents every ounce/28 g
- Postcard to Europe: 70 cents
- Airmail letter (maximal 1 ounce/28 g) to Europe: $1
- Aerogramm: 80 cents

Stamps are available in post offices as well as from machines in airports, railway stations, bus stations, hotel lobbies and drug stores.

US flags fly outside **post offices,** which have the following hours: Mon–Fri 9am–5pm or 6pm, Sat 8am–12noon. Smaller post offices close over lunch.

Mailboxes | Mailboxes are painted blue and have »US Mail« written on them in white, and a stylized eagle.

Telecommunications

Private telephone companies | The telephone system in the USA is in the hands of private companies. This has hardly any effect on service, except for international calls from some telephone booths, where the operator (tel. 0) has to make the call.

Hotel telephones | Telephone calls and faxes from hotel phones should be avoided since there are heavy surcharges.

Public telephones | Most public phones only operate on calling card or credit cards. There are still a few coin-operated phones around for local calls.

Toll-free numbers | Numbers with 800 or 888 can only be called within the USA and are toll free. Do not confuse them with 900 numbers, which usually connect to quite expensive commercial services.

Letters | The telephone dials also have letters on them, which are often used to help remember numbers (national breakdown service: tel. 1-800-AAA-HELP).

Calls within the USA | For local calls dial 1 and then the telephone number. For calls within the USA dial 1, then the area code and then the telephone number.

International calls | For international calls dial 011, then the country code, then the area code without the 0 and then the telephone number from private telephones. From public telephones dial 0. The operator will answer and give instructions.

To place a collect call dial 0 and then the telephone number. When the operator answers tell him to place a collect call.   Collect calls

Local call from public telephone: 35 cents. 3-minute long distance call to central Europe: depending on the time of day up to $15 (slightly reduced rates: 5pm–11pm; greatly reduced rates: 11pm–8am and on weekends).   Telephone charges

i   Telephone services

- Information inland: Tel. 411
- Information overseas: Tel. 1-555-1212
- Collect calls: Tel. 0
- Country codes from the USA to Europe:
  to UK: 0 11 44
  to Republic of Ireland: 0 11 353
  to Australia: 0 11 61
  to Canada: 1 (North American Numbering Plan)
- Country code from Europe to the USA:
  from UK and Republic of Ireland: 00 1
  from Australia: 0011 1
  from Canada: 1

Prepaid **phone cards** with often quite reasonable rates are recommended for international calls; they can be bought in shopping centres, at airports, at petrol stations etc.

In the USA a **triple band mobile phone** for 1900 MHz is necessary. Many European mobile phones do not work in the USA. The mobile companies have more information.

Prices · Discounts

Many hotels, restaurants, amusements parks etc. adjust their prices to the season. The rates are higher during the high season and summer vacations as well as around the main holidays. But prices could be reduced by half during the low season, when hotels and amusement parks have attractive special rates.   Seasonal prices

Marked prices are net prices without sales tax. Most items are charged with a state sales tax of currently 6%. Some cities, communities and counties also charge a general sales tax (usually 1%). Some towns also have a tourism development tax.   Net prices, sales tax

▶ WHAT DOES IT COST?

Double room
from $35

3-course Menu
from 15

Simple Meal
from $8

Cup of Coffee
from $1,50

Discounts   Children, students and senior citizens benefit especially from discounts. The spectrum covers everything from airline and railway tickets to special rates in hotels, amusement parks, national and state parks. It is worthwhile in any case to ask all tourist facilities about discounts when planning the trip.

Collect coupons!   Some tourist organizations publish brochures that can be found in various places including tourist offices, visitor centres, hotel receptions, petrol stations and supermarkets. Many of the businesses that place ads in these brochures also have coupons with many discounts, ranging from reduced hotel rates to super deals in the local factory outlet.

Shopping

Shop as you wish   The tourist sites all have a variety of opportunities for shopping. Every town worthy of the name has at least one shopping mall, one market place or one galleria to offer. These have then at least one large supermarket, one food court with various fast food vendors,

Sponges of all kinds are sold in Tarpon Springs on the Gulf Coast.

boutiques and specialty shops, services (doctor's offices, travel agencies etc.) and maybe even a restaurant or bar. The factory outlets, where designer goods (Tommy Hilfiger, Ralph Lauren, Levi's etc.) can be bought cheaply, are very popular. One of the largest outlet malls in the USA, Sawgrass Mills near Fort Lauderdale, attracts thousands of customers every day.

Typical Florida souvenirs are citrus fruits (especially grapefruits and oranges) as well as citrus products (especially juices, concentrates, jams, orange blossom honey). The shops will arrange to send entire lots to Europe if the customer desires. The great variety of seashells, which are mainly found on the Gold Coast, are also popular. Sponges, natural and artificial ones, are available in great variety in Tarpon Springs on the Gulf coast. Souvenirs from the amusement parks, like baseball caps, sunhats, shorts, t-shirts, sweatshirts from Kennedy Space Center, plush dolphins from SeaWorld, Marineland or Seaquarium, movie posters from Universal and/or Disney-MGM-Studios are always in demand. Some visitors to Florida may also like Indian arts and crafts; they are available not just in the Indian reservations but also in souvenir shops. Smokers will enjoy the hand-rolled cigars, which are available above all in Ybor City in Tampa, but also in many other shops in Florida.

Souvenirs

Every traveller can help protect endangered species of plants and animals as stipulated by the CITES agreement by refusing to buy souvenirs that were made out of endangered plant or animal products. This includes especially coral (especially black coral), tortoiseshell from wild turtles, living or preserved lizards or their skins, various species of birds (including parrots) as well as rare butterflies and other insects. Refrain from digging up rare plants or catching wild animals. It is strictly forbidden to export such »souvenirs« and offenders will be punished by law. A plea of ignorance is no excuse. The customs offices and WWF have more information on endangered species (www.wwf.org.uk).

Caution! Endangered species

Sport and Outdoors

Spectator Sports

Baseball is the most popular sport in America, but for the uninitiated it is difficult to follow. The top teams in Florida that play in the pro leagues are the **Florida Marlins** and the **Tampa Bay Devil Rays**. Baseball fever breaks out in spring. At that time many pro teams come to Florida for their spring training and for test games in the **Grapefruit League**.

Baseball

Wouldn't it be fun now: a ride across the turquoise water with a water scooter …

American football

American Football, game with a fascinating rhythm and tactics, is gaining a growing number of fans in Florida. The best teams include the **Miami Dolphins**, the **Jacksonville Jaguars** and the **Tampa Bay Buccaneers**.

College Football ▶

American football is especially popular in the colleges. The **Miami Hurricanes**, the **Gainesville Gators** and the **Tallahassee Seminoles** have all made a name for themselves. The college teams compete for important trophies every spring.

Basketball

Thanks to superstars like Kobe Bryant, LeBron James and Dirk Nowitzki, basketball fans flock to the National Basketball Association (NBA) arenas. The **American Airlines Arena on the Miami Bayfront** was built a few years ago in record time and became the new home of the Miami Heat.

Water Sports

Snorkelling, diving

The flat lagoons between the mainland and barrier islands or fringing reefs off the coast, which are often covered with sand dunes, are well suited to snorkelling and diving. Here is a colourful and diverse microcosm with a large number of fish, corals, molluscs and crustaceans. The waters are, for the most part, still very clean and offer excellent conditions for observing, photographing and filming. There are also shipwrecks – including some Spanish silver transports – on the ocean bottom that attract treasure hunters.

The best diving is in the Florida Keys. There are well-equipped diving stations on Big Pine Key and Cudjoe Key, in Islamorada, on Key Largo, Key West and Looe Key and in Tavernier. Along with the marine zone of Key Biscayne National Park the Key Largo Coral Reef Preserve, John Pennekamp Underwater Park and the coral limestone islands between Marathon and Key West are especially interesting. **The Gulf Island National Seashore** also offers good diving on the gulf coast of the Panhandle. The main diving stations are in Destin, Fort Walton Beach, Panama City and Pensacola. The many **spring basins inland** are also good places to dive. There are diving stations here as well (including Live Oak, High Springs).

◄ Diving areas

Surfing, jet ski, waterskiing, sail boarding: almost all larger tourist sites and beach hotels rent sailboats, motorboats, water scooters, water-skis, jet skis, surfboards, water sports and diving equipment for a minimal charge. But water sports equipment may only be used in the areas outside of the swimming areas.

! **Baedeker** TIP

Best Surf

The central east coast, especially the area around Sebastian Inlet and Cocoa Beach, has the best surfing conditions in the state.

There are numerous marinas in Florida, where boats can be rented for sailing trips with and without crews. There are many sailboats in the waters between Miami and the Bahamas, also around the Florida Keys as well as parts of the Gulf coast (including Fort Myers – Punta Gorda, Tampa Bay, Panama City, Destin – Fort Walton Beach, Pensacola). Island hopping by sailboat around the Keys as well as in the barrier islands off the east coast and the northern Gulf coast is also popular.

Sailing

Anyone who likes kayaking, canoeing and other sports boats or travelling by houseboat is in the right place in Florida. More than 1,600km/960mi of waterways are ideal for canoeists and kayakers. The **Atlantic and Gulf coast** as well as numerous waterways and lakes inland make all sorts of activities possible.
It is possible to boat around Florida's peninsula on the **Intracoastal Waterway** or across it on the **Okeechobee Waterway**. Adventurous routes through mangrove swamps offer the chance to see diverse reptiles, birds and insects up close, and to visit coral islands and lagoons.

Canoe, kayak, houseboat

Fishing is one of the most popular American hobbies. But in Florida the fishing season is strictly regulated. To fish in rivers, lakes and waters close to the coast, it is necessary to acquire a fishing licence (for a fee). They can be acquired at the local government revenue offices, in many marinas as well as in some of the shops that sell fishing equipment.

Fishing

► SPORT AND OUTDOORS

SPORT GENERAL

► The Florida Sports Foundation

2930 Kerry Forest Parkway
Tallahasse, FL 32309
Tel. (850) 488-8347
Fax (850) 922-0482
www.flasports.com
This organization publishes directories and brochures on various topics like golf (Florida Golf Guide), fishing and boating (Fishing & Boating Guide) as well as a guide to baseball spring training camps (Baseball Spring Training Guide).

GOLF

► The Florida State Golf Association

8875 Hidden River Parkway
Suite 110
Tampa, FL 33637

Tel. (813) 632-FSGA
Fax (813) 910-2129
www.fsga.org
Find out anything you want to know on golf and golf courses in Florida here.

CANOE AND KAYAK TOURS

► Florida Department of Environmental Protection

3900 Commonwealth Blvd.
Tallahassee, FL 32399-3000
Tel. (850) 488-3701
www.dep.state.fl.us
Get the very informative brochure Florida Canoe Trails here.

► Florida Paddlesports Association

Tel. (941) 494-1215
www.paddleflausa.com
More information here

Florida is considered to be the golfers' mecca – deservedly so.

HOUSEBOATS

► **Holiday Cruise Yacht Charters**
Tel. (239) 945-5459
www.houseboatrentals.com
Houseboats for the waters around
Fort Myers, Sanibel and Captiva

► **Houseboat Vacations of Florida Keys**
Tel. (305) 664-4009
www.thefloridakeys.com/
houseboats/
Houseboats for the waters around
the Florida Keys

► **Houseboat Rental Center**
Tel. (386) 763-1729
www.houseboatrentalcenter.com
Houseboats for all of Florida

HIKING AND BIKING

► **Florida Department of Environmental Protection, Office of Greenways & Trails**
3900 Commonwealth Blvd.
Tallahassee, FL 32399-3000
Tel. (850) 245-21 18
www.dep.state.fl.us
This office coordinates the protection of the Everglades.

► **Florida Trail Association**
5415 SW 13th Street
Gainesville, FL 32608
Tel. 1-877-HIKE-FLA
www.florida-trail.org
Both institutions have info material on hiking, biking and canoeing.

Deep sea fishing or big game fishing for large fish is possible from many ports. Fully equipped boats both with and without crews can be chartered there. Swordfish, sharks, barracuda, tuna are among the fish that can be caught off the coast of Florida. ◄ Deep sea fishing

Surf fishing requires robust equipment, since heavy weights and the appropriate rods are necessary to cast long distances and the fish that bite are generally strong. The line should be at least 150m/500ft long. ◄ Surf fishing

Other Active Sports

Florida is a mecca for golfers. Excellent greens are available not just on Amelia Island, in Palm Beach, Boca Raton, Bradenton, Fort Walton Beach, Jacksonville, Naples, Sarasota and around Orlando, but also in many other places. **World Golf Village** with the **World Golf Hall of Fame** near St Augustine is an attraction. Today the Sunshine State has way over 1,000 golf courses, many of which are open to non-members. Various hotels and holiday resorts with their own golf courses offer interesting package deals. Golf

Florida is also the Promised Land of tennis. The **tournaments on Amelia Island, Boca Raton and Key Biscayne** are well-known on television. Hotel guests can often play tennis on the hotel's own courts. It is also possible to watch top-quality seeded tennis matches. Tennis

Hiking, biking
Recently the number of hikers and trekking bikers has grown in Florida. Many tourist centres have come to recognize this and now there is an extensive network of hiking and biking trails. There is an effort to establish trails that connect the nature preserves. Abandoned paths and railway lines are being integrated into this endeavour. The national parks, state parks, recreational areas and some of the dunes have special trails (often plank walks) for hikers and bikers. The **Florida Trail** has about 2,000km/1,200mi marked hiking trails throughout the Sunshine State. So far some sections and connecting roads have been waymarked.

Florida from the air
Getting a bird's-eye view of Florida does not take magic. Biplanes with open cockpits and other small aircraft take off from many smaller airports on fascinating trips. Skydiving schools have opened in some of them and offer tandem jumps, among other things. A ride in a hot air balloon can also be exciting.

Time

Time Zones
Most of Florida is in the **Eastern Time Zone**, 5 hours behind Greenwich Mean Time.

Central Time ▶
The western Panhandle is in the Central Time Zone and is one hour behind the rest of Florida.

Daylight saving time ▶
Daylight saving time, when the clocks are set ahead one hour for the summer, runs from the first Sunday in April to the last Sunday in October.

Time Zones in the USA

Transport

Air traffic

The two most important air traffic hubs in Florida are Miami and Orlando, followed by Fort Lauderdale, Daytona, Tampa, Fort Myers, Jacksonvilleand Tallahassee. From these airports there are daily flights to many small airports in Florida and also to other destinations in the USA. Moreover many small landing strips in Florida are used on demand.

Airports

All larger airports are well-connected to regional roads. Moreover there are good local connections to the city centres or important locations further away. Many of the larger hotels, car rental agencies etc. have an airport shuttle service for their guests and customers. All of the larger car rental agencies are present in the larger airports so that there is no problem picking up a car for a trip through Florida.

Local travel connections

Rail Traffic

Passenger travel by rail is organized by **Amtrak**, which is responsible for passenger service and train schedules. The rails themselves and the train cars are owned and serviced by various companies. Amtrak trains run daily on the routes New York – Jacksonville – Miami or Tampa (Silver Service/Palmetto) as well as New Orleans – Pensacola – Orlando (Sunset Limited). The **Auto Train**, a comfortable car transport train, runs from Lorton (Virginia) – Sanford (Florida). Amtrak offers various rail passes, which can however only be bought outside the USA at reasonable rates. These rail passes are valid for 15 or 30 days. The **National Rail Pass** is valid for the entire USA. Now there is also a **Florida Rail Pass**, which is valid for Amtrak routes in Florida with unrestricted stopping.

Amtrak trains

> ! **Baedeker TIP**
>
> **Murder on the Mystery Train**
>
> Fort Myers has an attraction for Agatha Christie fans. On five evenings a week (Wed–Sat 6.30pm, Sun 5.30pm) the Murder Mystery Train leaves from Colonial Station for an unknown destination. En route the unbelievable happens: murder. The passengers then are asked to help hunt for the murderer. More information: tel. (239) 275-84 87, www.semgulf.com

The **Tri-Rail** passenger trains run daily between Miami, Fort Lauderdale and Palm Beach. This city express is an economical way to visit the holiday resorts on the south-east Atlantic coast. Occasionally local tour guides offer accompanied Tri-Rail sightseeing tours.

Excursion trains by **Seminole Gulf Passenger Service** run daily at least once on the route Naples – Fort Myers – Punta Gorda – Fort Ogden–

Seminole Gulf Railway

Arcadia during the high season. On set dates there is also a **Dinner Train** in the evening, where a set dinner is offered to passengers.

Bus Trips

Organized bus trips

Many European travel companies include organized bus trips through Florida in their catalogue. Travel agents have more information.

Bus travel by Greyhound

Buses of the Greyhound Inc. company are generally well-equipped and offer a comfortable trip. Greyhound buses cover routes between all important cities and tourist centres in Florida. The most important stops are Miami, Miami Beach, Orlando, Jacksonville, Tallahassee, Daytona Beach, Fort Lauderdale, West Palm Beach, Sarasota, Tampa and Key West.

Bus passes ►

The **Greyhound AmeriPass**, available for 4, 7, 15 or 30 days, and the **Greyhound DiscoveryPass** can also be recommended for tours of Florida. However these passes can only be bought outside of the USA. Ask a travel agents for information.

Taxis

Cabs

There is an ample number of taxis (cabs) in cities and major tourist centres. They can be stopped anywhere on the street by waving at them. Since the distances in the cities and tourist centres along the coast are often long, the fares can be quite high, The trip from Miami International Airport to Miami Beach, for example, costs at least $50 (without a tip)!

Public Transport

Means of transport

In the larger cities public transport services are good. Buses run along set routes in many towns. In Miami there is also Metrorail, a commuter train. Moreover downtown Miami has a completely automatic elevated railway called the Metromover, which can be used free of charge. Public transport fares are relatively reasonable and comparable to central European standards. Local transport buses generally only accept exact change. The bus drivers do not sell tickets or give change.

Travelling by Car

Every US state, along with the federal laws, has its own traffic regulations. Visitors from Europe will notice some differences. The following regulations should be observed:

Right of way

At unmarked intersections the one who gets there first has the right of way. Drivers may have to use hand signals.

Distances in Florida

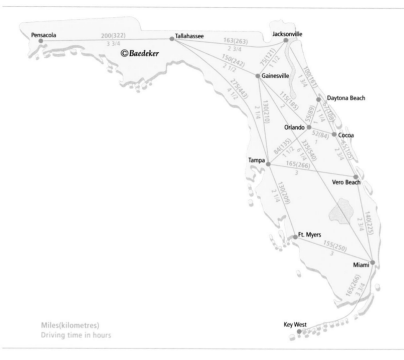

Pensacola · 200(322) 3 3/4 · Tallahassee · 163(263) 2 3/4 · Jacksonville
©*Baedeker*
150(242) 2 1/2 · Gainesville
75(121) 1 1/2
100(161) 1 3/4
275(445) 4 1/2 · 155(185) 2 · 57(105) 1 1/4 · Daytona Beach
130(210) 2 1/4 · Orlando · 52(84) 1 · Cocoa
84(135) 1 1/2 · 335(540) 6 1/4 · 25(105) 2 3/4
Tampa · 165(266) 3 · Vero Beach
130(209) 2 1/4 · 140(225) 2 3/4
Ft. Myers · 155(250) 3 · Miami
165(266) 3 3/4
Miles(kilometres)
Driving time in hours · Key West

At many intersections all lanes have stop signs. Every driver must stop here. The first one at the intersection may then proceed. ◄ 4-way stop

Seatbelts are required in Florida. Children under four years old may only ride in a children's seat. **Seatbelts**

In cities and residential areas the speed limits are between 20mph/32kmh and 35mph/56kmh; if there is a school, nursing home or hospital nearby the speed limit might even be only 15mph/24kmh! On roads leading out of town and country roads with two-way traffic speed limits are 45mph/72kmh. If the road runs through areas with wild animals, then the speed limit at night is only 35mph/56kmh. On multi-lane roads and motorways (highways) speed limits are 55mph/88kmh. On highways with little traffic the speed limit is 70mph/112kmh. **Speed limits**

No blood alcohol is allowed for drivers (0.0 per mille). »Driving under the influence« is punished severely. Opened liquor bottles may **Blood alcohol** only be transported in the boot; in campers only out of the driver's reach. People under 21 years old may not have any alcoholic products with them.

School buses On a street with two-way traffic, always stop when a school bus is dropping off or picking up passengers. If a school bus stops on a divided roadway then only the traffic flowing in the same direction as the bus must stop.

Traffic lights, right turns In the USA **traffic lights come after (!) the intersection**. Right turns on red are allowed after stopping and checking traffic. Right turn on red is not allowed when the sign »No turn on red« is present.

When the sun is low, when visibility is less than 300m/1,000ft, in rain and on long straight roads with oncoming traffic, low beam lights must be switched on.

i **Kerbstone colours**

- Red: no parking
- Yellow: general loading zone
- Yellow/black: truck loading zone
- Blue: handicapped parking
- Green: max. parking 10 minutes
- White: max. parking 5 minutes during business hours
- No colour: unlimited parking

Parking: parking is not allowed on country roads or motorways outside of towns as well as on many streets within towns. If a stop is necessary, pull over onto the shoulder of the road. Parking is not allowed in front of fire hydrants and in bus stops. Anyone who parks in a **no-parking zone** or blocks a driveway can count on getting towed away for a high towing fee.

U-turns U-turns are generally not allowed and marked by the sign »No U Turns«.

Passing on the right Passing on the right is allowed on multi-lane roads (interstates, many highways). When changing lanes to the right, it is advisable to be just as careful as when changing to the left.

Solid line Solid double lines may not be crossed, nor single lines on the driver's side. Many streets having turning lanes that can only be entered when the line is broken.

Rush hour lanes Multi-lane streets in metropolitan areas (especially around Miami – Fort Lauderdale) have lanes in areas where traffic can back up, which can be used during rush hour by cars with more than one occupant. Violations will be prosecuted by the police.

»Xing« The English word »crossing« is often shortened to »Xing« in the USA. The traffic sign marked »Ped Xing« refers to a pedestrian crossing. The sign »Gator Xing« means that alligators are likely to cross the road.

Hitchhiking is allowed in the USA but not on Interstates and on- and off-ramps. It should be noted that hitch-hiking is considered to be dangerous by Americans – for drivers and hitch-hikers.

Hitchhiking

When the police stop your car, remain seated in the car, open the window and leave your hands in sight on the wheel. Then wait for instructions from the officers.

Police stop

Interstates are like motorways and are recognizable by the blue-white-red signs. Interstates with two-digit even numbers run east-west, and those with two-digit odd numbers run north-south. Three-digit numbers refer to beltways around cities.

Interstates

Highways are basically multi-lane country roads. The white signs mark them as national (for example US 1) or state roads (for exam-

Highways

 TRANSPORT ADDRESSES

INLAND FLIGHTS

► **American Airlines**
Tel. 1-800-433-7300
www.aa.com

► **Continental**
Tel. 1-800-523-3273
www.continental.com

► **Delta Air Lines**
Tel. 1-800-221-1212
www.delta.com

► **United**
Tel. 1-800-864-8331
www.united.com

► **US Airways**
Tel. 1-800-428-4322
www.usairways.com

RAIL TRAVEL

► **Amtrak**
Tel. 1-800-USA-RAIL
www.amtrak.com

► **Tri-Rail**
Tel. 1-800-TRI-RAIL
www.tri-rail.com

► **Seminole & Gulf**
Tel. 1-800-SEM-GULF
www.semgulf.com

BUS TRIPS

► **Greyhound**
Tel. 1-800-231-2222
www.greyhound.com

RENTAL CARS

► **Alamo**
Tel. 1-800-GO-ALAMO
www.alamo.com

► **Avis**
Tel. 1-800-2304898
www.avis.com

► **Budget**
Tel. 1-800-527-0700
www.budget.com

► **Dollar**
Tel. 1-800-800-3665
www.dollar.com

► **Hertz**
Tel. 1-800-654-3131
www.hertz.com

ple SR 84 or FL 84). Their numbers also roughly correspond to the compass direction. ALT (alternative) or BUS (business) refers to bypasses. The most important difference between highways and interstates is the fact that highways are not limited access roads. Be careful at junctions and when turning left.

Toll   Toll refers to road use fees, which are charged on certain interstates and highways as well as for the use of some bridges, causeways and tunnels or underpasses. Keep some loose change in the car to avoid long lines at the manned booths.

Off-ramps   On divided roadways the off-ramps or exits are usually on the right, but when there is no room the exit may be placed on the left.

Petrol stations   Petrol stations are usually located in populated areas, near on- and off-ramps for highways and at intersections on country roads. **Unleaded gas** is sold in the categories **regular** and **super (premium)** as well as **diesel**. In order to start the pump turn the lever or lift the handle. Many petrol stations especially in the evening and at night require payment in advance. Often there are full service and self-service pumps.

A unique pleasure: driving through Florida with a rental convertible

The radio station WAQI Miami broadcasts all year 24 hours a day. It can be heard at channel 710.   Traffic radio

Rental Cars

Florida is best explored in a rental car, which can used to reach attractions that are off the beaten track. Some rental agencies have good deals, and the weekly packages are especially reasonable. But don't let the very low basic rates fool you. Instead watch out for adequate insurance rates (collision, third-party, deductible). Insurance packages can be expensive. Then state taxes are added and maybe even airport taxes, the latter only if an airport shuttle is used from the airport to the rental agency.   Preferred means of transport

Anyone who wants to rent a car must present a national or internationally recognized driver's licence and generally must be at least 21 years old. Some agencies allow people to drive from the age of 18, but charge a correspondingly expensive »underage« rate.   Driving licence, minimum age

Every rental agency has a counter at the airport, but the cars are claimed elsewhere. A shuttle bus will take you from the airport to the car depot.   Claiming a car
If the reserved car is not available, a car from the next higher category is made available for the same price. This can also be done with »upgrade coupons«, which some travel agencies and airlines give away.
Before leaving the agency's grounds check the car for defects and point them out immediately.
Rental agencies require a security deposit to rent a car, but most of them will accept a credit card instead.   ◄ Security deposit
The agencies offer a confusing array of different policies, not all of which are necessary. Here is a short explanation: **CDW** (Collision Damage Waiver), damage waiver for damage to the car (highly recommended); **LDW** (Loss Damage Waiver), damage waiver in case the car is lost or stolen; **PAI** (Personal Accident Insurance), accident insurance for occupants; **PEC** (Personal Effect Coverage), insurance for baggage; **LIS** or **SLI**: supplemental liability insurance to raise the liability level above the legal minimum.   ◄ Insurance

Travellers with Disabilities

Florida's building regulations are very friendly to the disabled. Public buildings, airports, ports, hotels and restaurants are equipped for the handicapped. Even the sidewalks are made for the handicapped. There are parking places for the disabled everywhere. The many at-   Disability-friendly Sunshine State

⏵ AIDS FOR THE HANDICAPPED

TRAVEL AGENTS IN THE USA

▶ **Flying Wheels Travel**
Tel. (507) 451-5005
www.flyingwheelstravel.com
This agent offers guided tours and
excursions in minivans equipped
for the disabled.

▶ **Accessible Journeys**
Tel. (610) 521-0339
www.disabilitytravel.com
This agency serves mainly people
with walking disabilities and
wheelchairs.

ORGANIZATIONS FOR THE HANDICAPPED

▶ **Florida Disabled Outdoor
Association (FDOA)**
Tel. (850) 668-7323
www.fdoa.org
This organisation offers especially
helpful information and internet
links.

▶ **Society for Accessible Travel
and Hospitality (SATH)**
Tel. (212) 447-7284
www.sath.org
Information and recommenda-
tions for people with all kinds
of handicaps are available at
this organisation. They also
publish Open World Magazine.
Their website has a list of web
addresses for individual attractions and travel agents along with
general information.

▶ **American Foundation
for the Blind**
Tel. (212) 502-7600
www.afb.org
People with visual impairments
will get help from this
foundation.

RENTAL CARS

▶ **Wheelchair
Getaways**
Tel. (859) 873-4973
www.wheelchair-getaways.com
They rent vehicles equipped for
the disabled. Agencies in West
Palm Beach, Fort Lauderdale, Miami, Naples, Fort Myers and
Jacksonville. The vehicles can be
picked up at the airports of the
above mentioned cities as well.

HELP IN UK

▶ **RADAR**
12 City Forum, 250 City Road,
London EC1V 8AF
Tel. (020) 72 50 32 22
www.radar.org.uk

HOTEL/TRAVEL ADVICE

▶ **Metro-Dade
Disability Services**
1335 N.W. Street
Miami, FL 33125
Tel. (305) 547-5445
They have a free guidebook for
physically disabled people entitled
»Directory of Services for the
Physically Disabled in Dade
County«.

tractions also offer aids for the handicapped. The large amusement
parks have wheelchairs to rent. Many of the beaches have surf chairs
which allow people who have difficulty walking to enjoy beach life.

Weights, Measures, Temperatures

Linear measures

1 inch (in;) = 2.54 cm
1 foot (ft;) = 12 in = 30.48 cm
1 yard (yd;) = 3 ft = 91.44 cm
1 mile (mi;) = 1.61 km

1 mm = 0.03937 in
1 cm = 0.033 ft
1 m = 1.09 yd
1 km = 0.62 mi

Linear
measures

1 square inch (in²) = 6.45 cm²
1 square foot (ft²) = 9.288 dm²
1 square yard (yd²) = 0.836 m²
1 square mile (mi²) = 2.589 km²
1 acre = 0.405 ha

1 cm² = 0.155 in²
1 dm² = 0.108 ft²
1 m² = 1.196 yd²
1 km² = 0.386 mi²
1 ha = 2.471 acres

Square
measures

1 cubic inch (in³) = 16.386 cm³
1 cubic foot (ft³) = 28.32 dm³
1 cubic yard (yd³) = 0.765 m³

1 cm³ = 0.061 in³
1 dm³ = 0.035 ft³
1 m³ = 1.308 yd³

Cubic measures

1 gill = 0.118 l
1 pint (pt)   = 4 gills = 0.473 l
1 quart (qt) = 2 pt = 0.946 l
1 gallon (gal) = 4 qt = 3.787 l

1 l = 8.747 gills
1 l = 2.114 pt
1 l = 1.057 qt
1 l = 0.264 gal

Liquid measure

1 ounce (oz;) = 28.365 g
1 pound (lb;) = 453.59 g
1 cental (cwt;.) = 45.359 kg

100 g = 2.527 oz
1 kg = 2.206 lb
100 kg = 2.205 cwt

Weights

Fahrenheit: 0 10 20 32 50 68 89 95
Celsius: -18 -12 -6.5 0 10 20 30 35

Temperature

Conversion:
Fahrenheit = 1.8 x Celsius + 32

$$\text{Celsius} = \frac{5\,(\text{Fahrenheit} - 32)}{9}$$

Men's clothing
For men's suits, coats and shirts measurements are identical in the UK and the USA.

Clothing sizes

Men's shoes:

UK	7	8	9	10	11
US	8	9	10	11	12

Women's clothing: Women's shoes:

UK	8	10	12	14	16	18	3	4	5	6	7	8
US	6	8	10	12	14	16	5.5	6.5	7.5	8.5	9.5	

Children's sizes:

UK	3-4 yrs	4-5 yrs	5-6 yrs	6-7 yrs	7-8 yrs
US	3	4	5	6	6X

When to Go

In the north four
seasons, in the
south two

North Florida has four seasons. Rain falls at all times of the year here. South Florida is different; it actually only has two seasons. The warm waters around Florida, high humidity and high evaporation make the weather summer-like and humid, from May to October extremely so.

From November to April the weather is cooler and dry for three to five months.

Temperatures From June to September the weather is quite hot. The highest temperatures can be found around the Keys and inland, where daytime temperatures during hot periods are frequently over 40°C/104°F. In the summer there are also severe thunderstorms with hail and tornados. The months of March, April and May as well as October and November are comfortable. The weather is mostly sunny then with summer-like temperatures. From December to February the weather in northern and central Florida can get quite cool. There can even be frost, which damages the citrus and vegetable crops severely.

The weather is getting better on Key West.

The Florida Panhandle has the greatest amount of rain, more than 1,500mm/59in fall annually. The Keys are dry and get only two thirds of the rain measured in the north, 1,000mm/39in.

Rain

Every year Florida has to face several tropical cyclones which either hit land or pass by, most of them between **June and October**. A hurricane can not only reach gigantic proportions, it also has massive destructive potential. In a six-week period in late summer 2004 no less than nine hurricanes wreaked havoc around Florida.

Hurricane season

The news programmes on the radio and TV broadcast weather reports regularly. The **NOAA Weather Radio Network** gives up-to-date information on the most recent developments in the weather over Florida, the Gulf of Mexico, the west Atlantic and the Caribbean Sea.

Weather reports

High season for north Florida is May to September. But in the sub-tropical south the high season is from mid-December until mid-April. The months of April and May as well as September, October and November are **low season** in all of Florida.

Hotels, amusement parks etc. are **full and expensive** on the weekends of President's Day, Easter, Memorial Day, 4th of July, Labor Day, Thanksgiving, Christmas, New Year's Eve and New Year.

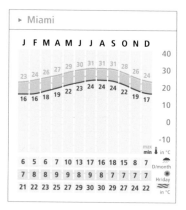

▶ Miami

	J	F	M	A	M	J	J	A	S	O	N	D
max	23	24	26	27	29	30	31	31	31	28	26	24
min	16	16	18	19	22	23	24	24	24	22	19	17
D/month	6	5	6	7	10	13	17	16	18	15	8	7
Hr/day	7	8	8	9	9	8	9	8	7	7	7	7
in °C	21	22	23	25	27	29	30	30	29	27	24	22

Tours

CAUTION

MANATEE AREA

ALONG THE ATLANTIC OR THE GULF COAST? A VISIT TO CAPE CANAVERAL, THE MEGA-AMUSEMENTS PARKS OR THE ALLIGATORS IN THE EVERGLADES? THIS MUCH IS CERTAIN: FLORIDA HAS SOMETHING FOR EVERYONE!

TOURS THROUGH FLORIDA

The attractions of the »Sunshine State« in the south-east of the USA are not only the climate and beautiful beaches, spectacular amusement parks, rockets to the moon and space shuttles, but also with large areas of protected nature. See the dolphins, manatees, alligators, sea eagles not only in a zoo, but also in their natural habitat and up close. The following pages have suggestions and tips for interesting excursions.

The three suggested routes can easily be combined into a big Florida tour, which would however take several weeks.

■■■ TOUR 1 South Florida
This circular route goes to some of the main attractions in Florida. Miami and Miami Beach are included, as are Cape Canaveral's rocket launching pads and the mega-amusement parks in Orlando and Tampa. The swamps of the Everglades, Florida Keys and Key West have not been left out.   ► **page 122**

Ideal beach near Fort Walton Beach

■■■ TOUR 2 North Florida
This tour also includes some highlights, like the big amusement parks in Orlando and the US space centre Cape Canaveral, but also St Augustine, the oldest city in the USA, and Tallahassee, Florida's capital. There are great beaches on Amelia Island, and manatees can be seen in the spring basins near Tallahassee and Crystal River.   ► **page 125**

Boating holiday off Key West

■■■ TOUR 3 Florida Panhandle
Florida's panhandle also has spectacular sights and great beaches. The mysterious spring basins near Tallahassee should not be left out, nor the U.S. Naval Aviation Museum near Pensacola and the miles-long beaches of fine-grained sand at Fort Walton and Panama City. And Apalachicola has oysters galore.   ► **page 128**

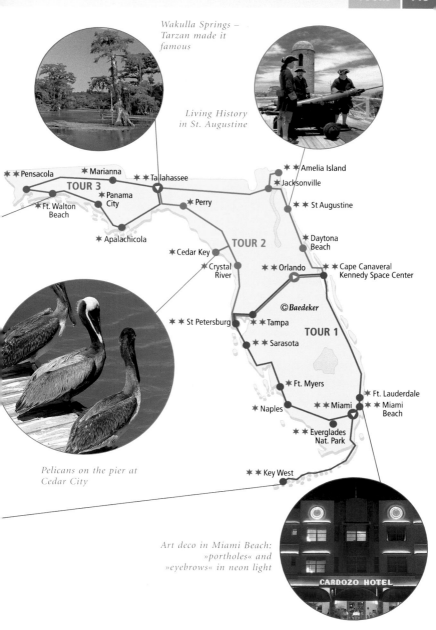

Wakulla Springs –
Tarzan made it
famous

Living History
in St. Augustine

** Pensacola   * Marianna
TOUR 3   * * Tallahassee   Amelia Island
* Panama   *Jacksonville
City   * Perry   * * St Augustine
*Ft. Walton
Beach

* Apalachicola   TOUR 2   * Daytona
Beach

* Cedar Key   * * Orlando   * * Cape Canaveral
*Crystal   Kennedy Space Center
River

©Baedeker

* * St Petersburg   * * Tampa   TOUR 1

* * Sarasota

* * Ft. Myers   * * Ft. Lauderdale
* * Miami
* Naples   * * Miami   Beach

* * Everglades
Nat. Park

Pelicans on the pier at
Cedar City

* * Key West

Art deco in Miami Beach:
»portholes« and
»eyebrows« in neon light

CARDOZO HOTEL

Travelling in Florida

Fun in the sun The sunshine state in south-east USA is one of the regions that continues to enjoy massive and growing numbers of holiday-makers despite »nine-eleven«, and deservedly so. The peninsula, which has been blessed with a pleasant climate, has a great deal to offer: wonderful **white beaches** which are not paved with beach towels; **lots of nature** including adventures with alligators, manatees, sea turtles, dolphins and colourful coral as well as **great cities** and **mega-amusement parks**, with lots to enjoy. Florida has lots to offer in the way of **culture** as well. The art deco architecture in Miami Beach and the Dalí museum in St Petersburg are examples.

By car Most holiday-makers and **tourists use a rental car to explore Florida** or a **camper**. The excellent network of **multi-lane highways** and **two-lane state roads, county roads** and local roads make driving around Florida easy. **In the metropolitan areas** (Miami/Fort Lauderdale/Palm Beach, Jacksonville, Orlando, Tampa/St Petersburg/Pinellas Coast) it is **easy to get lost** because of the many over- and underpasses, intersections and one-way streets. In areas where there is little traffic, like the Everglades, in the forested areas in northern Florida and on the Lost Coast the road system is well-developed. But be careful when you need petrol, since the stations are less frequent here.

Tourists in campers are **well catered-for** in Florida. Everywhere – in the national parks and state parks as well – there are well-equipped campgrounds and trailer parks. The **campsites** are mostly much **bigger than in Europe**.

! Baedeker TIP

Greyhound »Ameripass«

The economical »Ameripass«, available for 4, 7, 15 or 30 days, can be recommended for travelling around Florida and the neighbouring states. But this pass can only be bought outside of the USA.

Many tourists travel around Florida **by bus**, either in a package tour or independently. In all larger tourist centres there are travel agents who offer tours on comfortable and air conditioned buses, vans and limousines.

All important cities and tourist centres in Florida can be reached on well-equipped **Greyhound buses**, which also makes travelling comfortably on your own possible throughout the USA.

By public transport It is a little more difficult to explore Florida only on public transport (except for Greyhound buses). It works well in the metropolitan areas like Miami/Fort Lauderdale/Palm Beach and Orlando, where there is a good network of **bus routes**.

Rail ▶ Even though Florida's history and the history of tourism are inseparably connected to the railway, the rail passenger service only plays a minor role today. Passenger service has been stopped on some routes because it is no longer profitable. **Amtrak trains** only run on the routes (New Orleans) – Pensacola – Tallahassee – Orlando and (New York – Charleston) – Jacksonville –Orlando – Miami or Tampa. Metropolitan Miami can also be reached on the **»Tri-Rail« regional express**. In the less populated areas the standard of bus service varies greatly, so it can take a long time to get from one place to another. In some places citizens have started initiatives to reactivate and operate old railway lines as **museum trains or dinner trains**.

A unique way to explore Florida is by houseboat. Sail around the entire peninsula on the **Intracoastal Waterway** that runs between the barrier islands and the mainland. Some waterways, like St John's River, can be travelled well into the interior.

By houseboat

Fort Lauderdale is accessible by land and by water.

Tour 1 South Florida

Length of tour: about 930mi/1500km   **Duration:** at least 8 days

This tour introduces Florida's highlights. These include the twin cities of Miami and Miami Beach, the rockets at Cape Canaveral or Kennedy Space Center, the mega-amusement parks of Orlando and Tampa, the swamps of Everglades National Park and of course the Florida Keys island chain.

The tour begins and ends in Florida's metropolis ❶ ✳ ✳ **Miami** with its interesting sights. Don't miss Bayside Marketplace, the Miami Art Museum, Villa Vizcaya and the Miami Seaquarium. Little Havana as well as the suburbs of Coconut Grove and Coral Gables are worth a visit. Then go to ❷ ✳ ✳ **Miami Beach** with its world famous Art Deco District, its celebrity-filled South Beach and the excellent Bass Museum of Art. Anyone who has time should try out the nightlife, and maybe even see Madonna or Gloria Estefan.

When you have had enough of Miami and Miami Beach, follow highway A1A north. It follows the Atlantic coast to ❸ ✳ **Fort Lauderdale**, where the highlight is Las Olas Boulevard with its Museum of Art. Continue north on A1A through famous oceanside resorts like Pompano Beach, Deerfield Beach, Boca Raton, Delray Beach and Boynton Beach to sophisticated **Palm Beach**, where old and new money meets. Take some time to stroll along the breathtakingly expensive Worth Avenue or even have tea at the luxurious hotel The Breakers.

After Palm Beach the Atlantic coast quiets down. Via Jupiter, Port St Lucie, Fort Pierce and Vero Beach drive on to the so-called Space Coast with its wonderful beaches. From there it is not far to ❹ ✳ ✳ **Cape Canaveral/Kennedy Space Center**, the well-visited US space centre with its rocket launching pads and its excellent exhibitions. There is accommodation in Cocoa Beach, Melbourne or Titusville.

From Cape Canaveral it takes about one hour to get to the »world capital of amusement« in central Florida ❺ ✳ ✳ **Orlando**. It would take weeks to visit all the attractions here. The best are SeaWorld, Discovery Cove and Universal Studios. 20 minutes by car to the west is the mega-park Walt Disney World.

From Orlando or Disneyworld follow highway I 4 straight to ❻ ✳ ✳ **Tampa**, where the nicely renovated Ybor City, the Florida Aquarium and the Henry B. Plant Museum await interested visitors. Then relax in the amusement park Busch Gardens or just beyond Tampa Bay in ❼ ✳ ✳ **St Petersburg**, where the sun shines especially long and where there are wonderful beaches on the Gulf coast. Other highlights in »St Pete« are the Pier and the Dalí Museum.

Then follow the spectacular Sunshine Skyway (toll!) across the mouth of Tampa Bay to the south along the Gulf coast. The next stop is ❽ ✱✱ **Sarasota** with the imposing residence and the rich collections of the circus king John Ringling and his wife Mable. There are beautiful beaches around Sarasota. From here take a worthwhile detour to Myakka River State Park.

Popular attraction near Orlando

✱✱ Orlando *43 mi/69 km* ✱✱ Cape Canaveral
❺   ❹ Kennedy Space Center

88 mi/142 km

32 mi/52 km
❻ ✱✱ Tampa

❼ ✱✱ St Petersburg

32 mi/52 km
❽ ✱✱ Sarasota

66 mi/106 km

✱ Ft. Myers
❾
32 mi/52 km

✱✱ Miami
✱ Naples ❿
75 mi/38 mi/61 km
❶ ❷ ✱✱ Miami Beach
❶❶
121 km

179 mi/288 km

✱ Ft. Lauderdale
❸
26 mi/42 km

6 mi/10 km

✱✱ Everglades
Nat. Park

153 mi/246 km

✱✱ Key West
❶❷

Space shuttle en route to the launching pad

Relaxing in Miami Beach

Gator wrestling in the Everglades

The relatively new highway I 75 and the older US 41 continue south-wards past Venice and Port Charlotte, and finally reach the growing city of ❾✴ **Fort Myers**, where the legendary inventor Thomas A. Edison and the automobile manufacturer Henry Ford had their winter homes. From here make a worthwhile side trip to the beautiful beach at Fort Myers Beach or to the wonderful seashell-covered beaches on Sanibel and Captiva islands.

The next part of the tour goes to the luxury ocean resort ❿✴ **Naples** further to the south with its impressive Dockside and a long pier. Here again there are superb beaches like Vanderbilt Beach with its venerable Ritz-Carlton Hotel. Nearby there are several interesting nature reserves, like Corkscrew Swamp Sanctuary. A side trip to Marco Island is also charming.

Naples is the western gateway to ⓫✴✴ **Everglades National Park**. This swampy landscape between Naples and Miami is crossed by the Tamiami Trail (US 41), which was built with great effort at one time and today is a broad highway. Stop in Everglades City, where park rangers conduct interesting boat trips, or visit the Miccosukee Indian village and gain insight into their everyday life and their arts and crafts.

Tamiami Trail (US 41) leaves the Everglades in the far suburbs of Miami and ends at Calle Ocho (SW 8th Street) downtown ❶✴✴ **Miami**.

The last part of the route is a side trip via the Florida Keys down to ⓬✴✴ **Key West**. En route another detour leads to ⓫✴✴ **Everglades National Park**. At the southern edge of the Miami metroplex, near Florida City, County Road 9336 turns off into the Everglades and passes the administrative headquarters with its visitor centre.

The **Overseas Highway** (US 1) starts in Homestead or Florida City; it follows a railway line that runs to the coral islands of the Florida Keys and was destroyed in a hurricane in 1935; it ends in ⓬✴✴ **Key West**. Right at the beginning of the Overseas Highway, on Key Largo, is the turn-off to the north for an enjoyable side trip into the two marine nature preserves **John Pennekamp Coral Reef State Park** and **Biscayne National Park**. Don't fail to take a trip on a glass-bottomed boat over the colourful world of the coral reefs. Beyond Marathon the Seven Miles Bridge (see picture p. 132–133) crosses the ocean; a little way beyond it lies Bahia Honda with its wonderful beach. At Spanish Harbour is the boundary of the National Key Deer Refuge, where efforts are being made to protect the cute but endangered little key deer. The final destination is ⓬✴✴ **Key West** with its pretty old city, where Ernest Hemingway felt at home. Visit not only the home of the winner of the Nobel prize for literature but also the exhibition of the legendary treasure hunter Mel Fisher, which shows what he salvaged from sunken ships of the Spanish gold and silver fleet. When spending the night in Key West, don't miss the fabulous sunsets at Mallory Square. Sloppy Joe's Bar is the classic place to end the day.

Tour 2 North Florida

Length of tour: about 850mi/1370km   **Duration:** at least 6 days

The second tour of Florida explores the north and north-east. There are spectacular things to see here, too, starting with the mega-amusement parks of Orlando and the rockets of Cape Canaveral or Kennedy Space Center and ending at the mysterious spring basins, some of which are inhabited by manatees, near Florida's capital, Tallahassee, and Crystal River.

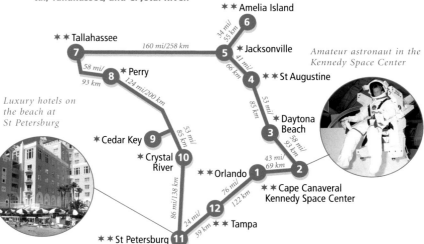

Amateur astronaut in the Kennedy Space Center

Luxury hotels on the beach at St Petersburg

Tallahassee 7 — 160 mi/258 km — 5 Jacksonville — 34 mi/55 km — 6 Amelia Island — 41 mi/66 km — 4 St Augustine — 53 mi/85 km — 3 Daytona Beach — 58 mi/93 km — 2 Cape Canaveral Kennedy Space Center — 43 mi/69 km — 1 Orlando — 76 mi/122 km — 12 Tampa — 24 mi/39 km — 11 St Petersburg — 86 mi/138 km — 10 Crystal River — 53 mi/85 km — 9 Cedar Key — 124 mi/200 km — 8 Perry — 58 mi/93 km — 7 Tallahassee

The trip begins and ends in ❶ ✳ ✳ **Orlando**, the »world capital of amusement« with its giant theme parks, which were already mentioned in Tour 1. From here drive eastwards one hour to reach the US space centre ❷ ✳ ✳ **Cape Canaveral/Kennedy Space Center**, which was also already mentioned in Tour 1. After the visit follow US 1 north to New Smyrna Beach, which was founded by Greek immigrants, and on to ❸ ✳ **Daytona Beach** with its famous auto beach and equally famous speedway for auto and motorcycle races. From Daytona Beach follow Highway A1A north along the coast and its wonderful beaches (including Flagler Beach). A few minutes north of Palm Coast is Marineland of Florida with its interesting dolphin shows. A short distance later at the mouth of the Matanzas River the historic Fort Matanzas is worth a short stop. Pass the beautiful Crescent Beach and St Augustine Beach to the next destination ❹ ✳ ✳ **St Augustine**, the oldest city in the USA with many interesting historic sights.

The former Ponce de León Hotel in St. Augustine

North of St Augustine, Highway A1A follows beautiful beaches to Jacksonville Beach, the recreational area of the city of ❺ ✳ **Jacksonville**, where this part of the tour ends. In Jacksonville there are several interesting museums to see. Do not miss making a detour to ❻ ✳✳ **Amelia Island**, Florida's historic northernmost island with its beautiful beach, the picturesque island capital of Fernandina and the historically interesting Fort Clinch.

Back in ❺ ✳ **Jacksonville** follow the I 10 westwards. En route stop in the pretty town of **Lake City**, from where there is a side trip to Osceola National Forest. Continue through the forested north of Florida to ❼ ✳✳ **Tallahassee**, Florida's historic capital with the old and new state capitol building, the Museum of Florida History and the San Luis Archaeological Site. From Tallahassee a detour into the surrounding area is also worthwhile, to Apalachicola National Forest or to **Wakulla Springs**, which was made famous by Tarzan actor Johnny Weismuller, and to St Marks National Wildlife Refuge with its interesting animal world.

From Florida's capital follow State Road 363 south to St Marks, where it crosses US 98. Follow US 98 south-east to ❽ ✳ **Perry**, which proudly calls itself the »Tree Capital of the South«. Do not miss the local outdoor museum. A few miles south-east of Perry the detour to **Lost Coast** the lonely Keaton Beach and the quaint fishing village Steinhatchee is rewarding. About an hour away cross the **Suwannee River**, a good place for boating and kayaking. Just before

Chiefland, State Road 230 turns off westwards to Manatee Springs, where you will see a manatee with a little luck. From Chiefland County Road 345 runs south to ❾ ✷ **Cedar Key**, which used to be an important wood export port.

After a stop in Cedar Key and maybe a canoe tour through the delta of the Suwannee River, follow State Road 24 back to US 19/98 and this in turn south to ❿ ✷ **Crystal River**, the last stop on this part of the tour. Here the river itself is the attraction, since about 200 manatees live in it. There is also an old Indian religious site here. From Crystal River follow US 19 south for a few miles to the wildlife park of **Homosassa Springs**, which is located on a natural spring pond. 22 mi/35 km further south the spring basin of **Weeki Wachee Springs** has been turned into a tourist attraction with acrobatic »mermaids« performing their feats under water.

The sponge-diving town of Tarpon Springs is on the Pinellas Peninsula with its beautiful swimming beaches. The next stop is ⓫ ✷ ✷ **St Petersburg** with its lively pier and interesting Dalí Museum. From there cross Tampa Bay to ⓬ ✷ ✷ **Tampa**, where the nicely decorated old residence of the tobacco industrialist Vincente Ybor, the Florida Aquarium, the Henry B. Plant Museum and of course Busch Gardens are all worth visiting. Leave Tampa on the I 4 going north-east and in one hour you will reach Walt Disney World and a little later ❶ ✷ ✷ **Orlando**, the starting point of the trip.

Wall paintings in Tampa's historic Ybor City

Tour 3 Florida Panhandle

Length of tour: about 440mi/710km   **Duration:** 3–7 days

The third tour explores Florida's northwest, also called the Florida Panhandle. It leads through a region that, unlike south Florida, is not known well in Europe, but which has natural and cultural charms of its own. The fantastic beaches along the Gulf coast and historical sites like Tallahassee and Pensacola show this.

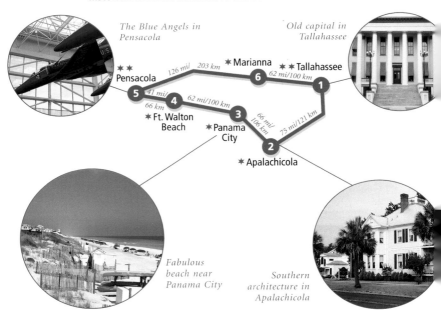

The Blue Angels in Pensacola

Old capital in Tallahassee

★★ Marianna ★★ Tallahassee
Pensacola 126 mi / 203 km 6 62 mi/100 km 1
5 41 mi/ 4 62 mi/100 km 3 66 mi/ 75 mi/121 km
66 km ★ Ft. Walton 106 km 2
Beach ★ Panama City
★ Apalachicola

Fabulous beach near Panama City

Southern architecture in Apalachicola

The trip begins and ends in ❶ ★★ **Tallahassee**, the state capital of Florida. There are some things to see here, like the old Capitol building, the Florida Museum of History and the San Luis Archaeological Site. The new Capitol building deserves a look, too; it is the tallest building in town. From Tallahassee follow US 319 south along the eastern edge of the **Apalachicola National Forest** down to Apalachicola Bay. A side trip to **Natural Bridge** and a Civil War battlefield on the way are worthwhile. The romantic **Wakulla Springs**, the setting of Tarzan movies with Johnny Weismuller, should not be missed; neither should a side trip to **San Marcos de Apalachee** and the eponymous nature reserve.

A few miles beyond the bridge over the **Ochlockonee River**, which is popular with canoers and kayakers looking for excitement, US 319 merges with US 98, a panoramic road along the Gulf coast of the Florida Panhandle. It leads to the friendly port of ❷ ✳ **Apalachicola**, which proudly calls itself the »world capital of oyster fishers«. Anyone who has never had fresh oysters can make up for it here. Off the coast of Apalachicola **St George Island**, a narrow barrier island, has beautiful beaches.

A few miles west of Apalachicola, State Road 30 leads to St Joseph Peninsula, which extends like a hook into the Gulf, and more excellent beaches. Via Port St Joe US 98 leads north-west along a beautiful coast to ❸ ✳ **Panama City** and **Panama City Beach**, a densely populated holiday resort that is already lively in spring. Further north-west are the super South Walton Beaches, where new holiday villages line up one after the other. **Seaside** with its innovative holiday architecture is worth seeing. Nearby is the beautiful **Grayton Beach** and the castle-like residence Eden Garden. A sand bar leads to **Destin**, the »world capital of sports fishermen«. From here cross Choctawhatchee Bay to ❹ ✳ **Fort Walton Beach**, where there are remains of old Indian cultures and an interesting museum on the US Air Force.

Right after Fort Walton Beach the **Gulf Islands National Park** begins with Santa Rosa Island, which is very narrow but nevertheless known for its wonderful beaches (Navarre Beach, Pensacola Beach) . Just before crossing to the historic port of ❺ ✳ ✳ **Pensacola** the Gulfarium and historic Fort Pickens are worth a visit. Pensacola itself has renovated historic buildings at the harbour and in the centre. The U.S. Naval Aviation Museum is one of Florida's best technical museums.

From Pensacola follow US 90 north-east. This and the interstate highway I 10 cross the hilly, forested and in part dried-out hinterland of the Florida Panhandle. **Blackwater River** with the forest of the same name, is very popular among adventurous kayakers; it is a part of the original north Florida landscape. Via Crestview and De Funiak Springs the route reaches the legendary Ponce de León Springs and a little while later the pretty town of ❻ ✳ **Marianna**, where the caves of the **Florida Caverns** make an interesting excursion.

Then drive south-east towards the border to Georgia. Near Chattahoochee is the **Apalachicola River** and Jim Woodruff Dam, which dams up Lake Seminole back into Georgia. The restful **Three Rivers State Park** was established here. From here it takes about an hour to get back to ❶ ✳ ✳ **Tallahassee**.

Sights from A to Z

WONDERFUL WHITE BEACHES AND PASTEL-COLOURED RESORTS, SWAMPS FULL OF ADVENTURE AND HISTORIC FORTS, GLITTERING CITIES AND WORLD FAMOUS AMUSEMENT PARKS – IN FLORIDA THERE'S LOTS TO DISCOVER!

✱ ✱ Amelia Island

H 2

Region: Central East
Population: 15,000

Elevation: 0 – 7m/23ft above sea level
Area code: 904

This paradise has been discovered already, but it is still possible to get away from the mainstream on its white beaches and in its historic towns: the island is a 45-minute drive north of Jacksonville and offers the best mix of beach life and culture on this part of the coast.

Wonderful beaches and historic buildings

The Ritz-Carlton usually means an expensive and somewhat snobbish holiday site. But the one on Amelia Parkway is refreshingly relaxing: guests walk through the lobby in shorts, and the personnel are not nearly as intense as in this luxury chain's other hotels. The same applies to Amelia Island: relaxed, informal and in parts still left in its natural state. What with the miles of beaches, dense forests of evergreen oak, red maple, cedars, pine, magnolia and palmetto brush, this is not surprising. The ecologically conscious islanders, including many endearing eccentrics, won't have it any other way either. History may have helped, too. When Flagler's East Coast Railroad passed by in the early 20th century, it brought tourism: steam ships had brought tourists until then, and the town of Fernandina, a Victorian gem, flourished as a transhipment port for wood and phosphate. Then the whole island seemed to fall asleep, and only the international tennis tournaments kissed it awake again in the 1970s. With them came the uniformity of golf courses, tennis courts and luxury resorts, above all in the south of the 20km/12mi-long and 5km/3mi-wide island. But fishing has remained the most important source of income along with tourism; Fernandina has been spared the effects of building developers. And the beaches … aah, the beaches!

What to See on Amelia Island

✱
Fernandina Beach Historic District

The houses reflect every building style used from 1870 to 1910, from whimsical Queen Anne to aristocratic Beaux-Arts. But the compact old city, which is has preserved monument status, is much older. There was a Spanish fort here in 1696. In the 18th century the island went back and forth between England and Spain. In 1811 the Spanish officially founded the town and named it after King Ferdinand VII: Fernandina was the last town that Spain founded in North America and was intended to stop US American expansion to the south. But then pirates and freebooters took over until it was occupied by American troops in 1817 and incorporated into the newly acquired state of Florida in 1821. In 1853 the city shifted to the south but the chequerboard pattern of the old city, which had Spanish ori-

▶ VISITING AMELIA ISLAND

INFORMATION

Amelia Island
Tourism Development
Council
102 Center Street
Fernandina Beach, FL 32034
Tel. (904) 277-0717
Fax (904) 261-2440
www.ameliaisland.org

WHERE TO EAT

▶ Moderate
Brett's Waterway Café
1 S. Front Street
Tel. (904) 261-2660
View of the bay at the end of Centre
Street. Eat freshly caught fish and
seafood while watching the fleet come
in. Relaxed atmosphere, nice terrace.
A tip: they make great Martinis!

▶ Budget
The Down Under
4883 Otis Trail
Tel. (904) 277-1557
Opposite Amelia Island on the mainland, under Shave Bridge. Simple
family restaurant. Meeting place for
the locals; hearty seafood.

WHERE TO STAY

▶ Luxury
Elizabeth Point Lodge
98 S. Fletcher Avenue
Tel. (904) 277-4851
Fax (904) 277-6500
www.elizabethpointlodge.com
24 rooms
At the end of Atlantic Avenue, right
on the beach: Wonderful B & B in
New England shingle-built style.
Beautiful terrace with rocking chairs,
comfortable rooms with fresh flowers
every day.

▶ Mid-range
Florida House Inn
20 S. 3rd Street
Tel. (904) 261-3300
Fax (904) 277-3831
www.floridahouse.com
15 rooms
Pastel-green B & B in the centre of the
old city with an illustrious guest list
including Ulysses Grant, José Marti,
some Rockefellers. The rooms are
furnished tastefully with venerable
furniture.

gins, remained. The streets that branch off from Centre Street lead
to picturesque residential areas with beautiful homes. Fairbanks
House (7th St., Italian Style), Fernandina Beach Courthouse (Atlantic Ave. corner of 5th St., Victorian Style) and Villa Las Palmas (304
Alachua St.; Spanish Mission Style) are especially worth seeing.
The main traffic artery of the old city is Centre Street, which contin-   ◀ Centre Street
ues to the east as Atlantic Avenue. The town's fishing fleet docks at
the west end in Fernandina Harbor Marina. Nearby in a beautiful
brick building is the Palace Saloon (117 Centre St.) of 1878, one of
Florida's oldest saloons. If you see a ghost here, it won't be because
of the alcohol: »Good ol' Charlie« Beresford, who was the bartender
here for 54 years, has been walking here since 1960. At least that's
what they claim on the ghost tours organized by the Amelia Island

Spanish colonial architecture in Fernandina Beach Historic District

⊙ Museum of History (233 3rd St.; hours: Mon–Sat 10am–4pm). The exhibition also presents the varied history of the island in an interesting and serious manner.

★★
Beaches

The main street (Centre St. or Atlantic Ave.) ends at the Atlantic to the west. Beyond the high dunes is **Main Beach**, with showers, toilets and parking. Adjacent to the south is **Peters Point Beach Park**, a wonderful beach that also has its own amenities, and **American Beach**. It is part of the beach community that was founded by Afro-American Life Insurance in 1935. American Beach flourished in the 1950s, when Ray Charles, Duke Ellington and Count Basie performed in the legendary nightclub Ocean Rendezvous. Wedged between the luxury resorts of the Ritz-Carlton Amelia Island and Amelia Island Plantation, the remaining 30 families have refused to sell to developers and golf course builders to date. The result is a section of beach that is free of apartment blocks and hotels.

★★
Fort Clinch State Park

From Main Beach a 5km/3mi-long walk leads to Fort Clinch State Park. In the fall whales can be seen here. The nature reserve includes dunes, the densely forested northern point of the island and beautiful beaches with shells and driftwood. The long pier is not only popular among anglers, but also among lovers – because of the wonderful sunsets.

The park is named after a fort, which was begun in 1847, occupied by Union troops in 1862 and finally abandoned in 1898. The main attraction of the fort are the communicative »re-enactors«; dressed in Yankee and Confederate uniforms they present living history and give informative guided tours. They even sleep in the fort in order to be as authentic as possible (2601 Atlantic Ave.; hours: daily 8am–6pm).

There is a nature reserve at the southern tip of Amelia Island (**Timucuan Ecological & Historical Preserve**), where the special conditions of a barrier island can be studied. Here there are also traces of settlements of the Timucuans, the Indians who lived in north-eastern Florida when the Spanish first came.

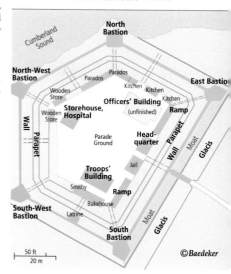

Fort Clinch Plan

©Baedeker

★ Apalachicola

E 3

Region: North-west
Population: 3,000

Elevation: 0 – 6m/20ft above sea level
Area code: 850

About 80% of all oysters harvested in the Sunshine State come from the banks in Apalachicola Bay. The »Oyster Capital« profits increasingly from the stream of tourists that has flowed into this part of the Gulf coast recently.

The fact that in 1850 Apalachicola had the third-largest harbour on the Gulf, an opera and a racetrack is no longer evident today. Only about 200 old houses, many encircled by verandas, remain as a reminder of the plantation owners who exported cotton from here. When the railway came, its tracks bypassed the flourishing port. The increasing size of ships made it impossible for them to dock in the harbour, which was located in a shallow, lagoon-like bay. Apalachicola managed to live on sponge diving and the trade in cedar wood for a while, but in the 1930s it declined for good. It was only the oysters and tourism that brought money in again. Today the quiet town is especially popular among young families from the cities. They are presently transforming Apalachicola into a pretty and, for its size, quite cosmopolitan town.

From exporting cotton to growing oysters

● VISITING APALACHICOLA

INFORMATION

Apalachicola Bay
Chamber of Commerce
122 Commerce Street
Apalachicola, FL 32320
Tel. (850) 653-9419
Fax (850) 653-8219
www.apalachicolabay.org

WHERE TO EAT

▶ **Moderate**
The Boss of Oyster
123 Water Street
Tel. (850) 653-9364
Fried, steamed or au gratin: in this rustic restaurant on the waterfront oysters are available in every variation with more than two dozen different toppings.

WHERE TO STAY

▶ **Mid-range**
Gibson Inn
Market and Ave. Streets
Tel. (850) 653-2191
Fax (850) 653-3521
www.gibsoninn.com
30 rooms
Victorian inn with rocking chairs on the veranda, where you can enjoy the breeze from the Gulf with a drink in the evenings.

What to See in and around Apalachicola

✳
Historic
downtown

The speed is slow and a breath of *Gone with the Wind* blows through the streets: hardly any other place in Florida has as many beautiful old wooden houses standing between the gnarled, moss-hung oaks. The ones worth noting include the Cotton Warehouse (1838; Water St. and Chestnut St.) and the Sponge Exchange (Commerce St. and Chestnut St.). Trinity Episcopal Church (6th and Chestnut St.; hours: daily 9am–5pm) was designed in the Greek Revival style in 1837 in New York and all of the building materials were shipped around the Keys. The John Gorrie Museum (6th St.; hours: Mon, Thu, Fri, Sat, Sun 9am–5pm) is housed in a simple bungalow and worth a visit; its display includes the ice-maker designed by the famous physician (▶Famous People).

Harbour

In Apalachicola's harbour and along US 98 there are many restaurants that serve fresh oysters – fried, steamed or in gratin, with or without spicy cocktail sauce. Note: unlike many Europeans, few Americans slurp fresh oysters right out of the shell!

✳ ✳
St George
Island State Park

The 24km/14mi drive east on US 98 is not too far to see this 15km/9mi-long beach, which many consider to be Florida's most beautiful. In Eastpoint turn right and cross the bridge. It connects the mainland with St George Island 6km/4mi off the coast. The island is only a few hundred yards wide but 45km/27mi long; as a barrier island it protects the coast. The state park itself is located at the eastern tip

Tasty oysters in Apalachicola

and preserves dunes, salt water marshes and 15km/9mi of the finest sand beach from construction. The first 7km/4mi are accessible by car, and the rest can be explored on foot.

Another beach regularly gets one of the top places in beach rankings. A few miles west of Apalachicola, FL 30 turns off US 98 onto a hook-shaped pencil-thin spit of sand. Past Cape San Blas, the south-ernmost point of the panhandle, through sparse pine forests on sand and dunes the road turns north again. The bare northern point is protected by the state park. Along with undisturbed sunbathing and swimming, it is a place to watch the pelicans glide over azure-blue waters.

✶ **St Joseph Peninsula**

> ! **Baedeker TIP**
>
> **Animal conservation**
>
> Extensive marshes, ponds and dunes, but above all impenetrable brush: that is what the barrier islands in the Gulf once looked like. St Vincent is one of the last refuges for alligators, sea eagles, wolves and sea turtles. But the island is only accessible by boat. The Apalachicola Chamber of Commerce has information on excursion boats, tel. (850) 653-9419.

21mi/34km west of Apalachicola, US 98 reaches **Port St Joe** (population 4,000), which was founded in 1835. The first constitutional assembly of the state of Florida met here in 1838. The Constitutional Convention Museum (hours: Thu–Mon 9am–noon and 1pm– 5pm) commemorates this event.

This large nature reserve starts one hour's drive north of Apalachicola. It has been a national forest since 1936, and its oaks, cedars and cypresses have recovered from exploitation. With savannahs, wetlands and rivers suitable for canoeing, it offers a wonderful alternative to the usual tourist activities.

✶ **Apalachicola National Forest**

Fort Gadsden ► Just after the park entrance a road turns off to Fort Gadsden State Historic Site. A few overgrown trenches and a visitor centre with a scale model, old muskets and Indian artefacts point to the exciting history of the site. In 1814 the British built the fort in order to recruit Indians and runaway slaves for the war against the Americans. Two years later it was destroyed by American troops, but during the First Seminole War it served as an American supply base.

✳ Boca Raton

J 6

Region: South-east
Population: 86,000

Elevation: 0 – 6m/20ft above sea level
Area code: 561

The name is Spanish and means »rat's mouth«; it probably came from Spanish sailors who anchored in this bay in the 17th century. It most certainly did not originate with today's residents.

Sophisticated resort

Boca Raton is one of Florida's wealthiest ocean resorts today and it can be assumed that the current residents did not name their thoroughly perfect paradise after a rodent. Smiling people in fashionable holiday clothing and armed with cream-coloured shopping bags under palm trees; uniformed personnel parking customer cars at supermarkets, and yuppies with constantly peeping cell phones driving their golf clubs around in jeeps set the scene: Boca Raton is rich and beautiful, and efforts are being made to keep it that way. This includes extremely strict building regulations: even McDonald's was forced to adjust its logo to fit. Whoever builds here has to have red tiles on the roof and arched entries for the house, office building or restaurant. Since star architect Addison Mizner (► Famous People) used this style and was creative here in the 1920s, nothing but his Mediterranean Style (► Arts and Culture) has been allowed. Mizner had ambitious plans for Boca Raton, including canals with gondolas and a cathedral for his mother, but they were given up with the Florida Land Bust in 1926. A few of his projects were completed however. His Boca Raton Hotel (now: Boca Raton Resort & Club), a pink, Moorish-style beach palace, is now the town's trademark.

What to See in Boca Raton

✳
Mizner Park

All roads lead to Mizner Park. It was built in the 1990s and has an overflowing calendar of events; its lawns are bordered by cobblestones and it is more than a chic mall for enthusiastic shoppers.

✳
Boca Raton Museum of Art ►

The pink museum, which was re-opened in 2001 at its new address in Mizner Park, is one of the best of its kind in the southern USA. The most interesting artists in Florida exhibit here. There is also a small but fine collection of 19th and 20th-century masters, including

► VISITING BOCA RATON

INFORMATION

Palm Beach County
CVB
1555 Palm Beach Lakes Blvd.
Suite 800
West Palm Beach, FL 33401
Tel. (561) 233-3000
Fax (561) 471-3990
www.palmbeachfl.com

WHERE TO EAT

► Moderate
Cap's Place
2765 NE 28th Court
Lighthouse Point
Tel. (561) 941-0418
The address for excellent seafood
since the 1920s. Take the launch
from Cap's Dock in the marina of
Lighthouse Point to the restaurant, an
old shack where US President Roosevelt and gangster boss Al Capone
once ate.

Zemi
5050 Town Center Circle
in Boca Center
Tel. (561) 391-7177

As elegant as the mall that houses
this nice restaurant. New American
cuisine. Pork steak in pear sauce is
especially recommended.

WHERE TO STAY

► Luxury
Boca Raton Resort & Club
501 E. Camino Real
Tel. (561) 395-3000
Fax (561) 447-3183
www.bocaresort.com
963 rooms and suites, 120 villas
Boca Raton's pride and joy has been
expanded several times since 1926
and as the perfect resort it has two
golf courses, tennis courts and fitness
rooms, five pools and ten restaurants.

► Budget
Ocean Lodge
531 N. Ocean Blvd.
Tel. (561) 395-7772
Fax (561) 395-0554
18 rooms
Clean, two-storey motel. 11 of the
rooms have kitchenettes. Pool and
terrace, beach across the street.

Picasso, Degas and Matisse (Mizner Park, 501 Plaza Real; hours: Tue, Thu, Fri 10am–5pm, Wed 10am–9pm, Sat, Sun noon–5pm).

Not only a hotel, but also a tourist attraction: guided tours through this pink palace, which can be seen from far off, explain not only how Addison Mizner managed to make the wood floors look so old (by having the construction workers apply their hobnailed shoes), but also who has slept in the ornate rooms and what happened there – both the important and the piquant (501 E. Camino Real).

✳ Boca Raton Hotel

Not artificial but original: the forest region between the Atlantic and Intracoastal Waterway was named after a native tree and protects one of the last original coastal regions in Florida. A boardwalk runs through palm-covered hammocks (wooded islands)and mangrove is-

✳ Gumbo Limbo Environmental Complex

lands, and ends at an observation tower with a beautiful view of the Atlantic. The residents of thisbiotope include rare brown pelicans, diverse amphibians and manatee, which can be seen with a little luck (1801 N. Ocean Blvd.; hours: Mon–Sat 9am–4pm, Sun noon to 4pm).

Some of the most beautiful beaches in the area are protected as state parks. In Boca Raton this includes South Beach Park (400 N. Ocean Blvd., changing rooms, toilets, open only in daytime) and Spanish River Park Beach a bit further to the north. Here nice trails lead through dense vegetation to an observation tower. Delray Public Beach (Ocean and Atlantic Blvds.), which is considered to be the cradle of surfing culture in Florida, is specially popular and the local teen meeting place on weekends. The regularly breaking waves really do attract whole packs of sun-tanned young men and women.

✳ Beaches

Beach life in Boca Raton is photogenic.

Around Boca Raton

The sun is all that reminds you that you're still in Florida. This wonderful traditional Japanese garden confuses many a visitor geographically. The peaceful site is 16km/10mi north-west of Boca Raton in Delray Beach and commemorates a group of Japanese farmers, who were settled here around 1900 by the East Coast Railway to grow tea and rice. The experiment failed. Only George Sukeji Morikami stayed and successfully switched over to pineapples. He later left his estate to the county (4000 Morikami Park Rd., Delray Beach; hours: museum Tue–Sun 10am–5pm; gardens Tue–Sat 10am–5pm).

✱
Morikami Museum & Japanese Gardens

The 60,000ha/148,000-acre wilderness is located 20km/12mi west of Delray Beach and is the northernmost point of the Everglades. It consists mainly of swamps and creepy cypress groves, and is home to thousands of alligators, varieties of cranes, wood ibis and more than 250 other bird species. The best way to explore this area is on the water: miles of canoe trails provide great photo motifs. Approach the swamp on foot via the short boardwalk trail which begins at the visitor's centre (10216 Lee Rd., Boynton Beach; hours: daily 6am to 6.30pm).

✱
Loxahatchee National Wildlife Refuge

🕐

✱ ✱ Cape Canaveral · Kennedy Space Center

J 4

Region: Central East

Elevation: 0 – 10m/33ft above sea level
Area code: 321

Take-off point into space: a visit to America's space port is a highly impressive experience – not just for rocket fans. The hangars and launching pads on the Atlantic coast document the unbroken optimism of a nation and man's unquenchable thirst for new limits.

The Cape: hundreds of successful space trips began here, including the Apollo missions to the moon, the Spacelab project and the space shuttles that are launched into orbit here. Presently 17,000 people are employed at Cape Canaveral. During the Apollo missions in the 1960s the number even reached 25,000.

America's space port was founded after World War II as a testing area for long-range missiles. In 1949 US President Harry S. Truman had Cape Canaveral, which reaches far into the Atlantic, closed off; at that time it was still unspoilt, even though city-dwellers from Miami and Jacksonville often went there. It was a good choice. Tests could be made over the Atlantic without endangering anyone and

History

the weather was good almost all year. The tests began the next year, first on modified V-2 missiles from German stocks, which could fly as high as 16km/10mi. Under the coordination of the German expert Wernher von Braun, rockets of increasing power were developed in the following years, including the Redstone and Polaris rockets for the army and navy. But it was the Sputnik shock in 1957 that really set the American space industry in motion. The success of the Russian Sputnik 1 space probe made Washington aware of the fact that Moscow was building better rockets. So in order to bundle American ambitions or »for the peaceful use and exploration of space« the space agency **NASA (National Aeronautics and Space Administration)** was founded on 1 October 1958.

Soon the entire coast between Fort Pierce and Daytona Beach had a new name: Space Coast. On 31 January 1958 the team of Wernher von Braun's colleague Kurt Debus put the 13.6kg/22lb satellite Explorer 1 into orbit. But while NASA was still being established, the Soviets put the first man in space. On 12 April 1961 the cosmonaut **Yuri Gagarin** went into orbit. Less than a month later the USA responded, by sending **Alan Shepard** on board Mercury 1 into space on 5 May. In the same month US President John F. Kennedy announced that within ten years manned expeditions would be sent to the moon. With that the Apollo programme was born. Merritt Island to the west became the launching pad for the gigantic Saturn V rockets and was named **John F. Kennedy Space Center (KSC)** after the president who was murdered in 1963. While unmanned rockets continued to be launched from Cape Canaveral, the KSC served as the take-off point for the moon. In 1966 the Apollo programme started and reached its climax with **Apollo 11**: on 20 July 1969 Neil Armstrong became the first human to walk on the moon. Other moon expeditions followed. Apollo 13 went down in history as a near-catastrophe. Shortly before reaching the moon and about 386,000km/240,000mi from the earth, one of the oxygen tanks on the mother ship Odyssey exploded. The landing on the moon was cancelled and the crew managed to save themselves through daring manoeuvres.

In December 1972, Apollo 17 the last expedition to the moon to date, started. Financially constrained, NASA then concentrated on the – cheaper – exploration of space from earth's orbit. On 14 May 1973 a Saturn V rocket brought the space lab **Skylab** into orbit. Until fall of 1973 three research teams spent a total of 513 days on board, conducting research on the sun and earth, and on the long-term effects of weightlessness. When Skylab burned up in late summer 1979 in the earth's atmosphere, NASA had already publicly presented the reusable **space shuttle Columbia**. The shuttles, which are carried into space piggy-back on rockets but land like airplanes, were supposed to operate often and cheaply, and carry cargo like satellites

← *Apollo 11 was launched to the moon on 16 July 1969.*

▶ VISITING CAPE CANAVERAL

INFORMATION

John F. Kennedy Space Center
Kennedy Space Center, FL 32899
Tel. (321) 449-4444
www.nasa.gov/centers/kennedy/

Florida's Space Coast
Office of Tourism
2725 Judge Fran Jamieson Way
Viera, FL 32940
Tel. (321) 637-5483
Fax (321) 637-5494
www.space-coast.com

Cocoa Beach Area
Chamber of Commerce
400 Fortenberry Road
Merritt Island
Tel. (321) 459-2200
Fax (321) 459-2232
www.cocoabeachchamber.com

WHERE TO EAT

► Expensive
Café Margaux
220 Brevard Avenue, Cocoa Village
Tel. (321) 639-8343
Creative French cuisine, excellent
service. Special recommendation:
lamb in Dijon mustard crust

► Moderate
Bernard's Surf
2 S. Atlantic Avenue
Cocoa Beach
Tel. (321) 783-2401
A local establishment and popular
among NASA employees: Bernard's
serves fish caught by its own fleet.
Under the same roof: the rustic
Fischer's Seafood Bar & Grill and
Rusty's oyster bar.

WHERE TO STAY

► Mid-range
Hampton Inn Cocoa Beach
3524 N. Atlantic Avenue, Cocoa Beach
Tel. (321) 799-0099
Fax (321) 799-4991
www.hamptoninncocoabeach.com
150 rooms and suites
Modern hotel right on the beach,
reliable quality.

► Budget
Campbell Motel
1084 N. Cocoa Boulevard
Cocoa Village
Tel./fax (321) 636-6111
18 rooms
Friendly and clean accommodation.

and spare parts. On 12 April 1982 the space shuttle Columbia made its maiden voyage with two astronauts on board. During the following two decades a total of five shuttles carried 61 satellites, transported about 700 pilots, crew members and passengers and flew over 700 million air kilometres (420 million miles). When the International Space Station »ISS« was being built in 1998 they acted as transports. But the space shuttles did not achieve the original goal of reducing flight costs: instead of the predicted 10 to 20 million US dollars, every trip cost about 500 million. Moreover two tragic accidents overshadowed the shuttle programme: on 28 January 1986 Challenger exploded 73 seconds after taking off. On 1 February 2003 Columbia burned up when it re-entered the earth's atmosphere.

swell; it is 6mi/10km long and divided into several recreational parks. Ron Jon's Surf Shop (4151 N. Atlantic Ave.) is a point of entry into the world of surfing; this retail cathedral for all followers of the cult is shaped like a sandcastle. The beach on the 270m/300yd-long Cocoa Beach Pier is dotted with fish restaurants and is a mecca for surfers with a lively clientele and all the necessary facilities.

> ## ! Baedeker TIP
>
> ### Surfin' USA
>
> If you are in Florida, try riding the waves on a surfboard! Friendly sun-tanned boys & girls give individual and group lessons. Further information: Ron Jon Surfing School, 150 E. Columbia Lane, Cocoa Beach, tel. (321) 868-1980, www.cocoabeachsurfingschool.com

Port Canaveral, a super-modern cargo and cruise port, grew up from the 1960s about a stone's throw from the space port. Cruise ships embark from here every day on excursions to the Bahamas and the Caribbean. Moreover many shrimp fishers and charter boats for big game fishing leave from Port Canaveral.

Located in the hinterland of the Space Coast on Indian River, the town of Titusville (population 40,000) owes its development from a small fishing port to a rapidly growing industrial centre to the events in the nearby US space port. Many employees of NASA and the US Air Force live here. **Titusville**

The Astronaut Hall of Fame on NASA Parkway has many mementoes of space travel. The impact of space travel on technical progress is also portrayed. In Space Camp children and teenagers can experience how astronauts are trained, what weightlessness is and what a space flight simulator feels like (hours: daily 9am–6pm). ◄ Astronaut Hall of Fame

ⓧ

✴ Cedar Key

Region: North Central
Population: 1,000

Elevation: 0 – 5m/16ft above sea level
Area code: 352

The most beautiful side trip in Florida: the sleepy fishing village on the Lost Coast of the Gulf of Mexico is not only at the end of the road, but also on an island. This guarantees character and tranquillity, as well as pleasant encounters in places where the locals eat.

Old Florida lies three miles off the coast. Connected to the mainland by a causeway, FL 24 from Gainesville ends at Cedar Key – the island, however, is called Way Key. It was settled in the 1840s and began to flourish when the railway arrived from Fernandina (►Amelia Island). This brought tourism and opened the markets in the north for the lumber industry. In 1865 Eberhard Faber Inc. built a sawmill **Cedar island**

and a pencil factory here. At one time Cedar Key was the second-largest city in Florida. But when the forests were used up, the income dried up, too. A hurricane in 1896 put an end to Cedar Key. The people who stayed anyway went back to the original sources of income: fishing and oysters. Enterprising city dwellers soon rediscovered this town on the largest barrier island in the Gulf. In the past years many run-down houses have been restored and occupied. A handful of nice restaurants, two interesting little museums and beautiful wilderness areas only accessible by boat are good reasons to spend a couple of quiet days here.

▶ VISITING CEDAR KEY

INFORMATION
Cedar Key Area
Chamber of Commerce
Cedar Key, FL 32625
Tel./Fax (352) 543-5600
www.fws.gov/cedarkey

Cedar Key National Wildlife Refuge
16450 NW 31st Place
Chiefland, FL
Tel. (352) 493-0238
www.cedarkeys.fws.gov

Manatee Springs
State Park
11650 N.W. 115th St.
Chiefland, FL
Tel. (352) 493-6072
www.floridastateparks.org/
manateesprings

WILDERNESS TOURS
Kayak Cedar Keys
Cedar Key
Tel. (352) 543-9447
www.kayakcedarkeys.com
See dolphins, sea turtles and cranes up close.

WHERE TO EAT
▶ Moderate
The Island Room at Cedar Cove
Cedar Cove Beach & Yacht Club
Tel. (352) 543-6520

Good pasta, seafood and steaks with a beautiful view of the bay towards the south.

▶ Budget
Captain's Table
On the dock
Tel. (352) 543-5441
Well-known restaurant where you can get fresh and well-prepared fish, oysters, prawns, shrimps etc.

WHERE TO STAY
▶ Budget
Dockside Motel
491 Dock Street
Cedar Key
Tel. (352) 543-5432
www.dockside-cedarkey.com
10 rooms
Simple accommodation on the pier, dolphins can be seen from the rooms with a Gulf view.

Cedar Inn
410 2nd Street
Cedar Key
Tel. (352) 543-5455
www.cedarinnmotel.com
12 rooms
Southern-style accommodation in the middle of Cedar Key. Pretty terraces with a view of the Gulf and Main Street, simple rooms.

What to See in and around Cedar Key

The remote location and the warm, humid climate take the hurry out of one's step. Cedar Key means quiet meandering on the covered sidewalks of Second Street, the main street, and strolling through the few side streets where pretty old wooden houses with verandas typical of the south pose under palm trees. The town's highs and lows are documented in the Cedar Key Museum (12231 SW 166 Court; hours: daily 9am–5pm) and the Historical Society Museum (D St. and 2nd St.; hours: Thu–Mon 9am–5pm). The former has a remarkable exhibition of all shells that can be found in the Gulf and reminders of the heyday of the American pencil centre founded by the German »pencil king« Eberhard Faber. The exhibitions in the Historical Society present artefacts of the Timuacan and Seminole Indians.

✻
Historic Cedar Key

West of Cedar Key a dozen islands have been under strict nature protection since 1929. The varieties of birds that live here include ibis, brown pelicans and varieties of deer as well as sea eagles and buzzards. Migrating birds rest here in March and April as well as in August and September. Rattlesnakes live in the dense thicket of the island interiors. The refuge can only be reached by boat from Cedar Key; various companies offer tours and rent kayaks. Exploring the island alone is restricted from March to July because of the brooding time, and is not recommended anyway because of the rattlesnakes.

Cedar Key National Wildlife Refuge

From Chiefland on US 19/98, FL 320 runs about 5mi/8km west to Manatee Springs State Park. The nature reserve on the lower Suwan-

Manatee Springs State Park

A manatee coming up for air

nee River was established in 1955 and is famous for its karst spring basin that shimmers in every shade of green and blue and is surrounded by cypresses and hardwood islands; its waters flow into the Suwannee River. Bathers and snorkellers enjoy the pleasant water temperatures. Divers explore the extensive cave system of this richly flowing spring. In the fall and winter manatee can be watched in the temperate waters, with a little luck. The park's services include a campground, canoe rental and a small shop.

★ Crystal River

G 4

Region: Central West
Population: 3,700

Elevation: 0 – 2m/7ft above sea level
Area code: 352

How do you protect hundreds of manatee from hundreds of thousands of tourists? The blessings and curses of manatee tourism can be studied well around the town of Crystal River in the sparsely populated Big Bend or on the Nature Coast.

Holiday resort with a history

Crystal River is the name of the town and the river. Both are about a two-hour drive from ►Tampa on Highway 19. The quiet town is a

Indian religious site on Crystal River

⊙ VISITING CRYSTAL RIVER

INFORMATION

**Citrus County
Visitors Bureau**
9225 W. Fishbowl Drive
Homosassa, FL 34448
Tel. (352) 628-9305,
Fax (352) 628-0703
www.visitcitrus.com

**Crystal River National
Wildlife Refuge**
Refuge Manager
1502 SE Kings Bay Drive
Crystal River, FL
Tel. (352) 563-2088
www.fws.gov/crystalriver/

ACTIVITIES

Swimming, snorkelling, diving, boating and watching manatee: numerous organizations in and around Crystal River offer manatee tours. The following companies have been established for many years and are known for their »soft« manatee tourism:

► Tour companies
Bird's Underwater Manatee Tours
320 NW US 19, Crystal River, FL
Tel. (352) 563-2763
www.birdsunderwater.com

Crystal Lodge Dive Center
614 N.W. US 19
in the Best Western Crystal

River Resort
614 N.W. US 19
Crystal River, FL
Tel. (352) 795-6798
www.manatee-central.com

WHERE TO EAT
► Moderate
Cravings on the Water
614 NW US 19
Tel. (352) 795-2027
Outstanding seafood, steaks and tasty salads. Great live music on the 1st and 3rd Saturdays of the month. Delicious tropical drinks.

WHERE TO STAY
► Mid-range
**Best Western Crystal
River Resort**
614 N.W. US 19
Crystal River
Tel. (352) 795-3171
Fax (352) 795-3179
www.crystalriverresort.com
114 rooms and suites
Very comfortable mid-range hotel with bright rooms, a swimming pool and a nice restaurant named Cravings on the Water right on the water. It also includes a marina for sailing enthusiasts. Exciting manatee tours can be booked here as well.

popular place to retire to when the Tampa Bay area becomes too noisy and busy. Before white people settled here in 1840, pre-Columbian Indians lived here, probably Timuacan. The pensioners and the natives were attracted by one thing above all: the – for once literally – crystal-clear waters of Crystal River, which is fed by several karst springs and flows into King's Bay at the end of its short course.

What to See in and around Crystal River

✳
Crystal River Archaeological Site

From about 200 BC until the 15th century there was an important Indian religious and cultural centre at Crystal River. Six massive hills have been identified, which probably served as sanctuaries and burial sites. In one of the burial sites more than 450 graves have been found. Steles, which are usually not found in North America, point to connections with the civilizations of Mexico or Central America. The little museum in the visitor centre for the archaeological site and the Indian culture is very informative (hours: outdoor area daily from 8am, museum Thu–Mon 9am–5pm).

Crystal River National Wildlife Refuge

Crystal River National Wildlife Refuge: the reserve consists of 20 islands in Kings Bay. The bay is fed by the Crystal River, into which more than two dozen springs flow. Since the water temperature rarely falls below 22°C/72°F during the course of the year, the bay is a good place for about one quarter of all manatees in Florida to winter. But what attracts the manatees, who are sensitive to cold, also attracts fishers, divers, snorkellers and tourists. Diving shops, marinas etc. in Crystal River owe their existence to the cute water animals.

A special corridor for swimmers and divers was established at the spring basin of Kings Springs. The places where manatees come often are marked with buoys and »no entry« signs.

i **Manatee Sanctuary**

■ Trespassers in a manatee sanctuary are fined heavily and might even face a prison sentence.

✳
Homosassa Springs Wildlife State Park

🕐

On US 19, about 7mi/11km south of Crystal River, it is possible to observe manatees without getting wet. They are astonishingly agile in their element – the manatees in this state park were injured and brought here to recover – and can be observed through the large windows of an underwater observatory. The 17m/56ft spring basin is also the habitat of various species of fish. The area around the basin is a birdwatchers' paradise (hours: daily 9am–5.30pm).

Yulee Sugar Mill State Historic Site ▶

About 2.5mi/4km south-west of Homosassa Springs the former sugar cane plantation of the railway magnate Yulee is open to the public. The sugar works were built in 1851 and have been carefully restored. An educational trail describes the process of making sugar.

Chassahowitzka National Wildlife Refuge ▶

South-west of Homosassa Springs there is a 120,000ha/297,000-acre nature preserve, which is only accessible by boat. The sensitive ecosystem is a refuge to countless aquatic birds and many wild animal species (including alligators, racoons, turkeys, wild deer, otters, red bobcats). The refuge administration in Crystal River (address see p.153) has more information.

Weeki Wachee Springs

44mi/70km south of Crystal River there is a special attraction: Weeki Wachee Springs. Up to 600 million litres (158 million gallons) of

Homosassa Springs

water per day bubble out of the natural spring basin, which is more than 80m/260ft deep. There is also an underwater show by imaginatively dressed »mermaids« several times a day, which can be watched through the glass windows of a special underwater room (hours: daily 10am–6pm).

Around the springs is a regular amusement park with a petting zoo, monkey cage, parrot show and nursery for wounded pelicans.

This park near Weeki Wachee Springs attracts families with children above all. There is a beach here and the river provides real jungle and wild water adventures (hours: late March to Labor Day, daily 10am–5pm).

◄ Buccaneer Bay Water Park

✳ Daytona Beach

Region: Central East
Population: 65,000

Elevation: 0 – 5m/16ft above sea level
Area code: 386

Where fast cars howl and choppers sputter... The trademarks of Daytona Beach are a beach that is always busy, where even cars are allowed, and a world-famous motor raceway. Auto racing fans from all over the world and thousands of motorbike drivers with their chromed machines meet here; students celebrate their spring break here as well.

Daytona Beach Map

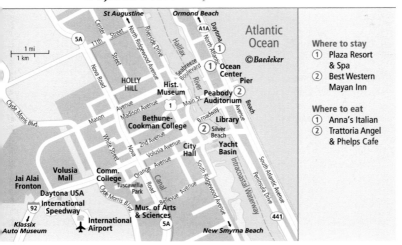

Where to stay
1. Plaza Resort & Spa
2. Best Western Mayan Inn

Where to eat
1. Anna's Italian
2. Trattoria Angel & Phelps Cafe

It all started with Olds, Chevrolet and Ford

The love affair between Daytona Beach and the car is almost 100 years old! At the beginning of the 20th century Ransom Olds, Louis Chevrolet and Henry Ford raced their latest models on the 40km/25mi-long beach, which the Atlantic had beaten solid. Rich New Yorkers – there were no highways yet – had their horseless carriages shipped here so that they could really step on the gas for once. Speed records were made and broken regularly: in 1931 Sir Malcolm Campbell shot across the sand along the edge of the water at a fabulous 441km/h (274mph), the highest speed ever measured on that beach. The natural surface was soon no longer considered to be safe, but only in 1959 could the National Association for Stock Car Auto Racing (NASCAR) move into the newly built 150,000-seat Daytona International Speedway. Races continue to take place here, including the legendary Daytona 500.

But it is still permitted to drive on the beach towards the heat-washed horizon – even if only at a maximum speed of 10 mph (16km/h). Cars roll up to »their« place and are parked at a right angle not too close to the water – because of the tides. Then the grill and beach umbrella is set up and the beer comes out of the cooler – that's when you have arrived in Daytona Beach!

A city changes its image

Since it was founded in 1872 Daytona Beach has gone through various phases. The last just ended a few years ago. At that time the city fathers decided that the reputation of Daytona Beach, which was strongly marred by the half million students who descended on it every year during spring break to drink and party, needed to be rescued and began an advertising campaign that was aimed at other tar-

▶ VISITING DAYTONA BEACH

INFORMATION

Daytona Beach Area CVB
126 E. Orange Ave.
Daytona Beach, FL 32114
Tel. (386) 761-7700
www.daytonabeach.com

DAYTONA USA
1801 W. International Speedway Blvd.
Daytona Beach, FL 32114
Tel. (386) 253-7223
www.daytonainternational
speedway.com

EVENTS

NASCAR Speed Weeks
Daytona 500
The auto races in February are the climax of the year. Reserving tickets early is highly recommended.

Bike Week – Daytona 200
Every year in early March way over 300,000 bikers of all ages in black leather outfits with their shiny Harleys, Hondas, BMWs and many other marques come to Daytona Beach for a boisterous meeting that culminates in the famous motorbike race that was first held on the beach in 1942.

Biketoberfest
In October bikers from all over the USA meet in Daytona Beach.

SHOPPING

Daytona Beach is not equipped for strolling and window-shopping. The only exception is Beach Street between Bay Street and Orange Avenue, also called the Riverfront Marketplace. Pretty clothing boutiques, galleries and antique shops can be found here.

Daytona Flea & Farmer's Market. more then 1,000 stalls (2987 Bellevue Ave., junction I-95/US 92; hours: Fri, Sat, Sun 8am–5pm).

FISHING

Fishing from Main Street Pier – a relaxing and also social alternative to grilling in the sun. Rods, bait and licenses are available in »bait shops«.

WHERE TO EAT
▶ Moderate
① **Anna's Italian Trattoria**
304 Seabreeze Blvd.
Tel. (386) 239-9624
Good Italian cooking. The home-made ravioli is excellent.

② **Angell & Phelps Cafe**
156 South Beach Street
Tel. (386) 257-2677
Restaurant with delicious American cooking, also good wines.

WHERE TO STAY
▶ Mid-range
① **Plaza Resort & Spa**
600 N. Atlantic Ave.
Tel. (386) 255-4471
www.plazaresortandspa.com
323 rooms and suites
Recently renovated, central location

② **Best Western Mayan Inn**
103 South Ocean Ave.
Tel. (386) 252-BEST
www.bwmayaninn.com
112 rooms and suites
Generously-sized and well-equipped rooms.

get groups. The results were questionable: instead of teenagers and students now tattooed motorsport fans – attracted by the many car and motorbike races all year – go overboard here.

The run-down beach front made up of silo-like hotels and motels was beautified and people interested in culture might even be surprised at what is offered. But it will take some time before Daytona Beach, where in 2003 Charlize Theron earned an Oscar for her performance in *Monster*, has lost its image as a cheap vacation place!

What to See in Daytona Beach

✳ Beaches People in all shapes, of every age and from every part of the country: the beach is up to 150m/500ft wide and seems to fade into the distance. One look and the world disappears. One of the beach's focal points is the 200m/650ft-long Main Street Pier on wooden piles. Fishermen can buy bait here in »bait shops« before casting their lines at the end of the pier. There is a restaurant, a bar, an observation tower with the optimistic name of Space Needle and the Sky Lift, a somewhat worn-out chairlift. The Boardwalk, a beach promenade with many bars and t-shirt shops, runs several blocks north to south from the lively end of Main Street.

> ## ! *Baedeker* TIP
>
> **Ride a Harley just once ...**
> America's largest Harley-Davidson shop is at 290 North Beach Street. The classic motorbikes are not only sold but also leased here (tel. 1-800-307-4464; www.daytonaharleydavidson.com).

Museums Beach life is the big thing, but Daytona Beach has some surprising cultural highlights. These include the Museum of the Arts & Sciences. The museum presents its varied collection in expansive rooms. It includes African masks, paintings and sculptures of early Cuban artists which were donated by the Cuban dictator Batista as well as the giant skeleton of a pre-historic sloth (1040 Museum Blvd.; hours: Tue–Fri 9am–4pm, Sat, Sun noon–5pm).

The Halifax Historical Museum, in a former bank with a classical portico, offers an exciting look at the speedy history of the city, which is documented by historical photographs (252 S. Beach St.; hours: Tue–Sat 10am–4pm).

The story of Afro-Americans in Daytona Beach is depicted by the Mary McLeod Bethune Foundation with memorabilia of the civil rights activist who was born here (640 Mary McLeod Bethune Blvd.; hours: Mon–Fri 9am–4pm).

✳ ✳ Daytona USA 4mi/6.5km inland is the holy of holies for American car freaks. The oval 3.5mi/5.5km-long racetrack is 13m/42ft wide and the curves have a steep incline (31%!), to make high speeds possible. Races are held on 10 weekends every year, with stock cars at up to 300km/h (180mph), motorbikes at speeds up to 270km/h (160mph) and go-

Fast cars on hot asphalt at Daytona

karts with speeds up to 200km/h (120mph). Many other events take place here apart from the races. Tickets sell out quickly. Reserving early is recommended, especially for the Daytona 500.

Local racing history is presented in the World Center of Racing Visitor Center in multimedia presentations (NASCAR office building east of the Speedway, 1801 W. International Speedway Blvd.; hours: daily 9am–7pm, tours daily 9.30–6pm).

A few minutes' drive away there is a treat for fans of old Harleys and Corvettes: the Klassix Auto Museum displays motor vehicles with lots of chrome from the time when air pollution and ecology were unknown (2909 W. International Speedway Blvd.; hours: daily 10am–6pm).

◀ **Klassix Auto Museum**

Around Daytona

About 6mi/10km north of Daytona lies Ormond Beach, which is characterized by modern apartment buildings and resorts and has a population of more than 40,000. After Flagler's East Coast Railroad came and the Ormond Hotel was built in 1887 with its golf course, the town became a sophisticated oceanside resort where the American plutocracy of the day – Vanderbilt, Rockefeller etc. – met in the winter months. Incidentally: the first auto race in the area took place in 1902 not in Daytona, but on the beach at Ormond.

Ormond Beach

Further to the north a road leads off to the ruins of a plantation that was founded in 1821 by Major C. W. Bulow. Until it was destroyed in the Second Seminole War, cotton, sugar cane and indigo were cultivated here. Only the foundations of the manor house are left. A footpath passes by the former slave quarters to the ruins of the sugar mill. The history of the plantation is displayed in the visitor centre (hours: daily 9am–5pm).

✷ **Bulow Plantation Ruins State Historic Site**

Ponce de León Inlet Lighthouse ✳

🕐 About 10mi/16km south of Daytona Beach the red brick lighthouse of 1887 rises to a height of 50m/165ft. Its platform offers a fantastic panoramic view. The former house of the lighthouse keeper has an exhibition on local seafaring history (hours: daily 10am–7pm).

New Smyrna Beach ✳

New Smyrna Beach (population 23,000), just 12mi/20km south of Daytona, is protected by a barrier island. In the second half of the 18th century Greek immigrants under the leadership of a Scots doctor tried to start a plantation here. The Scotsman named the location after the birthplace of his wife in Asia Minor.

New Smyrna Sugar Mill ▶

🕐 On the west side of town is a ruined sugar mill, the centre of a large sugarcane plantation from 1830 to 1835. After the army failed to move all of the Seminole Indians to the west of the Mississippi, Indians attacked the colony at New Smyrna in 1835, stole the cattle and slaves and set the plantation on fire. This was the start of the Second Seminole War (hours: daily 10am–5pm).

DeLand

This town about 25mi/40km west of Daytona has been spared from tourists so far. A New York manufacturer of Stetson hats, **Henry De-Land**, wanted to built a modern Athens in Florida in the 1870s and donated money to found a private university here in 1886. On the university campus an art gallery and a mineral collection can be viewed. The DeLand Museum on Woodland Boulevard has rotating exhibitions by famous artists. The Indian section has attractive basketwork and ceramics.

De León Springs ▶

About 5mi/8km north of De Land is the De León Springs State Recreation Area. On the property of a former sugarcane plantation there is a »fountain of youth« (a warm spring for bathing), diving, snorkelling, canoeing and a nature trail for hiking.

Spring Garden Ranch ▶

A few miles north of De Land, on US 17, several hundred horses are raised on one of the largest stud farms in Florida. The racetrack on the ranch holds top-quality races in the winter half of the year.

✶ ✶ Everglades National Park

H/J 7

Region: South-east	**Elevation:** 0 – 5m/16ft above sea level
Area: 5,661sq km/2,186sq mi	**Area code:** 305

As is often the case, the prettiest name is the one the Indians gave to this region: they called the giant wetlands »Pa-hay-okee«, »Grass River«.

Always in flux

They also showed their excellent powers of observation. For, to be exact, the Everglades are not a swamp but a river that flows so slowly that the current can barely be perceived by the naked eye: the water

In the middle of the Everglades, an anhinga dries its feathers.

in the 80km/48mi-wide but only knee-deep »river«takes more than a month to cross south Florida.

The Everglades used to cover about one third of Florida, but in the north and east were drained to create farmland. Along its eastern border the land is cultivated right up to the boundary of the national park in places. At first sight this flat swamp and marsh landscape seems monotonous, lost, even boring. But its truly incomparable charm can only be seen up close. The most fascinating aspect is that minimal differences in elevation have produced completely different ecosystems. While mangrove thickets extend along the coast, inland there are salt grass steppes, where hardy cacti flourish. Wherever there is fresh water classic wetlands evolved, with hammocks as the only features on the horizon. These tree islands consist of mahogany trees, strangler fig and gumbolimbo trees. Only a few inches deeper, reed grasses up to 3m/10ft high, called saw grass here because of their indented edges, form an impenetrable thicket. In the north there are endless, spooky cypress swamps.

For a long time the cultivation of this swamp wilderness was praised as a great technical feat. It was considered possible to fence in the rest and protect it in this way. But the fact that this wetland lives from flowing water was overlooked. Diking, channelling and above all over-draining are endangering the national park today, as are the fertilizer and insecticides that seep in from the surrounding farmlands. Efforts have been made for years to restore the ecological bal- **Endangered future**

⏵ VISITING EVERGLADES NATIONAL PARK

INFORMATION

Everglades National Park
40001 State Rd. 9336
Homestead, FL 33034-6733
Tel. (305) 242-7700
Fax (305) 242-7711
www.nps.gov/ever/

Everglades Area
Chamber of Commerce
P.O. Box 130
Everglades City, FL 34139
Tel. (239) 695-3941
Fax (239) 695-3172
www.evergladeschamber.com

SEASON

The best time for a visit to the Everglades are the dry winter months (Nov–April), when the animals and migrating birds collect near the water (brackish lakes, canals, etc.). In the rainy summer (May–Oct) the reed prairies are under water. The migrating birds are gone, but there are myriads of mosquitoes!

CAUTIONARY MEASURES

Caution absolutely must be taken when hiking away from the permanent trails, when camping or picnicking. Poisonous coral snakes, black water moccasin snakes and diamondback rattlesnakes live here along with a type of dwarf rattlesnake. Beware of the alligators at all times, but also of the »cute« racoons that love to inspect or beg for leftover food. Feeding the animals in the park is not allowed. There are poisonous plants as well, like poison ivy (rhus radicans) or poison-wood (metopium toxiferum), a relative of the staghorn sumac. Physical contact with these plants, especially their sap, can cause serious illness. Insect repellent is absolutely necessary.

ACTIVITIES

In the national park canoes and kayaks are the ideal mode of transport, and the only way to see the animal residents up close. The lengths of the canoe trails vary from a one-hour trip to an expedition of several days. Everglades City and Flamingo are good starting points. Canoes or kayaks can be rented for reasonable prices at the marina in Flamingo. In Everglades City Everglades National Park Tours (tel. 239/695-2591) rents canoes. Ivey House B & B (see below) organizes paddle tours of varying lengths through the mangrove forests of Ten Thousand Islands, which are guided by biologists and outdoor experts. Experts accompany the two-hour Tram Tours (daily 9.30am, 11am, 1pm, 3pm) from Shark Valley.

WHERE TO EAT

► Moderate

The Flamingo Restaurant
1 Flamingo Lodge Highway
(in Flamingo Lodge)
Tel. (239) 695-3101
Expansive dining room with a view of the water. Fresh fish, shrimps, steaks and ribs, simple salads.

Ghost Orchid Grill
107 Camellia Street
(in the Ivey House B&B)
Everglades City
Tel. (239) 695-3299
Best local restaurant, seafood according to modern Italian recipes. Gator chowder (alligator soup) is highly recommended.

► Budget

El Toro Taco
1 S. Krome Avenue
Homestead

Tel. (305) 245-8182
Homemade tortilla chips, fajitas and burritos, attentive service.

Joanie's Blue Crab Café
39395 Tamiami Trail, Ochopee
(about 500m/550yd past the Ochopee Post Office)
Tel. (239) 695-2682
hours: daily 9am–5pm
Classic swamp café, with stuffed owls and walls decorated with postcards from all over the world. The specialties are gator nuggets, sandwiches, black beans and rice.

WHERE TO STAY

Accommodations in or near the park are scarce and also simple. The Flamingo Lodge in Flamingo is the only hotel in the park. Near the park there are accommodations in Everglades City and Homestead.

▶ Mid-range
Ivey House B & B
107 Camellia Street
Everglades City

Tel. (239) 695-3299
www.iveyhouse.com
29 rooms
Pretty rooms with tropical decor, pool. Operator of canoe tours in the house.

▶ Budget
Captains Table Lodge & Villas
102 E. Broadway
Everglades City
Tel. (239) 695-4211
www.captainstablehotel.com
Simple accommodations with several clean rooms and apartments (with well-equipped kitchenettes for self-catering).

Everglades City Motel
301 FL 29
Everglades City
Tel. (239) 695-4224
Fax (239) 695-4444
www.evergladescitymotel.com
19 rooms
Large, simple rooms under royal palms.

ance of the Everglades, for example by retention basins in neighbouring pasturelands and with new laws. However, results are not living up to expectations: the politicians in Tallahassee and Washington are caught between ecologists on the one hand, and agriculture and real estate developers on the other. Half-hearted measures and laws that are modified later to benefit political lobbies are the result.

Drive through the Everglades NP (FL 9336)

Everglades National Park is located one hour's drive west of Miami and was founded by US President Harry S. Truman in 1947. It is the only sub-tropical protected area in North America. Its animal world is just as varied as its flora: alligators and the endangered American crocodile live here. Wild cats hunt deer, and dolphins disport themselves in the mangrove swamps. Moreover there are 345 different species of birds.

In a different world

ENDANGERED MONSTERS

They look like the perfect killing machines: there is hardly any other animal that man treats with as much caution. But Florida's alligators are by nature shy. Their cousins, the crocodile, are even an endangered species.

Reality puts the lie to the fearsome exterior of these primeval reptiles: **the American alligator was almost extinct in Florida in the mid-1960s** and survived only thanks to quickly established alligator farms. Of the American crocodile, less than 1,000 exist in Florida today. Their greatest enemy is man, who penetrates ever deeper into their habitat.

Shy Rambos

Once American crocodiles could be found everywhere from Lake Worth in the north to Florida Bay. They prefer quiet waters, and the last ones live in Crocodile Lake National Wildlife Refuge near Key Largo, in the Everglades and in the cooling-water channels of the Turkey Point atomic energy plant south of Miami.

The difference between the **American crocodile** and the American alligator is that the American crocodile has a longer, narrower snout, is grey-green and its lower teeth are visible even when its mouth is closed. It can get up to 23ft/7m long and weigh up to 550lbs/240kg. Its favourite foods include shellfish, fish, aquatic birds and smaller mammals. Since they are much less aggressive than their African cousins, people hardly ever see the American crocodile.

The **American alligator** is different. The black-brown-grey reptile with the

Has this alligator had enough to eat?

blunt snout, which can reach a length of up to 10–16ft/3–5m, even lives on the campus of the University of Florida in Gainesville, in Lake Alice, where freshmen occasionally confuse them with floating tree trunks. Since their comeback in the 1960s alligators appear regularly in the headlines in Florida as disruptors of barbecues, and for frightening children in the suburbs. Thus it is quite possible to

Common sense

The risks are small. But if a »gator« does cross your path, keep your distance in order to avoid the risk of an attack: It's hard to outrun a reptile that can reach speeds of up to **25mph/40kmh**. Never feed them or throw objects at them. When in a boat in alligator-infested waters, never let your arms or legs hang over the edge of the boat.

It's hard to outrun a reptile that can reach speeds of up to 25mph/40kmh.

meet up with an alligator when travelling in the state. In this case, it is good to know that alligators are by nature shy. Since the 1950s the Florida, Fish and Wildlife Conservation Commission has only recorded fifteen fatal attacks.

Tip: alligators and crocodiles of all sizes can be seen up close at:
Everglades Alligator Farm
40351 SW 192nd Ave.
Florida City
Tel. (305) 247-2628
hours: daily 9am–6pm

Feared hunter in the Everglades

The road FL 9336, which begins a bit south of Homestead and ends in Flamingo on Florida Bay, offers a good overview. At the entrance to the park the Ernest F. Coe Visitor Center (hours: daily 9am–5pm) with exhibits, brochures and mosquito spray is a good place to prepare for the tour. It is the first of five visitor centres in the national park, which are each located in a different biotope. The Royal Palm Visitor Center (hours: daily 8am–4.15pm) is located 2mi/3km further. Several walking and hiking trails start here. The 800m/2,600ft-long Anhinga Trail is a boardwalk through a sawgrass marsh where alligators, turtles, otters, anhinga (also called darters) and diverse types of cranes can be watched. The Gumbolimbo Trail winds through a thicket of royal palms and gumbolimbo trees. The Pineland Trail (11km/7mi west of the park entrance) runs through a fairytale-like palmetto thicket, and the Pahayokee Overlook Trail (21km/13mi west) ends at an observation platform over the »River of Grass«. The Mahogany Hammock Trail, a walkway through a jungle of mahogany trees, begins 32km/19mi after the park entrance.

Just before Flamingo about a dozen beautiful trails begin. The 400m/1,300ft-long West Lake Trail, located in the transitional zone to the coast, winds through a mangrove forest on the shores of West Lake, a brackish lake. The 2.6km/15mi-long Snake Bight Trail leads through a jungle of dozens of tropical hardwood trees, a paradise for bird lovers.

Flamingo ► Flamingo is located at the end of the road and 60km/36mi beyond the park entrance: a restaurant, a gas station, the Flamingo Visitor Center (hours: daily 7.30am–5pm), a campground, a few houses and a hotel with a marina. That's it. It almost seems as if more was going on here a hundred years ago. At that time Flamingo was a fishing village with about three dozen houses on stilts: it is said there were so many mosquitoes that they blotted out the light of the lanterns. That no longer happens today, and those who come here want to »get swamped«. Excursion boats, kayaks and canoes are available for this, especially those at the marina of Flamingo Lodge (►Experience the Everglades). In fact paddling along one of the eight canoe trails around Flamingo is the best way to see the Everglades and its inhabitants up close.

The Tamiami Trail (US 41)

The road across the southern tip of the Florida peninsula was built by two cities. In 1928 the two cities of ►Miami and ►Naples decided to build a road through the »River of Grass«. The results was Highway US 41, better known as the Tamiami Trail. Where once prisoners, immigrants and day labourers built the road through the swamp under the protection of alligator hunters, the drive along the northern edge of the national park takes three or four hours and leaves plenty of time for sightseeing.

The quick Everglades tour

First stop: the Shark Valley Visitor Center (hours: daily 8.30am to 5pm). A 15mi/24km-long paved trail starts here and runs far into the seemingly endless freshwater marsh. On a bus tour guided by park rangers (►Experience the Everglades) alligators, otters, racoons and countless varieties of marsh birds can be seen. But the view from the top of the observation tower at the highest point along the road is worth turning off for.

✴ Shark Valley

In contrast the popular Indian village a few miles further west leaves rather mixed impressions. It seems more like a necessary compromise. Miccosukee Indians sell pretty crafts at a few souvenir stands and picturesque workshops. Visitors are invited to ride the airboat into the swampy wilderness. And then muscular young Indians wrestle with alligators for the tourists and their cameras.

Miccosukee Indian Village

Along the Tamiami Trail airboat owners try to sell trips into the swamps of the Everglades. But in the national park itself, as in Big Cypress National Reserve to the north, trips on these fast and deafening propeller boats are not allowed.

◄ Important note

A few minutes drive to the west is Big Cypress National Preserve, the ecological continuation of Everglades National Park. Numerous endangered species of birds and animals live here, including wood storks, Florida panthers and snowy egrets. About halfway between Miami and Naples the Big Cypress Visitor Center at Oasis (hours: daily 9.30am–4.30pm) has information on ecology and the latest information on environmental protection.

🕐

Near Ochopee, a town scattered through an area of bush, there is a different kind of attraction: the little white house on the edge of the road with a huge American flag flying next to it is the smallest post office in the USA. Tourists love to send their postcards from here. The staff keep the 900 or so Indians, hunters and fishers who live here in touch with the rest of the world.

✴ Ochopee Post Office

To the west of Copeland lies a wonderful nature preserve, where dissolving limestone left long ridges (»strands«), which were transformed in the course of time to extremely photogenic cypress

✴ Fakahatchee Strand Preserve

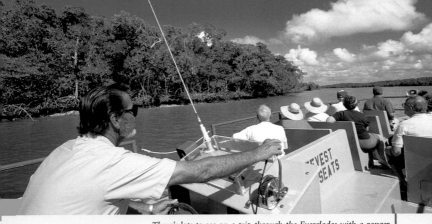

There's lots to see on a trip through the Everglades with a ranger.

swamps. The main entrance to this preservation area is a few minutes' drive to the west on the Tamiami Trail. A narrow half-mile-long planked walkway leads through the almost tropical jungle to an observation point, from where alligators, turtles and many kinds of birds can be seen.

Everglades City   Everglades City (population 500), the self-appointed »Gateway to the Ten Thousand Islands«, is located to the south. The small hamlet surrounded by lush green on the north-west boundary of Everglades National Park really is a good starting point for expeditions into the park. Boat trips through the Ten Thousand Islands, the mangrove labyrinth to the west, are on offer here. Canoes and kayaks bring you even closer, with or without a guide. However, choose wisely among the many tour guides who advertise on the edge of the road here!

★ Florida Keys

Region: South-east
Population: 80,000

Elevation: 0 – 3m/10ft above sea level
Area code: 305

Off the southern coast of Florida the USA ends in the form of an archipelago of droplets, the Florida Keys. There are over 400 islands, 30 of which are connected by the spectacular Overseas Highway. The Keys are a world of their own. The spirit of the Keys can already be breathed in on the magnificent road over the ocean. But anyone who wants to inhale it deeply has to go to the Back Country, to the islands that are only accessible by boat with their wonderful, tropically colourful underwater world.

Highlights Florida Keys

John Pennekamp
Coral Reef State Park
With diving mask, snorkel and fins through a colourful underwater world.
► page 170

Feeding tarpons
The up to 2.50m/8ft-long fish can be fed from Robbie's Pier on Islamorada: a wet and wild spectacle!
► page 172

Hidden Harbor
Turtle Hospital
In the turtle hospital in Marathon volunteers care for wounded turtles, victims of the tourist industry.
► page 174

Bahia Honda State Park
Caribbean island atmosphere with palm trees, beaches and rental surfboards.
► page 175

Juan Ponce de León, in 1513 the first European known to have visited these shallow waters, will hardly have noticed the brilliant reef dwellers. As a devout Catholic he named the coral islands that rise out of emerald green water »Los Martíres«: they reminded him – probably at a distance – of suffering people. During the next 300 years the Keys – the word derives from the Spanish word »cayo« for a reef or cliff – were a refuge for pirates. Only around 1800 did settlement begin on the larger islands. Fishing and »wrecking«, i.e. salvaging and hocking goods from ships that broke up on the reefs, brought money in – so much that Key West was the richest city in the USA for a short time around 1850.

Reefs and cliffs in emerald-green water

Up to the 20th century the Keys were accessible only by ship; then came Henry Flagler. »All we have to do«, the railway mogul is supposed to have said, »is to set one cement pylon after another, and we'll get to Key West in a hurry.« It wasn't that simple, but on 22 January 1912 the East Coast Railroad brought its 83-year old boss to Key West. For the next 20 years »Flagler's Folly« connected the Keys to the rest of the world. In 1935 a hurricane destroyed the causeway, but the islanders' new isolation did not hold long. Two and a half years later, on the ruins of the Flagler railway, US 1, a 113mi/182km-long Overseas Highway with 42 bridges, was opened. And the tourists soon followed.

The »Conches«, as the islanders are called, still live from tourism. Millions of tourists follow the highway every year to the Keys – with consequences for the animal world. Sea turtles, manatee and coral reefs are endangered by sailors; the delicate Key deer, which exist only here, by drivers of cars.

The greatest danger, global warming, remains invisible for the present. It will take a few years before the rising level of the ocean visibly starts to gnaw at the islands. Until then the Keys will remain a paradise for water sports, fishers and loafers, and Key West, the

Isn't it wonderful? A pretty spot on Islamorada

southernmost city of mainland USA, will remain America's most liberal venue for artists and drop-outs.

For a trip to the Keys from Miami, allow at least three days. The directions are child's play: the Overseas Highway is the only road. It begins in Florida City and ends in Key West. Little green markers on the right-hand edge of the road, called mile markers (MM), show the remaining distance to Key West.

Upper Keys

The Upper Keys are the islands furthest to the north of the entire chain. The largest – Key Largo, Tavernier and Islamorada – are a weekend venue for many people from the Miami area for diving and fishing, and are pretty well overrun by tourists. However, there are also worthwhile sights here.

Key Largo Key Largo has an area of 31sq km/12 sq mi and a population of 12,000. The main town has the same name but not much else apart from a few hotels and motels.

★★
John Pennekamp Coral Reef State Park John Pennekamp Coral Reef State Park is now run very professionally – thankfully, it has to be said (MM 102.5; hours: daily 8am–5pm). It was established in 1963 and named after an editor of the Miami Herald who fought for the protection of the Keys, and is

⏵ VISITING UPPER KEYS

INFORMATION

**Key Largo Chamber of Commerce
Florida Keys Visitor Center**
Milemarker 106
Key Largo
Tel. (305) 451-4747
www.keylargo.org

**Islamorada Chamber of
Commerce Visitor Center**
Milemarker 82.5
Islamorada
Tel. (305) 664-4503
www.islamoradachamber.com

ACTIVITIES

Along with the boating, diving and snorkelling tours that the park administration offers there are numerous tour companies in Key Largo (including Florida Bay Outfitters. MM 104, tel. 305/451-3018) that offer tours through John Pennekamp Coral Reef State Park.

Theater of the Sea and Dolphins Plus (Ocean Bay Drive, MM 100, tel. 305/451-1993) in Key Largo offer swimming with dolphins.

Boating is the most popular activity here. Dozens of rental agencies at Robbie's Pier in Islamorada as well as along the Overseas Highway hire out boats of every size and type. The same applies to fishing, the second most popular hobby of Key tourists.

WHERE TO EAT

⏵ Moderate
**Lorelei Restaurant &
Cabana Bar**
MM 82, Islamorada
Tel. (305) 664-4656
An institution: pass the giant mermaid to get to lobster, fish soup and shrimps.

▶ Budget
Harriett's Restaurant
MM 95.7, Key Largo
Tel. (305) 852-8689
Harriett likes to greet her guests personally in her simple canteen. Down-to-earth breakfast, hearty lunches. Her crab cakes Benedict are especially recommended!

WHERE TO STAY

▶ Luxury/Mid-range
Holiday Inn Key Largo
99701 Overseas Highway
Key Largo
Tel. (305) 451-2121
www.holidayinnkeylargo.com
130 rooms and suites
Beautiful holiday hotel with its own marina and extensive selection of water sports.

▶ Budget/Mid-range
Hotel Tavernier
MM 91.8, Tavernier
Tel. (305) 852-4131
www.taverniarhotel.com
18 rooms
Former cinema: tropics and tradition in pink, with a pretty English country restaurant.

the first underwater nature preserve in the USA; it includes the coral reef that reaches to Key West. The millennia-old coral deposits are home to a colourful hodge-podge world of tropical underwater flora and fauna. These can be seen from glass-bottom boats or on diving or snorkelling tours. The mangrove forests in the nature preserve are best explored in a kayak or canoe.

! **Baedeker TIP**

Bid the fish and crabs good night
Room service, pizza delivery and the daily newspaper in the morning: nothing special in a hotel. But in Emerald Lagoon off Key Largo all of this is available several feet underwater. Jules' Undersea Lodge, an underwater research station from the 1970s, has two comfortable bedrooms and a salon, and it is especially popular among divers on a honeymoon. Diving lessons are available, too, of course. Address: 51 Shoreland Drive, Key Largo, tel. (305) 451-2353, www.jul.com

At the edge of **Tavernier**, a village of 2,000 nestled sleepily among palmetto and hibiscus brush on the island of the same name, the Florida Keys Wild Bird Rehabilitation Center (MM 93.6; hours: daily 8.30am–5.30pm) is a little difficult to spot. Wounded wild birds are kept here after altercations with cars or motorboats and nursed by volunteers. Take a stroll through Tavernier's restored old city, which goes back 100 years to the time of the pineapple plantations, and a coffee break in the pink Tavernier Hotel, which started life as a cinema and was the hospital for hurricane victims in 1935. Not far away is Harry Harris Park (MM 92.5), a pretty site with a beach, picnic grounds and live music on the weekends.

Islamorada Beyond Tavernier the Keys Plantation, Windley, Upper and Lower Matecumbe are usually known under the combined name Islamorada and have a population of 7,000. If sports fishing is popular in the rest of the Keys, it is omnipresent in this 32km/19mi-long part. Islamorada, the self-proclaimed »sports fishing capital of the world«, seems to consist of marinas, boat ramps and tackle shops. Motorboats (the kind with a seat and safety belt in the back) as well as fishing tackle with and without a skipper can be rented everywhere. The coveted prizes are swordfish or marlin, which decorate billboards, cups and t-shirts.

Theater of the Sea ⏲ Inevitably all of the sights on land have some connection with the ocean. The Theater of the Sea (MM 84.5; hours: daily 9am–5pm) has put on dolphin and sea lion shows for over 50 years and also offers swimming with the dolphins.

Robbie's Pier Probably the cheapest – but by no means the worst – attraction on the Keys is **tarpon feeding** at Robbie's Pier (MM 77.5; daily). Ever since a compassionate shop owner named Robbie Reckwerth took in and fed a wounded tarpon 20 years ago, 80 to 100 of these fish, which can get up to 2m/6ft long and weigh up to 100kg/220lb, circle like minisubs under the water's surface and wait to jump for the herring that the tourists offer them.

Robbie's Pier is also the starting point for tours to **Indian Key** and **Lignumvitae Key**, which have been left in their natural state and are protected as state parks. Florida can be experienced here as it was before the Europeans came.

For loafing and swimming there is Anne's Beach (MM 73), a long, gently sloping beach with a beautiful picnic area.

Middle Keys

Pelicans glide by at eye-level and the mini islands have wonderful Shangri-La-like holiday resorts. The Overseas Highway fades into the blue mist on the horizon: between Duck Key and Bahia Honda the drive over the ocean becomes almost surreal. But a turtle hospital and other interesting sights keep tourists on the ground.

Indians, pirates, white settlers from the Bahamas, Flagler's railroad workers, hobby captains and tourists: the happenings in the 10,000-strong town on Vaca Key during the last 200 years are documented in the Museum of Natural History (MM 50.5; hours: Mon–Sat 10am–5pm, Sun noon–5pm) in refreshingly critical studies. Tropical Crane Point Hammock, a sub-tropical area of woodland, is also part

✳
Marathon
🕐

▶ VISITING MIDDLE KEYS

INFORMATION

**Greater Marathon
Chamber of Commerce**
12222 Overseas Highway
Marathon
Tel. (305) 743-5417
www.floridakeysmarathon.com

WHERE TO EAT

▶ Moderate
Herbie's
MM 50.5; tel. (305) 743-6373
Nice old-fashioned neighbourhood meeting place for over 30 years: oyster bar, fresh lobster, fresh fish.

Barracuda Grill
MM 49.5; tel. (305) 743–3314
Pretty bistro-style restaurant. »New« American cuisine, with good fish dishes and steaks.

WHERE TO STAY

▶ Luxury
Hawk's Cay Resort
MM 61, Duck Key
Tel. (305) 743-7000
Fax (305) 743-5215
www. hawkscay.com
177 rooms, 230 suites, spa, 3 restaurants
Holiday paradise on its own island, all types of water sports, swimming with dolphins.

▶ Mid-range
Lime Tree Bay Resort Motel
US 1, MM 68.5, tel. (305) 664-4740
www.limetreebayresort.com
Nice rooms, suites and cottages between Marathon and Islamorada or the border to Long Key Recreation Area.

of the museum and can be explored via a path of wooden planks. Other residents of the Keys are protected in a former striptease bar: animal-loving motel owners converted Fanny's Bar into the **Hidden Harbor Turtle Hospital** (2396 Overseas Highway, tel. 305/743–2552, tours on appointment) in 1986 and care for sick or injured turtles. In the **Dolphin Research Center** (MM 59, Grassy Key; hours: daily 9am–4pm) care that is appropriate to the species is important: 15 dolphins live in an expansive saltwater lagoon; they can be petted under supervision. The best spot for a picnic is Sombrero Beach, a beautiful, palm-lined beach with picnic benches and toilets.

Seven Mile Bridge, Pigeon Key

The 7mi/11km-long bridge from Vaca Key to Bahia Honda Key (photo see p.116–117) was completed in 1982 at a cost of $45 million. The feeling when driving high over the ocean really is intoxicating. The view of the old bridge built by the railway magnate Flagler, the middle section of which was torn down – it featured in the Schwarzenegger action movie *True Lies* – might inspire a side trip to Pigeon Key. The island is only accessible by bus (from Pigeon Key Visitor Center, MM 47) across the old bridge and until 1935 served as a camp for railroad workers; today it has a museum dedicated to »Flagler's Folly« (hours: daily 10am–4pm).

Great catches in the »world's fishing capital«

Lower Keys

Too far away for weekend trips from the mainland and only a half-hour drive from Key West, the islands between Bahia Honda Key and Coppitt Key have had only a slight brush with tourism. This makes them the best place to see flora and fauna.

Paths through tropical hammocks with palms, rare plants and exotic birds, mangrove forests and the most beautiful beach in the Keys: right after Seven Mile Bridge is a piece of postcard Caribbean. Boats, windsurfing boards, diving and snorkelling gear can be rented at Bahia Honda Marina (hours: 8am–sunset).

✱ ✱
Bahia Honda State Park

Key deer live here. The somewhat shy miniature deer with a maximum height of two feet at the shoulder do not get much bigger than an Alsatian dog; in the thicket of the nature preserve they are difficult to see. Along the side of the road there is a better chance of finding one – i.e. one that was hit by a car. With about 800 deer the population has recovered well – when the refuge was established in 1957 on Big Pine Key there were only 27 of them – but these relatives of the white-tailed deer are still endangered. To find out the best places to observe the deer, ask at the refuge office (Winn Dixie, Big Pine Key Plaza, Key Deer Boulevard). Via Cudjoe Key, where US American TV programmes are transmitted to the Caribbean and Cuba by means of Fat Albert, a dirigible that is anchored high above the island, as well as via Sugarloaf Key and the naval air station Boca Chica the road continues on to ►Key West.

✱ ✱
National Key Deer Refuge

Baedeker TIP

Relax!

By all means avoid travelling around the Keys on Friday afternoon or on Sunday evening! That is the only way to avoid the heavy traffic caused by holiday-makers from the metropolitan Miami area.

✱ ✱ Fort Lauderdale

J 6

Region: South-east
Population: 176,000

Elevation: 0 – 3m/10ft above sea level
Area code: 954

With more than 260km/160mi of mostly palm-lined canals, Fort Lauderdale rightly and proudly calls itself the »American Venice«. Countless artificial canals criss-cross the city and connect the Finger Islands, the exclusive residential areas with tropical gardens and private piers, which have been copied by many other towns in Florida meanwhile.

▶ VISITING FORT LAUDERDALE

INFORMATION
Greater Fort Lauderdale CVB
100 E. Broward Boulevard
Suite 200
Fort Lauderdale, FL 33301
Tel. (954) 765 - 44 66
Fax (954) 765 - 44 67
www.sunny.org

AIRPORT
Fort Lauderdale/Hollywood International Airport is integrated well into the network of North American airlines and can be reached from Europe daily without a problem.
The airport is served by city buses (Broward County Transit/BCT) and commuter trains (Tri-Rail). Numerous hotels and car rental agencies have their own shuttle buses.

CITY TOUR BY BOAT
Water Taxi
These water taxis run daily from 10am. They have 20 stops and run to all important attractions (schedules: tel. 954/467-6677, www.watertaxi.com).

Carrie B. Harbor Tours
These boats run to movie settings and the villas of the rich and beautiful (departures: Riverwalk, Las Olas Blvd., SE 5th Ave.; schedules: tel. 954/768-9920, www.carriebcruises.com).

Jungle Queen Riverboat
This paddle wheeler runs daily at 9am and 1.30pm from Bahia Mar Yacht Center through Fort Lauderdale's waterways on three-hour tours with live commentary (tel. 954/462-5596).

PROMENADES
The Beach Promenade between Sunrise Blvd. and SE 17th Street is the ideal place for strollers, the coffee bar in the Sheraton Yankee Trader Hotel (321 N. Beach Blvd.) a good place for people-watching. The River Walk meanders along with the New River and is another mecca for strollers, as is Las Olas Boulevard.

SHOPPING
Sawgrass Mills
One of the top shopping addresses is a giant outlet shopping mall on the north-western edge of Fort Lauderdale with about 300 factory outlets, boutiques and specialty shops of famous designers (including Calvin Klein, Jockey, MCM, Nike, Sergio's). There are also diverse attractions for young and old, food courts where delicacies from all over the world can be bought, and several restaurants (12801 W. Sunrise Blvd.; hours: Mon–Sat 10am–9.30pm, Sun 11am–8pm).

Las Olas Boulevard
Hard-core shoppers will find more than 100 luxury boutiques here.

Beach Place
This shopping centre on Beach Boulevard has mainly ready-to-wear fashion (Gap, Banana Republic etc.).

Swap Shop
Largest indoor flea market in southern Florida with a giant selection from more than 2,000 sellers (3291 W. Sunrise Blvd.; hours: Mon–Thu 9am–5.30pm, Fri–Sun 8am–6.30pm).

EVENTS
Las Olas Art Festival
Every year in mid-March an art festival takes place on Las Olas Boulevard with artists from all over the USA.

Fort Lauderdale Map

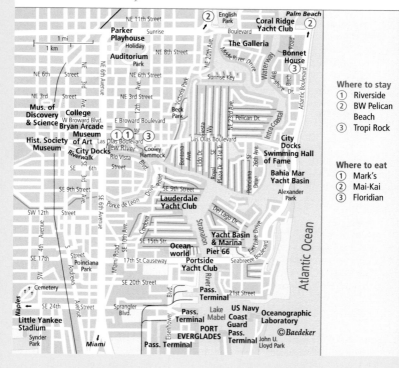

Where to stay
① Riverside
② BW Pelican Beach
③ Tropi Rock

Where to eat
① Mark's
② Mai-Kai
③ Floridian

Olde Florida Folk Festival

This festival in September is the high point of the festival calendar in Flamingo Gardens. On the programme are Anglo-American and Spanish-American folklore. There are also old crafts and Indian traditions to admire.

NIGHT LIFE

The Strip

The nightly entertainment route starts at the eastern end of Las Olas Boulevard and runs to Sunrise Boulevard on the beach. Here there are many restaurants, cafés, nightclubs, discos.

Seminole Paradise

The Indian reservation near Hollywood really has something to offer: apart from a casino there are 17 restaurants and 10 nightclubs, dance clubs and piano bars, which play everything from live jazz to rock 'n roll.

WHERE TO EAT

► Expensive

① *Mark's*

1032 E. Las Olas Boulevard
Tel. (954) 463-1000
At one time the first, but today still the best restaurant on the strip: excellent new American cuisine, inspired by Italian cooking.

▶ Moderate

② *Mai-Kai*
3599 N. Federal Highway
Tel. (954) 563-3272
Kitsch from the pre-Mickey-Mouse
era: a restaurant decorated like a
Polynesian village, with hula dancers
and fire-eaters.

▶ Budget

③ *Floridian*
1410 E. Las Olas Boulevard
Tel. (954) 463-4041
24-hour diner, called »the Flo«, for
more than 60 years the best source for
calorie-rich American breakfast.

WHERE TO STAY

▶ Luxury

① *Riverside*
620 Las Olas Boulevard
Tel. (954) 467-0671
Fax (954) 462-2148
www.riversidehotel.com
217 rooms and suites
The oldest hotel in the city (built in
1936) was recently renovated and has
an infectious Old Florida charm.

▶ Mid-range

② *Best Western Pelican Beach*
2000 N. Atlantic Boulevard
Tel. (954) 568-9431
Fax (954) 565-2662
www.pelicanbeach.com
159 rooms and suites
Swimming pool.
This hotel opened on the beach in
2004 and has very large rooms.

▶ Budget

③ *Tropi Rock*
2900 Belmar Street
Tel. (954) 564-0523
www.tropirock.com
30 rooms
Only a 2-minute walk to the beach and
a very nice sunroof.

Centre of the Gold Coast
The times when hordes of unleashed college students turned the town upside-down during the spring break are over. Today the city at the centre of the Gold Coast represents the classic example of a successful integration of city and beach. But that's not all. There are plans to build several new resort hotels in the next years. Fort Lauderdale's port, Port Everglades, where the new Queen Mary 2 spends the winter, has now become one of the most-visited cruise destinations in the world.
Greater Fort Lauderdale currently includes 30 towns and communities with a total population of about 1.7 million. The metropolitan area extends from Pompano in the north to Hallandale Beach in the south.

City history
During the Second Seminole War in 1838 a fort was built here and named after its commanding officer. But the actual founder was a businessman called Frank Stranahan, who started a trading post and a bank here in the 1890s and built the first road to Miami. In 1896 Flagler's railroad came, in the 1920s the land boom. During this time Charles G. Rodes, an architect and fan of Venice, transformed the swamps into canals that ran parallel through the city. They form the basic pattern of today's canals, which criss-cross the urban area.

Colleges all over the USA discovered Fort Lauderdale as the place to hold their swimming competitions. In 1960 this »youth movement« culminated in the successful teen movie *Where the Boys Are*, which put Fort Lauderdale on the map as a »party town«.

Many miles of palm-lined canals traverse the city. They not only connect exclusive residential areas, but also the office buildings downtown, the galleries and boutiques on Las Olas Boulevard as well as museums, theatres and nightclubs on Riverwalk. All the streets are numbered. Only the main streets that run through, like the large east-west streets between the beach and downtown, have names. The city centre is three miles (five kilometres) inland on New River and has excellent museums and an old city that is well worth seeing. Las Olas Boulevard reflects the zeitgeist with numerous small ateliers and boutiques. On the other side of the Intracoastal Waterway, Ocean Boulevard follows the white palm-lined beach for seven miles (eleven kilometres).

City and orientation

What to See in Fort Lauderdale

Even if the beach is irresistible, there are a few attractions between the sober office buildings downtown. A pedestrian promenade on New River, the **River Walk** connects the **Museum of Discovery and Science** with the IMAX 3D cinema (401 SW. Second St.; hours: Mon–Sat 10am–5pm, Sun noon–6pm) with the **Broward Center for the Performing Arts**, the city's modern cultural centre and theatre. The museum, which is specially attractive to children, has hands-on presentations on ecology and high-tech. Where else could you programme a robot yourself? The oldest house that is still standing is hardly older than the city's oldest residents. Frank Stranahan built

★ Downtown

Highlights Fort Lauderdale

Las Olas Boulevard
The unrivalled showpiece of Fort Lauderdale with chic boutiques and restaurants
▶ page 180

Fort Lauderdale Museum of Art
Truly a »shrine to modern art« with works by Henry Moore, Pablo Picasso and Andy Warhol as well as works by the CoBrA movement
▶ page 180

Flamingo Gardens
Picture-postcard Florida: long-legged pink birds, beautiful orchids and fragrant orange trees
▶ page 181

Butterfly World
Fantastic world of butterflies
▶ page 182

Sawgrass Mills
World class shopping centre with about 300 factory outlets of renowned designers
▶ page 176

the house that was later named after him in 1901 and used it first as a trading post for the Seminole trappers. A pretty little exhibition depicts this time (335 SE. 6th Ave.; hours: Wed–Sat 10am–3pm, Sun 1pm–3pm).

★ ★
Las Olas Boulevard

The main shopping street, between the art museum and the Atlantic, is nicely decorated. Nostalgic gaslights, chic boutiques, galleries, antique shops and restaurants set the scene. At the beginning of this street, which is equally frequented by tourists and locals, is the **Museum of Art**, a shrine to modern art with works by such artists as Henry Moore, Pablo Picasso and Andy Warhol, a collection of paintings by the American Impressionist William Glackens and many key works of the European CoBrA movement (1 E. Las Olas Blvd.; hours: daily 11am–7pm, Thu 11am to 9pm).

> **!** *Baedeker* TIP
>
> **Midnight jazz**
> Whether music lovers wear expensive Armani suits or worn-out jeans – the jazz in O'Hara's Pub (722 E. Las Olas Blvd., tel. 954/524 - 2801), probably the best jazz joint in town, unites them all.

★
Bonnet House Museum

This house that is surrounded by box-like hotels gives an idea of what Fort Lauderdale looked like 80 years ago. Built in 1921 by the eccentric artist Frank Clay Bartlett in plantation style in a luxuriant garden on the ocean, it now houses excellent animal sculptures (900 N. Birch Rd.; hours: Dec–April Tue–Sat 10am–4pm, Sun noon–4pm, otherwise Wed–Fri 10am–3pm, Sat 10am–4pm, Sun noon–4pm).

Int'l Swimming Hall of Fame & Aquatic Complex

All the big names in swimming are here, the Tarzan actor Johnny Weissmuller as well as the swimming star Mark Spitz, who won 7 gold medals at the Olympic Games in Munich in 1972. It includes an arena for swimmers, high board divers and scuba divers (1 Hall of Fame Dr.; hours: daily 9am–5pm).

★
Beachfront Promenade

Where students used to hold drinking binges and bikini contests during spring break, recent improvement efforts have transformed the place. Now skaters, bikers, joggers, Nordic walkers, volleyball players and above all families with children play here. Moreover street cafés, restaurants and boutiques attract strollers.

South of Fort Lauderdale

Port Everglades

Port Everglades, the port of Fort Lauderdale, south of the city, is the deepest seaport between Norfolk and New Orleans. It was only completed in 1989 but since then has developed into the second most important cruise port in Florida with well over two million passengers every year. In the northern part of the port the hyper-modern Convention Center (1950 Eisenhower Blvd./S.E. 17th St.) with hotels and a large shopping centre was opened in 1991.

South of Fort Lauderdale and the airport lies the town of Dania (population 30,000), which is divided by the A1A; it was founded in 1896 by Danish immigrants. Today Dania is a popular ocean resort with a beautiful beach. Dania's Main Street is well known for its many antique shops. And Dania's fishing pier is popular all year round to hobby and sports fishers. Everything worth knowing about big game fishing can be found out at the IGFA Fishing Hall of Fame (300 Gulfstream Way; hours: daily 10am–6pm).

Dania

⊕

This resort was only established in the 1930s, but it developed explosively after World War II and today has a population of far more than 125,000. Its appearance has changed markedly in the last years. The downtown area has been revived and now has many galleries, boutiques and sidewalk cafés. On the brand new Broadwalk along the beach the athletic, young and beautiful skate and bike.

Hollywood

In north-west Hollywood, on Seminole Way, there is a little Indian village. Here souvenirs and textiles that the Indians made themselves are sold, and Indian food can be tasted. A few older women demonstrate traditional crafts and young men show how to handle alligators and poisonous snakes (hours: daily 9am–7pm).
In order to earn money the Indians have built an ultra-modern entertainment complex with a casino, hotel, several restaurants and a few clubs, which is popular among nighthawks from the whole region.

✱
Seminole Okalee Indian Village & Museum

⊕

◄ Seminole Hard Rock Hotel & Casino

South-west of Fort Lauderdale, in the suburb of Davie, all Florida clichés have been put together: flamingos, alligators, a luxurious exotic plant world with beautiful orchids, Everglades swamp and orange trees. Pine Island Ridge Hammock is covered by ancient oaks with Spanish moss hanging from them and the Everglades Museum displays Seminole artefacts. A traffic museum displaying the typical Florida airboat and swamp buggy as well as a few old-timers is attached (Davie, 3750 S. Flamingo Rd.; hours: daily 9.30am–5.30pm, June–Sept closed Mon).

✱ ✱
Flamingo Gardens

North of Fort Lauderdale

To the north lies the popular ocean resort of Pompano Beach (population 101,000). The many canals are characteristic. Hotels, motels and other holiday complexes are strung out along the long beach. The 330m/1,000ft-long Fisherman's Wharf on the beach promenade is very popular.

Further to the north Ocean Boulevard (A1A) crosses **Hillsboro Inlet** with its many boats.

Florida's best-known feathered friends

From the Fish City Marina boats go out for big game fishing. On the other side a lighthouse of 1906 marks the entrance to the harbour. Numerous luxury villas line the beach.

★ ★
Butterfly World

Butterfly World west of Pompano Beach is worth a visit. The gardens with roses and orchids are trying to preserve various endangered butterfly species. With a little patience thousands of colourfully glittering butterflies and other insects can be seen. Hummingbirds also dart around (Tradewinds Park, Coconut Creek, 3600 W. Sample Rd.; hours: Mon–Sat 9am–5pm, Sun 1pm–5pm).

★ Fort Myers

H 6

Region: South-west
Population: 65,000

Elevation: 0 – 5m/16ft above sea level
Area code: 239

Fort Myers is located at the broad mouth of the Caloosahatchee River in the Gulf of Mexico; it is the rapidly growing centre of south-west Florida. Anyone for whom the Gold Coast has become too crowded lives, works and invests here. Fort Myers became famous because the inventor Thomas Alva Edison once had his winter home here. Fort Myers does not yet have the class of its more sophisticated neighbours Naples, Sanibel and Captiva. Not yet.

How to be a
»City of Leisure«

Only a quarter of a century ago, those who landed in Fort Myers had to carry their baggage across sun-dried grass to a shack of an »arrival hall«. In 1983 100,000 people flew to Fort Myers. Meanwhile Southwest Florida International Airport registers more than 5 million passengers. They go on to Fort Myers and a few other towns that only sprouted out of the ground in the last two decades.

Not bad for a city that started life as a fort during the Second Seminole War; it only saw its first settlers after the Civil War and in 1885 had a population of about 350 people, who raised tomatoes and sold their cattle to Cuba. But everything changed in 1885. **Thomas Alva Edison** (1847–1931) went ashore here during a cruise – and fell under a spell. From then on, the famous inventor whose doctor had advised him urgently to get a change of climate, spent every winter here. Other prominent people, including the automobile manufacturer **Henry Ford**, followed him. In the 1920s the railway and the newly opened Tamiami Trail made tourism available to all classes in the south-west. Building continued here even during the Depression. It was only slowed down by the »Florida Land Bust«, and the town's growth continued immediately after World War II. During the 1980s it grew out of all proportion. But only a few of the houses are higher than the palms that Edison once had planted.

▶ VISITING FORT MYERS

INFORMATION

Lee County VCB
12800 University Drive
Suite 550
Fort Myers, FL 33907
Tel. (239) 338-3500
Fax (239) 334-1106
www.fortmyers-sanibel.com

EVENT

Edison Festival of Lights
A festival of light is held from late January to mid-February in honour of the great inventor.

WHERE TO EAT
▶ Moderate
① **Veranda**
2122 2nd Street
Fort Myers
Tel. (239) 332-2065
Right in the centre of town with good, Mediterranean-style cooking

WHERE TO STAY
▶ Mid-range

Baedeker recommendation

① **The Outrigger Beach Resort**
6200 Estero Blvd.
Fort Myers Beach
Tel. (239) 463-3131
www.outriggerfmb.com
155 rooms and suites
Friendly Sixties-style beach hotel with an informal Tiki Bar at the pool.

② **Holiday Inn Riverwalk**
2220 W. 1st Street, Fort Myers
Tel. (239) 334-3434
www.holiday-inn.com
146 rooms and suites
Comfortable accommodation near the two main attractions.

What to See in Fort Myers

Efforts are being made here to preserve historic buildings. A good example of the style at the end of the 19th century is Burroughs Home, which is open as a museum today (2505 First St.; tours: Oct–May Tue–Fri 11am–3pm). Peck Street Station was closed in 1971 and restored since then; now it is the home of the Historical Museum. The part dedicated to the Calusa Indian culture and a historical model of the town are worth seeing (2300 Peck St.; hours: Mon–Fri 9am–4.30, Sun 1pm–5pm). Another attraction is the Manatee Park in the eastern part of town (3410 Palm Beach Blvd.; hours: daily 8am–5pm), where these playful animals can be watched.

Downtown

Fort Myers' main attraction is »Seminole Lodge«, Thomas Alva Edison's home at McGregor Road (no. 2350). Edison (1847–1931) came to Florida in the 1880s because his doctors had told him to spend winters in a warmer climate. At that time he was experimenting with bamboo fibres as the filaments in his new electric light bulbs. Bamboo and reed were abundant in this area so Edison had a holiday home built in 1886 on the Caloosahatchee River, where he

✷ ✷
Edison & Ford Winter Estates
⊙
Opening hours:
Tours:
daily 9am–5.30pm

Fort Myers / Cape Coral Map

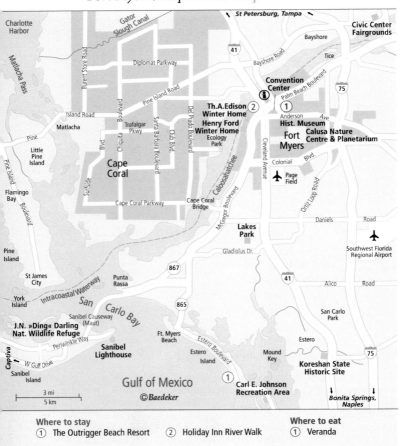

Where to stay
① The Outrigger Beach Resort   ② Holiday Inn River Walk

Where to eat
① Veranda

spent the next 46 winters. A banyan tree marks the entrance with its tangled air roots. This was a gift to Edison in 1925 from his friend, the rubber and tyre manufacturer Harvey Firestone (1868–1938). Edison was not only interested in fibre but also in plants that contained latex, which could be used to produce rubber.

The house is furnished as it was when Edison still lived here. The light bulbs are the kind that Edison produced in 1912. Edison developed numerous epoch-making technical devices in the workshop and laboratory. He registered more than 1,000 patents. The highlights of his work can be seen in the museum.

Incidentally, the pine building materials for the house which Edison designed himself reached the Gulf Coast by ship. This makes Edison's house the first pre-fab house in America. Edison was responsible for another novelty: the swimming pool in his garden was the first in the southern USA.

»Mangoes«, the neighbouring winter quarters of the car manufacturer Henry Ford (1863–1947), is also open for viewing. Ford, who was the first to produce cars on an assembly line, bought the estate in 1916 and spent the winters here near his friend Edison until his death. Ford sold the property in 1945. In 1988 the city of Fort Myers bought the villa and turned it into a museum.

The trademark of Fort Myers is Palm Alley. Royal palms imported from Cuba line McGregor Boulevard, which leads to the Gulf. The trees were planted in 1900 at Edison's suggestion, as he wanted to beautify the street that ran past his house.

✱ Palm Alley

Around Fort Myers

About 12mi/20km to the south is the seaside resort of Fort Myers on Estero Island. Here, especially around Times Square (intersection of Estero and San Carlos Blvd.), the activity never stops, due to the sol-

✱ Fort Myers Beach

This is what the genius inventor Thomas A. Edison's workshop looks like.

id front of motels, fast-food joints and t-shirt stores. En route to the south the scene quietens down and the barrier island, which is 7mi/ 11km long, but only a few hundred yards wide, has some of Florida's most beautiful beaches. At the southern end a causeway leads to the island Lovers Key, which is still quite undisturbed. The 2.5mi/4km-long beach can only be reached on foot or by bicycle from the parking lot.

Koreshan State Historic Site

About 16mi/25km south of Fort Myers lies the town of Koreshan on the Estero River, where a religious cult tried to realize its vision of the perfect city over 100 years ago. The members of the »Koreshanity« lived celibate in communes. They possessed no personal property. Their leader Teed planned a city for 10 million people; its broad boulevards were supposed to be 160km/100mi long. When Teed died in 1908 the community that he started sank into oblivion (Estero, South US 41/Corkscrew Rd.; hours: daily 9am–6pm).

Cape Coral

North of the Caloosahatchee River delta the town of Cape Coral is spreading out rapidly. It was only founded in 1958 and incorporated in 1970, but today it has a population of over 155,000 already. Cape Coral has the largest area available for development, about 300 sq km/ 115sq mi, of any city in Florida except ► Jacksonville. From the very beginning the houses built along the many canals that criss-cross the city were mainly single family homes with yacht moorings. This explains the almost affectionate nickname »Water Wonderland«.

> **! Baedeker TIP**
>
> **Tropical fruit galore ...**
> On Pine Island off the west coast all sorts of tropical fruits flourish, including mangos, papayas, guava and lychees. Sunburst Tropical Fruit Company offers tours of its plantation (reservations: tel. 239/283-1200).

Cayo Costa State Park

The islands of Cayo Costa and North Captiva as well as a few neighbouring islands at the entrance to Charlotte Harbor have been made into a state park. These islands are accessible only by boat; they still look as they did when the first Europeans arrived here. Mounds of clam and oyster shells bear witness to thousands of years of Indian settlement. On the Gulf side of Cayo Costa and North Captiva Island there are wonderful seashell sand beaches and dunes. In the summer sea turtles deposit their eggs here. The mangrove swamps on the land side are one of the largest breeding grounds for brown pelicans in Florida. Ospreys, bald eagles and frigate birds also nest here. Tourists can rent simple huts on Cayo Costa; on North (Upper) Captiva Island there is a little holiday resort with a marina that is not part of the State Park.

Gasparilla Island

This island, which has been taken over by wealthy Americans and Europeans, is accessible from the mainland by car from the northern

Brown pelicans in Cayo Costa State Park

entrance to Charlotte Harbor via FL 771 across a toll bridge. It is not certain if the island was named after a Spanish priest or a notorious pirate. Boca Grande, the main town on the island, is located at the end of FL 771; it has kept much of its original atmosphere. Nice restaurants have been integrated into the historical architecture. Boca Grande's main attraction are the glorious seashell sand beaches as well as the Port Boca Grande Lighthouse, which was built in 1888 at the end of the island.

Punta Gorda

This town of 17,000 residents, where Peace River runs into Charlotte Harbor, is the main town in an area that takes its character from cattle raising and fishing. In 1513 Ponce de León sailed into Charlotte Harbor and probably went ashore here. Spanish missionaries were active here in the 16th and 17th centuries; then pirates hid out here. Today's town was incorporated in 1885. Until 1904 Punta Gorda was the terminus of the Florida Southern Railway. From Long Dock ships sailed for ►Key West, Havana (Cuba) and New Orleans.

◄ Downtown

In place of the old pier on the banks of Peace River »Fishermen's Village« has sprung up. It is a complex of souvenir shops, restaurants, holiday apartments and entertainment as well as a yacht harbour. In the Charlotte County Museum fossils and remains of various mammals from the ice age are on display. At the west end of Marion Avenue Ponce de León Park commemorates the landing of the famous Spanish explorer in 1513.

Port Charlotte

The area north-west of Punta Gorda was still pastureland until the 1960s. Today Port Charlotte (population 47,000) is one of the large-scale projects of the General Development Corporation in Florida. The artificial city was conceived for a population of 80,000. About 60km/35mi of natural shoreline as well as 264km/158mi of artificial waterways, most of which open directly into the bay, make Port Charlotte a popular place to live and to holiday for water sports fans. Port Charlotte Beach with its fishing pier extends out from the south-western end of Harbor Boulevard.

From Port Charlotte take a boat trip to the islands of Useppa Island, Cabbage Key and Cayo Costa. Interesting boating tours of the waterways in the surrounding areas are also available (Babcock Wilderness Adventures or Charlotte Harbor Florida Water Safaris, among others).

Fort Pierce · Port St Lucie

J 5

Region: Central East
Population: 41,000

Elevation: 0 – 8m/26ft above sea level
Area code: 772

The boom in the centres of the Gold Coast appears to have passed by Fort Pierce. The city at the centre of the equally unpretentious Treasure Coast lives from citrus fruits first, and tourists second – despite the yacht harbour right in the centre of town.

A new tourist attraction

Fort Pierce began as a military post during the Second Seminole War and only started to blossom after Flagler's railway came. There was a naval base here during World War II. Modest tourism began in the 1950s – the nice old-fashioned motels and the piers that reach far into the ocean bring back memories of highway cruisers and drive-in-

► VISITING FORT PIERCE · PORT ST LUCIE

INFORMATION

St Lucie County
Chamber of Commerce
482 N. Indian River Drive
Fort Pierce, FL 34982
Tel. (772) 468-9152
www.stluciechamber.org

WHERE TO EAT

► **Moderate**
Mangrove Mattie's
S. Hutchison Island
1640 Seaway Dr., Fort Pierce
Tel. (772) 466-1044

Fresh fish and seafood with a view from the terrace onto Fort Pierce Inlet.

WHERE TO STAY

► **Budget**
Dockside Inn & Resort
1160 Seaway Drive
Fort Pierce, South Hutchison Island
Tel. (772) 468-3555
www.docksideinn.com
Nice place to stay with its own piers, pool and a large selection of water sports nearby.

diners. Since then Fort Pierce has developed the atmosphere of a working-class town. The nicely restored centre is unfortunately over-shadowed by the towers of a cement factory and there is a water fil-tration plant at the edge of town. But that doesn't matter. There are still things to see on the way across the lagoon called »Indian River« and out to North Hutchison Island, a barrier island off the coast that has remained largely undisturbed.

What to See in and around Fort Pierce

He said what he thought and was never averse to a fight. A. E. »Bea-nie« Backus (1906–90) was as rough as his town – and at the same time Florida's most famous landscape painter. Not far from the A1A across Indian River is the A. E. »Bean« Backus Museum, which is dedicated to the life and work of the painter who made Florida known throughout the world with his tropical subjects (500 N. Indi-an River Dr., hours: Tue–Sat 10am–4pm, Sun noon–4pm). A few blocks to the south there are free-roaming manatees in Moore Creek at the Manatee Observation & Education Center (480 N. Indian Riv-er Dr.; hours: Jan–June Tue–Sat 10am–5pm, Sun noon–4pm, other times Thu–Sat 10am–5pm). A guided tour through the marine re-search institute Harbor Branch Oceanographic Institution (5600 N. US 1; hours: daily 10am–5pm; bus tours: Mon–Sat 10am, noon and 2pm) gives information on modern aquacultures and includes a visit to a research ship. The Fort Pierce Inlet State Recreation Area (hours: daily 8am–sunset) at the southern tip of North Hutchison Island has beautiful beaches. Surf-ers also appreciate this beach.

One of the most unusual museum in Florida is situated in a round white house under palm trees: the **UDT-SEAL Museum** presents the work of the US Navy elite fighting troop as well as their undercover operations in the whole world (Hutchison Island, 3300 N. A1A; hours: Tue–Sat 10am–4pm, Sun noon–4pm). From World War II until the Vietnam War the elite units of the US navy were trained here.

Vero Beach, a town of 19,000 resi-dents, can be reached via the A1A, which traverses the length of North Hutchison Island, after 14mi/ 23km. Despite the fact that well-

Fort Pierce

Boating traffic on the Intracoastal Waterway

✳
Vero Beach
heeled winter residents have added a certain flair, Vero Beach has remained a nice small town with friendly people. Miles of beach on Ocean Drive, especially South Beach Park attract sun-worshippers and swimmers. At the northern end of the island Sebastian Inlet State Park (only open during daytime) also has a surf shop and kayak and canoe rental. The thunder of the regularly breaking waves can be heard from far off. In the **McLarty Treasure Museum** (13180 N. A1A, Sebastian Inlet State Recreation Area; hours: daily 10am–16.30) exhibitions of remains and salvage from sunken Spanish galleons graphically explain the origin of the name »Treasure Coast«.

Indian River
Still, dark and brackish, mostly only 1m/3ft deep, the so-called Indian River runs about 125mi/200km parallel to the Atlantic coast from New Smyrna Beach in the south to Stewart in the north – always protected by the off-coast barrier islands. The river, which is really more a lagoon, is especially shallow between Vero Beach and Sebastian and forms a labyrinth of marshes and islands, which provide a haven for countless varieties of birds. A channel has been dredged out for boats since Indian River is part of the Intracoastal Waterway. Parts of the lagoon have been reserved for different kinds of water sports.

Wabasso Island
The Environmental Learning Center (ELC), on Wabasso Island near Vero Beach in the middle of Indian River, reminds its visitors how delicate this biotope is. Open pools let visitors see typical local sea plants and animal life; a boardwalk leads through the thicket (hours: Tue–Fri 10am–4pm, Sat 9am–noon, Sun 1pm–4pm).

Port St Lucie
Port St Lucie, on the northern branch of the river of the same name, is one of the fastest growing cities in the USA. Where cattle were pastured until 1958 and orange pickers worked, a town sprang up in no time and now has a population of 145,000. Plots and houses were sold in Grand Central Station in New York, among other places, in the early days. On good days up to 300 contracts were signed there alone! A plot of land cost only a few dollars and a nice little house went for US$9,000. And the end of the »Port St Lucie Land Rush« is not in sight. Good infrastructure, which includes of course a marina with a yacht club as well as a golf course, attracts buyers.

Stuart
The fishing port of Stuart (population 12,000) 18mi/29km south of Fort Pierce does not hide its reputation as the sailfish capital of the world: yachts and sports fishing boats as far as the eye can see. Thousands of fishers go to sea from this port after sailfish (Istophorus americanus) with its striking back fin. Stuart is also popular because of its historical centre, which has been carefully restored and successfully revived with restaurants, bars, shops etc. The shoreline promenade and the houses along Flagler Avenue and Osceola Street are picturesque.

⋆ Fort Walton Beach · Destin

C 2

Region: North-west
Population: 25,000 (metropolitan area: 170,000)

Elevation: 0 – 8m/26ft above sea level
Area code: 850

What a beach, but what a beach! 25 miles/40 kilometres of fine white sand, flat, gently sloping beaches, emerald green water: year after year the readers of lifestyle magazines choose Fort Walton Beach as the most beautiful in Florida.

The best part: 60% of it is protected by law from any development whatsoever, which makes the »Emerald Coast« deservedly the most popular section of the Gulf Coast in the panhandle. The consequence has been a boom over recent decades. Apartment high-rises and huge American and international hotel chain complexes round Fort Walton Beach testify conspicuously to this. However, the town founded in the 19th century by Civil War veterans on the west bank of Choctawhatchee Bay and located on highway US 98, which is unabashedly called the »Miracle Strip«, does not live from tourism alone, but also from Eglin Air Force Base, one of the largest air force bases in the world and right on the city limits. Generations of American pilots were trained here, for missions to the Near East and other zones of conflict. But they leave hardly any mark on the city, apart from a few topless bars, pubs and vapour trails in the sky.

Tourism and military

▶ VISITING FORT WALTON BEACH · DESTIN

INFORMATION

Emerald Coast
Convention & Visitors Bureau
1540 Miracle Strip Parkway
Fort Walton Beach, FL 32548
Tel. (850) 651-7122
Fax (850) 651-7149
www.destin-fwb.com

EVENTS

Destin Deep Sea Fishing
Rodeo & Seafood Festival
Every year in October a large-scale deep-sea fishing competition is held in Destin with lots of prizes. There are also lots of good fish dishes available.

WHERE TO EAT

▶ **Moderate**
Old Bay Steamer
102 Santa Rosa Boulevard
Fort Walton Beach
Tel. (850) 664-2795
No view of the ocean in this restaurant, which is popular with the locals, but lots of tasty fish and seafood.

WHERE TO STAY

▶ **Budget**
Marina Motel
1345 E. Miracle Strip (Hwy 98)
Tel. (850) 244-1129
www.marinamotel.net
38 rooms. Comfortable motel opposite the beach at Beasley Park.

Perfect beach on the Emerald Coast near Fort Walton

History

The coast around Fort Walton has been settled for about 10,000 years. In the 5th century BC Mississippi Indians raised the first mounds for religious purposes. During the Civil War the few white settlers who lived in this area formed the »Walton Guards«, who defended the eastern entrance to Pensacola and the Santa Rosa Sound. Some of them returned to the coast after the war and started the settlement Fort Walton Beach.

What to See in and around Fort Walton Beach

✱
Indian Temple Mound & Museum
⊕

Drivers coming into town on Miracle Strip (US 98) passes a mound that was raised by Indians, probably in the 13th or 14th century, and is crowned by a reconstruction of an Indian cult hut. The museum associated with the site provides information on the infiltration of the Gulf Coast by Indian tribes, and displays Indian pottery from several periods (hours: Mon–Sat 10am–4pm, Sun 1pm–4pm).

✱
Air Force Armament Museum
⊕

Anyone interested in the air force should go to the Air Force Armament Museum, 6mi/10km north-east of town at the entrance to Eglin Air Force Base (access via FL 85). All of the US Air Force's weapons systems that were used from World War II to the Gulf War are exhibited here. A »Flying Fortress« from World War II can be seen as well as a B-52 long distance bomber, the legendary spy plane SR-71 »Blackbird« or an F-16 fighter jet. Of course, there are bombs, rockets and cruise missiles to see, too (hours: daily 9am–4.30pm).

A modern bridge on US 98 leads from the centre of town to the fabulously beautiful beaches of the barrier island; its eastern tip, which is outside the entrance to Choctawhatchee Bay, is called Okaloosa Island. Here too lots of new buildings have apparently sprung up out of the sand.

✳ ✳
Santa Rosa Island

Beyond the large bridge is the Gulfarium, which attracts many visitors especially in the school holidays by making it possible to observe dangerous sharks and moray eels from a safe distance, as well as peaceful sea turtles and dolphins. A few penguins, sea lions and otters also play in the pools (hours: May–Sept. daily 9am–6pm, Oct– April daily 9am–4pm, dolphin shows daily 10am, noon, 2pm, 4pm).

✳
Gulfarium

🕐

East of Fort Walton Beach another massive bridge on US 98 spans the entrance to Choctawhatchee Bay and after about 7mi/11km it reaches the fishing village of Destin, which is bursting at the seams today; countless yachts bob about in its harbour and marinas equipped with every variety of fishing equipment. The entire spit with the old harbour on its western tip is covered with hotels and holiday apartments today. The main attraction is the **Fishing Museum** off Emerald Coast Parkway (US 98). It exhibits a detailed history of fishing (hours: Tue to Sat 10am–4pm).

✳
Destin

> **!** *Baedeker* TIP
>
> **What a deal...**
> 8mi/13km east of Destin are the Silver Sands Factory Stores. In the giant designer factory outlet there are bargains galore, including articles by Tommy Hilfiger, Nike, Reebok (10562 Emerald Parkway/US 98; hours: March–Dec Mon–Sat 10am–9pm, Sun 10am–6pm, Jan, Feb Mon–Sat 10am–7pm, Sun noon–6pm; www.silversandsoutlet.com).

Follow US 98 eastwards and the sand dunes of Emerald Coastwill gradually disappear. What follows is a recreational area with an urban character. Massive high-rise complexes, endless shopping malls, broad highways, giant parking lots with golf courses and other sports complexes in between. The conglomerate with its sugar-white beach is called Sandestin or Santa Rosa Beach; today it takes up most of the spit of land between the Gulf and Choctawhatchee Bay.

✳
Santa Rosa Beach, Sandestin

East of Sandestin about 50mi/80km of more natural beaches where the leisure industry is less obvious. This section is called South Walton Beaches. Here, at Grayton Beach, Seaside and the new towns of WaterColor and Rosemary Beach, which were planned for tourists, lazy holidays for every taste can be had here.

South Walton Beaches

About 5mi/8km south-east of Santa Rosa Beach (via US 98) lies Grayton Beach, which is known as **one of the most beautiful beaches in the entire USA**. As early as 1880 the first wealthy retired persons from New England settled here. There was already a holiday

✳ ✳
Grayton Beach

hotel here at the end of the 19th century. The first of the wooden cottages that are typical of the coast between ▶Pensacola and ▶Apalachicola were built in the 1920s.

Grayton Beach State Recreational Area ▶

At the western edge of town there is a recreational area with mostly natural beaches and dunes. Native vegetation can be found here, too, including low-growing, long-needled cedars, palmetto brush and magnolias. In the early summer sea turtles deposit their eggs in the sand here. There is a camp ground, a bathing beach with water sports facilities and a nature trail.

✶ ✶
Seaside

A few miles to the east the artificially planned holiday resort of Seaside is separated from the other resorts only by a narrow strip of green, and is also located on a wonderful beach. It was planned and built in the 1980s with the aim of making an exceptional holiday resort.

Around an almost Baroque main square with pavilions, shops, restaurants and business services, holiday accommodation ranging from luxurious to simply rustic is grouped on lots of various sizes. Renowned architects from across the country have proven here that it is possible to build a modern beach resort without high-rises and highways that cut everything up. Pastel-coloured, Victorian-style wooden houses with towers, bay windows and other decorations predominate.

The wonderful beach at Seaside was only developed for tourism a few years ago.

Further to the east lies the holiday resort Seagrove, which is still under construction; it is similar to but at the same time more modern than Seaside. The demand for its plots of land and cosy little cottages is so great that more land is being added to the development.

About 3mi/5km north of Seagrove Beach there is another opportunity to experience the atmosphere of the Deep South; on the eastern tip of Choctawhatchee Bay the wood industrialist Wesley built a baronial plantation-style residence in the middle of a park where azaleas and magnolias bloom in spring. The manor house still has its valuable furnishings (hours: Thu–Mon 10am–3pm; park daily 8am–6pm).

About 26mi/42km north of Grayton Beach lies the town of DeFuniak Springs (population 6,000) with its listed Victorian buildings by a romantic spring-fed lake set in the charming hilly landscape of the Florida Panhandle. It was founded in 1881 when surveyors had to find a route for the Louisville & Nashville Railroad. They named the settlement after their boss. The public library of 1887 as well as Hotel DeFuniak from 1920 are especially nicely restored buildings.

A few miles to the east is the Ponce de León Springs State Recreation Area. A karst spring is the focal point of this park; it bubbles out of the horizontally layered limestone and forms a beautiful pond. The famous conquistador is supposed to have stopped here while searching for the fountain of youth. Swimming, fishing and exciting hikes through landscape full of wild game are possible here.

✱ Gainesville

Region: North Central
Population: 121,000 (city)
220,000 (metropolitan area)

Elevation: 52m/165ft above sea level
Area code: 352

About 40,000 students give Gainesville the zest that makes it attractive to visitors. Apart from a youthful appearance and pleasant nightlife the university city in north central Florida also has a sense of civic duty: its programmes for fitness at the workplace make it number one nationwide in the battle against obesity.

More than half of the businesses in the Gainesville area take part in the fitness campaign that began in 2003 – enough reason for the city fathers to call it the »most liveable city in Florida«. The Seminoles liked it here too: when Gainesville was founded in 1854, they fought bitterly against being relocated. In spite of the Third Seminole War

▶ **VISITING GAINESVILLE**

INFORMATION
Gainesville/Alachua County CVB
30 E. University Avenue
Gainesville, FL
Tel. (352) 374-5260
www.visitgainesville.net

SHOPPING
Butler Plaza
Miracle Mile/Archer Road
Largest shopping mall in the area.

Angel Gardens
10100 NW 13th Street
Browse for antiques and all sorts of
kitsch in an old farm house.

WHERE TO EAT
▶ **Moderate**
Paramount Grill
12 SW 1st Avenue
Tel. (352) 378-3398
Pretty restaurant, polyglot kitchen.

Steve's Cafe Americain
12 W. University Avenue
Tel. (352) 377-9337

New American cuisine, sophisticated
innovations. Nice bar.

WHERE TO STAY
▶ **Mid-range**

Baedeker recommendation

**Magnolia Plantation
Inn & Cottages**
309 SE 7th Street
Tel. (352) 375-6653
www.magnoliabnb.com
5 rooms, 7 cottages
Lovingly restored historic house in the
Second Empire style.

▶ **Budget**
Sweetwater Branch Inn
625 E. University Avenue
Tel. (352) 373-6760
Fax (352) 371-3771
www.sweetwaterinn.com
15 rooms
Victorian era style inn.

Gainesville started to grow. Kingsbury Academy moved from Ocala
to Gainesville in the 1860s and its incorporation into Florida Agricultural College later spurred the city's growth. In 1905 the college
became the University of Florida. Science and the cultivation of citrus fruits went hand in hand from then on and remain important
pillars of the university.

What to See in Gainesville

✳
Northeast
Historic
District

In the protected Northeast Historic District there are fine examples
of architecture from 1880 to 1930. From the courthouse that was
built in 1886 on the corner of E. University Ave. and N.E. 1st Street
only the bell tower has remained. The classical-style Thomas Center
(306 N.E. 6th Ave.) is used for exhibitions and events now. The earlier post office is now a theatre.

An extremely instructive nature exhibition is located on the university campus in the western part of town. Biotopes typical of Florida (including savannah, mangroves, hammocks) are constructed in dioramas with explanations. The anthropological and ethnographic department of the museum with excellent reconstructions of a Maya temple and Indian village are also worthwhile (SW 34th St./Hull Rd.; hours: Mon–Sat 10am–5pm, Sun 1pm–5pm).

✳ **Florida Museum of Natural History**

The university campus also has one of the largest art collections of the »Sunshine State«. The exhibits emphasize artefacts from pre-Columbian Mesoamerica, West African and Oceanian art, East Asian ceramics and also contemporary American art (SW 34th St./Hull Rd.; hours: Tue–Sat 11am–5pm, Sun 1pm–5pm).

✳ **Samuel P. Harn Museum of Art**

Around Gainesville

It is located about 4mi/6km north-west of Gainesville. The sinkhole is 37m/121ft deep and 152m/500ft wide; it was formed about 10,000 years ago when the ceiling of a river cave collapsed. Stairs lead down into the sinkhole with its luxuriant vegetation. The deeper you go, the cooler it gets. As a result plants grow in the sinkhole that are actually at home in the Appalachian Mountains further to the north. The visitor centre has detailed information (hours: Wed–Sun 9am to 5pm).

✳ **Devil's Millhopper State Geological Site**

Devil's Millhopper is eerie.

A side trip leads from Gainesville to the south (US 441). Paynes Prairie State Preserve begins at the city limits, a swampy grassland with several hardwood tree islands. This is what central Florida looked like 150 years ago: grassland spotted with hammocks and swamps and populated by many animal species. Bison, wild horses, wildcats, alligators and more than 270 varieties of birds can be seen here. There are hiking trails through the park and several observation towers (access: via I-75, exit 374; hours: daily 8am–sunset).

Micanopy

With its Victorian houses, this town 11mi/18km south of Gainesville is the perfect example of a rural town in the Deep South. It was named after a Seminole chief and started in 1821 with a post office. Not much has changed since then: Micanopy, dozing under old oak trees, pleases the eye with classic Southern charm – and the wallet with many interesting antique shops.

Marjorie Kinnan Rawlings State Historic Site

About 15mi/24km south-east of Gainesville lies the property where the American writer and Pulitzer prize winner **Marjorie Kinnan Rawlings** (1896–1953) lived from 1928 to 1941. In a typical Cracker-style wooden house under orange and pecan trees she wrote works like *The Yearling* or *Cross Creek*, in which she depicted life in the Florida of the 1930s. Ever since *Cross Creek* was filmed (1983) Rawlings' estate has taken on the character of a shrine for her fans (tours: Thu–Mon 10–11.30am and 1–4pm).

✳ Jacksonville

H 2

Region: North-east	**Elevation:** 0 – 7m/23ft above sea level
Population: 835,000 (metropolitan area: 1.1 million)	**Area code:** 904

Heavy industry, paper mills, large banks, harbours, military establishments: this major city in the extreme north-east of Florida has never been a tourist magnet. But those who look closer will see that something is going on. Galleries and hotels are opening, millions are being invested in museums. Sports has also recognized this in its own way: in 2005 the Super Bowl of the National Football League came to Jacksonville.

In the bend of a river ...

Locals call their city simply »Jax«, but even this nickname doesn't sound hospitable. Anyone who visited the city on the bend of the St John's River in the past, probably drove through quickly on his way to the beaches further east and ignored the anonymous forest of office buildings. The Super Bowl, the largest sporting event of the year in America, helped Jacksonville to lose this image a little in 2005.

● VISITING JACKSONVILLE

INFORMATION

Jacksonville & The Beaches Convention & Visitors Bureau
550 S. Water Street, Suite 1000
Jacksonville, FL 32202
Tel. (904) 798-9111
Fax (904) 798-9103
www.jaxcvb.com

SHOPPING

Riverside is known for its urban wear shops. Cool shoes are available especially on Riverside Street between Lomax and Post Street. Avondale is more chic. Prada, Lily Pulitzer and Fantini are in boutiques on St John's Street between Talbot and Pinegrove Street. San Marco Square is a good place to look for antiques, books and CDs.

NIGHT LIFE

Visitors tend to concentrate on the bend in the river downtown: Jacksonville Landing and Southbank Riverwalk, entertainment areas on opposite sides of the river, are the liveliest places in town evenings and on weekends.

WHERE TO EAT
► Moderate
① ***Mossfire Grill***
Riverside
1537 Margaret Street
Tel. (904) 355-4434
Spicy Southern food served in an amber-coloured designer ambience.

② ***Biscotti's***
Avondale
3556 St John's Avenue
Tel. (904) 387-2060
Lively restaurant with light bistro-style food.

► Budget
③ ***Sticky Fingers***
Atlantic Beach
8129 Point Meadows Boulevard
Tel. (904) 493-RIBS
Juicy steaks and ribs – with blues coming from the speakers and pictures of jazz musicians on the walls.

WHERE TO STAY
► Mid-range
① ***Inn at Oak Street***
Riverside, 2114 Oak Street
Tel. (904) 379-5525
www.innatoakstreet.com
6 rooms
Comfortable inn in historic Riverside. Some rooms have a whirlpool. A masseur is also available.

② ***Riverdale Inn***
1521 Riverside Avenue
Tel. (904) 354-5080
www.riverdaleinn.com
8 rooms
Beautiful Queen Anne-style residence. Restaurant »The Row« on the second floor.

► Budget
③ ***Omni***
Downtown
245 Water Street
Tel. (904) 355-6664
Fax (904) 791-4812
354 rooms
Modern city hotel, only a stone's throw from the popular Riverwalk, with a heated pool on the roof.

Highlights Jacksonville

South Bank River Walk
Stroll where wharfs and industrial complexes used to be.
► page 201

Museum of Science History
Spectacular insights into science and technology for young and old at the MOSH.
► page 202

Cummer Museum of Art & Gardens
Who would have thought it! Works by Albrecht Dürer, Lucas Cranach the Elder and Peter Paul Rubens in Florida.
► page 203

Jacksonville beaches
Well-known seaside resorts with wide beaches – some exclusive, some informal.
► page 205

North Bank

Downtown

The city centre has been renovated at a cost of millions. New skyscrapers glisten in the sunshine, including the Modis Building (see photo) and the post-modern style 40-storey Bank of America Tower, designed by Helmut Jahn, and are centred on the North Bank. Several bridges span the St John's River and connect parts of the city on the northern and southern banks.

The city's trademark is the Main Street Bridge, which can be raised to let large ships pass.

✳ Jacksonville Landing

Coffee shops, restaurants, street musicians, jugglers, body painters: this complex of glass, steel and sun umbrellas on the riverbank includes several dozen shops and various restaurants with a view of the river. Along the front of Jacksonville Landing the Northbank Riverwalk is a beautiful promenade from Berkman Plaza to Times Union Center for the Performing Arts.

✳ Florida Theater Performing Arts Center

East of Jacksonville Landing the Florida Theater Performing Arts Center glows after a refurbishing. It was built as a cinema in 1926–27 and recently renovated thoroughly. Painted terracotta figures and ornamental bands adorn the façade. The elaborately decorated theatre with massive beams now holds almost 2,000 guests for cultural events of all kinds.

Prime Osborn Convention Center

West of Jacksonville Landing is the convention centre, built in 1986. This modern structure incorporates Union Station, which was built in 1919 to plans by the New York architect K. M. Murchison. The massive former railway station with its 23m/75ft-high dome serves as the luxurious lobby of the convention centre today.

Museum of Contemporary Art

Contemporary art is exhibited here in an eminently innovative style. International and American artists are represented in the collection,

Jacksonville Map

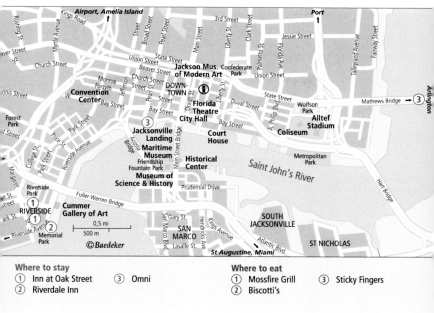

Where to stay
1. Inn at Oak Street
2. Riverdale Inn
3. Omni

Where to eat
1. Mossfire Grill
2. Biscotti's
3. Sticky Fingers

which has works by Helen Frankenthaler and Robert Rauschenberg (333 N. Laura St.; hours: Tue to Sun 10am–4pm, Wed to 9pm).

When white and black people still lived in different parts of town, LaVilla was the black neighbourhood of Jacksonville. Its cultural centre was the Ritz Theatre, where many famous musicians performed. The Ritz only survived the 1960s passion to replace old with new after a restoration and facelift. The LaVilla Museum relates an interesting part of Afro-American history (829 N. Davis St.; hours: Tue–Fr 10am–6pm, Sat 10am–2pm, Sun 2–5pm).

LaVilla

South Bank

The south bank of the St John's River has been the site of the South Bank Riverwalk since 1985. This attractive area with top-class hotels, restaurants and three museums is built on a former wharf and industrial property. The promenade offers a great view of the skyline on the North Bank. The focal point of Friendship Park is the fountain, which is illuminated at night and whose water plumes spray up to 36m/118ft high. With a diameter of 200ft/60m is the largest self-contained fountain in the United States.

✷ ✷
South Bank Riverwalk

Main Street Bridge is Jacksonville's trademark.

Jacksonville Historical Center ✱

The museum at the southern end of Main Street Bridge has displays on important periods in the city's history. The exhibits emphasis the Indian settlements in the city limits as well as the time when Jacksonville was a centre of the film industry (hours: Mon–Sat 10.30am–3.30pm, Sun 1–5pm).

Jacksonville Maritime Museum

On the other side of the bridgehead there is another little museum worth visiting, with its exhibits on the history of seafaring in northeast Florida. There are interesting ship models on display here (1015 Museum Circle, Unit 2; hours: daily noon–5pm).

Museum of Science & History (MOSH) ✱ ✱

This museum specializes in popular science and gives insight into the world of nature, history, science and technology. Next to the Science Theater and the planetarium the main attractions are the exhibits »The Living World« and »Atlantic Tails«, which are about natural history and several endangered species (including dolphins, manatees). The interesting presentation »Currents of Time« is devoted to the 12,000-year history of the settlement of northern Florida (1025 Museum Circle; hours: Mon–Fri 10am–5pm, Sat 10am–6pm, Sun 1–6pm).

San Marco ✱

This neighbourhood is located south of the Southbank Riverwalk and has kept its own charm. Many of the villas, which were built in the early 20th century – in part in art deco style and often right on the waterfront – have been skilfully renovated. The focal point is San Marco Square, where lifestyle and fashion fans will find what they want, as will fans of music clubs, bars and fine dining.

Riverside and Avondale

Riverside was founded in the 1850s and rebuilt after a fire in 1901. It is located next to Memorial Park and is probably the architecturally most diverse neighbourhood in Florida. Especially around Margaret Street there are wonderful examples of the Mediterranean Revival as well as colonial and neo-classical styles. Riverside Baptist Church, with its elements of Byzantine and Romanesque style, is especially impressive. It was built on Park Street in 1925 to plans by the renowned architect Addison Mizner from Palm Beach.

✶
Riverside

The cultural centre of the neighbourhood is this pretty art museum, which is located in a beautiful park on the western end of Fuller Warren Bridge (I-95). It is housed in the late 19th-century baronial villa of a lumber magnate. The collection is based on the art collection of the Cummer family. The spectrum covers everything from pre-Columbian art to Egyptian, Greek and Roman antiquity and European art of the 15th to 19th centuries. The showpieces are works by **Albrecht Dürer, Lucas Cranach the Elder and Peter Paul Rubens** (*Lamentation of Christ*).

✶✶
Cummer Museum of Art & Gardens

> ! **Baedeker TIP**
>
> **Relax after the museum**
> Not far to the west of the museum, also on Riverside Avenue, is the pretty Bohemian quarter named »Five Points« with several nice cafés and bistros

The collection of Meissen porcelain and the East Asian art objects are also worth seeing (829 Riverside Ave.; hours: Tue and Thu 10am–9pm, Wed, Fri, Sat 10am–5pm, Sun noon–5pm).

Riverside Avenue turns into St Johns Avenue further south and after 2.5mi/4km it reaches Avondale. It was designed in 1920 by Telfair Stockton as a neighbourhood for wealthy citizens and is still dominated by a small elite. The upper-class neighbourhood still has the atmosphere of the good old days at exhibition openings etc. The local art scene revolves around the exquisite R. Roberts Gallery (3606 St Johns Ave.; hours: Mon–Sa 10am–9pm). The designers and artists whose works have been exhibited here include Lily Pulitzer, Michel Delacroix, Prada and Fantini.

✶
Avondale

⊕

Other Attractions in Jacksonville

The campus of the university, which was founded in 1934, is spread out on the eastern banks of the St John's River. Important facilities include a centre for marine research, the Historic Society Library and the Alexander Brest Museum, which exhibits pre-Columbian art, ceramics, porcelain and glass from Europe and ivory carvings from the Far East. The house of the composer Frederick Delius (1862–1934) is also open to the public.

Jacksonville University

Jacksonville Zoo ✳ Jacksonville Zoo lies in the northern part of the city along the Trout River. Zebras, gazelles and lions roam in the »African Velt«; in the »Great Apes of the World« area gorillas, chimpanzees and other primates show off. The animal world of Central and South America can be seen in »Land of the Maya«; in the »Florida Wetlands« there are alligators and manatees (370 Zoo Parkway; hours: daily 9am–5pm).

Anheuser-Busch Brewery The production site of the largest brewery in America is also in the north of Jacksonville. They produce 8 million hectolitres (211 million gallons) annually. The entire southern USA is served from here (111 Busch Dr.; tours with tasting: Mon–Sat 9am–4pm).

Fort Caroline ✳ About 10mi/16km east of the city centre a replica of a wooden fort in the Timucuan Ecological & Historic Preserve on the banks of St John's River commemorates the French Huguenots, who built a base here in 1564 with the permission of the local Timucuan Indians (hours: daily 9am–5pm).

Mayport North-east of downtown Jacksonville is Mayport, an old fishing village. The harbour is a starting point for deep-sea fishing tours. Mayport Naval Station is one of the largest naval bases on the US eastern seaboard. The aircraft carriers and squadrons of the 6th fleet are stationed here (occasional tours, information: tel. 904/270-5226).

Fort George Island, Kingsley Plantation A ferry runs from Mayport to Fort George Island, one of the swampy islands in the mouth of the St John's River. In the 16th century the Spanish built a mission here. In 1730, when British troops entered Florida, the island got its present name. The governor of Georgia had the fort built. Toward the end of Spanish colonial rule

Popular among locals and tourists: the long beach at Jacksonville

three Americans started plantations here to raise cotton, sugar cane and oranges, including Kingsley Plantation. It is one of the few surviving examples of this type of estate in the south-east USA. The plantation was named after the planter Zephaniah Kingsley and consists of a main house, the cook house and the ruins of 25 of the slaves' quarters. Kingsley, who ran the plantation from 1819 to 1839, was married to a freed slave and business woman. He went with her to Haiti when the USA took over Florida and the slave laws became more restrictive (hours: Thu–Mon 9.30am–3pm).

Beaches around Jacksonville

South of the mouth of the St John's River there is a line of well-known seaside resorts stretching for 30km/18mi. They have names like Jacksonville Beach, Atlantic Beach and Neptune Beach. Jacksonville Beach, only a 20-minute drive east of downtown Jacksonville, offers all of the benefits of a tourist resort. The Seawalk and Seawalk Plaza, among other places, with their pretty shops and restaurants, grew out of a renovation programme. The 360m/1,180ft Jacksonville Pier, which is illuminated at night, is a popular meeting place for fishers and strollers.

★★ Jacksonville Beaches

> **? DID YOU KNOW ...?**
>
> ■ At South Ponte Vedra Beach, which ends just north of St Augustine, the Spanish conquistador Ponce de León landed and named the newly discovered land »La Florida«. He believed all of his life that he had discovered a large island.

Directly adjacent to the south is Ponte Vedra Beach, where exclusive villas and beach houses stand today. Golfers, too, can fulfil their wishes here: the Saw Grass Country Club Course is one of the best in Florida.

★★ Key West

H 8

Region: South-east
Population: 25,000

Elevation: 0 – 7m/23ft above sea level
Area code: 305

In Key West the Overseas Highway ends between flourishing bougainvillea and pastel-coloured Bahamas architecture. »Mainstream America« ends here too. What remains is a sensual still-life composed of shady verandas, free-roaming chickens and cats, dogs dozing under cars and streets named Caroline or Angela. Even the party zone Duval Street seems more Caribbean than US American.

The first Spaniards to sail by this bone-hard and bone-dry coral island named it Cayo Huesco (Bone Island). When the Americans took over a couple of centuries later, they misunderstood Cayo

Highlights Key West

Old Town
Brightly painted wooden houses dating from the 19th century.
▶ page 206

Sunset on Mallory Square
Especially beautiful sunsets are still greeted with applause. Acrobats and musicians shorten the wait with lively entertainment.
▶ page 209

Mel Fisher
Maritime Heritage Museum
Bloodthirsty pirate stories brought up from the briny deep.
▶ page 209

Ernest Hemingway Home & Museum
One of the most famous writers of the 20th century lived, wrote, boxed and drank here.
▶ page 212

Huesco as Key West. The southernmost island of the Florida Keys, only 90mi/145km north of Cuba, is the southernmost point of continental USA and also one of its strategically most sensitive places.

From pirates' nest to tourist stronghold
Cayo Huesco used to be a notorious pirates' nest. In 1845 Key West was an important port and the »Conches«, island residents who had come from the Bahamas, lived well from salvaging stranded goods. Around 1870 Key West was Florida's largest and richest city. The stately »Conch« homes today testify to the wealth of the »shipwreckers« and merchant captains. This all changed at the turn of the 20th century. Tourism gradually developed into the most important source of income. Henry Flagler's railway gave this process momentum when it reached Key West in 1912. At that time there used to be a ferry connection to Havana, Cuba. The multi-national background of the residents and the Caribbean lifestyle attracted artists and writers to Key West. In the 1930s and 1940s **Ernest Hemingway**, **Tennessee Williams** and at times **John Dos Passos** lived here.

Today Key West is one of the most visited tourist attractions in the USA and despite this activity it is still popular among artists, writers and people who opt out of established society.

? DID YOU KNOW …?

- Key West is considered to be the most tolerant city east of San Francisco. No one gets excited here when the county commissioner shows up as a drag queen in a bar on Duval Street and sings karaoke, and when other VIPs out themselves as gay or lesbian. »Live and let live« is the unwritten rule.

What to See in Key West

✳ ✳
Old Town
Old Town at the south-western end of the island, with its brightly painted wooden 19th century houses is the main attraction of Key

⏵ VISITING KEY WEST

INFORMATION

Florida Keys & Visitors Bureau
PO Box 1146
Key West, FL 33041
Tel. (305) 296-1552
Tel. 1-800-FLA-KEYS
www.fla-keys.com

ORIENTATION

It's easy to get your bearings here. The cheaper accommodation and fast-food restaurants are along US 1 (Roosevelt Blvd.) on the way into town. The main street, called Duval Street, cuts through the densely built-up Old Town. The better hotels and restaurants are here, most of them in old wooden houses, as well as most of the shops. On Mallory Square at the end of Duval Street people gather every evening to watch the sun go down. Bahama Village, once a hippy neighbourhood on the south side of town, has been up-graded by the appearance of trendy restaurants, but still appears very Caribbean and relaxed. It is best to leave the car in the parking lot, since traffic on Key West is very slow.

CITY TOURS

Pelican Path
This marked path (map and brochure available at the Chamber of Com-

Key West Map

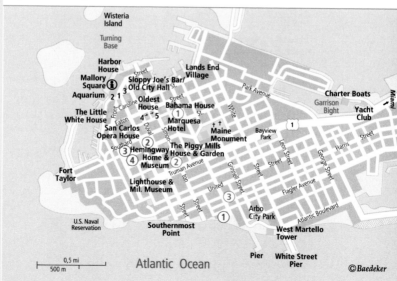

Wisteria Island
Turning Base
Harbor House
Mallory Square
Aquarium
The Little White House
San Carlos Opera House
Fort Taylor
Sloppy Joe's Bar/ Old City Hall
Oldest House
Bahama House
Marquesa Hotel
Hemingway Home & Museum
The Piggy Mills House & Garden
Lighthouse & Mil. Museum
Lands End Village
Maine Monument
Bayview Park
Park Avenue
Charter Boats
Garrison Bight
Yacht Club
Miami
Southernmost Point
Arbo City Park
West Martello Tower
White Street Pier
Pier
U.S. Naval Reservation
Atlantic Ocean
0,5 mi
500 m
©Baedeker

Where to stay
① Ambrosia
② Center Court Historic Inn
③ Key West Youth Hostel

Where to eat
① Louie's Backyard
② Mangoes
③ Blue Heaven
④ Banama Café

1 Mel Fisher Maritime Society Museum
2 Old Post Office/ Coast Guard Building
3 Audubon House
4 St Paul's
5 Old Stone Methodist Church

merce, 402 Wall Street) includes 49 historically interesting buildings.

Old Town Trolley
This old-timer bus also runs past all of the interesting spots (leaves from Mallory Square: daily 9.30–4.30pm).

Conch Tour Train
A »train« on tyres following a route that includes all of the most important sights (departures: daily from 9.30am Mallory Square Depot and 3850 N. Roosevelt Street; duration about 2 hours).

ACTIVITIES

Diving, snorkelling, deep sea fishing and »boating« are popular activities on Key West. Reef and wreck diving is available at Subtropic Dive Center (1605 N. Roosevelt Blvd.; tel. 305/296-9914, www.subtropic.com). Fishers can either rent a boat or join a group. Organizers of fishing tours have their stands around Mallory Square. Some organizers combine snorkelling with »Sunset Cruises«: snorkel during the day, enjoy sunset on a boat. Information at Sebago Watersports (201 William Street, tel. 305/292-4768, www.key westsebago.com).

BEACHES

Despite Key West's liberal lifestyle, bathing in the nude or topless is prohibited here, too. There are some pretty little sand and pebble beaches for sunbathing and playing in the surf. The largest one, Smathers Beach (S. Roosevelt Blvd.) is where the young people hang out. Fort Zachary Beach (via Truman Annex) offers shade under palm trees. Higgs Beach is the gay meeting place.

SHOPPING

Most of the shops are in Duval Street. Really nice shops and chic boutiques can be found above all in Simonton Street and in Caroline Street.

Fast Buck Freddie's
500 Duval Street
This shop is famous for its unusual swimwear.

Kermit's Key West Key Lime Shoppe
200 Elizabeth Street
Great Key Lime Pies are available here.

Key West Havana Cigar Company
1117 Duval Street
Passionate smokers can get exquisite hand-rolled cigars here.

WHERE TO EAT
▶ Expensive
① *Louie's Backyard*
700 Waddell Avenue
Tel. (305) 294-1061
»Shellfish paella« with a special touch, wild boar and lamb, among the hibiscus and bougainvillea – a feast for the senses!

▶ Moderate
② *Mangoes*
700 Duval Street
Tel. (305) 292-4606
See and be seen on the terrace while enjoying fresh fish, seafood and shrimp cocktails with lemon glaze.

③ *Blue Heaven*
729 Thomas Street
Tel. (305) 296-8666
Trendy venue for locals and visitors: Jamaica chicken, curry dishes and homemade granola.

▶ Budget
④ *Banana Café*
1211 Duval Street

Tel. (305) 294-7227
Bistro with tropical feeling and French cuisine. Excellent »crêpes gorgonzola«.

WHERE TO STAY

► Mid-range

① *Ambrosia House*
622 Fleming Street
Tel. (305) 296-9838
Fax (305) 296-2425
www.ambrosiakeywest.com
22 rooms, 6 suites, 1 cottage
Nicely hidden near Duval Street. The rooms are decorated with art by local artists and designers.

② *Center Court*
Historic Inn & Cottages
915 Center Street

Tel. (305) 296-9292
Fax (305) 294-4104
www.centercourtkw.com
4 rooms, 9 suites, 10 cottages
Amiable resort with pools, grounds with lush tropical vegetation.

► Budget

③ *Key West Youth Hostel*
718 South Street
Tel. (305) 296-5719
Fax (305) 296-0672
www.keywesthostel.com
96 beds, 14 private rooms
Pink youth hostel in the historic town centre. Snorkelling tours, bicycle rental.

West. Duval Street and its side streets are home to boutiques, art galleries, sidewalk cafés, restaurants and bars. Every evening **sundown is celebrated at Mallory Square** in a colourful carnival atmosphere.

This aquarium has pools for sea turtles, barracudas, mantas and sharks (1 Whitehead St.; hours: daily 10am–6pm; feedings: 11am, 1pm, 3pm, 4.30pm).

Key West Aquarium
ⓣ

Anyone who ever wanted to know everything about pirates will get expert information here: the new museum relates the wild stories of Cap'n Blackbeard and associates with many visual aids (524 Front St.; hours: daily 9am–7pm).

Pat Croce's Pirate Soul Museum

ⓣ

Spanish gold jewellery, silver coins and other treasures, which the treasure hunter Mel Fisher (d. 1998) salvaged out of the Spanish silver ships *Atocha* and *Santa Margarita* are exhibited here. The two ships sank in 1622 in a hurricane off the Marquesas. The museum also has lots of interesting information on underwater archaeology (200 Greene St./Front St.; hours: daily 9.30am–5pm).

★ ★
Mel Fisher Maritime Heritage Museum

ⓣ

In 1832 the painter of plants and animals J.J. Audubon (1785–1851) lived in this typical Conch house. Beautiful original etchings and valuable furnishings from the 18th and 19th centuries are displayed here. Sub-tropical and tropical plants bloom in the lush garden (205 Whitehead/Greene Street; hours: daily 9.30am–5pm).

★
Audubon House & Gardens

ⓣ

THE BEST PLACE ON EARTH

»This is the best piece of earth that I ever happened on. Flowers, tamarisk trees, guava trees, coconut palms ...« wrote the author and globetrotter Ernest Hemingway (1899–1961) from Key West to a friend in 1928. The restless writer put down stakes here for six years.

Key West and especially his villa on Whitehead Street were not only the home base that Hemingway returned to from his travels. In Key West's mild winters he wrote his most famous novels and short stories, for example *A Farewell to Arms, Snows of Kilimanjaro, Green Hills of Africa* and *For Whom the Bell Tolls.*

Journalism and Women

Hemingway grew up with his siblings in Oak Park, an upper-class suburb of Chicago. After graduating from high school he became a **reporter** for the *Kansas City Star.* In 1918 he volunteered for duty on the Italian front, where he was wounded seriously. After the war was over Hemingway returned to the USA and worked as a newspaper editor. In 1921 he married for the first time and moved to Paris

with his wife, Elizabeth Hadley Richardson. He wrote the first significant short stories there. They already show Hemingway's famous style, which was influenced by journalism in its use of short, terse sentences. The marriage to Hadley failed when Hemingway began an affair with **Pauline Pfeiffer**, a friend of his wife. After the divorce Ernest Hemingway married Pauline in May 1927 in Paris.

New Home on Key West

When the writer John Dos Passos enthused about the beauty of Florida, Hemingway and Pauline embarked for Havana in March 1928 and then crossed over to Key West. Most residents of Key West had something to do with the sea, and Hemingway too became an enthusiastic fisherman. Already in April he wrote to his editor

Hemingway's house in Key West is a tourist attraction today.

Max Perkins that he caught »the largest tarpon that they had seen here this season: 63lbs (29kg)«.

907, Whitehead Street

Hemingway and Pauline rented for the first three years, before they bought the **Spanish colonial villa** at 907 Whitehead Street in spring 1931 with the help of Pauline's Uncle Gus. Pauline had the neglected garden replanted and built the first swimming pool on Key West. The pretty house with its wrought-iron balcony all around is Hemingway's poet's garret and his home for the time with Pauline. Today a large colony of cats lives on the grounds, whose ancestors were brought there by Hemingway.

More Travels. More Marriages

Hemingway prospered; he enjoyed his wealth and his fame. In the winter of 1934 he returned with Pauline from his first safari in Africa. He hunted lions, cape buffalo and other large animals at Kilimanjaro. He later drew on his experiences there for his writing. In early 1937 Hemingway went to Spain as a war correspondent to cover the civil war. There he met the journalist Martha Gellhorn, whom he had met in Key West when she interviewed him. She became his third wife in 1940.

With the income from his novel *For Whom the Bell Tolls* he bought a finca on Cuba, in order to spend a few summers there. In the early 1940s the two reported from East Asia on World War II. He described the liberation of Paris and witnessed the battles for the Siegfried Line. His third marriage failed in late 1945.

In March 1946 he married Mary Welsh in the Cuban capital Havana. The finca La Vigia was to be his home for twenty years. He wrote one of his best works there, *The Old Man and the Sea* for which he was **awarded the Nobel Prize for literature** in 1954. Hemingway, who had survived war injuries, hunting accidents and two airplane crashes, had no more strength to write. He suffered from severe depression and spoke more and more often about killing himself. On 2 July 1961 Hemingway committed suicide.

Sloppy Joe's Bar, Captain Tony's Saloon

✳ Captain Tony's Saloon on Greene Street was called Sloppy Joe's Bar from 1933 to 1937. Here Ernest Hemingway liked to end the day on the barstool reserved for him. The ceiling and walls of the bar are plastered with business cards that guests left behind. The new Sloppy Joe's Bar is right around the corner in busy Duval Street. Hemingway pictures and memorabilia decorate the walls (201 Duval St.; hours: 9am–4am; daily live music).

Fort Zachary Taylor State Historic Site

The fort at the south-west end of the island was built from 1845 to 1866 as part of the US American naval defence system. It played an important role during the Civil War. The Union had a base here and used it to pursue blockade runners. During the Spanish-American War the fort was renovated. It has been a naval base since 1947. Cannons and weapons from the Civil War can be seen in the old fort (hours: daily 8am until sunset; guided tours: daily 2pm).

Ernest Hemingway Home & Museum

✳ ✳ Ernest Hemingway's house is one of the most-visited attractions on Key West. The house was built in Spanish colonial style in 1851; Hemingway bought the well-equipped house with a balcony around it in 1931.

The Nobel laureate for literature wrote some of his works here until 1961. The lush garden is the home of numerous descendants of Hemingway's cats (938 Whitehead St.; tours: daily 9am–5pm).

Key West's Shipwreck Historeum

The wreckers of Key West did their best business with the *Isaac Allerton*: the salvage that washed ashore brought in US$ 50,000. This unique museum documents the exciting, oft morbid history of the salvagers (1 Whitehead; hours: daily 9.45am–4.45pm).

Southernmost Point

✳ At the end of Whitehead Street a large colourful cement buoy (photo see p.147) marks the southernmost point of continental USA. From here Cuba is only 144km/86mi away, closer than Miami! The nearby lighthouse was built in 1847 and is now open as a museum.

Key West Lighthouse Museum

The wonderful panoramic view rewards the effort of climbing 90 steps through the narrow stairwell. It was inaugurated in 1848 and marked the beginning of the end of the lucrative wrecking trade. The little museum in the lighthouse keeper's house depicts this inglorious chapter of local history (938 Whitehead St.; hours: daily 9.30am to 4.30pm).

Bahama Village

Under siege by tourists, the neighbourhood between Thomas Street, Angela Street and Amelia Street clings to the old spirit of Key West. Most of the chickens live here; the simple wooden houses used to be the homes of cigar makers. Today the residents, mostly descendants of settlers from the Bahamas and Afro-Cubans, still go to church dressed in their Sunday best and love to reminisce about the cockfights that are now forbidden.

The cemetery in the north of Old Town (Margaret St. and Angela St.) is very photogenic and known for the humorous inscriptions on the gravestones: »Devoted Fan of Singer Julio Iglesias« on one; »I told you I was sick« on another. Monuments for Cuban patriots and sailors who died in the explosion of the »USS Maine« in 1898 in Havana seem almost out of place despite their appropriate earnestness. Because of the hard coral ground and the frequent floods, the dead are »buried« above ground: the caskets are mostly stacked on top of each other and look like a necropolis.

Key West Cemetery

Excursions from Key West

Excursions from Key West by boat or pontoon airplane to the Marquesas Keys to the west are worthwhile since they form the core of the Key West National Wildlife Refuge. Many kinds of birds can be observed in the nature preserve, including terns, egrets, cormorants and pelicans. Snorkellers and divers will see an enchanting underwater world with diverse coral formations and many colourful fish.

✱ Marquesas Keys, Dry Tortugas

About 110km/65mi west of Key West lies the Dry Tortugas, a group of tiny coral islands. Ponce de León discovered them in 1513 and named them after the sea turtles

> ! **Baedeker TIP**
>
> **Sunset Cruise**
> A special way to enjoy the sunset is on board a sailboat – with a well-filled coolbox and a nice crew. Organizers can be found in Duval Street in Key West.

that brood here. On Garden Key people interested in history can visit Fort Jefferson, which was built in 1846 to protect American ships. The brick fort was used between 1863 and 1874 as a prison for prominent political prisoners of the Civil War.

A rewarding trip: to the coral islands off Key West

✱ Kissimmee · St Cloud

H 4

Region: Central
Population: 55,000

Elevation: 19m/65ft above sea level
Area code: 407

The two towns in the heart of Florida, Kissimmee and St Cloud, are so to speak the gateway to entertainment. From here it is not far to the mega-amusement parks in ▸Orlando and ▸Walt Disney World.

From a farming village to an amusement hotspot

The picturesque, rural Florida with its lakes and cypress swamps, narrow country roads lined by spreading live oaks with garlands of Spanish moss swaying in the breeze can only be found off the beaten track. In 1878 the first white settlers came to this region. In 1891 the new settlement Kissimmee became the county seat, with a population of only 815. Favourable conditions for fruit and vegetable farming as well as two cigar factories soon attracted more settlers. Its modern development began in 1963 when Walt Disney thought that he had found the ideal conditions here for a perfect, clean amusement park. The rapid development of the Disney world of amusement encouraged other businessmen to set up their own projects in the wake of the Micky Mouse. Motels, shops and other attractions soon followed. Today the Kissimmee/St Cloud region is an urban area that revolves around amusement.

What to See in and around Kissimmee

Downtown

The old Main Street and Broadway Boulevard have been nicely renovated. Many little shops dot the scenery. The buildings that are particularly worth seeing are the Osceola Courthouse of 1889, Makinson's Hardware Store of 1895 and the Arcade Theater of 1925. In Lake Front Park the »Monument of States« is impressive.

Irlo Bronson Memorial Highway

The »main street of amusement«, Irlo Bronson Memorial Highway (US 192) runs through Kissimmee from west to east. Along this expansive axis attractions, hotels, motels, restaurants, malls, factory outlets etc. line up. There is a round-the-clock county fair atmosphere.

Old Town

Old Town was built in the style of the late 19th century; along with boutiques and restaurants there are also nice rides, like a Ferris wheel from 1928 and a merry-go-round from 1909. In Little Darlin's Rock'n Roll Palace 1950s nostalgia freaks will feel at home every night (US 192, about 1mi/1.5km before exit 25A on I-4; hours: daily 10am–11pm).

Splendid China

South-west of Walt Disney World the theme park »Splendid China« was opened a few years ago. Important natural and architectural monuments of old China were replicated here on a small scale, including the Great Wall, the »Forbidden City« and the Potala Palace in Tibet. Even the famous Leshan Buddha is here. There is also lots of information on Chinese culture (3mi/5km west on I-4, exit 25B, 3000 Splendid China Blvd.; hours: daily 9.30am–7pm).

The entrance to Gatorland Zoo between Kissimmee and ► Orlando is marked by the giant open mouth of an alligator. Along with various animals from all over the world there are about 5,000 alligators and crocodiles here. These animals are raised domestically. Various kinds of snakes can also be seen in the open enclosures. A »Gator Wrestlin' Show« and a »Gator Jumparoo Show« are held every day (14501 S. Orange Blossom Trail, intersection of Central Florida Greenway/FL 417/US 17/92/441; hours: daily 9am–5pm).

Gatorland

▶ VISITING KISSIMMEE · ST CLOUD

INFORMATION

Kissimmee CVB
1925 E. Irlo Bronson Memorial Highway
Kissimmee, FL 34744
Tel. (407) 944-2400
www.floridakiss.com

EVENT

Silver Spurs Rodeo
Every year in mid-February the largest rodeo east of the Mississippi is held in Kissimmee.

WHERE TO STAY

► Luxury
Gaylord Palms Resort
6000 W. Osceola Parkway

Tel. (407) 586-2000
www.gaylordhotels.com/gaylord-palms/
1,406 rooms, 115 suites, several restaurants and lounges, spa, convention centre, shopping arcade.
Nothing is lacking in this resort; there's something for every taste. Everything has a Florida theme.

► Budget/Mid-range
Days Inn Kissimmee
2095 E. Irlo Bronson Highway
Tel. (407) 846-7136
www.daysinn.com
120 rooms
Nice accommodation with spacious rooms and a swimming pool. Friendly service.

► Budget
Gator Motel
4576 W. Irlo Bronson Memorial Highway
Tel. (407) 396-0127
www.gatormotel.net
38 rooms
Cheap and clean accommodation in the middle of a well-tended garden.

✳ Lake City

G 2

Region: North Central
Population: 11,000

Elevation: 60m/200ft above sea level
Area code: 386

For many visitors to Florida from other US states, Lake City is the entrance to the »Sunshine State«, since it is located at the junction of interstate highways I-10 and I-75. But Lake City is also the starting point for nature lovers, hikers and canoeists who enjoy the nearby Osceola National Forest.

The city developed out of a large Indian village. A chief from this village played an important role in the Dade Massacre (1835), which started the Second Seminole War. The first white people settled here after the hostilities ended. Forestry and cattle raising supported the community at first. The discovery of phosphate deposits at the Suwannee River helped the economy to grow.

What to See in and around Lake City

Historic Districts

The city still has several well-preserved buildings from the 19th and early 20th centuries. Well-restored houses can be found along Main Street as well as in the Commercial District. There are attractive villas to be admired at Lake Isabella. The Columbia County Historical Museum is also sited here.

Florida Sports Hall of Fame

Near the intersection of I-75 and US 90 a popular exhibition is dedicated to the most popular sports in the Sunshine State as well as the most famous athletes and teams; the spectrum covers everything from bowling to motor sports.

Stephen Foster State Folk Culture Center

Near White Springs, 12mi/20km north-west of Lake City, a cultural centre on the Suwannee River is dedicated to Stephen Foster (1826–64), who composed and wrote texts for American folk songs. His songs *Old Folks at Home* and *Oh, Susanna* became world-famous.

✳ Osceola National Forest

Osceola National Forest to the north-east of Lake City was established in 1931 and with an area of 638 sq km/246 sq mi is the smallest of Florida's national forests. Expansive cedar forests, countless lakes, ponds and lagoons as well as cypress swamps, rubber trees and magnolias characterize the landscape. In the north the forested areas gradually give way to the Okefenokee Swamp.

An approximately 37mi/60km-long section of the **Florida Trail** runs through the forest from White Springs on the Suwannee River to the Olustee Battlefield. One of the most beautiful parts is Ocean Pond; adventurous nature lovers follow the Osceola Trail from the north shore into the damp hinterlands.

VISITING LAKE CITY

INFORMATION

Lake City – Columbia County Chamber of Commerce
106 S. Marion Street
Lake City, FL 32025
Tel. (386) 752-3690
www.springsrus.com

EVENTS

Olustee Battle Festival & Re-enactment
Every year in February the famous Civil War battle between Union and Confederate troops is re-enacted.

Florida Folk Festival
This folk festival takes place on the weekend around Memorial Day.

WHERE TO EAT

► Moderate

Bob Evans Restaurant
4730 US 90 West
Tel. (386) 752-8749
Very child-friendly restaurant with tasty American cooking.

WHERE TO STAY

► Mid-range

Best Western Lake City Inn
3598 US 90 W.
Tel. (386) 752-8301
www.bestwestern.com
83 rooms
Comfortable accommodation with spacious and well-furnished rooms.

► Budget

Motel 6
3835 US 90 W.
Tel. (386) 755-4664
www.motel6.com
110 rooms
The rooms are pleasantly furnished and very reasonably priced.

In 1864 thousands of Union and Confederate troops faced off near Olustee. The Confederates won and secured the supply lines for the South. A museum and an educational trail has more information on the battle.

◄ Olustee Battlefield State Historic Site

The Okefenokee Swamp is ideal for an excursion by nature lovers: the swampy region has an area of more than 2,000 sq km/772 sq mi and is located north of Osceola Forest; it stretches 40mi/64km northwards into the state of Georgia. The »land of swaying ground«, as it was originally called by the Choctaw Indians, is an important store of underground water. A labyrinth of lakes and waterways, cypress swamps and »floating« islands, which might sway when stepped on but which nevertheless carried entire woods and Indian villages, are fed by the Suwannee River, which runs into the Gulf of Mexico after more than 240mi/400km, and the St Mary's River, which runs into the Atlantic about 50mi/80km further east, as well as countless karst springs. The Okefenokee National Wildlife Refuge includes about 90% of the swamp and is a haven for endangered wildlife like black bears and wild cats as well as countless birds. About 10,000 alligators

✱ Okefenokee Swamp National Wildlife Refuge

Pretty 19th century architecture in Lake City

► Lakeland

live in the Okefenokee Swamp at present. There is more information on this interesting nature preserve at the Okefenokee National Wildlife Refuge Office (hours: Mon–Fri 7am–3.30pm) in Folkston, Georgia.

12mi/20km south-west of Lake City via FL 47 and FL 238 or US–27, **Ichetucknee Springs State Park** is located in very pretty countryside. Several rich karst springs feed the Ichetucknee River. So that future generations can continue to

Ichetucknee Springs State Park

enjoy this natural gem, only 3,000 visitors are allowed in every day. Near the springs traces of Indian settlement were found some time ago. The Spanish had a mission station here for a while when they first came to the New World.

Suwannee River

The Suwannee River flows out of the Okefenokee Swamp and meanders peacefully through northern Florida. It is popular among canoeists and fishers, and the numerous springs around Live Oak are ideal for snorkelling and diving.

Suwannee River State Park ►

About 14mi/22km north-west of Live Oak, at the confluence of the Suwannee River and Withlacoochee River, a bit of Florida's original landscape has been preserved.

✳ Lakeland

H 4

Region: North Central
Population: 90,000

Elevation: 67m/200ft above sea level
Area code: 863

The city halfway between ►Tampa and ►Orlando is an ideal base for day trips through rural Florida; it attracted people looking for rest and recreation long before Walt Disney turned his attention to the Sunshine State. Lakeland itself has – apart from water sports on a dozen lakes – a series of pleasantly unspectacular attractions.

Crisis and progress

In the past decades Lakeland has stubbornly continued to look ahead. There is nothing in this modern small town to recall the high unemployment of the 1980s. Citrus fruits and phosphate mining, Lakeland's two most important income producers, were going through their worst crises ever. The downtown area deteriorated. But then Lakeland changed its perspective. Energetic city fathers at-

VISITING LAKELAND

INFORMATION

Lakeland Chamber of Commerce
35 Lake Morton Drive
Tel. (863) 688-8551
www.lakelandchamber.com

EVENT

Sun'n Fun Fly-in
Pilots' meeting sponsored by the Experimental Aircraft Association (EAA), mid-April.

WHERE TO EAT

► **Expensive**
The Terrace Grill
329 E. Main Street
(in the Terrace Hotel)
Tel. (863) 688-0800
Fax (863) 688-0664
Best restaurant in the area. »Wood-grilled filet mignon« and other American classics are expertly prepared here.

► **Moderate**
Harry's Seafood Bar & Grille
101 N. Kentucky Avenue

Tel. (863) 686-2228
Culinary delights from Louisiana are served here: hearty »Cajun cuisine« and pretty spicy Creole cooking. Crawfish étouffé is especially recommended.

WHERE TO STAY

► **Mid-range**
Lakeland Terrace Hotel
329 E. Main Street
Tel. (863) 688-0800
Fax (863) 688-0664
www.terracehotel.com
88 rooms and suites
Elegant and tastefully furnished house from the 1920s.

► **Budget/Mid-range**
Jameson Inn
4375 Lakeland Park Drive
Tel. (863) 858-9070
Fax (863) 858-2491
www.jamesoninns.com
67 rooms
Friendly, colonial-style inn with a pool.

tracted new industry and increased their tourism advertising. Commuters who worked in Tampa or Orlando discovered Lakeland as a good place to live and the »Detroit Tigers« baseball team came here for »spring training«. Today the city has been comprehensively renovated.

What to See in and around Lakeland

The museum in the headquarters of the Experimental Aircraft Association (EAA) at Lakeland Regional Airport shows everything that ever took off. More than 70 flying machines are a source of entertainment, including bizarre homemade contraptions, remote-controlled drones and memorabilia of the aviator and millionaire Howard Hughes (4175 Medulla Rd.; hours: Mon–Fri 9am–5pm, Sat 10am–4pm, Sun noon–4pm).

Florida Air Museum at Sun 'n Fun

Florida Southern College

On the grounds of the college south-west of the town centre the architect Frank Lloyd Wright made his mark. The 18 buildings, which are connected by esplanades, embody what Wright called »organic architecture«: embedded in the natural environment and using local natural building materials. The Annie Pfeiffer Chapel and the only planetarium (111 Lake Hollingsworth Drive) that Wright ever designed are worth a look.

✳

Polk Museum of Art

Small but high-quality: this museum has valuable collections of pre-Columbian art from the Andes Mountains, European and Oriental ceramics as well as 18th and 19th-century American art. It also shows something of Florida's own art scene (800 East Palmetto St.; hours: Tue–Sat 10am–5pm, Sun 1pm–5pm).

Fantasy of Flight

15mi/24km north-east of Lakeland, near Polk City, more than two dozen antique airplanes are on display. The museum's showpieces are a Short Sunderland pontoon boat with four engines, a Grumman Wildcat fighter plane and a Supermarine Spitfire. They also offer flights in a biplane and balloon rides (on FL 559; hours: daily 10am to 5pm).

✳ ✳

Cypress Gardens Adventure Park

About a 20-minute drive east of Lakeland, near Winter Haven, lies the »mother of all American amusement parks«. In the 1930s a real estate agent recognized the charms of the local lakes. He had a combined botanical garden and amusement park built.

The **world-famous water-ski show**, still the park's main attraction, was developed during World War II by accident, more or less. A confusing newspaper article brought soldiers stationed near here in 1943 who expected to see a water-ski show. But no one in the park knew anything about it. The estate agent quickly got his kids and their friends together and they quickly improvised a show. The response was so great that hundreds came on the following weekend to see the show. The improvised act very quickly developed into »The Greatest American Water Ski Show«. After World War II Hollywood discovered Cypress Gardens as the setting for various films.

More than 8,000 different plants from all over the world flourish in the more than 90ha/222-acre park, including arrangements with roses, bougainvillea, hibiscus and chrysanthemums. »Southern Belles«, young women dressed in the antebellum style of the Deep South, pose in some of the most beautiful spots. The 47m/155ft-high observation tower offers a good overview of the whole park. Don't miss the »Wings of Wonder«, an aviary in which hundreds of colourful butterflies of all sizes flutter from blossom to blossom. Other attractions are Nature's Arena with an alligator show and an aviary for exotic birds.

Water-ski acrobatics ►

The breath-taking shows by water-ski acrobats that take place several times a day are still the most popular attraction. The absolute highlight of every show is the human pyramid (6000 Cypress Gardens

Blvd.; hours: weekends and high season, daily 10am–10pm; low season daily 10am–6pm).

A half-hour drive south-east, almost exactly in the geographic centre of Florida and nestled in pretty hills, lies **Lake Wales** (population 11,000) with its lovingly restored city centre. The pink Depot Museum (325 S. Scenic Hwy.; hours: Mon–Fri 9am–5pm, Sat 10am–4pm) depicts the beginnings of the railway, turpentine production as well as the industrial processing of citrus fruits.

An American pyramid: on water skis in Cypress Gardens

A few miles north of Lake Wales aromatic orange plantations surround the Historic Bok Sanctuary. The Dutch publicist Edward Bok (1863–1930) made botanical gardens here in the 1920s that are considered to be the most beautiful in Florida. They were designed by the landscape architect Frederik Law Olmsted on the top of Iron Mountain (at 90m/300ft one of the highest points in Florida); azaleas, cacti and magnolias bloom here in tropical profusion. The idyllic setting is dominated by the 60m/200ft-high Singing Tower, a daring mixture of Art Deco and neo-Gothic style. The limestone-and-marble tower is poetically reflected in a placid duck pond while a glockenspiel plays (Hwy. 17 A; hours: daily 9am–5pm).

✱
Historic Bok Sanctuary

⊕

Lake Okeechobee

Regions: South-east, south-west
Area: 1,810 sq km/700 sq mi

Elevation: 3m/10ft above sea level
Area code: 863

The fourth-largest lake in continental USA lies in the heart of rural Florida. Endless fields of sugar cane characterize the landscape. Cattle graze on green pastures and there are sleepy villages where the general store is also the post office and petrol station. The lake itself attracts anglers fishing for bass.

The »Great Water« of the Seminoles in the middle of southern Florida offers a welcome break from the bustle along the coast. People come here especially to fish, since the lake, which is only 15ft/4.5m deep, has more bass than anywhere else in Florida. The many boat rentals and fishing equipment suppliers as well as campgrounds and trailer parks along the shore in the towns of Clewiston and South Bay testify to this.

Fishing paradise

▶ VISITING LAKE OKEECHOBEE

INFORMATION

Clewiston Chamber of Commerce
109 Central Avenue
Clewiston, FL 33440
Tel. (863) 983-7979
www.clewiston.org

ACTIVITIES

Fishing is big here. Equipment and boats can be rented at »Big O Airboat Tours« (Roland Martin's Marina, Clewiston, tel. 863/983-2037, www.bigofishing.com), among other places.

WHERE TO EAT

▶ **Moderate**
Clewiston Inn Dining Room
108 Royal Palm Avenue

Clewiston, FL
Tel. (863) 983-8151
Best food in town. Spicy southern cuisine can be had here, especially catfish and fried chicken.

WHERE TO STAY

▶ **Budget/Mid-range**
Best Western of Clewiston
1020 W. Sugarland Highway
Clewiston, FL 33440-2707
Tel. (863) 983-3400
Fax (863) 983-3441
www.bestwestern.com
50 rooms
Comfortable, motel-like mid-range accommodation.

Deadly hurricane ▶ The lake, which is quiet most of the year, is part of a broad current of ground water that flows sluggishly between ▶Orlando and ▶Everglades National Park. On a hot Sunday, nothing would seem as impossible as what happened here in 1928. That year 2,400 people died when a hurricane roared over southern Florida and caused heavy flooding here. Afterwards a ring dike and a system of locks and canals were built to control the water level. Since they were completed the lake has served as a regulator during the hurricane season, and as a fresh-water reservoir. But its natural drainage into the Everglades to the south was blocked off, which has led to a serious conflict between the government and conservationists until today. Ecologists and aquatic engineers are now trying to keep the water around Lake Okeechobee as close to its natural level as possible.

> **!** *Baedeker* TIP
>
> **Take a dive ...**
> The quiet air space in the region and the flat landscape around Lake Okeechobee attracts skydiving fans. Skydiving novices can make a tandem jump here with a professional skydiver. More information is available at: Air Adventures of Clewiston, Airglades Airport, tel. (863) 983-6151, www.skydivefl.com

✳ Today the 36ft/11m-high **Herbert Hoover Dike** is the sight of the
Lake Okeechobee Scenic Trail ▶ Lake Okeechobee Scenic Trail, a 176km/109mi-long unpaved trail for hikers, bikers and horseback riders. The trail runs through towns

like Belle Glade, Okeechobee and Pahokee and offersnice views of the lake and fields, and constant opportunities to watch waterfowl. The best place to start a tour is Clewiston (population 6,500) on the southern shore, which calls itself »America's sweetest town« because of the surrounding sugar cane fields.

✳ Marianna

D 2

Region: North-west
Population: 7,000

Elevation: 36m/120ft above sea level
Area code: 850

A breath of the Old South is still in the air: Georgia and Alabama are only a short hop away. Beautiful old residences doze under magnolia trees, and the activity on Main Street is watched closely from shady verandas.

The town that proudly calls itself »City of Southern Charm« was founded in 1829, shortly after Florida joined the USA, by ranchers and cattle breeders from Georgia. Today Marianna is the county seat of rural Jackson County, where everything revolves around peanuts, soy beans and corn, and horse auctions are held regularly. The 19th-century manor houses are worth a closer look, but the real attraction lies outside of town.

City of Southern Charm

▶ VISITING MARIANNA

INFORMATION

Mainstreet Marianna
2880 Green Street
Marianna, FL 32447-0795
Tel. (850) 482-6046
Fax (850) 482-2199
www.cityofmarianna.com

WHERE TO EAT

▶ Moderate
Red Canyon Grill
3297 Caverns Road
Marianna, FL 32446
Tel. (850) 482-4256
Tasty home cooking, appreciated by »locals« and tourists alike.

WHERE TO STAY

▶ Budget/Mid-range
Best Western Marianna Inn
2086 Highway 71
Marianna, FL 32448
Tel. (850) 526-5666
www.bestwestern.com
74 rooms
Well-run inn with spacious rooms.

! *Baedeker* TIP

»Trip of a lifetime« for canoeists
Canoeists can make wonderful trips on the Chipola River. The river is considered to be one of the best waterways for canoeists in Florida!

Around Marianna

✳
Florida Caverns State Park

The main attraction is about 3mi/5km to the north outside of Marianna on FL 167: Florida Caverns. These dripstone caves were discovered by the Spanish in 1693. The system of karst caves was probably a hiding place for Indians, who hid there in 1818 from the approaching troops of US General Andrew Jackson.
Only part of the cave system, which was created for the most part by the Chipola River, is open to visitors. In a guided tour (daily 9am–4pm) wonderful stalactites and stalagmites can be seen.

✳
Falling Waters State Recreation Area

About 20mi/32km west of Marianna there is a natural phenomenon typical of the karst hillscape: Falling Waters. This is the only large waterfall in Florida. A small stream plunges about 20m/100ft into a rocky gorge and disappears into a deep cave system. Around it there are other sinkholes, with a difficult path leading to them. Above the waterfall a small lake is an inviting place to cool off. But watch out for alligators.

✳ Melbourne

J 4

Region: Central East	**Elevation:** 0 – 7m/22ft above sea level
Population: 77,000	**Area code:** 321

The rockets at nearby ► Cape Canaveral and the related development of high-tech businesses caused this town on the so-called Space Coast to expand dramatically in the 1980s. Thanks to the beautiful beaches, tourism has come to stay, too.

Railway brings growth

The first settlers in the Melbourne area were freed slaves who came here in the 1860s. The town got its name in 1879 from a postmaster who originally came from Australia. In 1894 the East Coast Railway of railway magnate Flagler arrived in Melbourne, which caused an enormous economic boom.

What to See in and around Melbourne

Melbourne

The **Brevard Museum of Arts & Science** has rotating exhibitions of works by famous artists and workshops on all sorts of subjects (1463 Highland Ave.; hours: Tue–Sat 10am–5pm, Sun 1pm–5pm).
The **little Brevard Zoo** has exotic animals including Australian kangaroos, wallabies and emus (3880 W. New Haven Ave., US 192; hours: daily 9.30am–5.30pm).
Eau Gallie Fishing Pier at the end of the causeway of the same name and Melbourne Beach Fishing Pier at the end of Ocean Avenue are popular meeting places for anglers.

From the southern tip of Merritt Island a 30m/100ft-long steel and concrete dragon watches over the boat traffic on the Indian River. This sculpture by Lewis Vandercar honours the legend of the dragon that rose out of the streams of the Indian River and chased away enemy Indians.

★ **Merrit Island Dragon**

The long and narrow barrier island off the coast is bordered by holiday resorts with romantic names. The resort named Satellite Beach is growing in leaps and bounds and has way over 10,000 residents. There are expensive holiday homes, some with yacht moorings, especially in Indian Harbour Beach. Paradise Beach and also Melbourne Beach have especially nice swimming areas.
To the south Melbourne Shores and Floridiana Beach are popular with tourists and locals alike.

★ **Beaches**

Further south Highway A1A crosses Sebastian Inlet. Deep sea fishers can go out to the Atlantic from Indian River since there is a gap here between the barrier islands. A larger part of the bathing and surfing beach has been declared a State Recreation Area.
McLarty Museum exhibits treasures salvaged from a Spanish galleon that sank in 1715 (hours: Wed to Sun 9am–5pm).

Sebastian Inlet

⊙

In Sebastian (between Melbourne and Vero Beach) finds made by Mel Fisher (1922–98) are on display. In 1985 the most famous and successful treasure hunter in the world and his team celebrated an outstanding achievement. After searching for years he discovered the wreck of the *Atocha*, which sank in 1622. This legendary ship was on its way back to Spain loaded with gold, silver, coins and jewellery. (1322 US 1; hours: Mon–Sat 10am–5pm, Sun 1pm–5pm).

★ **Mel Fisher's Treasure Museum**

⊙

▶ VISITING MELBOURNE

INFORMATION

The Melbourne – Palm Bay Area Chamber of Commerce
1005 E. Strawbridge Ave.
Melbourne, FL 32901
Tel. (321) 724-5400
www.melpb-chamber.org

WHERE TO STAY

▶ Luxury/Mid-range
Hampton Inn
194 Dike Road
Melbourne, FL 32904
Tel. (321) 956-6200
www.hampton.com
60 rooms and suites
Well-run inn with nice rooms and friendly service.

▶ Mid-range
Baymont Inn & Suites
7200 George T. Edwards Dr.
Melbourne, FL 32940
Tel. (321) 242-9400
www.baymontinns.com
100 rooms and suites
Modern accommodation for driving tourists with spacious rooms.

GOLDRUSH IN THE OCEAN

On 5 September 1622 a Spanish fleet of 9 ships left Havana harbour. It included the Nuestra Señora de Atocha and its sister ship Margarita, loaded with gold, silver and precious stones. The ships were actually supposed to wait, since there are often severe hurricanes in the Caribbean in September, but fear of robbery made the captains hurry and risk the dangerous journey.

Several days later only a few sailors were still alive. They tried to reach the coast of Florida holding on to planks. The treasures sank to the bottom of the sea. The fate of the two ships, which sank off the coast in a storm, was not unique. On their way home from the New World the ships had no choice but to sail through the **dangerous passage between Cuba and Florida** with its coral reefs and currents.

Blackbeard and Friends

Pirates lurked off the Florida coast as well, for the heavily laden ships were an easy prey here. They could be boarded from lighter ships or lured onto reefs with false lights. The pirate duo **Black Caesar** and **Edward Teach alias Blackbeard** were feared and famous then, and made the waters between Cuba, Florida and the Bahamas unsafe in the early 18th century. The pirate **Gasparilla** and his crew boarded or sank three dozen galleons from 1784 to 1795.

Treasures at the Bottom of the Sea

It is estimated that **more than 1,000 ships sank off the coast of Florida** from the 16th century. No wonder

The world-famous treasure hunter Mel Fisher with his young crew on board his research ship.

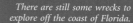

There are still some wrecks to explore off the coast of Florida.

then that divers from all over the world try their luck in these waters again and again. They use the most modern technology: computers calculate possible locations and the ocean bottom is searched by means of satellite-controlled navigation. New instruments register even small amounts of metal at unexplored depths. Thus there are occasionally spectacular finds that cover the high costs of the equipment.

Risky Business

But treasure hunting is risky and its outcome is uncertain. The professional treasure hunter **Mel Fisher** searched for 16 years for the two **galleons Atocha and Margarita** which sank on that September day in 1622. The search cost him over 8 million dollars, and his son and daughter-in-law lost their lives. No one believed any more that they would be successful when one of the divers in Fisher's crew suddenly swam into a wall of pure silver. Almost 1,000 bars of silver from Atocha were still neatly stacked on the ocean floor after centuries. Fisher also found the wreck of the Margarita in 1980 and salvaged **treasure worth US$ 350 million**; however, only after many days in court could he claim it for himself. The laws on treasure are unclear. Treasures found within the three-mile limit belong to

the government. Only wrecks that are found outside of the 24-mile limit belong to the finder. Between them there is a grey area in which ownership has to be determined in court. Spectacular finds in Florida did not come to an end with the discovery of Atocha and the Margarita. In 1987 Nuestra Señora de Maravilla, which rammed another ship fully laden in 1659 and sank, was discovered. In 1990 divers near the Dry Tortugas found another ship that had sunk in the 17th century.

Success on the Beach

In the face of competition from the professional treasure hunters, amateurs have hardly any chance of becoming millionaires overnight, since all the easily accessible places have been searched already. It is easier to find a spectacular treasure on the beach than when diving. After almost every hurricane, gold doubloons from colonial times are washed ashore on the beaches of southern Florida. One of the most valuable old pieces of jewellery ever found by treasure hunters turned up not on the ocean floor but on the beach: a **gold necklace** worth US$ 50,000.

For those not lucky enough to find treasure themselves, there us plenty to see in museums – for example in Mel Fisher's Museum in Sebastian.

★ ★ Miami

Region: South-east
Population: 380,000
(metropolitan area: more than 2.3 million)

Elevation: 0 – 7m/22ft above sea level
Area code: 305

»Welcome to Miami – Bienvenido a Miami!« – with this hit pop-star Will Smith paid homage to Florida's metropolis, where the air is scented with orange blossoms and arroz con pollo and where there are more statues of José Marti and Simon Bolivar than of Abraham Lincoln and George Washington. But the Spanish-speaking majority thinks in a thoroughly American way, as the dynamic skyline over the palm trees shows.

»It is my dream to see this wilderness transformed into a prosperous land.« Julia Tuttle (1840–98) had big plans for the settlement on Biscayne Bay, but she certainly didn't expect one thing: little more than one hundred years after its incorporation in 1896 Miami (»Mayami« meaning »large water« in the Seminole Indian language) is a boomtown bursting with life, which attracts 11 million partygoers and tourists from around the world annually.

Julia Tuttle started it all

It started with a bouquet of orange blossoms. That is what Mrs Tuttle, who had land on the Miami River and wanted a railway connection, sent to the railway magnate Henry Flagler in 1895. He had built his East Coast Railway as far as ► Palm Beach and considered his work to be completed. But then a cold snap destroyed the citrus crops in northern Florida and Julia Tuttle used the chance to advertise her wilderness in the south with blossoming orange branches. Flagler reacted immediately. As early as April 1896 his Florida East Coast Railroad reached Miami.

Orange blossoms, railroaders and Cubans

1896	The settlement on the large water (Indian »maya-mi«) was incorporated as a city; Flagler's East Cost Railroad reached Miami.
1930s	Miami, now a popular holiday destination, experienced an enormous building boom.
World War II	Miami was both a military hospital and boot camp for the US military.
1959	After Castro's revolution thousands of Cuban exiles settled in Miami.
1980s	Miami's new downtown began to grow.

← *Miami's imposing modern high-rise skyline*

Highlights *Miami*

Bayside Marketplace
Lively rendezvous
► page 231

Miami Art Museum
Works by leading contemporary North and South American artists are on display here.
► page 235

Villa Vizcaya
The winter home of the industrialist John Deering is simply overwhelming.
► page 238

Little Havana/Calle Ocho
The heart of Spanish-speaking Miami is Little Havana, especially on Calle Ocho.
► page 237

Coconut Grove
People-watching in one of the street cafés in »The Grove« is the best way to pass the time – and costs only as much as a caffè latte.
► page 238

Coral Gables
A walk through Coral Gables, the »City Beautiful«, goes by remarkable buildings like the Venetian Pool and the Biltmore Hotel.
► page 240

Miami Seaquarium
Sword whales, dolphins and a successful manatee-raising programme are worth a visit.
► page 243

The rest, as they say, is history. Spurred by the development of the sand dunes on the coast (today ►Miami Beach) Miami was already a popular holiday venue around 1910. It survived both the Florida Land Bust in the 1920s and two catastrophic hurricanes. The city celebrated the end of the depression with hotel architecture that was the most modern of its time. Soon Art Deco buildings were a part of Miami and Miami Beach like the sun, sand and beach.

During World War II shorts were traded in for uniforms. Soldiers were trained and the wounded were cared for in the south of Florida. After the war the GIs returned with their families to Miami to live.

National airlines discovered Miami. Miami Beach became the American Riviera: between 1945 and 1954 more hotels were built here than in all of the other states together. But Miami attracted not only tourists. In the 1950s organized crime came to the city. Almost all Mafia families on the east coast used Miami as the base for their activities in the Caribbean and Cuba. Gambling, prostitution, drug dealing – Miami became known as a dangerous place to be.

On 1 January 1959 Miami's future was decided once and for all. The success of Castro's revolution on Cuba brought a flood of exiles to Florida's metropolis, above all members of the deposed junta and almost the entire conservative upper class. In 1973 300,000 Cubans already lived in Miami. They were to change the face of the city for good. In the 1980s Fidel Castro emptied the Cuban prisons and sent another 140,000 compatriots, many of them criminals, to Miami.

Conditions in the already overflowing Cuban neighbourhoods led to riots. Many of the old-established residents left Miami.

But the city continued to grow. During the 1980s Miami's new Downtown was built. Other immigrants came from Latin America; street signs, billboards, displays all became bi-lingual. For the first time Miami was called »North South America«. Numerous businesses settled in Miami with feelers stretched out towards the markets of Latin America. Film and television discovered Miami. The TV series *Miami Vice* (1984–89) established the city's image as the playground of tough guys and easy girls and reflected its role in international drug dealing. Miami recovered from the activities of the Columbian drug cartel thanks to drastic police measures and to Hurricane Andrew, which blew through the city in 1992. The boom stayed. Today Miami is one of the most important centres of international finance and a wide-open door to Latin America as well as the largest cruise ship port in the world. The image stayed too: chic, cool, hot – and always a bit disreputable.

Downtown

The tourist focal point is Bayside Marketplace on the Miamarina, where mega-expensive yachts crowd in and excursion boats depart for Biscayne Bay. Incidentally: Miamarina includes the former Pier 5

✶ ✶
Bayside Marketplace

Cuban lifestyle at Bayside in Miami

▶ VISITING MIAMI

INFORMATION
Greater Miami CVB
701 Brickell Avenue, Suite 2700
Miami, FL 33131
Tel. (305) 539-3000
Fax (305) 530-3113
www.gmcvb.com

AIRPORT
The international airport, to which there are frequent connections from Europe, is just a few miles west of Downtown. There are good connections to local mass transportation. Hotels, car rental agencies etc. run shuttle buses to take guests to their destination in comfort. Plenty of taxi companies also serve the airport.

PUBLIC TRANSPORTATION
Tri-Rail
This regional express train runs from Monday to Saturday several times a day on the route Miami – Fort Lauderdale – Palm Beach.

Miami-Dade Transit
Miami's public transportation includes a dense Metrobus network with 70 routes, which include Miami's suburbs as well.
An elevated railway called the Metrorail runs through the city on a 22mi/35km long route from North Miami to Dadeland in the south. The trains run from 5.30am to midnight.
The driverless Metromover runs on two circular tracks in downtown Miami and connects all of the larger hotels, government offices and shopping centres daily between 6am and 10.30pm.

CITY TOUR
Miami is not the city to explore on foot. Public transportation doesn't always take you where you want to go. But the Metromover, a driverless elevated train, as well as the Metrorail and the Metrobus do run to some interesting places downtown and around. Organized city tours are recommended, most of which start from Bayside Marketplace.

SHOPPING/NIGHT LIFE
Bayside Marketplace
Miami's most popular venue is on Biscayne Bay and includes more than 150 shops, a food court and entertainment. The place is lively until 11pm. The drinks are cafe Cubano, mojito or even a caipirinha.

CocoWalk
CocoWalk is the heart of Coconut Grove. Enjoy the four dozen shops and boutiques with tasteful goods on three storeys or do some people-watching from one of the numerous restaurants. Busy until late at night.

Streets of Mayfair
In Coconut Grove, be sure to take a look at the Streets of Mayfair on Grand Avenue. There's lots to buy here as well and the southern atmosphere is lively until late at night.

EVENTS
Coconut Grove Arts Festival
On a weekend in February the first large arts festival of the USA takes place outdoors.

Carnival Miami,
Calle Ocho Festival
»Little Havana« is especially busy during carnival (Feb/March). There are colourful parades, Caribbean rhythms and salsa music on the streets.

Miami Downtown Map

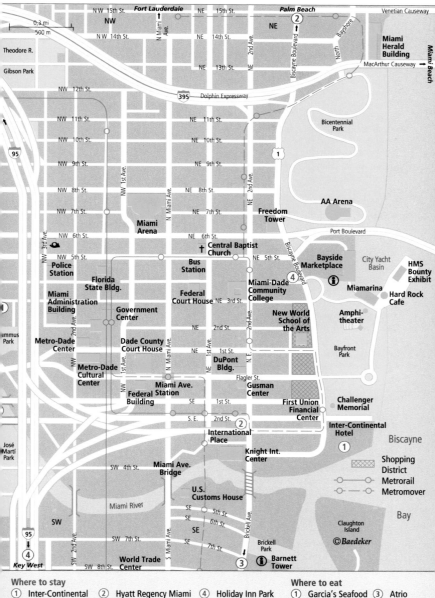

0,3 mi
500 m

NW 15th St. **Fort Lauderdale**   NE 15th St.   **Palm Beach** ② Venetian Causeway

NW
NE

Theodore R.

Gibson Park

NW 14th St. N Miami Ave.   NE 14th St.   Bayshore

Miami Herald Building

NE 13th St.   North   MacArthur Causeway →

Miami Beach

NW 12th St.   395 Dolphin Expressway

NW 11th St.   NE 11th St.

Bicentennial Park

NW 10th St.   NE 10th St.

95

NW 9th St.   NE 9th St.

NW 8th St.   NE 8th St.   2nd Ave.

NW 7th St.   NE 7th St.   **Freedom Tower**   **AA Arena**

NW 1st Ave.

N Miami Ave.

NW 6th St.   **Miami Arena**   NE 6th St.   Port Boulevard

† **Central Baptist Church**   Biscayne Boulevard

NW 5th St.   NE 5th St.   ④

Police Station   **Bus Station**   **Bayside Marketplace**   City Yacht Basin   **HMS Bounty Exhibit**

3rd Ave.

Florida State Bldg.   **Miami-Dade Community College**   ⓘ **Miamarina**   **Hard Rock Cafe**

Miami Administration Building   **Federal Court House** NE 3rd St.

Government Center   NE 2nd St.   **New World School of the Arts**   **Amphi-theater**

2nd Ave.

Metro-Dade Center

ammus Park

Dade County Court House   N Miami Ave.   1st St.   **Bayfront Park**

Metro-Dade Cultural Center   NW 1st Ave.   **DuPont Bldg.**

Miami Ave. Federal Station Building   Flagler St.   **Gusman Center**   **Challenger Memorial**

SE 1st St.   **First Union Financial Center**

José Martí Park

S.E. 2nd St. ②   **Inter-Continental Hotel** ①

International Place   **Biscayne**

Knight Int. Center   Shopping District

Miami Ave. Bridge   Metrorail

SW 4th St.   Metromover

U.S. Customs House

Miami River   SE 5th St.

SW 95   SE 6th St.   **Bay**

SW   SE   Claughton Island

SW 2nd Ave.   ©*Baedeker*

SW 7th St.   Miami Ave.   SE 7th St.   Brickell Park

95 ④   **World Trade Center**   ③ ⓘ **Barnett Tower**

Key West   SW 8th St.   Brickell Ave.

Where to stay
① Inter-Continental Miami
② Hyatt Regency Miami
③ Miami River Inn
④ Holiday Inn Park Port of Miami

Where to eat
① Garcia's Seafood
② Chef Allen's
③ Atrio
④ Norman's

WHERE TO EAT

► Expensive

③ *Atrio*
1395 Brickell Avenue
Tel. (305) 503-6500
Progressive »American cuisine« on the 25th floor of the Conrad Miami Hotel with a breathtaking view of the skyline of downtown Miami.

④ *Norman's*
Coral Gables
21 Almeria Avenue
Tel. (305) 446-6767
Norman Van Aken is a trendsetter in »New World cuisine«.

► Moderate

② *Chef Allen's*
19088 NE 29th Avenue
Tel. (305) 935-2900
Master chef Allen Susser prepares excellent dishes in an Art Deco ambience.

► Moderate/Inexpensive

① *Garcia's Seafood*
398 NW North River Drive
Tel. (305) 375-0765
Red snapper and stone crabs are available in the middle of »Little Havana«.

WHERE TO STAY

► Luxury

① *Inter-Continental Miami*
100 Chopin Plaza
Tel. (305) 577-1000
www.intercontinental.com
640 rooms and 36 suites
Post-modern hotel skyscraper with lots of marble. The lobby holds *The Spindle* by Henry Moore.

② *Hyatt Regency Miami*
400 SE 2nd Avenue
Tel. (305) 358-1234
Fax (305) 358-0529
www.miami.hyatt.com
610 rooms and 50 suites
The tastefully furnished rooms offer a wonderful view of Biscayne Bay and the harbour.

► Budget/Mid-range

Baedeker recommendation

③ *Miami River Inn*
118 SW South River Drive
Tel. (305) 325-0045
Fax (305) 325-9227
www.miamiriverinn.com, 40 rooms
Small but high-class: a protected historic building and very comfortable B&B dating from 1908.

④ *Holiday Inn Port of Miami*
340 Biscayne Blvd.
Tel. (305) 371-4400
Fax (305) 371-2862
www.ichotelsgroup.com
200 rooms and suites
Recently renovated hotel at the harbour, appreciated by tourists and business travellers.

of the harbour and became known as the mooring of Sonny Krockett's houseboat in the TV series *Miami Vice*. There is a promenade here, where people go to be seen; the outdoor stage occasionally hosts pop music stars and the best salsa bands perform in the Latino café. In the nearby Hard Rock Café there's always something going on. The gallerias offer souvenirs for every taste and strong café Cubano.

Bayfront Park with the skyscraper backdrop of Biscayne Boulevard has three important monuments: the Torch of Friendship symbolizes Miami's variegated relationship to Central and South America; the World War II Memorial commemorates the American soldiers who were killed in World War II; the Challenger Memorial honours the crew of the Challenger spacecraft that was lost in 1986.

Bayfront Park

Miami's main artery is the southern part of the palm tree-lined Biscayne Boulevard, where the first skyscraper boom began in the 1920s. **Freedom Tower** (600 Biscayne Blvd.), which was built in 1925 and still stands apart, is reminiscent of this time. The richly decorated tower was once the headquarters of the daily newspaper *Miami News*. Cuban refugees were housed here in the 1960s. A small exhibition on the ground floor depicts the sufferings of Cuban exiles during the Castro regime and their achievements in the USA. In 2000 the super-modern **American Airlines Arena** was built diagonally opposite as the new home of the »Miami Heat« basketball team. On the southern edge of Bayfront Park unusual skyscrapers characterize the skyline: in 1972 the 139m/456ft-high One Biscayne Tower was completed. Next to it is the 55-storey First Union Financial Center (200 S. Biscayne Blvd.), the highest building in Florida.

✳
Biscayne Boulevard

Loud, lively and multilingual, Flagler Street runs into town from Bayfront Park and gives the best impression of downtown Miami. Wealthy tourists from Latin America stock up on consumer goods here; European visitors think they are in Caracas. The street first runs to Guzman Cultural Center, which was opened in 1926 as the Olympia Theater and later converted into a cultural centre. On the other side of the street is the Alfred I. DuPont Building (169 E. Flagler St.); it was built in 1938 as the headquarters of the Florida National Bank, which was controlled by the DuPont family.

✳
Flagler Street

Metro Dade Cultural Center (Nr. 101 W.) is accessible over a ramp and built around a post-modern piazza; in it the Historical Museum of Southern Florida offers an exciting dramatization of 10,000 years of history in Florida. The exhibition begins with the Indians who built their shell mounds in mangrove swamps. Then there are treasures of the Spanish galleons, which were salvaged off the coast of Florida. Another topic is the explosive development of the city of Miami. There is also an excellent presentation entitled Tropical Dreams: A People's History of South Florida (hours: Mon–Sat 10am–5pm, Thu 10am–9pm, Sun noon–5pm).

✳
Miami Dade Cultural Center

🕐

The south-western part of the cultural centre houses the exquisite Miami Art Museum (MAM). It exhibits not only works by renowned US American artists, but also works by Latin American artists since 1940. The highlights include works by Max Ernst, Jasper Johns, Alexander Calder and Robert Rauschenberg. The packaging artist

✳ ✳
Miami Art Museum

Downtown Miami at sunset: on the left the NationsBank Tower is illuminated.

Cristo is also represented. The museum's entrance is decorated by a black marble sculpture *Cheval Majeur* by Raymond Duchamp-Villon (101 W. Flagler St.; hours: Tue–Fri 10am–5pm, Sat, Sun noon–5pm).

NationsBank Tower

South of Flagler Street is Miami's landmark: the NationsBank Tower, which is illuminated at night. This 52-storey skyscraper was built in 1987 to designs by I. M. Pei (in cooperation with Spillis Candela & Partners). The colourful lighting is by Douglas Leigh. On St Patrick's Day, for example, the building is bathed in Kelly green and on Valentine's Day in red light.

N. E. 1st Avenue

On N.E.1st Avenue, which runs through the middle of downtown Miami, two buildings are worth mentioning. One is the Catholic Gesù Church, which was built in 1925 and has stained glass windows from a workshop in Munich, Germany. The other, not far to the north, is the **U.S. Federal Courthouse** with its Moorish inner courtyard, which was built in 1931. A brilliant mural shows the development of Florida from wild swampland to a progressive civilized state.

Brickell Avenue

Biscayne Avenue ends at the Miami River. In the 1980s impressive high-rise architecture was built here. The bridge across the Miami River connects the busy city centre with the well-to-do residential areas between Biscayne Bay and Brickell Avenue. Brickell Avenue was originally conceived as a residential street for wealthy families; today it is lined with the marble and glass palaces of over 100 financial institutions. The street is called the »Wall Street of the South« and not without reason. The futuristic buildings of the architectural cooperative Arquitectonica are remarkable. The best-known is Atlantis (2025 Brickell Ave.; photo see p.57), which became a sensation for the square hole in its façade – with a palm tree and a red spiral staircase. Brickell House (no. 501), which was built in 1871 at Brickell Park, is also noteworthy.

From the southern end of Brickell Avenue the Rickenbacker Causeway (toll) runs across the shallow Biscayne Bay to Virginia Key and further to the island of Key Biscayne.

Rickenbacker Causeway

Little Havana

South-west of downtown Miami there is a neighbourhood populated by many Cuban exiles, who came to Florida in several waves after 1959. Between SW 12th Avenue and SW 27th Avenue there is a colourful, mixture of shops, small markets and friendly restaurants in a relaxed atmosphere; café cubano and mojito are available everywhere and in the evening the rhythmic sounds of salsa and dancon can be heard. This area is now called Little Havana. The street language is Spanish.

Neighbourhood of Cuban exiles

The busy main street of Little Havana is Calle Ocho (SW 8th St.), the annual scene of the boisterous Carnaval Miami Festival with its hours-long parades of salsa bands. Calle Ocho, which starts at the banking palaces of Brickell Avenue as SW 8th Street, runs west through Little Havana and then becomes Tamiami Trail (US 41).

✷ ✷
Calle Ocho

There are interesting buildings and monuments along Calle Ocho. In the eastern part of Little Havana, just before the busy interstate I-95, is the **Teatro Martí**, the oldest theatre of the Cuban exiles, which was founded in 1963. On the little square where SW 13th Street runs into Calle Ocho a marble monument was solemnly unveiled in 1971 with an eternal flame in memory of the members of Brigade 2506, who lost their lives in April 1961 during the failed invasion of Cuba. To the west at the intersection of SW 15th Avenue is the park that was originally named after Máximo

? DID YOU KNOW ...?

■ Curiouser and curiouser:
Teatro Martí is located in the Riverside Commercial Building, which was built in 1926 as the headquarters of the Ku Klux Klan.

Gómez, the leader of the Cuban liberation army, but which is now known as Domino Park. Older Cuban exiles meet here to play dominoes.

A few blocks further to the west the Latin American Art Museum exhibits works by contemporary Cuban and Latin American artists (2206 8th St.; hours: Tue–Fri 11am–5pm, Sat 11am–4pm).

Latin American Art Museum
⊙

Move by move: this applies to the chess-playing Cubans on Calle Ocho in Little Havana.

Orange Bowl North of the Latin Quarter the Orange Bowl (1501 NW 3rd St.) is a very popular attraction. In the home of the »Miami Hurricanes« football team rock and pop concerts attract thousands of fans. Of course, the local heroes Gloria Estefan and Ricky Martin have performed here, too.

Coconut Grove

Where the rich live The area of Miami's southern suburbs was established around 1840 by »Conchs«, immigrants from the Bahamas. Later wealthy people from New England came and built their winter homes here. Artists and hippies joined them. Simple half-timbered homes and buildings made of Coquina limestone as well as Mediterranean villas in the middle of profusely blooming gardens give the settlement lots of atmosphere. The heart of the neighbourhood is the intersection of Grand Avenue, Main Highway and McFarlane Road.

★ ★ Villa Vizcaya Not far south of Rickenbacker Causeway is the beautiful Villa Vizcaya in the middle of classical-style gardens. The building was built from 1912 to 1916 as the winter residence of James Deering, who produced harvesters, and was built in Italian Renaissance style. In the opulently furnished rooms of the palace a collection of French, Spanish and Italian art as well as valuable furnishings, carpets and sculptures – and a collection of old Baedekers – can be admired (3251 S. Miami Ave.; hours: daily 9.30am–4.30pm).

North of Villa Vizcaya lies another prestigious building that was built in the first quarter of the 20th century in the Mediterranean style. Today it houses a natural science exhibition as well as a space travel show and a planetarium. In cooperation with the Smithsonian Institution the museum was expanded to a »Science Center of the Americas« (3280 S. Miami Ave.; hours: daily 10am–6pm).

Miami Museum of Science & Planetarium ★

About 2mi/3km further south-west lies Miami City Hall, a remarkable example of Art Deco architecture at Dinner Key. It was built in 1933 as the terminal for seaplanes. The last seaplane took off from here in 1945. Nine years later it was converted to City Hall.

Miami City Hall

Westwards toward the centre of town (Grand Avenue/Main Highway) is the town centre of Coconut Grove. In the 1960s there was a colourful mixture of simple shops, cafés and galleries; in the 1970s and 1980s it mutated to a chic shopping zone. In the 1990s the area was discovered by young people and tourists. The selection in the shops changed with the times. Today there are pretty street cafés, cinemas and shops that sell beach fashions, CDs, DVDs etc. Venues like CocoWalk, which was built in 1990, the Streets of Mayfair and Commodore Plaza have remained popular.

Coconut Grove Village ★ ★

Villa Vizcaya: Italian flair in Coconut Grove

CocoWalk is a popular place to shop.

Coconut Grove Playhouse
At the south-western edge of Coconut Grove Village stands the local theatre, which was built in 1926 in the Moorish style. It became known as the place where Beckett's drama *Waiting for Godot* was first performed in America. Today cabaret programmes and musicals are performed here, too (3500 Main Highway; info tel. 442 - 26 62).

The Barnacle State Historic Site
Nearby at Dinner Key Channel there is a piece of the original Florida. A wooden house stands here on stilts; it was built in 1891 by Ralph Munroe, the most famous sailboat builder of his time. He imitated the building style of the Conchs, who had found an interesting solution to the problem of ventilation in a tropical climate. The rooms and covered verandas are grouped around the »barnacle«, the octagonal living room in the middle. The original furnishings have been preserved, as has the boathouse with workshop (3485 Main Highway; tours: Fri, Sat, Sun 10am, 11.30am, 1pm, 2.30pm).

Coral Gables

★★ Mediterranean ambience
The suburb of Coral Gables sprawls west of Coconut Grove. It was built in 1926 by **George Merrick** to designs by his father as an upper-class residential neighbourhood with generous parks and sports facilities; here too Mediterranean architecture, which was fashionable at that time, was used. Eight city gates were planned originally, but only four were actually built, all of them in the north of the suburb. Anyone driving west on the Tamiami Trail will pass by three of them, the Douglas Entrance, the Granada Entrance and

the Prado Entrance. They were modelled on triumphal arches that can be found in Madrid, Toledo and Seville. The main artery is Coral Way, which traverses Coral Gables from east to west. The Spanish Renaissance Coral Gables City Hall at the intersection of Coral Way and LeJeune Road is an architectural attraction.

Coral Gables is still elegant and beauty-conscious – so much so that not even the residents are allowed to park a pickup truck in their driveway. As an irony of history, today more and more wealthy YUCAs (»Young Urban Cuban Americans«) live on the streets with Spanish names.

From City Hall the Miracle Mile, the eastern arm of Coral Way (SW 22nd Avenue), runs towards Miami. After a period of stagnation the broad thoroughfare was revived. Here stands the Colonnade Building with its rotunda, wonderful marble interior, beautiful ornamentation and Spanish tile roof; it was designed and used by Merrick. Next to it stands the Colonnade Hotel; this skyscraper was built in 1985.

★ Miracle Mile

West of City Hall the childhood home of George Merrick is worth noting. It was restored in the style of the 1920s and is a museum today (907 Coral Way; tours: Wed, Sun 1pm–4pm). Two interesting buildings near Merrick House are Poinciana Place (937 Coral Way), which was built in 1916, and Casa Azul (1254 Coral Way) (1924) with its spectacular roof of glazed blue tiles.

Merrick House

⊙

Just before Merrick House DeSoto Boulevard branches off from Coral Way towards the south-west and DeSoto Plaza. On the way is the picturesque Venetian Pool, a very pretty swimming pool that was built in an abandoned coral limestone quarry; films were made here with the Tarzan actor Johnny Weissmuller and the actress Esther Williams. Towering coral limestone constructions, a casino, Venetian-style arched bridges, little waterfalls and artificial caves attract not only tourists, but also many local people (2701 DeSoto Blvd.; hours: mid-May–Aug Mon–Fri 11am–7.30pm, Sat, Sun, holidays 10am–4.30pm, at other times Tue–Sun 10am–4.30pm).

★★ Venetian Pool

⊙

The artist Denman Fink designed the fountain on DeSoto Plaza in front of the Venetian Pool in the 1920s.

◄ DeSoto Plaza

DeSoto Boulevard ends in front of the Biltmore Hotel, which opened in 1926. The centre of the 275-room complex is the 100m/330ft-high tower, which was probably modelled on the Giralda in Spanish Seville. The hotel lobby, with its Italian marble and Spanish tiles, is a feast for the eyes, and has already impressed such guests as Judy Garland and Ginger Rogers. The luxury hotel was used as a military hospital during World War II and afterwards as a veterans' hospital. It then fell into disuse and deteriorated from 1968 to 1986. Parts of it at least have been renovated. Fashion photographers, film makers and bridal couples use it as a backdrop today. Around the hotel there

★★ Biltmore Hotel

are two golf courses, a polo field and more than a dozen tennis courts. During the hotel's heyday Italian gondoliers brought guests to the beach at Biscayne Bay via a »Canale«.

Lowe Art Museum

The campus of the University of Miami (14,000 students) is located at the southern edge of the Biltmore Hotel property; it was founded in 1926. The art museum here holds outstanding Pueblo and Navajo Indian arts and crafts. Another highlight is the Kress Collection with works from the Renaissance and the Baroque, including paintings by Tintoretto and Jordaens. In the Beaux-Arts Gallery works by famous artists of the 19th and 20th century can be seen. Paintings by Frank Stella and Roy Lichtenstein as well as ceramics by Pablo Picasso have pride of place (1301 Stanford Dr.; hours: Tue, Wed, Fri, Sat 10am–5pm, Thu 1pm–7pm, Sun 1pm–5pm).

Fairchild Tropical Gardens

Only a few minutes' drive south of Coral Gables lies Matheson Hammock Park. There are virgin hardwood groves here as well as a beautiful beach. The south-west part of the park has been dedicated to the botanist David Fairchild in the form of a tropical garden. Thousands of varieties of plants are cultivated here, including more than 100 species of palm tree. In the Gate House Museum of Plant Exploration there is information on the many-facetted history of botany (10901 Old Cutler Rd.; hours: daily 9.30am–4.30pm).

South Miami

The area south-west of Coral Gables has been developed all the way to the ► Everglades National Park and consists of residential areas with malls, golf courses and parking lots, petrol stations, used car lots and waterbed dealers. Anyone driving this way should stop at two attractions.

Miami Metrozoo

The zoo was heavily damaged by hurricane Andrew in August 1992, but afterwards rebuilt according to the most modern scientific standards. More than 100 species of animals live in areas modelled on natural biotopes. The main attractions are the Bengal tigers, koala bears, gorillas, reptiles, a few giant aviaries (more than 300 different kinds of birds) and a petting zoo (12400 SW 152nd St.; hours: daily 9.30am–5.30pm).

Gold Coast Railroad Museum

Nearby train lovers will be tempted by the highly polished old locomotives and wagons of the Gold Coast Railroad Museum. The star of the museum is a Pullman wagon that was used by US Presidents Roosevelt, Truman and Eisenhower. »California Zephyr« trains as well as an extra-powerful diesel locomotive that belonged to NASA can be viewed. On weekends rides on steam and diesel engine locomotives are offered (12450 SW 152nd St.; hours: Mon–Fri 11am to 4pm, Sat, Sun 11am–4pm).

Key Biscayne

Sting in faded shorts, Paris Hilton with or without her lapdog: when Miami's gossip columns reports on celebrity sightings, the name Key Biscayne comes up often. A few miles south-east of Miami lies this 7mi/11km-long barrier islandwith its beautiful beaches, expansive sports facilities, most luxurious residences and several gourmet restaurants. Key Biscayne is known above all to golfers and tennis players as the venue for important tournaments. Get to the island via Brickell Avenue or Bayshore Drive across the Rickenbacker Causeway (toll).

Exclusive recreational and residential area

South Florida's largest tropical seawater aquarium is situated at the southern tip of Virginia Key. In the late 1950s numerous episodes of the worldwide popular TV series with the clever dolphin Flipper were filmed here. Presently the female orca whale Lolita is the absolute star of the seawater circus. The large aquarium holds thousands of sea creatures. The artificial coral reefs and the underwater station, where the feeding of the sharks can be watched, are also worth seeing. In Lost Islands Wildlife Habitat endangered species are presented, including manatees (4400 Rickenbacker Causeway; hours: daily 9.30am–6pm).

✱✱ Miami Seaquarium

Lively dolphins in the Seaquarium

The new nature centre is dedicated to the grand old dame of ecology (► Famous People) and has interesting aquariums, beautiful walks through almost untouched hammocks and beach tours guided by experts in the field. The writings of Marjorie Stoneman Douglas are also interesting (6767 Crandon Blvd.; hours: daily 10am–4pm).

✱ Marjory Stoneman Douglas Biscayne Nature Center

One of the most beautiful beaches in the Sunshine State lies practically at Miami's front door: the 2mi/3km-long beach slopes so gently to the Atlantic that it's possible to walk all the way to the sandbanks far out in the water. With a little luck some dolphins may swim by (4000 Crandon Blvd., parking lots).

✱ Crandon Park Beach

On the southern end of Key Biscayne, Crandon Boulevard ends at the entrance to this beautiful nature reserve that protects the dunes. No less beautiful than Crandon Beach, the 1.2mi/2km-long beach is also the site of Florida's oldest lighthouse. Built in 1825, the Cape Florida Lighthouse (tours: daily 10am and 1pm) was besieged by Indians and burned down during the Second Seminole Wars. The 31m/100ft-high lighthouse was rebuilt shortly afterwards and still offers a point of orientation for ships.

✱ Bill Baggs Cape Florida Recreation Area

PARADISE IN DANGER

Massive, colourfully shimmering coral reefs, myriads of brilliant fish, sea anemones, sponges, lobsters, sea urchins – a mysterious underwater world awaits snorkellers and divers at the southern tip of Florida, where coral reefs grew in warm waters that are still teeming with life.

The coral reefs are more than 180 miles (300 kilometres) long and protect Florida's Atlantic Coast from the Dry Tortugas in the south to Biscayne Bay and Miami in the north. It is the **third-largest coral reef in the world**, and it protects and nourishes a great variety of creatures.

Flower-like Creatures

A coral reef consists of millions of calcified skeletons of dead coral polyps. These tiny creatures are only a few millimetres in size, and shaped like sacks with tentacles at the head. They are connected to the ground and cannot move. For this reason they were taken to be plants for centuries. Only in 1744 did the French biologist Peysomel discover that these flower-like creatures were not plants. The polyps take in calcium from sea water to build skeletons that stabilize their jelly-like bodies. New polyps are formed by gemmation (budding) and remain connected to the mother polyp.

Polyps with Different Functions

The polyp heads grow gradually from thousands of individual creatures. Different functions are distributed within these heads: there are **dactylozoids**, which provide protection and have poisonous stinging capsules on their tentacles, and **gastrozoids** that eat and digest. Since the polyps are connected, the ones that are not able to take in food are nourished by the others.

Corals get their colours from algae, which also provide oxygen, sugar and other products that are vital to their metabolism. The algae in turn benefit from the coral, which provide them with carbon dioxide and minerals.

The underwater world of the coral reef off Key Biscayne shimmers in every colour imaginable.

A Reef is Born

The lower layers of polyp heads die off regularly, and together with encrusted algae and crustaceans form more or less steep reefs and sometimes even cliffs. With their many caves and crevices they offer ideal living conditions for many denizens of the sea. They also serve as an ideal breeding ground for many kinds of tropical fish and other fish.

Endangered Ecosystem

No other reefs in the world are visited as frequently by snorkellers and divers as those off the coast of Florida. In nature reserves like John Pennekamp Coral Reef State Park the underwater world can be observed from glass-bottom boats. But for how long? Scientists have watched **these reefs die slowly** for years. **Disease and hazards** are spreading. The reefs have pale areas where the polyps have died and no new ones are being formed. In order for polyps to form, the right water temperature, salt content and the light incidence are necessary; moreover the water must be relatively calm. Any variation in these components could endanger the reefs. A minimal warming of the sea water by about 1°C (1.8°F) over an extended period of time makes the polyps expel algae that vital to the survival of the corals and kills them.

The greatest danger to the reefs is the **rise in temperature of the oceans** caused by global warming. Moreover, chemicals, fertilizer, insecticides and pesticides in sewage pollute the waters around Florida's peninsula.

Should even more coral die this would, of course, be the death knell to all other plants, animals and forms of life in symbiosis with the reefs. It would indeed be the end of a truly unique ecosystem.

Biscayne National Park

Largest marine nature reserve of continental USA
Biscayne National Park was established in 1980 and is located about a one-hour drive south of Miami; it is the largest marine nature preserve in the continental USA. It protects an area of 275 sq mi/712 sq km including 44 barrier islands, coral reefs, mangrove forests and costal swamplands. The reef itself is located several miles off the coast and offers refuge to about 50 different types of coral as well as a variety of tropical fish and shellfish.

Dante Fascell Visitor Center
Dante Fascell Visitor Center, accessible via North Canal Street (SW 328 Street), is located 9mi/15km east of Homestead on Convey Point. The informative exhibitions are devoted to the complicated natural history of Biscayne Bay (hours: daily 9am–5pm).

✶ ✶ Coral reefs
The coral reefs that grew before the Keys in the open sea are a special attraction, but for some time now they have been endangered by environmental pollution. The warm Gulf Stream that flows by here enables various kinds of coral to flourish. The corals are a home to an unbelievable variety of fish. Sponges, shrimps, crayfish and lobsters can also be seen. Moreover sea turtles live in this region as well. Divers explore the wrecks of ships that ran aground here on the reefs in the past. In 1733 alone 19 Spanish galleons sank here during a hurricane on their way to Europe.

Mangrove Coast ►
On the main land the Mangrove Coast is mainly intact. With their tangle of roots the mangroves capture the finest sediment and filter the water. They are the nursery for the fish who live in the bay and offer ideal living conditions for tideland and sea birds.

Keys ►
The Keys in the nature preserve have a vegetation that is unique in the USA. The islands bear a variety of tropical hardwoods and bushes that are otherwise only found in the Caribbean.

On Elliott Key a few miles off the coast there is a dock, a campground and a pretty beach. The ranger station, which has information on the problems of the nature preserve, is only open occasionally in the winter.

Florida City · Homestead

The East Coast's salad bowl
The fertile coastal plain on the southern edge of metropolitan Miami is one of the most important areas in the USA for cultivating vegetables. The completely frost-free climate allow several harvests every year for lettuce, tomatoes, avocados, onions etc. Recently decorative plants, flowers, herbs and spices have been added.

Andrew was here ►
In August 1992 the Homestead – Florida City area was devastated by Hurricane Andrew. More than 170,000 people were left homeless, and almost all the crops were destroyed as well as the nearby Homestead Air Force Base. In the meantime life has started up again; all signs of the devastation are gone.

North Miami · Port of Miami

Opa Locka in northern Miami was a model of settlement building in the 1920s. The architect Glen Curtiss designed it in Moorish style. The streets are shaped like a sickle and named after characters in *Arabian Nights*. The City Hall and the Heart Building (Opa Locka Hotel) with domes and minarets are worth seeing. In May an Arabian Nights Festival is held here.

Opa Locka

In the suburb of North Miami to the east the ultra-modern North Miami Civic Complex with its **Joan Lehman Museum of Contemporary Art** attracts friends of contemporary art. Original exhibitions that like to break with conventions are the trademark of the house. They attract visitors from the avant-garde American urban scene. The exhibits include works by Keith Haring, Jasper Johns, Roy Lichtenstein, Claes Oldenburg and Robert Rauschenberg (770 NE 125th St.; hours: Tue–Sat 11am–5pm, Sun noon–5pm).

North Miami Civic Complex

The port of Miami is located on the artificial Dodge Island and Lummus Island and is the most important sea-passage terminal in the world. More than a dozen cruise ships can dock here at one time. About 4 million passengers pass through every year, most of them to the Bahamas or the Caribbean. The harbour was expanded in the 1990s. Meanwhile giant container ships can dock here as well. A tunnel between Watson Island and the Port providing direct access to the interstate highway system is planned. It will relieve downtown Miami of Port passenger and cargo traffic.

Port of Miami

Causeways

North of the harbour »streets on stilts« connect the mainland with the islands and the vacation city of Miami Beach. The MacArthur Causeway runs from the mainland to Watson Island. While Watson Island is presently in a state of flux, there is still plenty to see. In 2003 the Miami Children's Museum moved to Watson Island. The large facility offers activities, hands-on exhibits and resources designed to make learning fun (980 MacArthur Causeway, tel. 305 373-5437).

Causeways

Jungle Island is presently the largest facility on Watson Island. The former Parrot Jungle has been expanded to include more animals (including a liger, a cross between a lion and a female tiger), activities and access to the beach with a giant slide (1111 Parrot Jungle Trail, hours: daily 10am–6pm). Island Gardens, a large combination residential, hotel, shopping and entertainment complex with a marina for luxury yachts, will be completed by 2010. The Japanese Garden is presently being remodelled and an Aviation Center for seaplanes and helicopters is also under construction.

★
Jungle Island

✶ ✶ Miami Beach

Region: South-east
Population: 92,000

Elevation: 0 – 3m/10ft above sea level
Area code: 305

Before setting the sun illuminates the pastel-coloured houses in the Art Deco district. Inside are the sounds of salsa music, clinking glasses and laughing voices. Miami Beach is Florida's party town, where Jennifer Lopez, Paris Hilton and friends turn night into day and paparazzi lie in wait for hung-over celebrities.

In 1868 the farmer Henry B. Plum saw palms on an island while sailing along Florida's Atlantic coast. He tried his luck with coconuts and built the first house. But the impenetrable mangrove swamps and the clouds of mosquitoes prevented more than that. In 1894 Plum gave up and sold his land to John Collins, a successful farmer from New Jersey. He only saw his property two years later when he came to Miami on one of the first trains. But he could not pay for his dream of building a bridge from the mainland to the sandy island. Enter Carl Fisher, the owner of the Indiana Speedway. The bridge was built and Collins' property turned into a winter resort with golf course and tennis courts. Miami Beach was born! Meanwhile railway magnate Henry Flagler advertised in the cool northern USA for the new winter holiday venue and had the luxurious Royal Palm Hotel built.

Stormy beginnings

Miami Beach was incorporated in 1915. Fisher's advertising campaigns – in cold New York he set up billboards proclaiming »It's June in Miami« and attracted investors and visitors – were also successful. America's millionaires wanted their place in the sun: in the 1920s the

---

Highlights Miami Beach

Art Deco Historic District
The world's largest collection of Art Deco buildings is one of the top attractions in southern Florida.
▶ page 253

South Beach
Bronzed guys and girls, an electrifying atmosphere: the ways leading to this palm-lined beach are the catwalks of the rich and beautiful.
▶ page 253

← *Art Deco in Miami Beach*

Ocean Drive
Scantily dressed Latinas, Latinos wearing gold rings, muscular Afro-Americans and red-faced Yankees in Bermuda shorts: the cafés on Ocean Drive are the place to watch people.
▶ page 254

Shopping on Collins Avenue
Credit cards were never busier: in an Art Deco setting on south Collins Avenue, shopping for clothes is even more fun than usual.
▶ page 255

super-rich such as media tsar William Randolph Hearst and the industrialist Alfred DuPont had their winter residences built on »Millionaire's Row«. Real estate prices skyrocketed. While Miami Beach in 1921 had 5 hotels and 9 apartment buildings, 4 years later it already had 56 hotels, 178 apartment buildings and 858 private homes. The hurricane in 1926 ended the building boom, but Miami Beach stayed in business. In 1928, at the height of prohibition, mafia gangs under Al Capone took over the alcohol business in Miami.

 VISITING MIAMI BEACH

INFORMATION

Greater Miami CVB
701 Brickell Avenue, Suite 2700
Miami, FL 33131
Tel. (305) 539-3000,
Fax (305) 530-3113
www.gmcvb.com

AIRPORT

Miami's international airport lies about 7mi/11km west of Miami Beach and is easy to reach with public transport. Many hotels in Miami Beach run shuttle buses to bring guests comfortably to their destination. Plenty of taxi companies also serve the airport.

PUBLIC TRANSPORTATION

Miami-Dade Transit
Miami's public transport runs the dense Metrobus network with 70 routes, which also serves Miami Beach.

The South Beach Local
This special bus runs daily through the entire South Beach Area on a circular route.
Hours: Mon–Sat 7.45am–10pm,
Sun 10am–1am. A ticket costs 25 cents.

CITY TOUR

Art Deco District tour
A walking tour through the Art Deco District takes about two hours and is well worthwhile. Information at: Art Deco District Tour, 1000 Ocean Drive, South Beach, tel. (305) 672-2014.

SHOPPING

Collins Avenue
Collins Avenue between 6th Avenue and 8th Avenue is a place for upmarket shopping. Designer shops here include Armani, Nike and Polo Sports.

Lincoln Road Mall
Only a few steps further is the bustling Lincoln Road Mall, where almost anything can be bought. Tourists and locals alike come here.

Bal Harbour Shops
Luxury by Chanel, Gucci, etc. is available in this posh shopping centre with about 100 shops on Collins Avenue about a 20-minute drive north of South Beach.

Aventura Mall
One of the largest malls in metropolitan Miami is in North Miami Beach. More than 250 shops offer nice things for the »normal« budget. It's not surprising then to find department stores like Bloomingdale's, JCPenney and Sears Roebuck here.

EVENTS

Art Deco Weekend
Held every year on a weekend in

Miami Beach Map

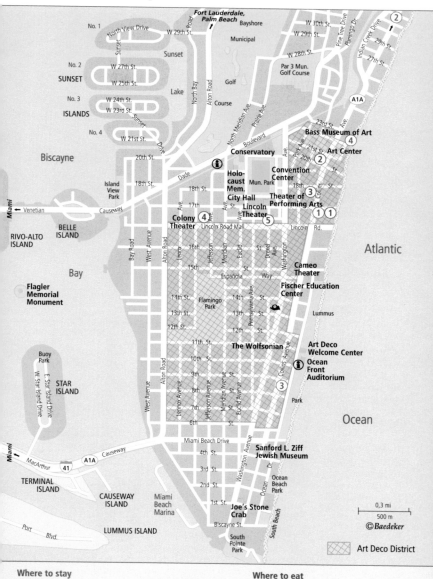

Where to stay
1. Delano
2. Fontainebleau Hilton
3. Casa Grande
4. Holiday Inn South Beach

Where to eat
1. Blue Door
2. Mark's South Beach
3. Raleigh's
4. Pacific Time
5. Yuca

January in Miami Beach's Art Deco District: a popular festival involving many artists and musicians.

Miami Boat Show

More than 2,300 exhibitors take part in the world's largest fair of its kind. There is much to see in the Miami Beach Convention Center, in Sealine Marina and in Miamarina.

NIGHT LIFE

Miami Beach's nightlife is incomparable, as TV fans know. Collins Avenue throbs, for example at the Rose Bar in the Delano Hotel (1685 Collins Ave), in Marlin (1200 Collins Ave) and at the Sky Bar (1901 Collins Ave). Current hip addresses include Tides (1220 Ocean Drive) and especially Lola.

WHERE TO EAT

► Expensive

① *Blue Door*

1665 Collins Avenue
Tel. (305) 674-6400
Gourmet restaurant in the Art Deco Delano Hotel.

② *Mark's South Beach*

1120 Collins Avenue
Tel. (305) 604-9050
Gourmet restaurant with star chef Mark Militello. Fresh seafood, luscious prosciutto.

► Moderate

③ *Raleigh's*

1775 Collins Avenue
Tel. (305) 534-6300
New American cuisine is served here.

④ *Pacific Time*

915 Lincoln Road
Tel (305) 534-5979
Excellent south-east Asian cuisine as well as Indian and Mediterranean dishes.

⑤ *Yuca*

501 Lincoln Road
Tel. (305) 532-9822
»New World cuisine« with a Latin American touch, for example a Peruvian tamal verde.

WHERE TO STAY

► Luxury

① *Delano*

1685 Collins Avenue
Tel. (305) 672-2000
www.delano-hotel.com
238 rooms and suites
An Art Deco jewel that became a society venue after renovation by star designer Philippe Starck.

Baedeker recommendation

② *Fontainebleau Hilton*

4441 Collins Avenue
Tel. (305) 538-2000
www.bleaumiamibeach.com
1,504 rooms and suites.
Newly renovated, excellently run top-class hotel with every imaginable comfort; also known as a film setting.

③ *Casa Grande*

834 Ocean Drive
Tel. (305) 672-7003
www.casagrandesuitehotel.com,
32 suites
Art deco luxury hotel on South Beach. Early reservations an absolute must!

► Mid-range

④ *Holiday Inn South Beach*

2201 Collins Avenue
Tel. (305) 779-3200
www.ichotelsgroup.com
355 rooms and suites
Well equipped rooms, fitness centre, tennis courts and access to the beach, valued by tourists and business travellers.

1886	The first house was built on the island.
Late 19th century	The financiers John Collins and Carl Fisher as well as railway magnate Henry Flagler made Miami Beach into a winter resort.
1915	Miami Beach was incorporated.
1920s	Wealthy Americans built their residences.
1928	At the height of prohibition Al Capone made his ill-gotten gains.
1930s	Art Deco architecture flourished.
1941	After the Japanese attack on Pearl Harbor, Miami Beach was made into a military hospital.
50s and 60s	Building boom. The »sub-tropical Manhattan« was built.
1997	The murder of the fashion designer Versace marked the climax of a wave of violence.

In the 1930s and 1940s the growth continued and Art Deco began to flourish. Architects designed buildings with the forms of eclecticism, Mediterranean architecture and the streamlines of new means of transportation.

After the Japanese attack on Pearl Harbor (1941), the Miami Beach hotels were temporarily turned into training camps, military hospitals and private quarters. After the war a broader social spectrum was attracted to Miami Beach. In the 1950s and 1960s the city where houses until then barely reached over the palm trees turned into a sub-tropical Manhattan with every sort of skyscraper. »Millionaire's Row« was replaced by »Hotel Row«. But the 1980s saw a crisis in the tourism industry. Not until new tourist markets were opened in Europe, Asia and South America, and southern Florida was discovered by the media did Miami Beach experience another renaissance, which not even the murder of the fashion designer Versace on the steps of his home on Ocean Drive in 1997 could affect.

✳ ✳ South Beach · Art Deco Historic District

Athletic boys, bronzed models, a square mile of colourful houses amongst art and kitsch – and all of it in sensual Caribbean surroundings: visitors don't know where to look first. South Beach, also called »SoBe«, is Miami Beach. The area between Dade Boulevard in the north and 1st Street in the south is to blame for Miami Beach's reputation as a hip party zone. But while it is possible to see enough of scantily clad people, the unique architecture exerts a longer-lasting fascination. South Beach has the largest collection of Art Deco buildings in one place: several hundred of them. It was placed under monument protection in 1979 but in the early 1970s the Art Deco

Historic District (▶Baedeker Special p.256) at 6th Street, Alton Road, Collins Avenue and Dade Boulevard almost disappeared: investors wanted to tear down the entire neighbourhood and build apartment blocks. The fact that this did not happen is mainly due to the Miami Beach Art Deco Preservation League. Under its leadership the aged buildings from the 1930s and 1940s were restored and put to use again as hotels in lemon yellow, Caribbean blue apartment buildings and neon-lit cafés.

★ ★
Ocean Drive

Ocean Drive is the catwalk of the young, rich and beautiful. 1963 Mustangs and brightly polished Harleys cruise up and down the street; light airplanes trailing advertising banners announce the next party venue. Many of the buildings are pretty street restaurants, chic bars and hotels with lobbies that are worth a look inside. Many have been in the movies and were used as locations for shows such as *Miami Vice* to *CSI Miami*. The finest Art Deco buildings are the sky-blue **Wave Hotel** (no. 350), the geometrical **Park Central** (no. 640), the **Colony Hotel** with its changing colours from baby blue to flamingo pink (no. 736), **Waldorf Towers** with its towers and lighthouse décor (no. 850) and the white, ivy-covered **Cardozo** (no. 1300) – the latter is the family business of Gloria and Emilio Estefan.

Art deco on the world-famous Ocean Drive in Miami Beach

There is natural green and blue across the street in Lummus Park: the park with its palm trees and paths for strollers and bikes separates Ocean Drive from the popular palm-tree-lined Lummus Park Beach (between 5th Street and 23rd Street).

South Beach has been »in« for years – for the publicity-hungry, for gays and lesbians as well as for everyone else. The broad beach is a party venue all year round. And since the violent death of the fashion designer Versace, whose villa is nearby, South Beach has practically become a pilgrimage site.

✳ ✳
South Beach

The main axis of Miami Beach is Collins Avenue, often called »The Strip«. It is also flanked by Art Deco buildings. Architect L. Murray Dixon designed **Tiffany** (801 Collins Ave.) and **Fairmont** (1000 Collins Ave.). **Essex House** (1001 Collins Ave.) was built in 1938 to plans by Henry Hohauser in the so-called Nautical Modern style. Roy F. France created the skyscraper **St Moritz** (1565 Collins Ave.) in 1939. The apartment building **Surfcomber** (1717 Collins Ave.) was only built after World War II to designs by the architectural office of MacKay & Gibbs. Three of the largest Art Deco hotels are the **National** (1677 Collins Ave.), a lemon yellow dream with an expansive swimming pool, the **Delano** (1685 Collins Ave.), where Sandra Bullock, Dennis Rodman, Will Smith and Barbra Streisand have stayed, and the **Ritz Plaza** (1701 Collins Ave.), a completely symmetrical construction crowned with towers. Streamlining and construction details are reminiscent of 20th-century means of transportation like airplanes, rockets and submarines.

✳ ✳
Collins Avenue

Washington Avenue is Miami Beach's main street and has more Art Deco buildings. Built in 1924, the **George Washington Hotel** (534 Washington Ave.) was one of the first beach hotels in Miami Beach. Further noteworthy buildings include the **Hotel Taft** (1044 Washington Ave.), which was built in 1936 by Henry Hohauser, the **Main Post Office** (1300 Washington Ave.), which was built in 1939 in the so-called Deco Federal Style with a decorated rotunda, as well as the **Old City Hall** (1130 Washington Avenue), which was built in 1927. The **Sanford L. Ziff Jewish Museum** presents Florida's Jewish tradition, which goes back to the 18th century, and is housed in Beth Jacob Synagogue, which was designed in 1936 by architect Henry Hohauser (301 Washington Ave.; hours: Tue–Sun 10am–5pm). A warehouse that was built in 1927 with a Moorish façade holds part of the **collection** of the eccentric art lover **Mitchell Wolfson**. Exhibits in-

✳
Washington Avenue

 Baedeker TIP

Winter delicacies

The restaurant Joe's Stone Crab (11 Washington Ave.) is at its busiest from October to March. That's when it serves the delicacy that made it famous: crayfish. Reservations: Tel. (305) 673-0365

TROPICAL ARCHITECTURE

Pastel-coloured houses that seem to swim like a swarm of fish through Florida's shimmering heat: no building style fits the truly relaxed atmosphere of Miami Beach as well as Art Deco. The bright city on the sea has the world's largest collection of these fanciful houses. The Art Deco District of Miami Beach is one of the top attractions of the Sunshine State.

All of it was new: the style, the forms, the colours, even the daring with which all of these contrary elements were combined.

A New Style from Europe

Art deco, which was named after an exhibition held in 1925 in Paris called »Exposition Internationale des Arts Decoratifs et Industriels Modernes«, had a very eclectic approach to past and contemporary forms. It drew equally on the decorative art of Viennese Art Nouveau, the forms of Maya and Aztec architects and the 4,000-year-old ornamentation of Mesopotamia and Egypt. Cubism and Futurism also influenced the concept of these houses. Streamlines and lack of ornaments were the trademarks of this new style. The

entrances were emphasized, as were the roofs and roof structures: the houses now got stepped gables inspired by Mesopotamian ziggurats. **Geometrical symmetry** was praised as it had never been before.

Successful Leap to the New World

From Europe, where it had already influenced buildings in Paris around 1900, Art Deco came to America in the 1930s. The USA was pursuing the American dream and developing into an economic super-power, fascinated by everything that symbolized progress. **The Chrysler Building in New York** carried Art Deco to lofty heights; many of the skyscrapers built in Manhattan at this time had Art Deco elements. The new style was

»Tropical« Art Deco façade decoration

Much-photographed Art Deco hotel in Miami Beach

novel and exciting. It was inspired by the aerodynamic design of the cars, trains and planes that were coming off the assembly lines by the tens of thousands, promising a new beginning after the dark years of the Depression.

Miami Beach: Capital of Art Deco

Making use of chrome, aluminium and vivid colours, it was not only progressive but also thoroughly humorous – especially in Miami Beach from the mid-1930s. A small group of local architects around Henry Hohauser (1895–1963) created »Miami Beach Art Deco« by adding tropical elements like stylized flamingos, flowers, pelicans, cranes and suns, which at first attracted derision as being kitschy, to the previous form vocabulary of Art Deco. Depending on the ornamentation, variants of the style were known as **»Streamline Moderne«**, **»Tropical Deco«** and **»Depression Moderne«**. How to recognize **»Nautical Deco«**? Correct: round porthole windows, long balconies resembling sundecks on ships and shady »eyebrows« over the windows.

Renaissance in the 1980s

By the late 1960s the days of the approximately 400 Art Deco houses in Miami Beach appeared to be numbered. The neighbourhood was run down, its residents aging and poverty-stricken.

Profit-oriented investors set their sights on the houses. They were saved in 1976, when concerned residents under the leadership of the feisty Barbara Baer Capitman founded the **Miami Design Preservation League** (MDPL). Their most difficult job was to convince lurking investors and chronically broke home-owners of the potential of the neighbourhood as a tourist attraction. In 1979 the MDPL achieved its aim of having the area added to the National Register of Historic Places. It was the first time that 20th-century objects were listed as historic buildings. In 1980 **Andy Warhol** came. This was a turning point: the world-famous performance artist and collector of Art Deco was guided through the neighbourhood by Barbara Baer Capitman – and followed by a mass of international journalists; he thus brought the work of the MDPL to international attention. Since then the league has watched over the Art Deco Historic District with Argus eyes.

clude decorative art, including posters and advertising from 1880 to 1945 (The Wolfsonian, 1001 Washington Ave.; hours: Mon, Tue, Sat, Sun noon–6pm, Thu, Fri noon–9pm).

Española Way

Española Way between 14th and 15th Street is also worth a visit. The Spanish-style street was built in 1925 and attracted artists above all. Today small galleries can be found here and a weekend market keeps it lively. At the beginning of Española Way the Cameo Theater (1938; architect: Robert Collins) stands out.

Euclid Avenue

On Euclid Avenue, note the following Art Deco buildings: The Denis (no. 841; 1938; architect: Arnold Southwell), The Enjoie (no. 928; 1935/1936; architect: Albert Anis and Henry J. Maloney) as well as The Siesta (no. 1110; 1936; architect: Edward A. Nolan).

21st Street

There are some wonderful Art Deco buildings along this street as well. This includes the former luxury hotel Plymouth (no. 226; 1940; architect: Anton Skislewicz) and the adjacent Adam's Hotel (1938; architect: L. Murray Dixon). Henry Hohauser's masterpiece is considered to be Governor (no. 435), built in 1939. The nearby Tyler Apartment Hotel (no. 430; 1937; architect: L. Murray Dixon) also stands out. Abbey (no. 300; 1940; architect: Albert Anis) is also interesting. On the corner of Washington/21st St. is the clubhouse of the Municipal Golf Course by August Geiger (1916).

Bass Museum of Art

The art museum in Collins Park was built in 1930 by Russell T. Pancoast, who used elements of Mayan architecture. The impressive reliefs are by Gustav Bohland. Inside the works of old and new masters are exhibited, including pictures by Albrecht Dürer and Peter Paul Rubens (*The Holy Family*) as well as some works by Impressionists (2121 Park Ave.; hours: Tue–Sat 10am–5pm, Sun 1pm–5pm).

Collins Park Hotel

Offset wings, pilasters and zigzag motifs are the characteristics of the adjacent Collins Park Hotel, which was built in 1939 according to plans by Henry Hohauser.

Lincoln Road

Two blocks to the north of Española Way is the gallery row of Miami Beach. Artists converted the derelict office buildings on Lincoln Road to workshops and shops with the help of government funding in the 1980s. Today Initiative 52, which is now called ArtCenter, has studios and galleries in three buildings (no. 800, 810, 924), which give an excellent impression of the art scene in Miami Beach.

Colony Theater ►

Designed by R. A. Benjamin in 1934 the theatre is a model of Art Deco in Miami Beach (1040 Lincoln Rd.). It was renovated extensively and reopened in 1976; today it is a focal point of cultural life in the city. The Lincoln Theater, a utilitarian Art Deco building from 1935–36 designed by Robert E. Collins, is the home of the **New World Symphony**.

Lincoln Theater ►

✳ Mount Dora

H 4

Region: Central
Population: 11,000

Elevation: 56m/170ft above sea level
Area code: 352

About an hour's drive north-west of ► Orlando Florida shows a completely unexpected side to its personality. Forested hills, almost mountains, lakes sparkling in the sunlight and green meadows with grazing cattle and horses, old live oaks make the area »Florida's Switzerland«.

In 1880 the town was founded and named after a certain Dora Ann Drawdy, who lived here with her husband. In the 1920s Mount Dora was a centre of orange cultivation. In 1930 US president Calvin Coolidge spent the winter in the local Lakeside Inn. Then the town sank into oblivion. Only recently has the pretty town on the lakeside been discovered as a weekend refuge by harried city dwellers.

From cultivating oranges to tourism

 VISITING MOUNT DORA

INFORMATION

Mount Dora Chamber of Commerce
341 Alexander Street
Tel. (352) 383-2165
Fax (352) 383-1668
www.mountdora.com

SHOPPING

Village Antique Mall
405 N. Highland Ave.
Hours: daily 9am–6pm
More than 80 antique dealers under one roof.

Renninger's Antique Center
20651 US 41
Hours: Sat and Sun 8am–4pm
180 dealers on the eastern edge of town.

Farmer's Market
on US 41 at the eastern edge of town
Hours: Sat and Sun 8am–4pm
There is a wide selection of regional products available here.

WHERE TO EAT

► **Moderate**
The Goblin Market Restaurant
331 N. Donelly Street
Tel. (352) 735-0059
Creative cooking in a nicely restored old warehouse.

WHERE TO STAY

► **Mid-range**

Baedeker recommendation

Heron Cay Lake View B & B
495 Old Highway 41
Tel. (352) 383-4050
Fax (352) 383-7653
www.heroncay.com
6 rooms
This Victorian jewel has a view of wonderful sunsets over Lake Dora and a hearty and sumptuous breakfast in the morning.

Mount Dora and Surroundings

Victorian architecture

Many of the pretty Victorian buildings have been lovingly restored recently. Some of them now house cafés, snack bars and antique shops. Beautiful houses can be found on Donelly Street and Fifth Avenue. The 600m/2,000ft-long Palm Island Boardwalk, which runs through a sub-tropical swampland and offers nice views of the lake – and with a little luck some alligators – is a nice place to stretch your legs.

Wekiwa Springs State Park

About 12mi/19km to the south-east, near Apopka, is a bubbling crystal-clear source called Wekiwa Springs; many visitors come to canoe on the Rock Spring Run and the Wekiwa River or just enjoy the beautiful natural setting. Archaeologists have discovered that the Timucuan Indians already lived on the shores of the Wekiwa River 5,000 years ago.

Leesburg

The town of Leesburg (population 19,000), site of one of the world's largest cool houses for citrus juice concentrate, lies only a few minutes' drive west of Mount Dora in the lake-rich heart of Florida. It is an excellent place for exploring central Florida on a houseboat. There are hundreds of lakes in the area. East of the town are the more than 30ha/74-acre Venetian Gardens, an attractive place for bathing, boating and relaxing.

✶ Naples

H 6

Region: South-west	**Elevation:** 0 – 3m/16ft above sea level
Population: 23,000	**Area code:** 239

The most millionaires per capita, the most golf courses, and a biblical average age: this town two hours west of ►Miami on the Gulf of Mexico has lots of labels. But like everything else, there are two sides to the issue. For some it is a millionaires' row suffering from its own wealth, for others it is an island of civilization light years away from the next large city. Naples has a tradition of dividing opinion.

Attractive seaside resort

The town was founded by wealthy real estate speculators in 1886; the first hotel opened before the first rail or even road access was laid. When the railway came (1926) and the Tamiani Trail (1928) was built, Naples became an oceanside resort. While investors advertised in the north with slogans like »This bay is even more beautiful than the one at Naples, Italy« and indirectly gave the town its name, the price of land rose quickly more hotels and homes were built. The

▶ VISITING NAPLES

INFORMATION

Naples Area Chamber of Commerce
Information Center
2390 Tamiami Trail N.
Tel. (239) 262-6141
www.napleschamber.org

WHERE TO EAT

► Expensive
① **Chop's City Grill**
837 5th Ave. S., tel. (239) 262-4677
The best steaks far and wide, extensive wine list.

► Moderate
① **Yabba Island Grill**
711 5th Avenue, tel. (239) 262-5787
This place is always full, probably because of its tasty Caribbean dishes and wonderful rum cocktails.

WHERE TO STAY

► Luxury
① **Ritz-Carlton Vanderbilt Beach**
280 Vanderbilt Beach Rd.
Tel. (239) 598-3300
www.ritzcarlton.com
460 rooms and suites
Old-established luxury hotel with its own beach, golf course, tennis courts, spa etc. and excellent cuisine.

② **Hotel Escalante**
290 Fifth Ave. S.
Tel. (239) 659-3466
Fax (239) 262-8748
www.hotelescalante.com
71 rooms and suites
Cultured Mediterranean-style inn in a sub-tropical garden; beach and shopping right around the corner.

► Mid-range
③ **Cove Inn**
900 Broad Ave. S.
Tel. (239) 262-7161
Fax (239) 261-6905
www.coveinnnaples.com
50 rooms
Friendly accommodation with pastel-coloured rooms right on Naples Bay and a beautiful view of the bustling yacht harbour.

»millionaire's row« was built, a series of baronial beach homes, which are part of the old part of town today called »Olde Naples«. Hollywood discovered the new town as a winter residence, especially Greta Garbo, Hedy Lamarr and Gary Cooper, who held wild parties in Club 41.

During World War II bomber pilots were trained nearby. In 1960 Hurricane Donna destroyed large parts of town, but then Naples – thanks also to the insurance premiums – began a building boom that still continues and apart from many hotel and apartment blocks on Vanderbilt Beach north of Naples has produced many new villas and industrial parks for high-tech and service industries.

Naples *Map*

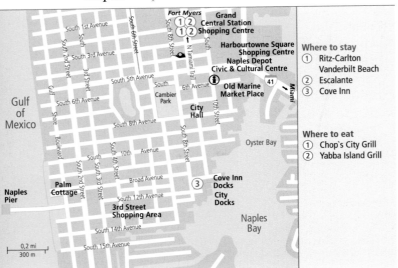

Fort Myers
Grand
Central Station
Shopping Centre
Harbourtowne Square
Shopping Centre
Naples Depot
Civic & Cultural Centre
Old Marine
Market Place
Miami
City
Hall
Oyster Bay
Cambier
Park
South 1st Avenue
South 3rd Avenue
South 5th Avenue
South 6th Avenue
South 8th Avenue
South
10th   Avenue
Broad Avenue
South 12th Avenue
South 14th Avenue
South 15th Avenue
Gulf
of
Mexico
Naples
Pier
Palm
Cottage
3rd Street
Shopping Area
Cove Inn
Docks
City
Docks
Naples
Bay
0,2 mi
300 m

Where to stay
① Ritz-Carlton
Vanderbilt Beach
② Escalante
③ Cove Inn

Where to eat
① Chop's City Grill
② Yabba Island Grill

What to See in Naples

Olde Naples

The »old city« of Naples has a grid pattern between the bay and the gulf. The heart of town is at the old docks south of South 5th Avenue. The former site of a fish factory, **Old Marine Marketplace** at Tin City (1200 5th Ave. S) is now a photogenic ensemble of colourful warehouses with restaurants and souvenir shops, a place for browsing and dining. The 300m/1,000ft-long wooden **Naples Pier**, which stretches out into the Gulf of Mexico and is used by fishers, brown pelicans and sun-worshippers alike. It was built already in 1888–89 and has been renovated several times since then. The area for elegant and expensive shopping is 3rd Street and 5th Avenue. The shady side streets are a good place to stroll under palm trees along well-watered lawns and beautiful villas and to work up an appetite for dinner.

Other attractions in town

North-west of the »old city« are the **Caribbean Gardens** (1590 Goodlette-Frank Rd.; hours: daily 9.30am–5.30pm), a lovingly run zoo whose main attractions are tigers from Indochina, islands inhabited by monkeys and alligator-feedings. Next to the zoo is The Conservancy of Southwest Florida's Naples Nature Center (14th Ave.; hours: Mon – Sat 9am–4.30pm). The long name hides a veritable wilderness. On a boat ride visitors can see alligators and many kinds of waterfowl up close; exhibitions explain the complicated ecosystem. On the way to Vanderbilt Beach stop at the Naples Philharmonic Center with the attached **Naples Museum of Art** (5833 Pelican Bay

Blvd.; hours: May–Oct Tue–Sat 10am–4pm, Sun 1pm–4pm, Nov–May Tue–Sat 10am–5pm, Sun 1pm–5pm). Beyond the glass-domed lobby, paintings and sculptures by contemporary artists are on display.

South-east of the city centre on the other side of Naples Bay, this museum illuminates local history from the first period of Indian settlement up to the present. Outside it the typical Seminole »chickees« have been set up (3301 Tamiami Trail East/Airport Rd.; hours: Mon–Fri 9am–5pm, Sat 10am–4pm).

Collier County Museum

Around Naples there are more than 35mi/60km of wonderful beaches. In »Olde Naples« all streets end within sight of Naples Municipal Beach, as it sparkles between the old villas. To the north lies Lowdermilk Park (Banyan Blvd. and Gulf Shore Blvd.). Clam Pass County Park consists of a dense mangrove jungle, with a long planked walkway over tideways and marshes to dunes and a wonderful natural beach. Kayaks and canoes are available for renting. To the north Vanderbilt Beach County Park adjoins with its luxury hotel. Delnor Wiggins Pass State Recreation Area on a barrier island to the north also has wonderful beaches.

★ ★ Beaches

Naples Pier is more than 1,000ft (300m) long.

Around Naples

Bonita Springs

14mi/22km north of Naples and on the north-west edge of Big Cypress Swamp, Bonita Springs (population 14,000) lies on the Imperial River, which has a good reputation among anglers. Right on the Gulf Coast the two holiday resorts Bonita Shores and Bonita Springs attract families with children. The long beach entertains young and old.

★ ★
Corkscrew Swamp Sanctuary

Corkscrew Swamp Sanctuary lies 10mi/16km east of Bonita Springs is a nature reserve called with up to 500-year-old swamp cypresses. The giant trees are densely covered with ferns, orchids and other epiphytes. In the winter endangered American wood ibis brood in the trees. The National Audubon Society, which runs the park, had a 2.5mi/4km-long walkway made so that visitors can explore the area without getting their feet wet in this original piece of Florida (access via CR 846, 375 Sanctuary Rd.; hours: Oct–April daily 7am–5.30pm, other times daily 7am–7.30pm).

★
Marco Island

The island lies about 20mi/30km south of Naples; bridges connect it with the mainland (US 41 or FL 92 or 951). It is about 10km/6mi long and 6km/3.5mi wide, has a population of about 10,000 and is the northernmost of the Ten Thousand Islands, a labyrinth of mangrove islands off the coast of the Everglades. Archaeological excavations have uncovered evidence of a 5,000-year-old Indian settlement. In 1922 an investor named Collier bought a large part of Marco Island in order to build a deep-sea or oil harbour here. Large deposits of oil were expected in this area. Marco Island has been a popular tourist venue since the 1960s. Wonderful beaches and excellent fishing attract visitors. The interior of the island is criss-crossed by canals bordered by luxury villas with private yacht moorings.

Old Marco Village ▶

Old Marco Village on the northern end of the island is very nice. Old buildings with friendly shops and restaurants make for a lively atmosphere. The harbour is now a shopping centre with an old-world atmosphere.

Beaches ▶

Next to the broad main beach with its fine-grained sand, which is lined by sophisticated hotel and apartment buildings, Tigertail Beach in the north-western part of the island is worth a visit; it is best reached via Hernando Drive.

★
Collier-Seminole State Park

This nature reserve has both cypress swamps and hardwood hammocks with a few royal palms and almost impenetrable mangrove thickets on the coast. Hiking, biking and canoeing trails make it possible to »take only pictures and leave only footprints«. A few nature trails and a 13mi/21km-long canoe trail make exploration possible. The visitor centre has information on the condition of the ecosystem and the local flora and fauna. The Indian settlement history in this area is also part of the exhibition.

★ Ocala

G 3

Region: Central
Population: 46,000

Elevation: 15m/50ft above sea level
Area code: 352

Almost everyone drives by and misses a landscape with gentle hills, moss-covered oaks and green pastures where thoroughbred horses graze. The proximity of the entertainment giants in ►Orlando is both a curse and a blessing to Ocala: around the centre of rural Marion County things still looks as they did before Mickey Mouse arrived.

A square surrounded by the tiny »Ocala Historic District« and the carefully restored main street, Fort King Street: Ocala wants to appeal not just to tourists but also to its residents. Most of them are descendants of the »Florida Crackers«, the hard-working farmers who made the land arable in the 19th century and who fought in the Seminole Wars. Ocala appears solid and down-to-earth; Timucuan Indians lived here 400 years ago and still do today.

City of crackers and horses

VISITING OCALA

INFORMATION

Ocala Marion County Chamber of Commerce
110 E. Silver Springs Blvd.
Tel. (352) 629-8051
Fax (352) 629-3529
www.ocalacc.com

EVENTS WITH HORSES

The horse auctions during Ocala Week (October) in the South-eastern Livestock Pavilion and in the Ocala Breeders Sales Complex attract customers from all over the world. For the annual Arabian Extravaganza in spring thoroughbred horses are »dressed in their best«. On the Classic Mile Horse Race Track west of town high-class horse races are held all year.

WHERE TO EAT

► **Moderate**
Reno's Grille
30 S. Magnolia Avenue

Tel. (352) 402-0097
Delicate alligator meat in tequila lemon sauce: Ocala's newest restaurant offers imaginative Florida cuisine.

WHERE TO STAY

► **Luxury**
Seven Sisters Inn B & B
820 SE Fort King Street
Tel. (352) 867-1170,
www.7sistersinn.com
13 rooms. Excellent Queen Anne-style inn. Rooms with fireplaces, jacuzzi and furnishings from all over the world.

► **Mid-range**
Ritz Historic Inn
1205 E Silver Springs Blvd.
Tel. (352) 671-9300
www.ritzhistoricinn.com
32 rooms. More charming and personal than the many big-chain hotels on the street to Silver Springs.

The descendants of the Crackers raised cattle on the fertile pasture-land that is blessed with clear spring water and when horseback riding became a sport, they added horses. Today Ocala is known as the home of thoroughbred horses and prize-winning racehorses.

Base for excursions ▶ Ocala is recommended as the starting point for excursions in the area. The city fathers also point to the attractions in the area as an argument for the high quality of life here.

What to See in Ocala

Brick houses, old art and fast cars Next to the old part of town, which is also called »Brick City« because of the brick houses there, Ocala has two museums that could not be more different. On the eastern edge of town **Appleton Museum of Art** (4333 NE Silver Springs Blvd.; hours: Tue–Sat 10am–5pm, Sun noon–5pm) holds the art collection of a Chicago industrialist that covers over five millennia. The excellent exhibition ranges from Greek antiquity to ethnological collections from Africa.

The southern suburb of Belleview boasts a thoroughly American museum, the **Don Garlits' Museum of Drag Racing** (13700 SW 16th Ave.; hours: daily 9am–5pm), which is dedicated to the patron of this high-speed sport. The most famous dragster pilot in the USA displays his legendary racing cars, the »Swamp Rats«, here. The car with which he drove 323.04mph (520kmh) in 2002 is also exhibited. For lovers of veteran cars, Don Garlits' Antique & Classic Car Collection is right next door (hours: daily 9am–5pm).

Around Ocala

Excursion through horse country to Orange Lake A charming trip goes from Ocala on CR 475 north of Orange Lake. The route runs through Riddick, the centre of thoroughbred breeding in Florida. Rolling hills and many miles of fencing between the roads and the green pastures characterize the countryside, as do the hammocks with centuries-old live oaks covered with Spanish moss. Between them are picturesque farms and studs. The trip ends at Orange Lake (19 sq mi/50 sq km), known to fishing fans for its sizeable bass.

Silver Springs Silver Springs, a few miles east of Ocala, is one of the most attractive places in the region. Already in the 19th and early 20th centuries when paddle wheelers sailed on the Silver River, this pond of warm spring water at 23°C/73°F attracted visitors. On the pond and the Silver River, which is fed by 17 springs, glass-bottom boats allow guests to see the exotic underwater world. Silver Springs has often been used as a film setting. In 1942 several Tarzan movies with Johnny Weissmuller and in 1982–83 the

? DID YOU KNOW ...?

■ With up to 23 cubic m/sec (over 6,000 gal/sec) of water Silver Springs is one of the strongest artesian wells on earth.

Swimming at Alexander Springs

diving scenes from the James Bond movie *Never Say Never Again* were made here. Around Silver Springs an amusement park has grown up with many attractions. On the Lost River Voyage or a Jeep Safari original Florida landscape can be discovered. Then there is a petting zoo for children and an alligator and snake show. For anyone looking for more action there is the nearby Silver Springs Wild Waters (hours: late March–Labor Day daily 10am–6pm). ⏲

East of Silver Springs lies the Ocala National Forest; it has an area of about 500 sq mi/1330 sq km and has been a nature reserve since 1908. A piece of the wooded landscape typical of central Florida has been preserved here. It is characterized by pines on sandy knolls that rise up like islands out of the brush known as »Big Scrub«. Swamp cypress dominate in the lowlands. Hardwood tree islands (hammocks) with magnolias, oaks, laurel trees and palm trees enliven the scenery. The forest is a refuge for many kinds of animals. Apart from snakes, alligators and racoons there are also black bears and Florida pumas. Of course, there are also many interesting kinds of birds, including bald eagles. Because of its many lakes, springs and slowly meandering rivers the forest region is a paradise for campers, canoeists, divers and other outdoor enthusiasts. Seasoned hikers enjoy the approx. 60mi/100km-long Ocala Hiking Trail. Juniper Springs, Alexander Springs and Salt Springs are wonderful spots which have campgrounds, canoe rentals, nature trails and other tourist facilities.

✳ **Ocala National Forest**

> ! **Baedeker TIP**
>
> **Like Tarzan and Jane...**
> Make your childhood dream come true: swing like Tarzan or Jane on a vine from tree to tree or drop into the water at Juniper Springs in Ocala National Forest.

✱ ✱ Orlando

Region: Central
Population: 225,000 (metropolitan area: about 1.8 million)

Elevation: 32m/100ft above sea level
Area code: 407

30 million visitors annually, 110,000 hotel rooms and the numbers are growing. Endless queues at the attractions, coupon books as thick as the telephone book with »special offers«. Visitors can be overwhelmed by Orlando. But even if you are allergic to mice, at least make a short stop in the world capital of amusement.

Orlando is a thoroughly American fairy tale. Even those who just drive by on Interstate 4 are not completely immune to its remarkable success story. Office, apartment and hotel towers in all colours line both sides of the multi-lane highways. Digital billboards advertise Disney, Burger King and the dentist. It only took 35 years for the city to grow from a rural town in central Florida to a billion dollar a year money-making machine. The end of the boom is not in sight. Even the hurricane year 2004, when Orlando stood in the path of storms, only slowed down business for a couple of days.

Not bad then for a city that doesn't even know for sure where it got its pretty name. According to one of the many theories it was named after Orlando Reeves, a corporal who was killed here in 1836 by Seminoles when he woke up his comrades with a warning shot. Later veterans of the Seminole Wars settled down here. In 1843 the brothers Aaron and Isaac Jernigan built a ranch and trading post at Lake Holden, which attracted more settlers. In the 1860s the area was already covered with ranches and cotton plantations; in 1872 Orlando was incorporated.

A billion-dollar money machine grows up

A certain William Holden planted the first orange grove in 1875, and a little later citrus fruits surpassed cattle as the most important source of income. In 1880 the railway came – and with it the first tourists, who stayed in elegant hotels on Orange Avenue and relaxed around the 54 lakes within the city limits. Unimpressed by cold spells – in 1886 and 1894–95 the entire citrus crop was ruined by cold snaps – Orlando continued to grow, but more slowly. In 1929 a fruit fly plague caused the citrus industry to collapse. Then came the Depression. World War II helped the monoculture to diversify and up to the beginning of the 1960s the space industry and its suppliers settled in Orlando, spurred on by the Cold War and the nearby space industry in Cape Canaveral. Then Orlando made the most important deal in its history.

← *Spiderman and his foe at Universal Orlando*

Highlights in *Orlando*

Charles Hosmer Morse Museum of American Art
Beautiful art nouveau glass and stained glass by Louis Comfort Tiffany and other artists, including work by the artist-poet John LaFarge and the architect Frank Lloyd Wright can be seen in Orlando's Winter Park suburb.
► page 279

Discovery Cove
A trend-setting water theme park with an expansive lagoon and a new kind of dolphin programme.
► page 280

SeaWorld Orlando
Lots of fun for over 30 years with trained dolphins, »killer« whales, sea otters, sea lions etc. Interesting theme areas, including »Manatees – the Last Generation?« and a few wet »thrill rides« attract children and adults.
► page 280

Universal Orlando
Next to Walt Disney World second-to-none high-tech thrills. Successful films like *Earthquake*, *Jurassic Park*, *Terminator 2* and *Spider Man* in 3D, also roller coasters and top-class stunt shows.
► page 281

Walt Disney came. The »father« of Donald Duck and Mickey Mouse bought land south-west of Orlando through front men for a new mega-resort. As soon as the transaction became public, real estate prices skyrocketed. Orlando experienced a land boom the likes of which Florida had never even known in the 1920s. On 1 October 1971 Walt Disney World's Magic Kingdom opened its doors. The ultra-modern amusement park set new standards in the industry and in the next decades made Orlando the entertainment capital not only of the USA, but of the whole world. Other theme parks came, with Universal Studios leading the way and then SeaWorld Orlando, Disney's biggest competition.

The fast pace infected the city of Orlando too. The day when the goings-on around Orange Avenue could be watched from a rocking chair on the porch were over. At the beginning of the third millennium Orlando is one of the fastest-growing metropolitan areas in the USA. Even without Disney & Co. it is the talk of the nation: the NBA basketball team Orlando Magic plays here. The city has kept its love of green spaces. It has 47 parks with old oaks and pretty lakes to help soothe the jangled nerves of residents and visitors.

Downtown Orlando

Orange Avenue Orlando's grid-like city centre is small and manageable on foot; tourists generally do not go there since it offers no more than the usual office buildings found in American cities of this size.

The main street, which is filled with office employees around the lunch hour, is still the north-south Orange Avenue. Along with a lot

Orlando Map

Paradise Heights
Lockhart
Orlando College
Jacksonville
Charles Hosmer Morse Museum of American Art ⑤
Clarcona Road
Ben White Raceway
Lee Road
Clarcona
Orlando Avenue
Winter Park
Ocoee Apopka Road
Ocoee
Silver
Star
Road
Rollins College
Science Center & Planetarium
Florida's turnpike
Pine Hills
441
17 92
Leu Botanical Gardens
East Colonial Drive
West Colonial Drive
Beulah
Orlovista
Church Street ②③①
Expressway
City Hall
East - West
④
Kirkman Road
Mystery Fun House
17 92
Conway
Windermere
4
Edgewood
Hoffner Road
Lake Butler
Isleworth
Lake Cane Hills
Pine Castle
Lake Conway
merport each
Universal Studios
Oak Ridge Road
Bay Hill
Wet'n'Wild Fun'n'Wheels ③
Tangelo Park
④
Sky Lake
Belle Isle
Colonial Plaza Mall
Lake
①
Sand Lake Road
Tibet
Doctor Philips
Big Sand Lake
Morningside Park
Bee Line Expressway
Taft
✈ Orlando International Airport
gic gdom
Ripley's Believe It or Not ②
Convention Center
Sea World
Central Florida
Parkway
Orange Avenue
Williamsburg
Boggy
LT DISNEY WORLD
Lake Buena Vista
Meadow Wood
Central Florida Greenway
World Drive
Water Mania
Shingle
Gatorland Zoo
441
EPCOT Disney/ MGM Studios
17 92
Buena Ventura Lakes
nimal ngdom
4
192
192
Xanadu House of the Future
Indian Wells
Lake Cecile
Orange Blossom Tr.
Florida's Turnpike
3 mi
5 km
©Baedeker
Sherwood Forest
Alligatorland Safari Zoo
Siesta Lago
192
Medivial Times
Kissimmee
Miami
Flying Tigers Waterbird Air Museum
East Lake Tohope- kaliga

Where to stay
① Eo Inn
② The Veranda
③ Clarion Universal
④ Sandy Lake Towers

Where to eat
① Christini's
② Café Tu Tu Tango
③ Dexters of Thornton Park
④ Numero Uno
⑤ The Briarpatch

▶ VISITING ORLANDO

INFORMATION

Orlando/Orange County CVB
8723 International Drive
Suite 101
Orlando, FL 32819
Tel. (407) 363-5872
Fax (407) 354-0874
www.orlandoinfo.com

AIRPORT

Orlando's international airport, which serves all of the major US airlines and a few smaller ones, is only a few miles east of the city centre. All of the large amusement parks, hotels and car rental agencies are easy to reach by shuttle bus. Regular buses run all day at short intervals between the airport and downtown Orlando.

CITY TRANSPORT

Orlando has a well-developed bus network, which also includes the large amusement parks. Moreover, there are many taxi, minibus or van and limousine services.

PARKS AND PRICES

A visit to a mega-amusement park is not exactly cheap. On the other hand, the admission price includes all the rides, shows and other attractions. The single-day ticket for Wet 'n Wild (www.wetnwild. com) costs about US$37 for an adult and about US$31 for a child.
A day at SeaWorld (www.seaworld.-com) costs about US$65 for an adult and about US$54 for a child.
Anyone who wants to visit more than one park should buy the »4 Park Orlando Flex Ticket« (about US$195 for an adult and about US$160 for a child); it is valid for 14 days at SeaWorld, Universal Studios/Islands of Adventure, Wet 'n Wild and Busch Gardens in Tampa.
A day at Universal Orlando costs about US$80 for an adult and about US$70 for a child; the 2-day-ticket costs about US$86 (adult and child). There are different multi-park tickets here as well (www.themeparks. universalstudios.com).

SHOPPING

As is fitting for a tourist venue of this magnitude, which has a high disposable income among locals as well, there are any number of factory outlets in Orlando, especially on International Drive. The largest are Belz Factory Outlet World (hours: Mon–Sat 10am–9pm, Sun 10am–6pm) and Orlando Premium Outlet (hours: Mon–Sat 10am–10pm, Sun 10am–9pm). Florida Mall in downtown Orlando with its 270 specialty shops and one of the best food courts far and wide is by far the largest shopping centre in central Florida. Quality is available at Orlando Fashion Square opposite the Orange County Convention Center as well as in Universal's CityWalk and Downtown Disney Marketplace.

WHERE TO EAT

▶ Expensive

① **Christini's Ristorante Italiano**
7600 Dr. Phillips Blvd.
Tel. (407) 345-8770
Excellent Italian food. Special tip: pork chops marinated in port wine.

▶ Moderate

② **Café Tu Tu Tango**
8625 International Drive
Tel. (407) 248-2222
Trendy food, and the artworks are for sale too: stone-baked pizza, sushi, sandwiches, vegetarian dishes.

③ **Dexters of Thornton Park**
Thornton Park
808 E Washington Street
Tel. (407) 648-2777
Ahi, tuna, tacos, exotic spices, creatively prepared. Pretty decor, often live music.

► **Budget**
④ **Numero Uno**
Downtown, 2499 S Orange Avenue
Tel. (407) 841-3840
Lots of Cuban cooking for little money. We recommend »Moros y Christianos« (black beans with rice).

⑤ **The Briarpatch**
Winter Park, 252 Park Ave. N.
Tel. (407) 628-8651
This place has served homemade breakfast and lunch for a quarter of a century. Try the eggs Benedict and homemade ice-cream!

WHERE TO STAY
► **Mid-range**
① **Eo Inn**
Thornton Park, 227 N. Eola Drive
Tel. (407) 481-8485
Fax (407) 481-8495
www.eoinn.com
19 rooms. Elegant boutique hotel with a wellness area. It also has a pretty view of Lake Eola.

② **The Veranda Bed & Breakfast Inn**
Thornton Park
115 N Summerlin Avenue
Tel. (407) 849-0321
Fax (407) 848-0321
www.theverandabandb.com
12 rooms
Romantic B & B on Lake Eola. Good shopping opportunities nearby.

► **Budget**
③ **Clarion Universal**
7299 Universal Blvd.
(east of International Drive)
Tel. (407) 351-5009
Fax (407) 352-7277
www.clarionuniversal.com
298 rooms and suites
Cheap and clean accommodation with a pool and restaurant near Wet 'n Wild.

④ **Sandy Lake Towers**
6145 Carrier Drive
(International Drive Area)
Tel. (407) 996-6000
Fax (407) 996-6010
www.sandylaketowers.com
204 rooms and suites
Brand-new double towers in bright pink. The top floors have a great view of Wet 'n Wild, Universal and Walt Disney World.

of non-descript functional architecture, several buildings nevertheless make their mark, including the post-modern City Hall, which was opened in 1992, and the 1930s Art Deco McCrory Five & Dime Building (Orange Ave. and Pine St.). Near the First National Bank, which was inspired by ancient Egyptian architecture, Orange Avenue crosses Church Street with its Church Street Station, a mini-entertainment zone located around the old railway station. In front of the restored railway station the steam locomotive *Old Duke* is worth a photo; it was built in 1912 for transcontinental rail traffic and used in various Hollywood films. Rosie O'Grady's Good Time Emporium, a bar in the style of the Roaring Twenties, will satisfy your thirst and entertain you with can-can dancers on the stage. The Cheyenne Saloon, a giant three-storey nightclub with live music, is another place to party all night.

The County Courthouse holds the **Orange County Regional History Center** (65 E Central Bld., hours: Mon – Sat 10am–5pm, Sun noon–5pm). Its outstanding exhibits depict the history of the region. Note especially the documentation of the Afro-American community in Orlando as well as the exhibition »The Day We Changed«, about the changes that Walt Disney brought to the region.

Loch Haven Park

Regional cultural centre

A few minutes' drive along the I-4, about 3mi/5km north-east of downtown, leads to Loch Haven Park with its three artificial lakes. With three museums and the Civic Theater of Central Florida the park is the cultural centre of the region. The **Orlando Museum of Art** (2416 N Mills Ave.; hours: Tue–Fri 10am–4pm, Sat, Sun noon–4pm), which concentrates on American art since the 19th century as well as African art, is considered a gem by insiders. The **Orlando Science Center** (777 E Princeton St.; hours: Sun–Thu 10am–6pm, Fri, Sat 10am–9pm) covers scientific topics as diverse as Florida's geography, the canals on Mars and the human body.

Harry P. Leu Gardens ▶

The wonderful gardens of the entrepreneur Harry P. Leu (1920 N. Forest Ave.; hours: daily 9am–5pm) are a true oasis of peace. The rose garden has more than 1,000 different varieties that bloom all year. Moreover, the largest collection of camellias in the USA can be admired here as well as magnolias, orchids and azaleas. The Butterfly

Nightlife in downtown Orlando

Garden has colourful butterflies from all over the world. Leu House (tours: daily 10am–3.30pm) is the place where the »green« business-man worked. ⊙

✷ Winter Park

The wealthy town of Winter Park borders on the north. This truly pleasant place has not lost any of its relaxed charm since it was founded in 1887 as an artists' colony. The local attractions reflect the residents' lifestyle. The Albin Polasek Museum & Sculpture Gardens (633 Osceola Ave.; hours: Tue–Sat 10am–4pm, Sun 1pm–4pm) exhibits the work of this artist of Czech descent in light-flooded rooms and a garden with palm trees. His sculptures that capture movement made him one of the most important 20th-century American artists. No less inspiring is a stroll through Kraft Azalea Gardens (Alabama Drive) on the beautiful Lake Maitland with its thousands of azaleas and various types of palm trees.

Albin Polasek Museum & Sculpture Gardens ⊙

On Winter Park's main boulevard this museum exhibits works by Louis Comfort Tiffany (1848–1933), which are among the finest art nouveau works to have been produced. Numerous paintings, stained glass windows, lamps etc. come from Tiffany's earlier house in New York City. Other important artists are also represented, including the art nouveau French glass painter Emile Gallé, the American painter and writer John LaFarge and the architect Frank Lloyd Wright (445 Park Ave. N.; hours: Tue–Sat 9.30am–4pm, Sun 1pm–4pm).

✷✷ Charles Hosmer Morse Museum of American Art ⊙

The best reason to drive further north past Winter Park is the Audubon of Florida – National Center for Birds of Prey. The conservation league, along with an informative visitor centre, has the largest rehabilitation clinic for wounded birds in the eastern USA. Visitors can see birds of prey that are native to Florida like ospreys and bald eagles up close.

Maitland

✷ International Drive

Begun in the early 1980s and continuously expanded since then, the 4.5mi/7km-long thoroughfare south-west of downtown Orlando is so to speak the umbilical cord to which all of the famous theme parks in the area are connected. It has earned its nickname of »Orlando's Most Dynamic Destination«. Its sidewalks and bike paths are lined by more than 100 hotels, some of which have spectacular architecture, along with three very big theme parks and countless

Pure energy ...

> **❗ Baedeker TIP**
>
> **Practice free falling ...**
>
> ... at Sky Venture Orlando. After instruction by professional jumpers, practice the proper posture – weightless on giant airbags. Address: 6805 Visitors Circle. Hours: Mon–Fri 2pm–11.30pm, Sat, Sun noon–11.30pm.

smaller amusements, about 150 restaurants, 500 designer shops, department stores and factory outlets and several entertainment complexes.

★ ★
Discovery Cove

Spoiled for choice! One of the most unusual attractions is undoubtedly Discovery Cove, a SeaWorld affiliate that was opened in 2000. For a fee visitors can swim with the three dozen dolphins in the expansive lagoon. The visitor limit of only 1,000 a day (the larger neighbouring parks admit to 50,000 a day!) means that you can enjoy the dolphins in peace. Other attractions, including snorkelling in a coral reef and a tropical river half a mile long, both inhabited by swarms of tropical fish, are included in the steep admission fee (6000 Discovery Cove Way; Reservations required!, tel. 407/370-1428, www.discoverycove.com).

Titanic – The Exhibition

This park feeds a dark fascination. From the famous staircase where Leonardo DiCaprio alias Jack Dawson walked in the legendary blockbuster film, to the original deckchairs and yellowed photos: Titanic fans will get their money's worth here (8445 International Drive; ⏱ hours: daily 9am–9pm).

★
Wet 'n Wild

This water park offers plenty of opportunities to get wet, what with rides like Raging Rapids (rapids with waterfall) and The Surge (one of the longest waterslides in the USA). The giant slide named Stuka is nothing for weak nerves: plummet down the steep 76m/250ft-long slide almost at free fall into a pool. The Black Hole is another white-knuckle experience: a plunge on a small raft into total darkness (6200 International Drive; hours vary depending on the weather, ⏱ spring daily 10am–6pm, summer daily 9am–9pm, fall and winter daily 10am–5pm).

Ripley's Believe it or not! Museum

This attraction was founded by Robert L. Ripley. Young and old will be astonished at the most unbelievable exhibits in the crooked »Sinking Building« (8201 International Dr.; hours: daily 9am–11pm).

★ ★ ## SeaWorld Orlando

⏱
Opening hours: Depending on the season and weekday daily 9am to 7pm or 10pm

Accessible via International Drive, SeaWorld Orlando lies 10mi/16km south-west of downtown Orlando (access via I-4, exit 72) and is one of the most beautiful amusement parks in the world and offers pure entertainment – above and below the water. In 1973 Busch Entertainment, the entertainment branch of the mega-brewery Anheuser-Busch, opened SeaWorld, which has been improved and expanded several times and includes an imposing sea water aquarium, an artificial reef with swarms of colourful inhabitants, pools for sting rays, a dolphinarium, and facilities for penguins, seals and otters as well as a flamingo garden. The shows with trained dolphins and orcas or »killer whales« have always been the public's favourite.

The nice thing about this park is that it does not overwhelm the senses: it has a manageable size and everything is easy to see on foot.

The personal atmosphere gives visitors a chance to relax. In the dolphin nursery young dolphins are raised. In the area called *Manatees: The Last Generation?*, manatees can be watched up close. For most tourists in Florida this is the only chance to take time to observe these endangered animals. In the Sea Lion & Otter Stadium the two sea lions Clyde and Seymore appear as pirates and the agile sea otters play tricks on them. An elephant seal takes part, too.

The sea water aquarium is breathtaking: visitors can walk through the glass tunnel and watch mantas, barracudas, sharks and other beauties of the deep. But no trip to Sea-

Dolphins are masters at synchronized jumps.

World is complete without a visit to **Shamu Stadium**: the orca whale Shamu and his companions show their acrobatics and make the water splash over the first 14 rows of visitors! And this would not be Orlando, if there were no roller coasters and other »thrill rides«.

✳ ✳   Universal Orlando

Here everything bangs, explodes or takes off. Universal Orlando, an affiliate of Universal Studios in Hollywood, focuses on »action«. It offers some of the best high-tech attractions ever.

Universal Studios in Orlando opened in 1990. After a rocky start this Hollywood theme park earned its place next to Walt Disney World. With the help of creative minds that switched over from Disney-MGM Studios to Universal Orlando a second theme park was conceived and built a few years later. In 1999 Universal Islands of Adventure opened, a tour de force aimed at youths and adults that was inspired by Hollywood blockbusters and features hair-raising roller coasters and the craziest technical effects. With City Walk, which was opened the same year, an entertainment zone for adults that connects the two parks, Universal confirmed its interest in older customers.

🕐
Opening hours: Daily 9am–6pm, and on weekends to 7pm. During the high season and on special occasions the park often stays open until 10pm or even midnight.

Look familiar? **Famous movie sets** await visitors here. Scenes from *Ghostbusters* were filmed here, the on-location shots for the *Blues Brothers* there, as well as various mafia films. Altogether the sets from about three dozen movies were set up here, including that of the Hitchcock classic *Psycho*, the house of Norman Bates.

✳ ✳
Universal Studios

These areas offer spine-tingling pleasure, and especially on weekends and during the high season the fans form long queues. In **E.T. Adventure** Steven Spielberg's most popular extra-terrestrial needs our help to save his home planet. In **Earthquake – The Big One** visitors can experience an earthquake with a magnitude of 8.3 on the Richter scale while riding a subway in San Francisco: suddenly the earth shakes, subway shafts collapse, masses of water flood the tunnel and a tank explodes.

Ultra-modern high-tech effects tests the visitors' perception of reality in computer animated shows. **Terminator 2** 3-D Battle across Time uses three giant screens and live shows on stage to make the audience feel a part of the action. The latest digital technology, high-tech simulators, aroma sprays and shaking seats in **Shrek 4-D** produce an event in which Shrek, Princess Fiona and Donkey start out on new adventures. **Revenge of the Mummy – The Ride**, also new, plunges visitors into deep darkness at first and then – by means of the latest technology, some of it in-house proprietary technology, and any number of talking mummies and crawling scarabs – takes them on the worst ride of their lives.

★ ★
Stunt shows

Stunt shows use tried and true methods. In the **Horror Make-Up Show** the audience gapes while arms are cut off and other »cosmetic surgery« is performed – not for weak nerves! It is no exaggeration to say that this also applies to **Fear Factory live**, where visitors can themselves try out breathtaking stunts – before an audience.

Roller coasters rocket, people scream and squeal, and things crash and rattle here as if there was no tomorrow: welcome to **Islands of Adventure**, the mecca of adrenaline junkies! The park, which no less a person than Steven Spielberg helped design, brings dinosaurs to life and offers the very latest in entertainment in the form of roller coasters, »thrill rides«, that truly deserve respect.

These can be tried out in the theme areas Marvel Super Hero Island and The Lost Continent. For example the **Incredible Hulk** Coaster races through corners and loops at a speed of up to 55mph (90kmh). The hanging ride called

Thrilling Hulk coaster

Duelling Dragons consists of two spirals that turn around each other, where two ride constructions repeatedly race at each other at top speed only to miss each other by inches at the last minute. **Doctor Doom's Fearfall** is also not for faint hearts and weak stomachs: a rocket-like start »shoots« participants almost 60m/200ft straight up only to bring them back to the starting point in an almost free fall. The latest attraction is **Simpsons – The Ride**: a thrilling roller-coaster trip through the world of yellow-skinned Homer, Marge, Bart. Lisa and Maggie Simpson.

The Amazing Adventures of Spider-Man (photo see p.272) is an absolute delight to roller coaster fans. Wearing 3D eyeglasses the participants' cars first get shaken up only to plunge down a 100m/330ft skyscraper canyon in New York by means of computerized effects and three-dimensional video projections. But Spiderman arrives in the nick of time.

◄ Amazing Adventures of Spider-Man

For families whose kids always want dinosaurs the Jurassic Park theme area is the highlight of the visit. Here they will meet the dinosaurs that Spielberg taught how to walk in his top-selling movies. The zone is conceived as a tropical jungle and in the Discovery Center similar to the visitors' centre in the movie, visitors can learn everything about the pre-historic beasts. Various dino-relevant attractions await, including Jurassic Park River Adventure, where a gentle raft ride turns into a nightmare when the passengers have to flee a hungry T-Rex by going over the edge of an almost 30m/100m-high waterfall.

◄ Jurassic Park

Around Orlando

Follow along FL 50 east towards Titusville for about 25mi/40km to reach Christmas, a town with a reconstructed fort from the time of the Seminole Wars. Documents, historic maps, weapons and utensils of the first settlers as well as pictures of the Seminole chiefs depict the time when this land was grabbed by the white people.
Incidentally: many visitors mail their Christmas cards from the post office in Christmas, Florida (1300 Fort Christmas Rd.; hours: Tue–Sat 10am–5pm, Sun 1pm–5pm).

Fort Christmas

The town, which the founder named after his French hometown, lies 23mi/37km west of Orlando. The almost 70m/230ft-high Florida Citrus Tower is a landmark that can be seen from far off; its observation platform offers a beautiful view of the hilly countryside with its many lakes and citrus plantations (open: daily 8am–5pm). In the fruit plantations around Clermont more than 17 million orange and grapefruit trees are cultivated. During a »Citrus Grove Tram Tour« visitors can find out more about the cultivation of citrus trees. From October to June freshly picked oranges and grapefruits are packed and shipped from the Citrus Packing House. Freshly pressed orange juice, jams and other sweets are available here, too.

Citrus plantations of Clermont

Sanford About 20mi/32km north of Orlando, on the road to ▶ Daytona Beach, this town of 24,000 lies on the idyllic Lake Monroe. It started out in 1837 as a trading post and up to a few years ago it was the centre of a larger fruit and vegetable farming region. Until today it remains the »gateway to southern Florida«, above all for tourists who come to the Sunshine State by auto train.

! *Baedeker* TIP

Fine wine

About 7mi/10km north of Clermont on US 27 the Lakeridge Winery & Vineyards is a recommended stop. The personnel inform guests on wine-growing under local conditions, where the grape harvest is usually finished by July or August. The cellar, where good wines can be tasted, is also open for viewing (hours: Mon–Sat 10am–5pm, Sun 11am–5pm; www.lakeridgewinery.com).

South of Sanford General Hutchinson Parkway leads to Big Tree Park whose main attraction is a 42m/140ft-high, approximately 3,500-year-old swamp cypress, one of the oldest living trees in the entire USA.

Monroe Harbor is the base for relaxing boating excursions on the lake itself (some with a paddle-wheeler) as well as on the St John's River.

✶ ✶ **Palm Beach**

J 6

| **Region:** South-east | **Elevation:** 0 – 5m/16ft above sea level |
| **Population:** 100,000 | **Area code:** 561 |

Is Palm Beach in Florida the wealthiest city in the world or is it Malibu in California? One thing is certain: the city fathers watch over their billionaires with Argus eyes. In early 2005 they even refused to give Donald Trump permission to have fireworks at his wedding celebration. Visitors who earn as much in a year as the lady at the next table donates during a charity function can't believe their eyes ...

Playground of the jet set Teenagers in Rolls Royce convertibles, power shopping and a city ordinance that prohibits clothes-lines: located on a palm island off the Gold Coast, Palm Beach with its grandiose villas and its Tiffany, Armani and Gucci shop windows, is the winter quarters of the American rich and famous and their equally rich and/or famous friends. From November to April »one« meets in the Palm Beach Polo & Country Club or in the brand-new ballroom of Trump's Mar-a-Lago-Estate on Ocean Boulevard, where the construction magnate likes to have world-famous stars like Céline Dion and Gloria Estefan perform in front of small groups of his friends. This is a busy time

It doesn't get any more exclusive: shopping at Tiffany's in Palm Beach. →

Highlights *Palm Beach/West Palm Beach*

The Breakers
The unchallenged flagship of the hotel trade in Florida is also the place where old and new money meet.
▶ page 286

Whitehall
Today the winter palace of the restless railway magnate Flagler is a museum.
▶ page 289

Worth Avenue
»It's worth it« – the motto of one of the

most exclusive shopping streets in the world where all of the labels are also exclusive.
▶ page 290

Norton Museum of Art
Art lovers consider this to be the »first address«: paintings by impressionists like Gauguin and Matisse as well as modern American artists, including Edward Hopper and Andy Warhol.
▶ page 290

too on exclusive Worth Avenue, where the architect Addison Mizner (▶ Famous People) made his mark with Mediterranean houses, arcades and inner courtyards. Then there are the many gourmet restaurants and hotels right on the beach, neighbours to the Kennedys, Rockefellers and Vanderbilts.

History Yes, you guessed right: Palm Beach has always been rich. It all began when the Spanish freighter *Providentia*, loaded with coconuts from the Caribbean, ran aground in 1878 off the coast of the 22km/13mi-long and only 1km/0.6mi-wide island. Railway magnate Henry M. Flagler, who explored the area in the early 1890s, saw the potential of the palm-tree covered island bordered by the deep blue and turquoise Atlantic. In 1894 he had his Florida East Coast Railroad extended to Lake Worth and built the legendary Royal Poinciana Hotel on Palm Beach. A year later the Palm Beach Inn was added, later to be known as Breakers. Naturally, the elegant hotels attracted an illustrious clientele. John D. Rockefeller stopped here, the newspaper tsar Randolph Hearst and US President Harding as well. In 1918 Addison Mizner stepped off the train and gave the city its Mediterranean appearance. At that time the service personnel lived beyond Lake Worth in West Palm Beach on the mainland. Meanwhile the former suburb has developed into the 80,000-strong centre of Palm Beach County. Electronics companies have settled here, as have tax accountants and real estate agents who control their territory in Palm Beach from here.

What to See in Palm Beach

★ ★
The Breakers Since 1926 this beautiful palace has been Palm Beach's landmark and its calling card! It is a luxury hotel with 540 rooms in the style of an

▶ VISITING PALM BEACH

INFORMATION

Palm Beach CVB

1555 Palm Beach Lakes Blvd.
Suite 800
Palm Beach, FL 33401
Tel. (561) 233-3000
Fax (561) 471-3990
www.palmbeachfl.com

BEACHES

The most beautiful beaches are privately owned and off limits, but that's no reason to do without a swim. Midtown Beach at the east end of Worth Avenue is a public beach. The one in Phipps Ocean Park further to the south is quieter.

SHOPPING

Even by American standards Worth Avenue in Palm Beach is second to none in shopping. Every exclusive label is present. But a bulging wallet or a platinum card is also necessary. This may be hard to believe, but the city of billionaires also has second-hand shops! As an alternative to paying a four-figure sum for a tuxedo, go to Déjà Vu (219 Royal Poinciana Way) or The Church Mouse (374 S County Rd.).

NIGHT LIFE

Palm Beach prefers to keep itself to itself after dark: nightlife generally takes place in the form of private parties, balls and charitable events. For dancing it's best to go to West Palm Beach, where bars, restaurants and music bars around Clematis Street stay open until 4am.

One of the best places in Florida for live music for the last 15 years has been the Respectable Street Café (518 Clematis St., tel. 561/832 - 9999, www.respectablestreet.com).

WHERE TO EAT

▶ Expensive

① **L`Escalier at the Florentine Room**
in: The Breakers Hotel
1 S. County Road
Tel. (561) 659-8480
Eating is an event here: under heavy chandeliers and magnificent frescoes expert »garçons« serve prize-winning New French cuisine.

② **The Grill at the Ritz-Carlton**
100 S. Ocean Boulevard
Tel. (561) 533-6000
From November to May Chef Sean McDonald creates culinary delicacies. These are accompanied by wines from all over the world.

▶ Moderate

③ **Café Mediterraneo**
200 Clematis Street
Tel. (561) 837-6633
Italian specialties like gnocchi Sorrentina and pollo Milanese are served here in a nice setting.

④ **Tsunami**
West Palm Beach
651 Okeechobee Blvd.
Tel. (561) 835-9696
It is known for style and substance: an elegant interior delights the eye, and the best sushi pampers the palate.

WHERE TO STAY

▶ Luxury

① **The Breakers**
Palm Beach, 1 S. County Road
Tel. (561) 655-6611
Fax (561) 655-8403
www.thebreakers.com
560 rooms and suites. This traditional luxury hotel with its elegant rooms,

contemporary Kid's Club and five heavenly restaurants is and remains the first address in Florida.

② *Biba*

320 Belvedere Road, West Palm Beach
Tel. (561) 832-0094
Fax (561) 833-7848
www.hotelbiba.com
43 rooms and suites
Chic boutique hotel with sake bar and zen garden. Room interiors with clear lines and warm colours.

► **Mid-range**

③ *The Colony Hotel*

Palm Beach
155 Hammon Ave.
Tel. (561) 655-5430
Fax (561) 659-8104
www.thecolonypalmbeach.com
83 rooms and suites
Good accommodation between the Atlantic and Worth Avenue with friendly and obliging service.

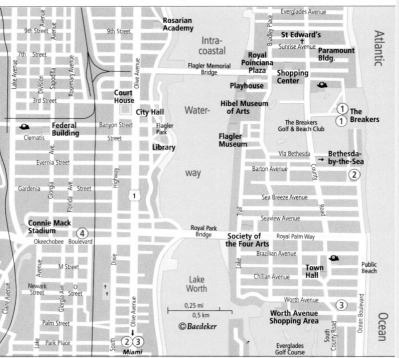

Palm Beach Map

©Baedeker

Where to stay
① The Breakers
② Biba
③ The Colony Hotel

Where to eat
① L'Escalier (Florentine Room)
② Ritz-Carlton
③ Café Mediterraneo
④ Tsunami

Traditional venue of American money: the luxury hotel The Breakers

Italian palazzo which is located right on the water and despite its size does not appear ostentatious. It is still the place where the city's old and new money meet. It has the number of golf courses, spa clubs and beauty salons appropriate to a hotel of its class. With the Flagler Club on the top two floors of the seven floors it has an even more elegant hotel in a hotel: for guests in the 28 suites, 28 butlers stand ready to redefine the word »service«.

On the west side of the island railway magnate Henry M. Flagler (► Famous People) had a 55-room palace built in the Beaux-Arts style with the lyrical name of Whitehall as a wedding present for his third wife. The couple lived here every winter from 1902 until Flagler's death in 1913 and thus inaugurated high society here. As was customary for the »Gilded Age« around 1900, every room was decorated extravagantly along a different historical theme. Thus there is a Louis XV ballroom, a Swiss billiard salon and a Louis XIV concert hall. After Flagler's death Whitehall changed hands several times and in 1959 was even scheduled to be torn down. Today the building is a protected monument that gives the visitor an impressive picture of the restless builder. In the expansive garden, which is separated from the street by a beautiful wrought iron fence, stands The Rambler, Flagler's private railway coach, in which he made the first train trip to Key West in 1912 (Whitehall Way, Cocoanut Row; tours: Tue–Sat 10am–5pm, Sun noon–5pm).

✷ ✷
Whitehall (Flagler Museum)

A few minutes' walk further south, along the Intracoastal Waterway, are – in sub-tropical vegetation – the stucco buildings of this non-profit organization. It was founded in 1936 by wealthy art-loving residents in order to satisfy the community's cultural needs; the facility was designed by the famous architect Mizner and houses a worthwhile library, interesting rotating exhibitions and beautiful sculpture gardens with samples of all the varieties of plants that flourish in

✷
Society of the Four Arts

⊙ southern Florida (2 Four Arts Plaza; hours: Dec – April Mon–Sat 10am–5pm, Sun 2pm–5pm).

✳ ✳
Worth Avenue

»It's worth it!« – the 200 exclusive shops on this most elegant shopping street hope to attract their wealthy clientele with this motto. And since they know that billionaires can't resist a bargain, they offered reduced parking rates – »no matter if you spend one or a hundred thousand dollars ...«. All famous labels are represented here: Hermès, Chanel, Louis Vuitton etc. Some of the newer trendy labels like Victoria's Secret and Banana Republic have sneaked in, too. Fine restaurants and a Mediterranean atmosphere, for which Addison Mizner was once again responsible,

! **Baedeker** TIP

Cycling through paradise
The best way to experience Palm Beach with its people, dogs and cars is on a bike and on Lake Trail. The most beautiful villas and yachts can be admired at leisure this way. Bike rental: Palm Beach Bicycle Trail Shop, 233 Sunrise Ave., tel. (561) 659-4583.

make a shopping trip along this astronomically expensive street, from which small diversions lead into quiet inner courtyards, an almost obscene pleasure.

✳ ✳
Luxury villas

Some of the most beautiful villas from the 1920s were also designed by Addison Mizner. Especially fine examples can be seen on South Ocean Boulevard, including the villa of the cosmetics queen **Estée Lauder** (no. 126), a house built in 1919 where ex-Beatle **John Lennon** relaxed decades later (no. 720), and not least the castle-like Villa Mar-a-lago (no. 1100), which was built by the Cornflakes heiress Marjorie Merriweather Post and bought in 1985 for the bargain price of 8 million dollars by the billionaire Donald Trump.

What to See in West Palm Beach

✳
Raymond F. Kravis Center for the Performing Arts

The focal point of the old centre of West Palm Beach is the Raymond F. Kravis Center for the Performing Arts (701 Okeechobee Blvd.), which was completed in 1992, with its generously proportioned theatre and concert hall. The architecturally very attractive cultural centre was designed by the Canadian-German architect Eberhard Zeidler. The Palm Beach Symphony and the Philharmonic Orchestra of Florida regularly perform here.

✳ ✳
Norton Museum of Art

In 1941 an industrialist from Chicago founded the Norton Museum, considered by art lovers to be an extremely high-class address. Its collection includes important works by French impressionists like Gauguin, Matisse and Monet. The American collection includes such heavyweights as Edward Hopper, Jackson Pollock, Georgia O`Keeffe ⊙ and Andy Warhol (1451 S Olive Ave.; hours: Mon–Sat 10am–5pm, Sun 1pm–5pm).

In this museum in Dreher Park technical and natural phenomena can be explored. In the Native Plant Center almost all of the local flora is represented, and in the Aquarium Florida's aquatic fauna can be seen. For anyone who wants to take a look at the universe there is a planetarium or observatory with a large telescope (4801 Dreher Trail; hours: Tue–Sat 10am–5pm, Sun noon–5pm, Fri also 6.30pm–10pm; laser show Fri 8pm and 9pm).

South Florida Science Museum, Planetarium & Aquarium

The Dreher Park Zoo with its native and exotic animals is also popular. Some can be even petted. The stars in this zoo are the Florida panthers, which now are rarely found in the wild (1301 Summit Blvd.; hours: daily 9am–5pm).

◄ Dreher Park Zoo

Around Palm Beach

15mi/24km to the west lies a safari and amusement park where lions roam around free. Visitors drive their cars through the grounds. Keep windows and doors closed for safety reasons! In Safari Village there is a petting zoo as well as a dinosaur and reptile park (2003 Lion Country Safari Rd., Loxahatchee; hours: daily 9.30am–4.30pm).

✶
Lion Country Safari

North of Palm Beach the metropolitan area of ►Miami and the so-called Gold Coast ends. On the next 80mi/130km of coast there are surprisingly large stretches of open land between individual towns, seaside resorts and brand-new retirement communities. The boom that rolled over the Gold Coast in the last decades has reached this Treasure Coast only in greatly reduced form.

Treasure Coast

Singer Island, unfortunately an almost completely built-up barrier island, still has the John D. MacArthur Beach State Park hidden away behind sand dunes; it offers good swimming and hiking as well as a nature centre with information on the highly sensitive ecological system (10900 State Rd. 70; hours: daily 8am–sunset).

Singer Island

Juno Beach (population 4,000) is a typical retirement community: during the winter months the population triples. This settlement with its beautiful beach was bypassed by Flagler's railway because the railway magnate could not come to an agreement with the owners of the local railway line. Thus Juno Beach missed its chance to become a millionaires' row.

✶
Juno Beach

Between May and September the excellent Marine Life Center of Juno Beach (14200 US 1; hours: Mon–Sat 10am–5pm, Sun noon–3pm) conducts tours to the nesting places of the sea turtles in Loggerhead Park. These primeval-looking animals come on land here in June and July in order to bury up to 100 eggs in the sand.

Juno Beach (cont'd)

The seaside resort of Jupiter is located about 7mi/11km further to the north (population 50,000). Its prominent landmark is the red brick Jupiter Lighthouse (US 1 and Beach Rd.; hours: Tue–

✶
Jupiter

Henry B. Plant

22 January 1912: Flagler's train arrives in Key West

POINTSMEN FOR THE ECONOMY

Florida would never be what it is today had not three men and one woman set a new course in the 19th century. By building the railway they created the necessary conditions for turning the swampy peninsula into a tourist paradise.

The idea came from US Senator Yulee: before the American Civil War he built the first railway from the Atlantic port Fernandina straight across north Florida to the Gulf Coast port of Cedar Key in order to transport cedarwood, sugar cane and cotton. Smaller businessmen joined in and laid their own tracks, which however were not connected to each other.

Henry M. Flagler

When the businessman Henry M. Flagler visited Florida in 1879 – his ailing wife came here to recuperate – he saw a market opportunity. At that

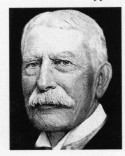

Henry M. Flagler

time Florida was already an insider's tip among wealthy convalescents, but getting there was still difficult and there was no appropriate accommodation. Flagler, who had become wealthy in the oil business with **John D. Rockefeller**, had the financial means to develop Florida. He bought up existing train lines and connected them. He created a consolidated rail network along the east coast of the USA. At especially beautiful locations, like St Augustine, he had elegant Mediterranean-style luxury hotels built. In 1894 Flagler's railway builders constructed the enchanting Palm Beach. Flagler bought a hotel there and converted it into the legendary The Breakers. Flagler's ideas bore fruit. The wealthy from the cold north-east USA came to Florida by the thousands.

Julia Tuttle Attracted Flagler

The winter of 1895 set Florida tourism back. Cold spells not only destroyed the citrus crops but also drove away the tourists. This was Julia Tuttle's hour. She owned a plantation

in southern Florida on the Miami River and had already asked Flagler several times to extend his railway to the south, but without success.

Now she sent him a branch of blooming orange blossoms – which convinced him. Julia Tuttle and Henry M. Flagler became business partners. In April 1896 the first train reached the then quite small settlement of Miami. This was the start of its uninterrupted rise to Florida's metropolis. But Flagler's rise, too, was unstoppable: he pushed his East Cost Railroad south as the Overseas Railroad over the Keys to Key West by building bridges at great expense. On 22 January 1912 Flagler took the first train to Key West. This enterprise cost several millions and 700 workers their lives, but now it was possible to take the **train from New York to Key West**. Then, on Labor Day 1935, a hurricane destroyed the tracks over the Keys and blew a train filled with passengers into the sea. The railway was not reconstructed.

Henry B. Plant

What Flagler did successfully on the East Coast, Henry B. Plant did on the **Gulf Coast**. Like Flagler he recognized Florida's tourist potential when his wife came here to convalesce. He developed south-west Florida and from Tampa expedited freight to Key West and Cuba. He attracted many tourists to Florida's Gulf Coast, which was known for its wonderful beaches and sunny weather, with his comfortable trains and hotels. In 1895 already he had a railway network of over 1,400 miles (2,400 kilometres).

And today?

The heyday of the railway is history now. Trains still run from New York or Washington to Orlando and Miami, but now most tourists travel by air or in their own cars to the »Sunshine State«. A few shorter sections have been reactivated recently as museum trains for leisure trips through the countryside.

Sun 10am–5pm). It was built in 1860 and is considered to be the town's birthplace. Loxahatchee River Historical Museum (805 US 1; hours: Tue–Fri 10am–4pm, Sat, Sun 1pm–4pm), which has the hard life of the early white settlers as its main topic, is worth a visit.

Burt Reynolds Ranch ▶ But some stop here for only one reason: Burt Reynolds! The Burt Reynolds and Friends Museum (100 N. US 1; hours: Fri–Sun 10am–4pm) was founded in 1999 on the ranch of the popular Hollywood actor; it has memorabilia on Burt Reynolds' films, including the canoe from *Deliverance*, as well as »holy relics« of famous Reynolds associates, like baseballs signed by the legendary Mickey Mantle and Muhammad Ali's boxing gloves.

Jupiter Island Beyond Jupiter Inlet, on the beautiful barrier island Jupiter Island, a visit to Blowing Rocks Preserve (574 S. Beach Rd.; hours: daily 9am–4.30pm) is worthwhile. This section of coast consists of porous coral limestone. High tides or high seas force sea water through holes and pipes in the stone and cause fountains to spray up to 15m/ 50ft high.

✷ Hobe Sound National Wildlife Refuge About 7mi/11km further to the north is the wonderful nature reserve on Hobe Sound. Apart from a magnificent beach and imposing dunes there are also several square miles of sea-water marsh in its original state. Every year in the summer many sea turtles come to the nature reserve in order to lay their eggs on land undisturbed.

✷ Jonathan Dickinson State Park A few miles further inland the Jonathan Dickinson State Park (16450 SE Federal Highway; hours: daily 8am–sunset) offers a completely different picture. From Hobe Mountain, a giant sand dune, there is a view of uninterrupted thicket made up of cedar and palmetto. The course of the Loxahatchee River is lined by mangrove forests and cypress swamps. The reserve is a refuge for numerous endangered species, especially manatees and sea turtles. These gentle creatures can best be watched from a canoe (canoe rental in the park).

✷ Panama City · Panama City Beach

D 2

Region: North-west	**Elevation:** 0 – 9m/30ft above sea level
Population: 48,000	**Area code:** 850

Anyone who asks about museums and art galleries here will be rewarded with an amused look. In Panama City Beach, the centre of the 18mi/30km long »Redneck Riviera«, everything revolves around having fun on the white sand beach and in the warm blue waters. The endless rows of faceless hotels make no apology for being there.

Panama City Map

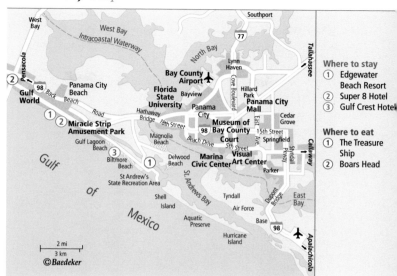

Where to stay
1 Edgewater Beach Resort
2 Super 8 Motel
3 Gulf Crest Hotel

Where to eat
1 The Treasure Ship
2 Boars Head

But there's one thing to be said about Panama City Beach: it never tried to be anything else. With its twin, Panama City on the other side of St Andrews Bay, it has been the venue for millions of holiday makers from Alabama, Mississippi and Georgia ever since beach holidays were invented. The families of Southerners relax on the indisputably beautiful beaches. For a long time it was contemptuously called »Baja Georgia« or even the »Redneck Riviera«, because of the predominance of people from the Deep South on the beaches. In spring tens of thousands of college students invade, ready for anything. The beach parties are broadcast live by radio stations from all over North America. Anyone looking for cultural stimuli and more depth should keep on driving. Panama City Beach consists of sports bars with dozens of TV screens and old-fashioned motels, go-cart tracks and Coney Island-style amusement parks, and hotels that look like they were built in a day. Highway US 98, which is called »Front Beach Road« within the city limits, is the main drag day and night where everything happens.

Redneck Riviera

What to See in Panama City & Beach

In the centre of this bustling port and industrial city some historical buildings have been nicely restored. There are good restaurants here too. The marina at the end of Harrison Avenue has room for more than 400 yachts and fishing boats. In the **Junior Museum of Bay**

Downtown Panama City

⏵ VISITING PANAMA CITY BEACH

INFORMATION
Panama City Beach CVB
17001 Panama City Beach Parkway
Panama City Beach, FL 32413
Tel. (850) 233-5070
www.thebeachloversbeach.com

WHERE TO EAT
▶ **Moderate**
① **The Treasure Ship**
3605 Thomas Drive
Tel. (850) 234-8881
Enjoy fresh fish on a replica of a galleon.

② **Boars Head**
17290 Front Beach Rd.
Tel. (850) 234-6628
Restaurant with good food and an excellent wine list.

WHERE TO STAY
▶ **Luxury**
① **Edgewater Beach Resort**
11212 Front Beach Rd.

Tel. (850) 235-4044
www.edgewaterbeachresort.com
520 apartments
This is the place to relax; it has its own swimming facilities, spa zone and golf course.

▶ **Budget/Mid-range**
② **Super 8 Motel**
11004 Front Beach Rd.
Tel. (850) 234-7334
www.super8.com
96 rooms
Modern motel with functionally furnished rooms.

③ **Gulf Crest Resort**
8714 Surf Drive
Tel. (877) 851-4853
www.resortquestnwflorida.com
Giant and somewhat impersonal holiday facility with two pools, spa and diverse other amenities. The apartments are quite spacious.

County young visitors are introduced to natural phenomena as well as the culture of the Indians of this region. A 19th-century pioneer homestead has also been reconstructed along with a barn and smoke house (1731 Jenks Ave.; hours: Mon–Fri 9am–4.30pm, Sat 10am–4pm).

Miracle Strip The Miracle Strip of Panama City Beach hops day and night with its many amusement parks, bars, discos and other attractions. Tourism began to develop here in the 20th century. Above all during »spring break« thousands of young people from Alabama, Georgia and other states come here to party. There are several amusement parks, including Miracle Strip Amusement Park, the largest of its kind in northern Florida, and Shipwreck Island Water Park, a combination of amusement park and fun swimming pool attract young and old. When visitors tire of giant water slides, bungee jumping and roller coasters, the long City Pier or one of the walkways that run into the dunes are great places to enjoy the sunset.

The aqua park is arranged like a sub-tropical garden and shows dolphins, sea lions, sea otters and sharks in their natural element. The dolphin shows always attract large crowds. Anyone can go into the water with the playful animals, for a fee of course (15412 Front Beach Rd.; hours: daily from 9am–evenings).

Gulf World Marine Park

It's interesting to speculate on how strong the nerves of early divers were while viewing this museum! From the old diving bells to diving helmets from the 18th century and claustrophobic diving suits from the time of World War II, this exhibition run by the Institute of Diving documents man's early efforts to live and work under water (17314 Panama City Beach Parkway; hours: daily 9am–5pm).

Museum of Man in the Sea

The nature reserve at the east end of Panama City Beach has the most beautiful stretch of sand (2.5mi/4km long) on the Redneck Riviera. It was founded in 1951 and was military property before that. Today it shows what this section of coast looked like before mass tourism developed here. Walk through dunes and sea water marshes on the Heron Pond Trail and watch cranes and ibis (4607 State Park Lane; hours: daily 8am–sunset).

★ St Andrew's State Park

> **!** *Baedeker* TIP
>
> **Nothing but sun ...**
>
> ... on this 6mi/10km-long beach on Shell Island, a delightful little island in St Andrew's Bay. Get there by boat from St Andrew's State Park (daily 9am–5pm every 30 minutes).

Spring on the »Redneck Riviera«

Around Panama City Beach

There are charming and easily accessible places for excursions nearby, for example the seaside resorts to the north-west, Seaside and Grayton Beach (▶ Fort Walton Beach, Around), Florida Caverns (▶ Marianna) one hour's drive north-east and the historic town of ▶Apalachicola to the south-east.

★ ★ Pensacola

B 2

Region: North-west
Population: 60,000

Elevation: 0 – 12m/40ft above sea level
Area code: 850

White beaches, warm temperatures and hospitable southern atmosphere are the attractions of this city at the extreme end of the Florida Panhandle. Since the old town has been restored, tourists are discovering that Pensacola is more than an air force base on the Gulf of Mexico.

Pensacola – and not ▶ St Augustine or Jamestown (Virginia) – very nearly became the oldest city in the USA. Spanish conquistadors knew and appreciated the natural harbour of Pensacola Bay, which is protected by the barrier islands Perdido Key and Santa Rosa Island, in the 16th century. In 1559 Don Tristan de Luna went ashore with soldiers and colonists near the present air base. Three years later a hurricane destroyed the settlement, which was never rebuilt. Colonization only began seriously in the early 18th century when the Spaniards arrived on the Castillo San Carlos de Austria. During the Spanish-French War Pensacola was fought over and changed hands

several times. In 1763, at the end of the Seven Years' War it went to the British, but reverted to Spain in 1781 already. Then Pensacola became a safe haven for pirates, runaway slaves and Indians. In 1821 Pensacola briefly felt the hand of history as the place where Florida was turned over to the USA. The United States expanded the harbour into a navy base. During the Civil War the fort was held by Union troops and played an important role in the blockade of the Confederate states. Reconstruction after the Civil War was made easier by a lumber boom, which was however already over in 1900. Then came commercial fishing and carried the economy for a while until the US navy set the course for modern urban development by building an air base. Today Pensacola is the economic centre of the region and thanks to its location and cultural heritage a rising holiday venue. In this it profits from the nearby Gulf Islands National Seashore, where many holiday resorts have been built recently.

 VISITING PENSACOLA

INFORMATION

**Pensacola Visitor
Information Center**
1401 E. Gregory Street, Pensacola, FL
Tel. (850) 434-1234
Fax (850) 432-8211
www.visitpensacola.com

CITY TOUR

A trip on the trolleybus which leaves from the Visitor Center for the local tourist sites explains why Pensacola is often called »Five Flags City« (Mon–Fri 9am–4pm).

EVENT

Fiesta of the Five Flags
Every year at the end of May an extravagant celebration is held in every neighbourhood of the city. The highlight of the festival is the re-enactment of the landing of the city's founder Don Tristán de Luna on the white Pensacola Beach to be met by the Indian chief Mayoki.

WHERE TO EAT

► **Expensive**
Jackson's
400 S. Palafox Street
Tel. (850) 469-9898
Presently the best restaurant in town, it serves innovative »Southern cuisine«.

► **Moderate**
Dharma Blue
300 S. Alcaniz Street
Tel. (850) 433-1275
Light and wholesome »fusion cuisine«. The terrace is especially nice.

► **Budget**
Flounder's Chowder House
800 Quietwater Beach Rd.
Tel. (850) 932-2003
Fresh fish and seafood – and the brilliant sunset from the terrace is for free.

WHERE TO STAY

► **Mid-range**

Baedeker recommendation

Clarion Suites & Convention Center
20 Via de Luna Drive, Pensacola Beach
Tel. (850) 932-4300, Fax (850) 934-9112
www.clarionsuitesresort.com
Not a giant hotel block, as one might presume from the name, but an expansive resort right on the beach consisting of pretty cottages with verandas and kitchenettes.

Pensacola Grand Hotel
200 E. Gregory Street
Tel. (850) 433-3336,
Fax (850) 432-7572
www.pensacolagrandhotel.com
212 rooms and suites
A 15-storey building with spacious rooms and a unique past: the lobby was originally a railway depot.

► **Budget**
Seville Inn & Suites
223 E. Garden Street
Tel. (850) 433-8331
Fax (850) 432-6849
126 rooms
Pleasant modern rooms near the historic district in town.

What to See in Pensacola

Seville District ✳

What a conglomeration of people! When Pensacola began to grow up at the end of the 17th century it was the meeting place of Indians, freed slaves, white settlers from the most varied backgrounds and all sorts of seafarers from the Caribbean. They plied their trades at the harbour jetty of Seville District east of Palafox Street. The most successful then settled in ostentatious residences in the quarter bordered by Government Street, Adams Street, Tarragona Street and Alcanz Street.

Historic Pensacola Village ✳

About **two dozen lovingly restored buildings** today form Historic Pensacola Village (hours: Tue–Sat 10am–4pm), the city's largest attraction. The village is characterized by Spanish, Creole and British colonial architecture. Dorr House (311 Adams St.) was built in 1871 and is a rare example of the Greek Revival style in Florida. Lavalle House (205 E Church St.) was built in 1805 by Carlos Lavalle in the so-called French Creole style and has furnishings from this period. Julee Cottage (210 E Zaragoza St.), a modest, leaning wooden house dating from 1804 belonged to Julee Panton, a freed black slave. A few steps further the Museum of Industry (200 E Zaragoza St.), housed in an old railway car, is dedicated to the development of industry in this part of Florida. Right next door in an old warehouse the Museum of Commerce (201 E. Zaragoza St.) presents the development of transportation by means of a reconstructed street scene

Spanish colonial architecture on Seville Square in Pensacola

from 1890. Lear-Rocheblave House (214 E. Zaragoza St.), also nearby, dates from 1890; it is a beautiful Victorian house surrounded by a veranda. A few blocks away the Pensacola Historical Museum is dedicated to the eventful history of the city (115 E Zaragoza St.; hours: Mon–Sat 10am–4pm).

The historic business district of Pensacola runs from the harbour to Wright Street. Many of the beautiful houses are **reminiscent of New Orleans**: wrought-iron balconies decorate the façades, pedestrians stroll under shady arcades. Spanish neo-Renaissance and Mediterranean styles predominate, especially at Palafox Square, the heart of the old city centre. The Saenger Theater (118 Palafox St.), which opened in 1925, is worth a visit. Its opulent terracotta ornaments are a beautiful example of Spanish neo-Baroque. If it is open, go inside: the interior is even more extravagant!

✶
Palafox Historic Business District

Only a few steps further there is an opportunity, rare in Florida, to find out about the Civil War. The Civil War Soldiers Museum (108 S Palafox Place; hours: Tue–Sat 10am–4pm) has the collection of a Pensacola doctor and documents the every day life of the recruits and the city's role in the bloody conflict. On Plaza Ferdinand T.T. Wentworth Jr. Florida State Museum was built in 1907 as a neo-Renaissance palace with red roof tiles. It is devoted to the history of the Florida Panhandle. The Jackson Memorial in front of the museum commemorates the swashbuckling American general who took over Florida here from the Spaniards in 1821.

◄ Civil War Soldiers Museum
🕑

Around Pensacola

You can't help but be impressed: this is one of the largest and most interesting air and space museums in the world. The halls and hangars on the grounds of the Naval Air Station (NAS) a few miles southwest of the city centre display more than 100 aircraft from almost 100 years of American naval flying. The exhibits range from biplanes from World War I to Hornet fighters that were used only recently in the Near East. Sea planes, the bridge of an aircraft carrier, the deep-blue jets of the famous aerobatic and formation team Blue Angels and the command capsule of the space lab Skylab, which was flown by navy pilots, are highlights of the exhibition. The IMAX cinema screens films on the everyday life of a jet pilot (1750 Radford Blvd.; hours: daily 9am–5pm).

✶ ✶
National Museum of Naval Aviation

🕑

Pensacola's natural harbour was so important to the city fathers that they had four forts built to protect it from enemy attacks. Fort Barrancas, on a cliff above the harbour entrance which looks across to Perdido Key and Santa Rosa Island, was built between 1834 and 1844 by American troops on the foundations of British and Spanish forts and is open to the public today in conjunction with a visit to the National Museum of Naval Aviation (see above; hours: daily 9am to 5pm).

✶
◄ Fort Barrancas

🕑

Legendary Blue Angels jets on display at the National Museum of Naval Aviation

★★
Santa Rosa Island, Perdido Key

Lucky residents and guests of Pensacola! Right in front of their porches are the fine white sandy beaches of two barrier islands – Perdido Key and Santa Rosa Island, which is only a few hundred yards wide but about 50mi/80km long, extending all the way to ▶ Fort Walton. Sections of special historical or ecological interest are part of the Gulf Islands National Seashore.

★
Pensacola Beach ▶

From Pensacola drive across the 3mi/5km-long Pensacola Bridge to the suburb of Gulf Breeze on the spit of land between the bay and the gulf. From there a short bridge connects to Santa Rosa Island. Right behind this bridge lies the seaside resort of Pensacola Beach; along the white beach the chain of snack bars, restaurants, taverns, hotels, motels, giant apartment blocks, t-shirt stands as well as bike and surfboard rentals seems endless. There is also a 400m/1,300ft-long pier.

> ! **Baedeker TIP**
>
> **Sunset with manta and dolphins**
> The best way to end the day: while the sun sinks spectacularly into the Gulf of Mexico, dolphins and mantas cavort in the sea. Pensacola Beach Pier is the best place to watch this show.

★
Fort Pickens ▶
⏱

At the western end of Santa Rosa Island the imposing Fort Pickens (tours: March–Oct daily 9.30am–5pm) stands guard on the white sand. Built in 1834, the fortress defended the entrance to the harbour along with Fort McRee on Perdido Island opposite and Fort

Barrancas on the mainland. The massive ruins, especially the dark corridors and courtyards deserve a closer look. A small museum is dedicated to the most famous prisoner at Fort Pickens: from 1886 to 1888 the Apache chief Geronimo was imprisoned here with 17 of his braves.

Only a 20-minute drive north-east of Pensacola, this forest is famous for its rivers Juniper Creek, Sweetwater Creek, Coldwater River and Blackwater River. The town of Milton on the southern edge of the forest took advantage of this by calling itself the »canoeing capital of Florida«. Indeed, canoeing tours on the rivers meandering through untouched forests are a delight. In Milton several tour organizers rent canoes and kayaks, and also offer day trips or longer tours.

★
Blackwater River State Forest

★ Perry

F 2

Region: North Central
Population: 7,000

Elevation: 13m/42ft above sea level
Area code: 850

An old part of Florida lies on the route to the Panhandle. This land was not developed by railway barons and their friends but by farmers and day-labourers, the »Florida Crackers«. In Perry a museum is dedicated to the people who helped make the land of Florida cultivable.

The city fathers have proudly named their town the »Tree Capital of the South«. In this way they commemorate Perry's role in the lumber boom around 1900. The region's wealth of lumber was recognized at the end of the 19th century; the settlement that was founded in 1857 became the centre of the industry. The production of turpentine was another important forest industry, but by the end of the 1930s large parts of the region

? DID YOU KNOW …?

■ The Crackers were the first white settlers in Florida. The expression »Cracker« comes from whip cracks, with which the poor pioneers drove their cattle and yoked oxen.

were deforested. Sawmills and paper factories had to close, and many people moved away. Today US 98 keeps the place alive: with its motels along the highway Perry is a welcome break for tourists on the way south.

What to See in and around Perry

The museum was opened in 1973 in fragrant woods south of town and gives an impression of the development of forestry and the lumber industry in Florida. The most important types of trees are pre-

★
Forest Capital State Museum & Cracker Homestead

● VISITING PERRY

INFORMATION

Perry-Taylor County
Chamber of Commerce
428 N. Jefferson Street
Perry, FL 32347
Tel. (850) 584-5366
www.taylorcountychamber.com

EVENT

In October the Florida Forest Festival takes place with various events related to forestry (like sawing contests), exhibitions and music.

WHERE TO EAT

▶ **Moderate/Inexpensive**
Roy's Restaurant
Steinhatchee, on Hwy. 51
Tel. (352) 498-5000
Popular venue for locals and tourists. It has a giant salad bar and good fish dishes.

WHERE TO STAY

▶ **Mid-range**
Steinhatchee
Landing Resort
228 NE Hwy 51
Steinhatchee, FL 32359
Tel. (352) 498-3513
www.steinhatcheelanding.com
29 cosy Cracker-style cottages.

▶ **Budget**
Days Inn Perry
2277 S. Byron Butler Parkway
Perry, FL 32348
Tel. (850) 584-5311
www.daysinn.com
60 rooms
Centrally located motel with spacious and well furnished rooms as well as a nice outdoor swimming pool.

sented ,as well as a broad selection of products made from wood fibre or tree sap. The exhibition focuses on the history of local forestry and the production of turpentine. Next to the museum there is a reconstructed Cracker homestead with its outbuildings. In 1863 a pioneer family settled here and earned their living from the forest industry typical to the area. The main house is a simple log cabin with the veranda and outside kitchen typical of the South. The entire farmstead is surrounded by a log fence (204 Forest Park Dr., US 19/ 27A/98; hours: Thu–Mon 9am–noon and 1pm–5pm).

Keaton Beach, Steinhatchee

A charming side trip goes via CR-361 south to the Gulf Coast, which is still largely undeveloped here and thus called the Lost Coast. A drive of about 20mi/35km leads to the beautiful Keaton Beach, site of a very popular restaurant. 20mi/35km further on the somewhat dusty lumber and fishing settlement of Steinhatchee (population 800) at the mouth of the river of the same name, which is a centre of sports fishing. Steinhatchee was founded in the 1870s, as the first settlers brought cedars that had been cut down in the hinterland to the coast, tied them into rafts and floated them along the coast to ▶Cedar Key. Meanwhile tourism has arrived.

✶ ✶ St Augustine

Region: North-east
Population: 13,000

Elevation: 0 – 10m/30ft above sea level
Area code: 904

This beautifully tended settlement on Matanzas Bay welcomes visitors with open arms. European guests especially find this to be true. They feel at home immediately under the palm trees of the old town, which could easily be in Spain or Mexico. No wonder: St Augustine is the oldest city in North America, and its residents are the most history-conscious of Floridans.

Narrow, winding alleys, Spanish houses with wrought-iron gates that lead to shady inner courtyards, romantic balconies and expansive plazas with palmettos and trees covered in Spanish moss: St Augustine is a trip through time. It started in 1513 with Ponce de León. In that year the Spanish seafarer arrived – supposedly, since there is no evidence to sustain the claim – here on »pascua florida« (Easter Sunday) and claimed it for his king, naming it »Florida«. However, only when the French settled further north near today's ► Jacksonville did the Spanish government remember what it had. With orders to kill all Protestants in the New World, General Don Pedro Menéndez de Avíles landed here in 1565 with 600 soldiers. After founding the Castillo de San Augustín he led his army northwards, burned down the French Fort Caroline and annihilated everyone in the fort.

Then the Spanish settlement of St Augustine developed into the administrative base for about 30 Spanish bases on the Florida peninsula. The settlement was attacked repeatedly by pirates looking for booty. One of the most famous buccaneers, Sir Francis Drake, plundered the growing colonial city in 1586. John Davis, another pirate,

Oldest city in the USA

Highlights in *St Augustine*

Castillo de San Marcos
This masterpiece of Spanish colonial fortification protected the city and secured the sea passages for Spanish ships returning home.
► page 307

Old Town
The historic old city of St Augustine has been restored and maintained beautifully; several very interesting museums attract visitors.
► page 310

Old St Augustine Village Museum
Do not miss this museum. It comprises a whole block of historic buildings from various periods of city history.
► page 311

Anastasia Island
From St Augustine cross the Bridge of Lions to the barrier island with its brilliant beaches.
► page 313

⏵ VISITING ST AUGUSTINE

INFORMATION

St Augustine, Ponte Vedra & The Beaches VCB
88 Riberia Street
St Augustine, FL 32084
Tel. (904) 829-1711
www.getaway4florida.com

PARKING

Parking space is extremely rare in St Augustine. It is best to park in the garage with Spanish colonial-style architecture on the northern edge of the old city (6 S. Castillo Drive).

CITY TOUR

The old town can easily be explored on foot. The visitor centres (10 Castillo Drive, hours daily 8am–5.30pm) at the large parking lot on the northern edge of the old city and at Castillo des San Marcos provide maps of the town. »Sightseeing trains« and horse-drawn carriages start from there.

WHERE TO EAT

► Moderate
① **Harry's Seafood Bar & Grill**
46 Av. Menendez
Tel. (904) 824-7765
Hearty and spicy southern specialties and wonderful fish dishes – including lobster and shrimps – are served here.

► Budget
② **O. C. White's**
118 Av. Menendez
Tel. (904) 824-0808
Popular venue for local people and tourists, who enjoy the coconut shrimps, Caribbean chicken or even a Porterhouse steak.

③ **Spanish Bakery**
St Augustine Beach
42½ St George Street
Tel. (904) 471-3046
Tasty snacks and good lunches.

WHERE TO STAY

► Luxury
① **Casa Monica**
95 Cordova Street
Tel. (904) 827-1888
Fax (904) 819-6065
www.casamonica.com
138 rooms and suites
The castle-like hotel was built in 1888 and re-opened in 1999 after comprehensive renovation and modernization. Spanish colonial ambience, first-class service.

► Budget/Mid-range
② **Best Western Spanish Quarter Inn**
6 Castillo Drive
Tel. (904) 824-4457
Fax (904) 829-8330
www.bestwestern.com
40 Zimmer
Comfortable accommodation near Castillo de San Marcos. The old town is within walking distance.

③ **Ramada Inn**
116 San Marco Avenue
Tel. (904) 824-4352
Fax (904) 824-2745
www.ramadainnhistoric.com
100 rooms
This well-run modern house is located at the edge of the old town.

The Old St Augustine Village Museum (246 St George St.; hours: Mon–Sat 10am–4.30pm, Sun 11am–4.30pm) is a highlight. The ensemble consists of ten historic buildings in their original locations. They were built between the late 18th century to the early 20th century and thus represent some of the important periods of city history. The oldest building is also the most interesting: built in 1790, the Prince Murat House was the home of Achille Murat, Napoléon's nephew and Prince of Naples. Exiled from post-Napoleonic France, the prince occupied the house in 1824 and then stayed here several times thereafter. A small exhibitions displays correspondence between Murat and Napoleon Bonaparte as well as some nice reports on the prince's charismatic personality.

★ ★
Old St Augustine Village Museum

The two stone lions that guard the photogenic Bridge of Lions can be seen from the cathedral. The Spanish-Moorish style drawbridge over the bay has connected the old city with the beaches on Anastasia Island since 1927. It is presently being restored thoroughly.

★
Bridge of Lions

South of the plaza there are more attractions for visitors. The Spanish Military Hospital, however, is no for the faint-hearted. Guides full of anecdotes describe the military hospital from the second Spanish colonial period and can tell grisly stories about each of the surgical instruments (3 Avíles St.; hours: Mon–Sat 10am–5pm, Sun noon–5pm).

Spanish Military Hospital

🕐

Casa Gonzales is probably the oldest house in the USA.

Oldest House – Casa González-Alvarez

✳ The »oldest house« in St Augustine is easy to recognize by the four flags hanging outside, which flew over the city in the last 400 years. The complex consists of several buildings and is named Casa González-Alvarez after its two owners, whose beginnings go back to 1702, as well as a house that now holds the Manucy Museum of St Augustine History. It exhibits old maps and photos and various items from the Spanish colonial period (14 St Frances St.; hours: daily 9am–5pm).

Lightner Museum

✳ From the southern edge of the Plaza de la Constitución King Street leads out of the Spanish colonial centre of St Augustine towards the west. A few minutes' walk behind Government House is the Lightner Museum. It is housed in the luxurious Alcazar Hotel, which was built in the flamboyant style of the railway magnate Flagler and then went broke during the Depression in the 1920s.

The representative building holds the collections of the Chicago publisher Otto Lightner, who bought the empty hotel in 1948. Several floors hold everything from Egyptian mummies to stuffed birds, rare minerals, historic steam engines and automatic musical instruments (75 King St.; hours: daily 9am–5pm).

Flagler College ▶ Once there do not miss the artistic Tiffany stained-glass windows of Flagler College with its towers, diagonally opposite. This building was once the legendary Ponce de León Hotel.

Zorayda Castle

Also on the south side of King Street, but beyond Granada Street, a large palace was built in the Moorish style in 1883. It is modelled after the Alhambra in Granada. Various antiquities are exhibited here as well, including a more than 2,000-year-old Egyptian carpet with a cat pattern (83 King St.; hours: daily 9am–5pm).

What to See outside the Old Town

Fountain of Youth Archeological Park

In 1513 – as far as the legend and the local advertising goes – Ponce de León landed here, north of today's Castillo, in order to search for the mythical fountain of youth. He did not find the fountain, but archaeologists found the remains of a pre-Columbian Timuacan Indian village. A guided tour shows gardens, excavation sites and the fountain, whose story was just too good for it not to be »reconstructed«. The place has all the marks of a tourist trap, but despite the kitsch it also possesses charm (11 Magnolia Ave.; hours: daily 9am–5pm).

Mission of Nombre de Dios

The grounds of the first mission station in North America facing the Intracoastal Waterway are a nice place to relax. In 1565 Pedro de Menéndez de Avíles is supposed to have landed and celebrated the first mass in America with his priests here. Along with the church and a 63m/210ft cross the little chapel of Our Lady of La Leche is worth looking at. It is the oldest church in the USA dedicated to the Virgin (27 Ocean Ave.; hours: daily 8am–5.30pm).

Around St Augustine

From St Augustine highway A1A crosses the Bridge of Lions to a narrow barrier island off the coast. Anastasia Island is known for its enchanting beaches and high dunes. The nicest is St Augustine Beach in Anastasia State Recreational Area. Unfortunately large parts of the dunes are now covered with holiday houses, but there are regular gaps that make the beaches accessible.

✷ ✷
Anastasia Island

> ## ❗ *Baedeker* TIP
>
> ### A good wine ...
>
> Spanish monks were the first to grow grapes for wine here. In 1996 the San Sebastian Winery followed, which now produces table wines, champagne and sherry (157 King St., tel. 904/826 - 1594, hours Mo–Sa 10am–6pm).

Just a few miles beyond the bridge there is an interesting alligator farm. Large reptiles have been raised here since 1893. The unchallenged star is Maximo, an Australian crocodile almost six metres (20 feet) long. There are also several albino alligators from Louisiana. Colourful waders, geese, swans and cranes can be seen in swamps and ponds (999 Anastasia Blvd.; hours: daily 9am–5pm).

St Augustine Alligator Farm Zoological Park ⏲

Not far from the alligator farm is a 50m/165ft-high lighthouse built in 1874 on the foundations of the previous lighthouse; its black and white spiral motif makes it a popular photo motif and its observation platform offers a wonderful panoramic view. But be warned: 219 steps have to be climbed to get to the top! The lovingly restored lighthouse-keeper's house has a little exhibition on the hard life of the lighthouse-keeper (81 Lighthouse Ave.; hours: daily 9am–6pm).

✷ St Augustine Lighthouse & Museum ⏲

About 14mi/22km south of St Augustine lies a small Spanish fort that was built in the entry to the Intracoastal Waterway. In 1565 the slaughter of the French Huguenots by the Spanish took place here; the French had built Fort Caroline further to the north at the mouth of the St John's River. From the visitor centre on the A1A a park ranger takes visitors to the fort by boat.

✷ Fort Matanzas

About 20mi/32km south of St Augustine, on the other side of the Matanzas Inlet, highway A1A runs to **Marineland of Florida**, which was renovated thoroughly in 2005. This tourist attraction originally opened in the 1930s and is thus one of the oldest of its kind. The

Fort Matanzas from the Spanish colonial period

🕐 park stages programmes with dolphins. Every effort is made to offer ecology-friendly tourism (hours: daily 8.30am–4.30pm).

✳
Flagler Beach A few miles to the south lies the superb, largely undeveloped Flagler Beach with its dunes, a good place for recreation. In the summer sea turtles lay their eggs in protected areas.

✳
World Golf Village & Hall of Fame About 12mi/20km north of St Augustine a super-modern golfing meccawas opened in 1998 right on the I-95. The core of the facility with two 18-hole golf courses is a luxury hotel and the Golf Hall of Famewith an IMAX cinema. The most famous golfers of all time are commemorated and the development of the sport with the little white
🕐 ball is presented (hours: Mon–Sat 10am–6pm, Sun noon–6pm).

✳ ✳ St Petersburg

G 5

Region: Central West	**Elevation:** 0 – 14m/46ft above sea level
Population: 255,000	**Area code:** 727

Juan Ponce de León would probably turn over in his grave: the fountain of youth that the Spanish sea-farer searched for in vain is in St Petersburg. Really in St Petersburg? In Florida's most famous residence for senior citizens? Yes, since the residents have gotten 10 years younger in the last three decades; the average age now is 39.

Successful rejuvenation
Of course, St Petersburg cheated a bit. Since there was no spring that promises eternal youth, it began to attract high-tech businesses in the 1990s. The young hardware and software developers stirred up the nightlife in the otherwise quiet pensioners' colony. New trend hotels, gourmet restaurants and bistros accelerated the rejuvenation. The skyline grew, too. Since 1998 the city has invested 1.5 billion dollars in apartment and office buildings. It added new concert arenas, a modernized event calendar with top-class events and a dozen new art galleries. Today both senior citizens and punks with rainbow-coloured hair enjoy »St Pete«. But St Petersburg has kept its unique charm despite changing its appearance: downtown its palm tree-lined streets open to Tampa Bay and still have the aura of a seaside resort. The pelicans still sit in a line along the pier and in the yacht harbour; sailboats anchor off shore, and dolphins play in the surf.

History
In 1875 General John Williams from Detroit bought about 700ha/1,700acres of land on the Pinellas Peninsula in order to build a holiday resort with beautiful parks and broad boulevards. 13 years later his vision grew with the arrival of the Orange Belt Railway of the Russian entrepreneur Peter Demens. The Russian named the city after his hometown: St Petersburg.

► VISITING ST PETERSBURG

INFORMATION

St Petersburg/Clearwater Area Convention & Visitors Bureau
13805 58th St. N., Suite 2-200
Clearwater, FL 33760
Tel. (727) 464-7200
Fax (727) 464-7222
www.floridasbeach.com

SHOPPING

BayWalk
153 2nd Avenue North
The BayWalk Entertainment Center gave the somewhat quiet city centre the necessary vitamin shot a few years ago. Apart from trend boutiques the shopping centre, built in the Californian mission style, also has restaurants, bars and cinemas as well as beautiful courtyards for relaxing.

Haslam's Book Store
2025 Central Avenue
Hours: Mon–Sat 10am–6.30pm
Florida's largest bookstore is a must for bookworms: Haslam's Book Store in St Petersburg has more than 350,000 new and used books!

NIGHT LIFE

BayWalk
The new BayWalk Entertainment Center in St Petersburg with its restaurants, bars and cinemas is a good address in the evening and at night, too.

Jannus Landing Courtyard
220 1st Avenue North
Tel. (727) 896-1244
Famous musicians appear all year round in this wonderful outdoor arena in St Petersburg.

Coliseum Ballroom
535 4th Ave.; tel. (727) 892-5202

This wonderfully old-fashioned ballroom is where St Petersburg's seniors dance the »Java« etc.

EVENTS

Fun 'n Sun Festival
A colourful programme including a bathtub regatta in April or May on Clearwater Beach.

Kahlua Cup
In November the Clearwater Yacht Club sponsors a regatta and the coveted cup for sailors from all over the world.

DOLPHIN WATCHING

Hubbard's Sea Adventures
Madeira Beach
John's Pass Village
Tel. (727) 393-1947
The best dolphin-watching tours in the area.

WHERE TO EAT

► **Expensive**

Baedeker recommendation

① **Marchland's Grill**
in the Renaissance Vinoy Resort
501 5th Ave. NE
St Petersburg
Tel. (727) 894-1000
Nostalgic elegance and French-Mediterranean inspired cuisine: the gnocchi with wild mushrooms and the bouillabaisse are especially to be recommended.

► **Moderate**
② **Bridie Gannon's Pub**
200 E Tarpon Ave.
Tarpon Springs
Tel. (727) 942-3011

St Petersburg Downtown Map

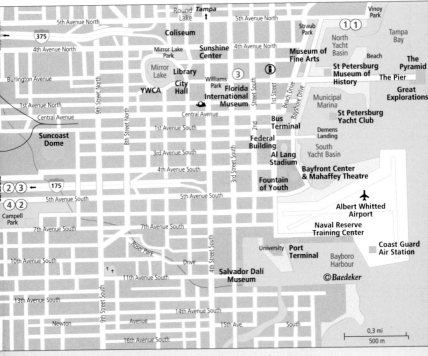

Where to stay
① Renaissance Vinoy Resort
② Don CeSar
③ The Heritage Holiday Inn
④ Beach Heaven

Where to eat
① Marchand's Grill
② Bridie Gannon's Pub
③ Hurricane

Shepherd's pie and Irish dishes. Live music on weekends.

▶ **Budget**

③ *Hurricane*
807 Gulf Way, Pass-a-Grille
St Pete Beach
Tel. (727) 360-9558
www.thehurricane.com
Fine dining in a beautiful Victorian house. Fish and seafood as well as aperitifs are also served on the roof terrace.

WHERE TO STAY

▶ **Luxury**

① *Renaissance Vinoy Resort*
St Petersburg
501 5th Ave. NE
Tel. (727) 894-1000
Fax (727) 822-2785
www.renaissancehotels.com
360 rooms and suites
The best inn downtown with its own golf course tempts guest with Mediterranean elegance. Many VIPs have stayed here.

② **The Don CeSar**
Beach Resort & Spa
St Pete Beach, 3400 Gulf Blvd.
Tel. (727) 360-1881
Fax (727) 367-6952
www.doncesar.com
350 rooms and suites
Cool marble floors and elegant stucco ceilings, wonderfully furnished rooms and suites with an ocean view: the landmark of St Pete Beach offers pure luxury with lots of culture.

► **Mid-range**
③ **The Heritage Holiday Inn**
St Petersburg
234 3rd Ave. N.

Fax (727) 823-1644
www.theheritagehi.com
81 rooms
The former Martha Washington Hotel has managed to preserve its old-fashioned charm under the management of Holiday Inn.

④ **Beach Heaven**
4980 Gulf Boulevard
St Pete Beach
Tel. (727) 367-8642
Fax (727) 360-8202
www.beachhavenvillas.com
18 rooms and suites.
Pink and turquoise Art Deco inn on the beach.

Outdoor dining in »St Pete«

The invention of air conditioning in the 1950s made the city more attractive to seniors and it soon became a pensioners' colony. But since the 1990s the city has worked successfully on changing its image. The weather helped. The sun shines here almost every day, a fact that earned St Petersburg an entry into the Guinness Book of Records.

What to See in St Petersburg

★★
The Pier

The landmark of St Petersburg – and the best place for people-watching – reaches 730m/2,400ft into Tampa Bay. Something is always going on here. It starts at the five-storey pyramid with various restaurants, shops and souvenir stands. Its observation terrace offers a good view of the city skyline (800 2nd Ave. NE; hours: Mon–Thu 10am–9pm, Fri, Sat 10am–10pm, Sun 11am–7pm).

★
St Petersburg Museum of History

How old – and yet young – the city is can be seen in the permanent and the rotating exhibitions. The people who made »St Pete« can be seen here: the first citrus farmers, angry creditors chasing the highly indebted Peter Demens, the seaplane that began commercial flight here in 1914 (at the beginning of the sea bridge, 335 2nd Ave.; hours: Mon noon–7pm, Tue–Sat 10am–5pm, Sun 1pm–5.30pm).

Masterpieces by Salvador Dalí in St Petersburg

This museum is housed in a former department store and cooperates with the Smithsonian Institution; it puts on exhibitions on exciting periods of history. One such exhibition on the Cuban crisis was so successful while it ran that it has been installed as a permanent feature. Other recent favourites have been: the Sinking of the Titanic, Alexander the Great, The Treasures of the Czars (100 2nd St. N.; hours: Mon–Sat 10am–5pm, Sun 1pm–5pm).

★
Florida International Museum
🕐

One block north of the pier a neo-classical villa holds an exquisite art collection. It covers works from antiquity to items from pre-Columbian America, Far Eastern art, famous French impressionists and modern American artists like Georgia O`Keeffe (255 Beach Dr. NE; hours: Tue–Sat 10am–5pm, Sun 1pm–5pm).

★
Museum of Fine Arts
🕐

South of downtown a modern gallery has dedicated itself since 1982 to the work of the Catalan Surrealist Salvador Dalí (1904–89). The exhibition shows 95 oil paintings, more than 100 drawings and water colours, prints and sculptures by Salvador Dalí from 1914 to 1980. These include several masterpieces like *The Ecumenical Council*, *The Persistence of Memory* (»melting clocks«) and The First Days of Spring. A large library with publications on Dali and Surrealism is attached to the museum (1000 3rd St. S.; hours: Mon, Tue, Wed, Sat 9.30am–5.30pm, Thu 9.30am–8pm, Fri 9.30am–6.30pm, Sun noon–5.30pm).

★ ★
Salvador Dalí Museum
🕐

The Sunken Gardens are located north of the city centre. They were built in the 1930s and are the home of abundant tropical and subtropical vegetation and a fine large butterfly aviary. There are also daily shows with trained parrots (1825 4th St. N.; hours: Mon–Sat 10am–4.30pm, Sun noon–4.30pm).

★
Sunken Gardens
🕐

Pinellas Suncoast

St Petersburg Beaches, Pinellas County Beaches, Holiday Islands: there are various names for the 50km/30mi-long Gulf Coast of the Pinellas Peninsula's barrier islands. With 361 sunny days a year and snow-white endless beaches their future was determined: the leisure industry has covered them with hotels, restaurants, marinas, diving, fishing and other water sports facilities, so much so that the communities merge with each other. American families and European package-tour travellers are the target audience of all this, since they appreciate the proximity of Florida's top amusement parks. The at-

Holiday paradise

! **Baedeker TIP**

Bikers and skaters watch out!
Instead of driving along the »Sun Coast« in stop-and-go traffic, try a bike or even roller skates on the 50m/80km long Pinellas Trail. This paved bicycle path follows an old railway line and connects St Petersburg with Tarpon Springs. It isn't that busy yet either.

mosphere is accordingly noisy and informal. Many beaches are so full in the winter that traffic moves at a snail's pace. But there are also quieter and less developed parts.

✳ **St Pete Beach**

It all started in St Petersburg's resort. Tourists bathed here in the bath-water warm Gulf of Mexico as much as one hundred years ago. Several causeways lead across Boca de Ciega Bay to the six-mile-long beaches of the traditional resort town. Watersports lovers are spoiled for choice here: everything goes! The landmark is the pink Don Cesar Resort (3400 Gulf Blvd.) on the beach. This luxury hotel is decorated with Moorish elements and slender towers; a few years ago it was renovated at a cost of millions and is now once again resplendent in the atmosphere of the 1920s. Pass-a-Grille is adjacent to the south on a small spit of land. This beach belonging to a French fishing town that was founded in 1911 is a bit quieter and has an undisturbed view of the islands in Tampa Bay.

✳ **Fort DeSoto Park**

South of Pass-a-Grille lies Mullet Key, an island that guards the entrance to Tampa Bay. The nature reserve for birds and plants is named after the massive Fort DeSoto, which was built here in 1898 at the time of the Spanish-American War. However it was spared its baptism of fire since the war was ended before the fort was completed.

✳ **From St Pete Beach to Sand Key**

North of St Pete Beach lies **Treasure Island**, a 3.5/6km mi-long barrier island that is connected to the mainland by two bridges. The name is reminiscent of earlier times when pirates hid here; settlers dug up almost the whole island looking for buried pirate treasure. Here, as on the neighbouring Madeira Beach, beach tourism is important. Madeira Beach also has St John's Pass Village, a fishing village built in early 20th-century style, where a creaking wooden sidewalk leads to pretty little shops, pleasant fish restaurants and bars. Boating trips and dolphin-watching tours can be undertaken from here, too.

Family oriented attractions lie to the north: **Reddington Beach**, North Reddington Beach and Reddington Shores. A change from sunbathing can be found in Indian Shores at the Suncoast Seabird Sanctuary (18328 Gulf Blvd.; hours: daily 9am–sunset), which opened in 1971. It is the largest clinic for wounded birds in the USA, caring for cranes, pelicans and ibis as well as seabirds. Most of the injuries are caused by direct or indirect contact with people: pollution and fishing lines are the most common culprits.

The next of the barrier islands is **Sand Key**, the longest on this section of coastline, where an incredibly beautiful beach surrounded by palm groves, Sand Key Park (1060 Gulf Blvd.), makes a dive into the surf irresistible.

Pure relaxation: the Don CeSar Resort on the beach at St Petersburg →

Clearwater Beach

Opposite Sand Key Park lies Clearwater Beach, the next holiday island that is completely dedicated to sun-worshippers. Several miles of the finest sand beaches are bordered by hotels, motels, restaurants and organizers of all sorts of fun sports. The seaside resort of the same name, which lies on a narrow stretch of sand between the Gulf and Clearwater Harbor, appears much more relaxed with its quiet side streets than the neighbouring communities. Locals and tourists meet at Clearwater Public Beach with its 330m/1,100ft-long pier. The sunsets here are fabulous.

The Clearwater Marine Aquarium is worth seeing. Injured dolphins, sea lions and sea otters are cared for here (249 Windward Passage; hours: Mon–Sat 9am–5pm, Sun 10am–5pm).

Caladesi & Honeymoon Islands

The island hopping ends in Clearwater Beach. Cross Memorial Causeway to get back to the mainland and continue north. Just before Dunedin there is an unusual sight: undeveloped, natural islands! In 1921 Caladesi Island and Honeymoon Island were torn apart by a hurricane and then made into state parks. They show what the barrier islands looked like 120 years ago. Honeymoon Island can be reached via Causeway Boulevard (toll) and has wonderful beaches with showers and changing rooms.

A boat runs to Caladesi Island, whose beaches appear regularly in the lists of best beaches found in lifestyle magazines. Caladesi Island is also one of the places in Florida where sea turtles can lay their eggs undisturbed on the beach on summer nights. Park rangers conduct nature walks on this subject.

Tarpon Springs

Tarpon Springs (population 24,000) at the northern end of the Pinellas Suncoast, with its Greek flair, is the most unusual site on the

Natural sponges of all sizes on sale in Tarpon Springs

Suncoast. Canals called »bayous« wind through the town. Restaurants and bakeries have Greek names, and Greek music spills out of the dark kafenions. One third of the population is of Greek origin, and descended from the Greek sponge divers who came here around 1900 from Key West. They began to harvest natural sponges from the sponge reefs on a large scale using the know-how that they brought along from the Aegean. In 1939 the local sponge-diving fleet had about 200 boats. But the next year bacteria attacked the sponge reefs and at the same time the production of synthetic sponges ruined the market for natural sponges. Only recently has the demand for natural sponges revived the business.

A stroll along this boulevard is charming. In the old Sponge Docks natural sponges are for sale. St Nicholas Boat Line (693 Dodecanese Blvd., tel. (727) 942-6425) offers half-hour boat tours and explains everything about the local sponge industry. In the Konger Coral Sea Aquarium (850 Dodecanese Blvd.; hours: Mon–Sat 10am–5pm, Sun noon–5pm) divers can be watched feeding sharks and tarpons several times a day.

✶
◀ Dodecanes Boulevard

⏱

Spongeorama (510 Dodecanes Blvd.; hours: daily 10am–5pm) also informs on the local sponge industry and about the Greek immigration one hundred years ago.

◀ Spongeorama
⏱

This church was dedicated in 1943 and copies Hagia Sophia in Constantinople; it is worth a stop. It is decorated with icons and Greek marble (Pinellas Ave./Orange St.; hours: daily 10am–4pm).

✶
◀ St Nicholas Orthodox Cathedral

This masterpiece of engineering, a 20km/12mi-long highway on stilts (I-275/US 19; toll), curves elegantly across the entrance to Tampa Bay. The core is a 7km/4mi-long bridge whose centre is suspended from two giant pylons, which allow ocean-going ships to pass.
The old bridge was rammed in 1980 by a freighter and collapsed partially. Several cars plunged into the water and more than 30 people were killed. Today parts of the old bridge serve as a fishing pier.

✶
Sunshine Skyway

✶ ✶ Sanibel & Captiva Islands

G 6

Region: South-west
Population: 6,000

Elevation: 0 – 2m/7ft above sea level
Area code: 239

No house is higher than the palm trees. In view of the wonderful beaches, this might suggest that the islanders are insular and unwelcoming. In fact they took revenge in the 1970s for the bridge that was built from the mainland in 1963 against their will with the strictest land-use laws in Florida. Thus there are no hotel or apartment blocks here, but only smiling and mostly very wealthy people.

▶ VISITING SANIBEL AND CAPTIVA

INFORMATION

Sanibel & Captiva Islands Chamber of Commerce
1159 Causeway Road
Sanibel Island, FL 33957
Tel. (239) 472-1080
Fax (239) 472-1070
www.sanibel-captiva.org

Lee County CVB
12800 University Drive
Fort Myers, FL 33907
Tel. (239) 338-3500
Fax (239) 334-1100
www.fortmyers-sanibel.com

PARKING

Parking spaces are scarce on the two islands, especially at the public beaches. During the high season the traffic is really bad.

BIKING

Probably the best way to get around on the two islands is on a bike. Sanibel alone has about 20mi/32km of bike paths. All of the attractions can be reached by bike from Periwinkle Way (main street on the island).

SHELL COLLECTING

The magic word here is »shelling«: every high tides brings new shells to the beaches of Sanibel and Captiva. They come in all shapes and colours. Empty shells may be taken along without restrictions, but living shells may not and the fines if caught are high. The best time to collect shells is from February to April.

BOATING EXCURSIONS

From the dock of the South Seas Plantation, excursion boats run to the neighbouring uninhabited and paradise-like islands Cabbage Key, Useppa Island, Boca Grande and Cayo Costa. Dolphins can be seen on such a tour as they play in front of the boat's bow.

WHERE TO EAT

▶ Expensive

Mad Hatter
Sanibel Island
6460 Sanibel-Captiva Rd.
Tel. (239) 472-0033
Romantic restaurant with a view of the Gulf of Mexico. Creative »fusion cuisine«, inspired by recipes from all over the world.

▶ Moderate

Mucky Duck
Captiva Island
Andy Rosse Lane
Tel. (239) 472-3434
English pub right on the beach. Great atmosphere, great sunsets.

▶ Budget

Hungry Heron
Sanibel Island
2330 Palm Ridge Rd
(in Palm Ridge Place)
Tel. (239) 395-2300
Giant sandwiches, homemade French fries. Popular venue for locals.

WHERE TO STAY

▶ Luxury

Casa Ybel Resort
Sanibel Island
2255 W Gulf Drive
Tel. (239) 472-3145
Fax (239) 472-2109
www.casaybelresort.com
114 suites
This holiday heaven right on the beach with its excellent restaurant is one of the best of its kind in the Sunshine State.

► Luxury/Mid-range
West Wind Inn
Sanibel Island
3345 West Gulf Drive
Tel. (239) 472-1541
Fax (239) 472-8134
www.westwindinn.com
103 rooms
Beautiful resort on the beach; many rooms have an enchanting view of the beach. Nice pool bar.

► Budget/Mid-range
Kona Kai Motel
Sanibel Island
1539 Periwinkle Way
Tel. (239) 472-1001
Fax (239) 472-2554
www.konakaimotel.com
13 rooms
Comfortable Polynesian-style motel with a large pool.

Natural beauty

Not even Hurricane Charley, which uprooted most of the cedars on Periwinkle Way, the main street on Sanibel Island, and tore the rest of the place apart in August 2004, could mar the natural beauty of the islands for good. There are no forests of billboards or neon lights on these two barrier islands that are connected by a bridge. Everything revolves around peace and quiet on this part of the southern Gulf Coast. It is not therefore not surprising if the residents might occasionally be unfriendly to tourists. In the winter months, especially, their paradise is full to bursting.

History

The two islands that are separated by the narrow Blind Pass were discovered early. Juan Ponce de León supposedly named the larger island Sanibel, after his queen San Ybel. No one really knows where the other name comes from. But this area used to be a popular refuge for pirates. It is said that José Gaspár, the most fearful of them, held kidnapped women captive on Captiva Island. Toward the end of the 19th century a few »Crackers« settled on the islands and tried to raise limes and coconuts, but without success. Then they tried tourism: in 1938 the first holiday resort opened.

Blue, yellow and green, and every shade between can be found on the island **beaches**. Sanibel Island has four public beaches, all of them on the Gulf side – five, counting the thoroughly acceptable Causeway Beaches by the bridge. Lighthouse Beach is at the east end of the island and also has a lighthouse of 1884 that can be viewed, a pretty pier and a board walkway through

Mangrove thicket on Sanibel

They are world famous: the shell-covered beaches of Sanibel.

★★
Beaches

the neighbouring wetlands. Gulfside City Park, accessible via Algiers Lane, has nice picnic benches under shady gnarled cedars and wonderful sand. Tarpon Bay Beach at the end of Tarpon Bay Rd. is a short walk away from the parking lot. Bowman's Beach, the quietest of the four, can be reached via Bowman's Beach Rd. and is the only beach with picnic grills – and quiet corners where even Americans might undress.

What to See on Sanibel

★★
Bailey-Matthews
Shell Museum

☉

Very interesting for nature lovers. More than 30,000 shells from all over the world and all the types that wash up on the beaches here are displayed. Crafts using shells are also on show, including some from Barbados and Mexico. Shell-collecting novices can have their finds identified (3075 Sanibel-Captiva Rd.; hours: daily 10am–5pm).

★
Sanibel Historical
Village &
Museum

Everyday life on the island 100 years ago is the subject of this open-air museum, which is made up of several buildings. A stroll through the palm-shaded grounds leads to the Rutland Home, a settler's house from 1913, to Bailey's General Store with an old gasoline pump and to Miss Charlotta's Tea Room. The museum employees like to tell anecdotes from Sanibel's past (850 Dunlop Rd.; hours: Nov–mid-Aug. Tue–Sat 10am–4pm).

★★
»Ding« Darling
National Wildlife
Refuge

This reserve, named after the popular caricaturist J. N. »Ding« Darling, protects 2,000ha/5,000 acres of untouched mangrove, marsh and swamp area on the side of the island facing the mainland. On the 5mi/8km-long Wildlife Drive tourists can watch countless migratory birds from their cars in the winter, and in the summer ibis, roseate spoonbill, grey heron as well as the almost-extinct white heron. A 2mi/3km-long walkway leads to observation points from where alligators and sea otters can be seen. In the modern visitor centre there is information on the nature preserve (1 Wildlife Drive; hours: daily 8am–sunset).

A paddling tour through the mangrove wilderness of the »Ding« Darling NWR is an authentic Florida experience. The visitor centre rents canoes.

What to See on Captiva

Captiva, five miles (8km) long and half a mile wide, is Sanibel's little sister. The few residents of the island mainly live from tourism.

Turner Beach at Blind Pass is the main reason for day visitors to come here: some come only because of the spectacular sunsets. The northern tip of the island is taken up by the luxurious South Seas Plantation Resort. On the grounds of a former copra plantation surrounded by thick mangrove forests, it is one of the best venues for tennis-playing visitors to Florida.

Excursion to Cabbage Key

From the South Seas Plantation Resort excursion boats sail north to the neighbouring Cabbage Key, where there are neither streets nor cars, but only a pier and Cabbage Key Inn with 6 rooms, 7 cottages and a restaurant. Jimmy Buffett is supposed to have been inspired by the cheeseburgers made here to compose his hit *Cheeseburger in Paradise*. The restaurant also has the most expensive wallpaper around: diners glue dollar bills to the wall. There are supposed to be about 25,000 dollars there now!

★ ★ Sarasota

G 5

Region: Central West
Population: 55,000

Elevation: 0 – 9m/30ft above sea level
Area code: 941

Before World War I wealthy visitors discovered what was then a sleepy fishing village with beautiful beaches. Since then Sarasota has evolved into one of the most attractive recreational resorts on Florida's Gulf Coast.

Refuge for the wealthy and art lovers

The white beaches on the offshore islands of Lido Key, Siesta Key and Longboat Key, which stretches northwards towards Bradenton, a year-round mild sub-tropical climate, a relaxed southern lifestyle and excellent recreational opportunities are the factors that attract pensioners and a growing number of people looking for relaxation.

The first white settler came in 1842. In the 1880s a large number of Scottish immigrants came, but in 1910 Sarasota was still a sleepy fishing village. Only a little later wealthy people from the east coast discovered Sarasota Bay.

It got its nickname »City of the Arts« from the circus impresario and art collector John Ringling and his wife Mable. Their art collection is one of Florida's main attractions. Since 1959 Sarasota has had an opera house with its own opera company and its own orchestra. Asolo State Theater has made a name for itself far beyond Florida's borders, and famous performers of modern and classical music often appear in Van Wezel Performing Arts Hall.

What to See in Sarasota

✱ Downtown

The old city centre was built in the 1920s in the Mediterranean style and has recently been regenerated. Expensive jewellery and antique shops, art galleries etc., which confirm Sarasota's reputation as a city with money, can be found in the exclusive Palm Avenue, and on western Main Street the shopping centre Kress International Plaza is worth a look. In the 1930s it was built in Art Deco style and today holds boutiques, a food court and a permanent exhibition featuring local artists. The Sarasota Opera Association is at home in the Edwards Theater (Pineapple Ave./First Street).

✱ Bayfront

Van Wezel Hall (777 N. Tamiami Trail), a modern functional building with a pink, shell-shaped roof, catches the eye on the attractive Bayfront. It is the venue for theatre performances, concerts etc. Another architecturally dominant sight right on the water is the peach-coloured office complex Sarasota Quay, built in 1988. At the end of Main Street the city marina and Island Park are located right on the bay. Boat excursions start from here.

Sarasota Jungle Gardens

Lavish sub-tropical vegetation and exotic animals can be found south of town. There are shows every day with parrots as well as an exciting reptile show with snakes and alligators. The Kiddy Jungle caters ⏲ for the little ones (3701 Bayshore Rd.; hours: daily 9am–5pm).

✱ Marie Selby Botanical Gardens

Since 1975 botanists from this organization in the southern part of Sarasota have undertaken expeditions into tropical rainforests and put together a large collection of epiphytes and orchids. The botanical garden is also home to two models of elegant southern architecture: the former Selby family residence and Christy Payne Mansion, which now holds the Museum of Botany & Art (811 S. Palm ⏲ Ave.; hours: daily 10am–5pm).

► VISITING SARASOTA

INFORMATION

Sarasota Convention and Visitors Bureau
655 N. Tamiami Trail
Sarasota, FL 34236
Tel. (941) 957-1877
Fax (941) 951-2956
www.sarasotafl.org

EVENTS

Sarasota Music Festival
This top-class music festival takes place in May and June.

Suncoast Offshore Grand Prix
On the last weekend in June or the first weekend in July speedboat captains compete for trophies.

WHERE TO EAT

► Moderate
Bijou Café
1287 1st Street
Tel. (941) 366-8111
J. P. Knagg's restaurant not only serves excellent roast shoulder of lamb but also wonderful crab cakes.

WHERE TO STAY

► Luxury/Mid-range

Baedeker recommendation

Hyatt Sarasota
1000 Blvd. of the Arts
Tel. (941) 953-1234
Fax (941) 952-1987
www.sarasota.hyatt.com
294 rooms and suites
High-class accommodation in a beautiful location with its own marina and a wonderful lagoon-like swimming pool.

► Budget/Mid-range
Golden Host Resort
4675 Tamiami Trail
Tel. (941) 355-5141
Fax (941) 355-9286
www.goldenhostresort.com
80 rooms
Centrally located and comfortable, with a pool in the middle of a fragrant garden, where families with children feel at home.

The work of a research station is presented to the public here. Many forms of life that occur in the Gulf of Mexico can be observed, including seahorses and squids. The shark aquarium attracts many visitors (1600 Ken Thompson Parkway; hours: daily 10am–5pm).

Mote Marine Aquarium
🕐

✶ ✶ Ringling Center for the Cultural Arts

Sarasota's main attraction is the museum of the circus king John Ringling , about 3mi/5km north of the city centre on Bayshore Road. Ringling gave it to the state of Florida in 1936. The neo-Renaissance style complex was built from 1927 to 1930 and stands in the middle of well-tended gardens with wonderful views of Sarasota Bay. The art museum holds not only an important collection of ancient Cypriot art, but also an excellent display of European masters of the 16th,

**✶ ✶
John & Mable
Ringling Museum
of Art**

John and Mable Ringling Collections

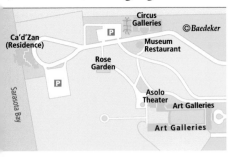

Circus Galleries

©*Baedeker*

Ca'd'Zan (Residence)

Museum Restaurant

Rose Garden

Asolo Theater

Art Galleries

Art Galleries

Sarasota Bay

17th and 18th centuries, including famous works by Lukas Cranach, Peter Paul Rubens, Anthony van Dyck and others. Replicas of famous statues, like Michelangelo's *David* adorn the inner courtyard.

The museum annex has rotating exhibitions of contemporary art (hours: daily 10am–5.30pm, Thu–10pm).

In the year 1950 the Ringling Museum acquired the beautiful interior of the Baroque theatre in Asolo, Italy. It was transported to Florida and rebuilt at great cost. From 1960 until the new Asolo Center for the Performing Arts was completed in 1989 it was used as a theatre.

✳ Circus Gallery

The extensive exhibition contains articles reminiscent of the heyday of John Ringling's circus. Along with old circus wagons, costumes and posters there is also a pretty miniature circus. Special exhibitions are dedicated to famous artists and clowns.

✳✳ Ca' d' Zan

Located right on Sarasota Bay, Ca' d' Zan is the baronial winter residence of John and Mable Ringling. »John's House«, a very luxurious 30-room villa, was built in 1926 in the style of a Venetian Renaissance palace. It is one of the most beautiful examples of historicist architecture of the 1920s. The old tiles for the roof and the 30m/100ft-high tower were imported from Barcelona. The windows are glazed with Venetian glass. From the terrace marble steps lead down to the water, where Mable Ringling's Venetian gondola was tied up.

Museum of Cars & Music

Not far from the Ringling museums, this most unusual museum invites a visit. In addition to highly polished antique cars, it has a particularly good collection of old music boxes and historic mechanical musical instruments. The oldest instruments date from the 18th century (5500 N. Tamiami Trail/US 41; hours: Mon–Sat 9am–6pm, Sun 10am–6pm).

Around Sarasota

✳ St Armands Key

The Ringling Causeway connects St Armands Key and Lido Key with the mainland. St Armands Key was bought in the 1920s by the circus magnate John Ringling and is known today for its exquisite shops and restaurants. The Circus Ring of Fame was built in 1988 and is dedicated to famous circus artists. Lido Beach is one of the most popular beaches in Sarasota; it is about half a mile long and has picnic areas and playgrounds.

On the island Siesta Key an artist's colony was established some time ago. Crescent Beach is one of the most beautiful beaches in Florida. Large parts of the island are occupied by fine residential estates today. Some of the older houses hidden in luxurious gardens were built in the »Sarasota Style«, which was created by the architects Ralph Twitchell and Paul Rudolph in the 1920s.

Siesta Key

The nature reserve is located about 19mi/30km south-east of Sarasota on FL 72. The ecosystem on the Myakka River is still intact for the most part. Open land, broad expanses of water, swamps with hammocks (tree islands), large cedar forests and palmetto prairie make for a varied landscape. The area is known for its wealth of deer, wild turkeys, alligators and aquatic birds. Bald eagles, herons and cranes are common. The visitor centre at the park entrance has information on the area. Park rangers offer bird-watching tours and campfire programmes. Hiking trails, including the wonderful Myakka Trail, and canoe trails cover the State Park.

* *
Myakka River State Park

> **! Baedeker TIP**
>
> **Airboat to wild animals**
>
> An airboat leaves from the Visitor Center of Myakka River State Park on wilderness tours into the nature reserve. En route wild turkeys and of course alligators might appear. Information: Tel. (941) 361-6511

The residence of the circus king looks like it should be in Italy.

Historic Spanish Point About 10mi/16km south of Sarasota is Historic Spanish Point, where old Indian »mounds« (grave sites) have been found. In 1867 a family settled here and named the site after the Spanish fishermen who used the coast as their base. In 1910 the famous women's rights activist Mrs. Potter Palmer bought the property. This famous widow of the Chicago hotelier had her winter residence The Oaks built here. Her arrival in Sarasota was a stroke of luck, for she brought welcome publicity to the young city.

✶ Venice South of Sarasota lies the town of Venice (population 5,000). The fishing village began to flourish in the 1920s when a colony for pensioners was built here. The stock market crash in 1929 brought the boom to an abrupt end, and the community did not flourish again until the 1960s, when the Ringling Bros., Barnum and Bailey circus set up its winter base here. Today Venice is a popular holiday site with beautiful beaches, marinas and good fishing. Every year around Christmas the world-famous circus pulls in the crowds with daring artistic feats and animal shows.

✶ Bradenton Bradenton, founded in 1878 by Dr. Joseph Braden, today it numbers 55,000 residents and is located a short drive north of Sarasota at the delta of the Manatee River. It is a commercial centre and also a popular place for fishing expeditions out into the Gulf of Mexico or on the Manatee River. Bradenton Beach is great for beach holidays. The fortress-like building of the city founder is in the eastern part of town; for the early European immigrants it served as a refuge against Indian attacks. The Manatee Village, located between 6th Ave. E and 15th St. E, includes the old church (1887), the old court house (1860), Wiggins Store (1903) and the old school house (1908) as well as Stephen's House, built in 1912 in the typical Cracker style.

✶ South Florida Museum ▶ ⊙ The natural and cultural history of the region is explained here. Indian artefacts are on display, as are Spanish colonial relics. There is a special exhibition on the manatees that live in the local waters (201 10th St. W.; hours: Mon–Sat 10am–5pm, Sun noon–5pm).

De Soto National Memorial North-west of Bradenton, at the mouth of the Manatee River in Tampa Bay, the Spanish conquistador Hernando De Soto is commemorated; he is supposed to have landed in this area with an army in May 1539. De Soto led the first expedition of Europeans to explore the south-east of what is now the USA up to the Mississippi River.

Gamble Plantation ⊙ Gamble Plantation, north-east of Bradenton on the northern banks of the Manatee River delta, is a protected monument. It is the only remaining plantation house in southern Florida. Robert Gamble, a major of the Confederate army, had a sugar plantation with a refinery here in the mid-19th century; it was operated by about 200 slaves. The manor house of 1844 has been restored (tours: daily 8am–sunset).

West of Bradenton the two islands Longboat Key and Anna Maria Island have beautiful seashell sand beaches, where the modern holiday colonies Bradenton Beach, Holmes Beach and Anna Maria have grown up. The best-known addresses are the Longboat Key Club with its championship gold courses and Colony Beach & Tennis Resort.

✳
Longboat Key, Anna Maria Island

Sebring

H 5

Region: Central
Population: 10,000

Elevation: 40m/130ft above sea level
Area code: 863

Anyone interested in auto racing knows Sebring, since Grand Prix races take place here every year on the third weekend in March.

Sebring is located in the fertile hills of central Florida, where citrus fruits and avocados are cultivated. The elevation as well as lakes and waterways keep the climate pleasant.

Sebring was only founded in 1911. The railway arrived shortly afterwards, and it developed into a winter resort in the 1920s. During World War II an air base was built near Sebring. After the war the city acquired the land and built the racetrack there.

History

The motors have been humming in Sebring for five decades.

What to See in and around Sebring

Sebring International Raceway

Sebring International Raceway is located south-east of town on the grounds of the former military airport; it is a 4mi/6.5km-long circuit on which important races have been held here since 1950. The highlights are the »12 Hours of Sebring« in March and the »Sebring Historic Fall Classic« in October. After Indianapolis and ▶ Daytona Sebring is the third most important address for thousands of auto racing fans.

Downtown

The historic centre has an attractive appearance with its brick houses around Circle Park, Main Street and Commerce Avenue. From City Pier there is a beautiful view of Lake Jackson. The Cultural Center Complex houses a theatre and the Highlands Museum of Arts with its interesting art collection.

▶ VISITING SEBRING

INFORMATION

Sebring Chamber of Commerce
227 US 27 North, Sebring, FL 33870
Tel. (863) 385-8448
Fax (863) 385-8810
www.sebringflchamber.com

Sebring International Raceway
113 Midway Drive
Sebring, FL 33870
Tel. (863) 655-1442
Fax (863) 655-1777
www.sebringraceway.com

AUTO RACING

12 Hours of Sebring
Top-class Grand Prix auto race for sports cars in March.

Historic Fall Classic
In October veteran sports cars race for points.

EVENT

Roaring Twenties Festival
In May the city centre revives the Roaring Twenties. One of the highlights is the Twenties-style street market.

WHERE TO EAT

▶ **Moderate**
Chicanes
(in the »Inn on the Lakes«)
3100 Golfview Road
Tel./Fax (863) 471-9400
Wonderful fresh fish and other tasty dishes are prepared by the innovative kitchen staff. The beautiful view of the lake is free.

WHERE TO STAY

▶ **Mid-range**
Inn on the Lakes
3100 Golfview Road
Tel./Fax (863) 471-9400
www.innonthelakessebring.com
160 rooms and suites
Elegant and traditional house with a spa, pool and very spacious rooms.

Kenilworth Lodge
1610 Lakeview Drive
Tel. (863) 385-0111
www.kenlodge.com
107 rooms and suites
This luxurious and well-run hotel on Lake Jackson was opened in 1916.

Lake Jackson is very busy in the summer thanks to several beautiful and well-tended beaches. Not just swimmers, but sailors, paragliders and water-skiers find the right facilities here.

Lake Jackson

The oldest State Park in Florida lies a few miles to the west of Sebring is; it was opened in 1931 and can best be reachedvia US 27 and CR 634. The nature reserve has an almost untouched and typical hammock flora with hardwoods and palms on areas that look like geological upheavals and are surrounded by cypress swamps and cedar forests. Deer, racoons, alligators and many kinds of birds (including bald eagles) populate the area, which can be explored on several nature trails. In the interpretive centre there is information on flora and fauna; register for guided nature walks here (hours: daily 8am–5pm).

✳
Highlands Hammock State Park

🕐

✳ ✳ Tallahassee

E 2

Region: North Central
Population: 177,000

Elevation: 58m/200ft above sea level
Area code: 850

The city is only a half-hour drive from the coast and has succeeded in preserving some of the charm of the Old South. Old oaks, densely covered with Spanish moss, tidy lawns and pretty 19th-century houses characterize the »biggest small town in Florida«.

The tranquil capital of the »Sunshine State« is located in northern Florida at the beginning of the Panhandle. The »old fields« – the meaning of the Indian name of the settlement – are spread out over several hills and surrounded by cedar forests and lakes.

Florida's capital

Before the Europeans arrived there was already a flourishing settlement of agrarian Indians. In 1528 the Spanish first moved through the region, and eleven years later the conquistador Hernando de Soto spent the winter here. In the 16th century Franciscans founded San Luis Mission, which was at times the central Spanish settlement of the Apalachee region. Conflicts between the rival colonial powers Spain, France and Great Britain led to attacks by the English at the beginning of the 18th century. Many Spanish settlements were destroyed at the time and the native Apalachee Indians were driven away. A little while later the unpopulated territory was settled by other Indians, who were then driven out during the Seminole Wars. White settlers came in increasing numbers. They started cotton and sugar cane plantations. In 1824 Tallahassee became the capital of Florida, which led to more people moving in. A city fire in 1843 decimated the city and a yellow fever epidemic slowed the development of the city. Tallahassee only recovered around the turn of the last century. Since the 1940s the enormous migration to Florida has also reached the capital of the state.

● VISITING TALLAHASSEE

INFORMATION

**Tallahassee Area
Visitor Information Center**
106 E. Jefferson St.
Tallahassee, FL 32301
Tel. (850) 606-2305
Fax (850) 487-4621
www.seetallahassee.com

PARKING

Parking is a problem in Tallahassee as elsewhere. Anyone interested in the city centre should use the underground parking garage at Kleman Plaza west of City Hall. Tourists get an hour of free parking from the visitor information centre (106 E. Jefferson St.).

CITY TOUR

Tallahassee has a well-developed bus network. From the visitor centre (106 Jefferson Street) the »Old Town Trolley« runs regularly between 8am and 6pm on a circular route through the city centre. The stops are close together and important sights are within easy walking distance. The trolley is free!

EVENT

Market Days
The popular market days are held on the first weekend in December and offer beautiful works of art for sale.

WHERE TO EAT

► Moderate
① **Barnacle Bill's**
1830 N. Monroe St.
Tel. (850) 385-8734
Informal restaurant with excellent fish cuisine.

WHERE TO STAY

► Luxury/Mid-range

Baedeker recommendation

① **Governor's Inn**
209 S. Adam Street
Tel. (850) 681-6855
Fax (850) 222-3105
www.thegovinn.com
40 rooms, 8 suites
This elegant hotel (protected monument!) is in the centre of town. Mahogany furniture embellish the tasteful rooms.

► Budget/Mid-range
② **Econo Lodge**
2681 N. Monroe Street
Tel./Fax (850) 365-6155
www.choicehotels.com
80 rooms
Motel north of downtown with comfortable rooms and good service. Continental breakfast is free.

③ **Doubletree Hotel Tallahassee**
101 S. Adam Street
Tel. (850) 224-5000
www.doubletree.com
240 rooms and suites
Modern hotel in the heart of downtown with well-equipped rooms, a restaurant and a bar. Many of the journalists who reported on the irregularities of George W. Bush's election in 2000 stayed in this hotel.

Tallahassee Downtown *Map*

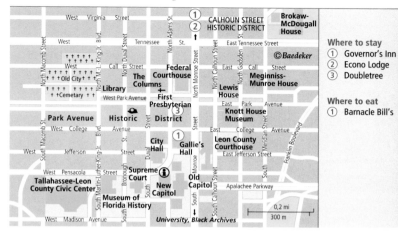

West Virginia Street

CALHOUN STREET HISTORIC DISTRICT

Brokaw-McDougall House

Where to stay
① Governor's Inn
② Econo Lodge
③ Doubletree

Where to eat
① Barnacle Bill's

©Baedeker

0,2 mi / 300 m

What to See in Tallahassee

Florida's capital is known for its beautiful »canopy roads«, avenues that are lined by broadly spreading, live oaks covered in Spanish moss, whose tops spread above the streets. The first avenue, Old St Augustine Road, was built already in the 16th century and connected San Luis Mission with the capital at that time, St Augustine. Other pretty canopy roads are Miccosukee Road, Centerville Road, Meridian Road and Old Bainbridge Road.

✱ ✱
Canopy Roads

The old capitol of Florida with its gleaming white façade and conspicuous red and white striped canopies over the windows stands on the highest hill in downtown Tallahassee. It was built in 1839 and renovated in the style of the late 19th century. The governor's room as well as the assembly halls of the state supreme court, the state senate and the state house of representatives are open to the public (400 S.; tours: Mon–Fri 9am–4.30pm, Sat 10am–4.30pm, Sun, holidays 1pm–4.30pm).

✱ ✱
Old State Capitol

The new capitol was inaugurated in 1978. This 22-storey building is still the tallest building in Tallahassee and a symbol for the dynamic economic development of the »Sunshine State«. In the entry hall is the large bronze seal of the state of Florida. The observation gallery offers a wonderful panoramic view (S. Duval St.; tours: Mon to Fri 8am–5pm).

◄ New State Capitol

In front of the Old Capitol stands the Union Bank, which was built in 1841. It was at one time the most important bank for the plantation owners (Apalachee Parkway; hours: Mon–Sat 10am–1pm, Sun 1pm–4.30pm).

Union Bank

What a contrast: the old and the new Capitols in Tallahassee.

Adam's Street Commons

North of the two capitol buildings two city blocks of old Tallahassee have been restored. Cobblestone streets, restaurants, bars, boutiques and Gallie's Hall, which was the city theatre at the end of the 19th century, make Adam's Street Commons a popular venue.

✳ Museum of Florida History ⏱

Two blocks to the west the R. A. Gray Building, which was built in 1976, holds the state archives, a library and above all an excellent exhibition on the state. The almost 3m/10ft-high skeleton of a mastodon that was found in Florida is impressive (500 South Bronough St.; hours: Mon–Fri 9am–4.30pm, Sat 10am–4.30pm, Sun noon to 4.30pm).

✳ Park Avenue Historic District

From the museum follow Bronough Street north to Park Avenue with its old trees and several historic buildings. On the corner of Bronough St./Park Ave. a formal columned building named The Columns attracts attention. It is one of the oldest buildings in the city and was built in 1830 by the president of the Bank of Florida. Today it is the seat of the Tallahassee Chamber of Commerce. Only a few steps above it is the First Presbyterian Church, the oldest church in the city. The population took shelter in this neo-Classical style brick building, which was built in 1838, during the Seminole Wars. Until the Civil War the gallery was reserved for slaves. On the other side of Monroe Street, Tallahassee's main north-south axis, lies the pretty Lewis Park. Here there are several typical southern-style villas with verandas and columned porticoes, which were built before the Civil War. **Lewis House**, which belonged to a wealthy banker's family from 1850 to 1993 is an especially impressive example of southern archi-
⏱ tecture (316 E. Park Ave.; hours: Mon–Fri 10am–3pm). **Knott House** opposite is also open to visitors. It was the residence of the Union

General Edward McCook, built in 1843 and bought in 1928 by William Knott, Florida's secretary of the treasury. He had the imposing portico added and furnished the house with valuable Victorian furnishings (301 E. Park Ave.; tours: Wed–Fri 1pm–4pm, Sat 10am to 4pm).

It is worth taking a stroll through the upper-class neighbourhood on northern Calhoun Street. Wealthy citizens lived here during the 19th century. Thus there are some fine examples of the Greek Revival and neo-classical styles Brokaw-McDougall House which was built in 1856 at the south-western edge of the neighbourhood, is now a museum. Sometimes it is used by the government of the state of Florida for special events (329 North Meridian St.; hours: Mon–Fri 9am to 1pm).

★
Calhoun Street Historic District

North-west of Calhoun Street Historic District is the residence of the governor of Florida in a formal park. The building with its entry flanked by Corinthian columns is open for viewing (700 N. Adam St.; tours: March–mid-May Mon, Wed, Fri 10am–noon).

Governor's Mansion

What to See in the Outer Districts of Tallahassee

In 1923 a New York financier laid out wonderful gardens about 5mi/ 8km north of the city centre. His widow turned them over to the state of Florida. In the winter when the camellias are in flower it is beautiful here, but also in the spring when azaleas and magnolias bloom. A look inside Maclay House, which was built in 1905, is also worthwhile.

★
Maclay State Gardens

When undeveloped land was being prepared for building in 1987, the remains of the Spanish conquistador Hernando de Soto's camp from 1539 were found quite by accident east of the town centre (Goodbody Lane/Lafayette Street). There is a little exhibition in the restored hunting lodge of Governor J. W. Martin (1925–29).

DeSoto Archaeological & Historic Site

On the campus of Florida Agricultural & Mechanical University at the southern edge of town, an exhibition focuses on the history of Afro-Americans with documents on slavery as well as testimonies to the cultural contributions of black Americans (hours: Mon–Fri 9am to 4pm).

Black Archives Research Center & Museum

This museum is located in the western part of town near the airport and shows what rural Florida was like in the 19th century, for example on Big Bend Farm. The elegant Maison Bellevue was once occupied by the widow of Napoleon I's nephew, who went to America after the Battle of Waterloo and settled as a plantation owner near Tallahassee (3945 Museum Dr.; hours: Mon–Sat 9am–5pm, Sun 12.30pm–5pm).

Tallahassee Museum of History & Natural Science

★★
San Luis Archeo-
logical & Histori-
cal Site

On a hill in the western part of town traces of the settlement of Apalachee Indians were found, as well as the remains of a mission station founded in 1656 by Franciscans and a late 17th-century Spanish fort. During the heyday of the settlement (around 1670) more than 1,400 people lived here together – Indians and Spaniards. After English attacks the settlement was abandoned. Presently there is an outdoor museum here with replicas of the mission church and the Franciscan priory, an Indian meeting house and the house of the Apalachee chief. Reconstruction of the Spanish fort is planned. The visitor centre is located in a typical southern-style house of the 1930s (2020 ⏰ Mission Rd.; hours: Mon–Fri 9am–4.30pm, Sat 10am–4.30pm, Sun noon–4.30pm).

Lake Jackson
Indian Mounds

About 6mi/10km north-west of the city centre, at the southern end of Lake Jackson, there is a field of mounds. It is assumed that from about 1200 to 1500 there was an Indian chief's residence or a cult centre here. At least one of the mounds was a grave. The high quality of the burial goods indicates close relations with other pre-Columbian cultures in south-east USA (access: via US 27 N. and Crowder ⏰ Road; hours: daily 8am–6pm.

Around Tallahassee

★
Pebble Hill
Plantation

The drive from Tallahassee on US 319 north-east into the state of Georgia is an opportunity to get to know a bit of plantation America. About 20mi/32km north of Florida's capital, the giant Pebble Hill Plantation and its castle-like manor are open to the public. Pebble Hill was built in the 1820s. Later it was the winter home of a wealthy family from Cleveland, Ohio. In the extravagantly furnished manor house the aristocratic lifestyle of the former plantation owners can ⏰ be seen up close (tours: Tue–Sat 10am–4pm, Sun 1pm–4pm).

Thomasville
(Georgia)

About 12mi/20km further to the north-east, the city of Thomasville (population 20,000) has beautiful 19th-century buildings. The city used to be known for its pleasant climate and had elegant hotels. Even American presidents came here to hunt quail and play golf. The Historic District has been restored to its former Victorian glory. The shops on the earlier Main Street (Broad/Jackson St.) look like they did in the late 19th century.

Monticello

From Tallahassee follow US 90 east for 26mi/42km to Monticello (population 3,000), where time seems to have stood still. Cotton brought prosperity to this town, which was founded in 1827. A massive city hall and beautiful antebellum houses testify to this today.

★★
Wakulla Springs

A side trip 16mi/26km south of Tallahassee to Wakulla Springs is worthwhile, either via US 319 or Woodville Highway (FL 363) and FL 267. The most copious karst springs in Florida spill over 54,000 litres per second through a widely spread cave system and into a spring pond. The area around Wakulla Springs, a state park, is a small piece of the original Florida landscape. Crystal-clear water, lush vegetation, and exotic animals like alligators, sea turtles and anhingas (birds) were captured in the 1930s and 1940s by cameras for films. The area was used as the **location of Tarzan films** with the actor Johnny Weissmuller and for other jungle movies. Today it is a popular recreational site. Swimming and trips in glass-bottom boats are possible here.

In 1937 Wakulla Springs Lodge was built on the shore; in the entryway »Old Joe« is the first thing that everyone looks at. This alligator lived in Wakulla pond until the ripe old age of 200, when he was shot in 1966 by an unknown person.

26mi/42km south of Tallahassee, on Apalachee Bay, the Spanish built a fortress in 1679, which was bitterly contested later. In May 1800 the fort was taken by W. A. Bowles, a former British officer, and 400 Indians. Bowles declared himself to be the king of Florida. But he only reigned a few weeks until the Spanish re-took the fort. In 1818 General Andrew Jackson took the fort. After Florida joined the USA, the fort was abandoned. From 1861 to 1865 Confederate troops occupied it in order to blockade the mouth of the St Marks River. There is a museum here (hours: Thu–Mon 9am–5pm).

★
San Marcos de Apalache State Historic Site

Once the setting of Tarzan movies: Wakulla Springs

✳ **St Marks National Wildlife Refuge**

The mouth of the St Marks River is the core of a nature reserve with an area of 263 sq km/101 sq mi. The marshes and swamps of Apalachee Bay is characterized by swampy bayous, hammocks, and oak and cedar woods. Many aquatic birds and alligators live here. Bald eagles and sea hawks can also be seen. About 3mi/5km south of the turnoff of FL 267 from US 98 there is a nature centre (hours: Mon to Fri 8am–4pm, Sat, Sun 10am–5pm).

☉

St Marks Lighthouse ►

A road leads through the nature reserve to the lighthouse of St Marks, which was built in 1831. From the observation platform and several trails that run through the grounds many varieties of animals can be seen.

✶ ✶ Tampa

G 4/5

Region: Central West	**Elevation:** 0 – 17m/55ft above sea level
Population: 330,000	**Area code:** 813
(Tampa Bay area: 3.3 million)	

Everyone drives by – to Busch Gardens, which is mentioned in the same breath with Tampa, or across Tampa Bay to the fabulous beaches on Pinellas Peninsula. Too bad. They miss the mightily pulsating heart of the booming Tampa Bay Area.

The port city at the mouth of the Hillsborough River has lots to offer. The city centre, with its sparkling office buildings, is the result of a building boom in the 1980s and 1990s. It has several important art and cultural sites. Historic areas like Ybor City and Old Hyde Park with their shops and restaurants are attractive places to stroll.

Young and dynamic

It's hard to believe that this dynamically growing port and industrial city – the gateway to the fabulous beaches on the Gulf of Mexico – is less than 100 years old. Spanish conquistadors were the first white people in Tampa Bay, but the systematic development of the area only started 300 years later. In 1824 US Americans built Fort Brooke at the mouth of the Hillborough River in order to keep the Seminole Indians under control. A little fishing village named Tampa developed in the shadow of this fort, but it remained unimportant until the South Florida Railroad of the railway magnate Henry B. Plant came in 1885 and the mouth of the Hillsborough River was developed into a deep-sea harbour. Then things happened quickly. In 1886 the Spanish cigar manufacturer Vicente Martínez Ybor moved his production from Cuba and Key West to Tampa. Thousands of Cuban workers came. After the luxurious Tampa Bay Hotel opened in 1891, Tampa became fashionable as a winter residence. Phosphate mining in the interior also added to the development. Tampa's port and the shipping industry also added to its prosperity.

Highlights in Tampa

Former Tampa Bay Hotel
Built by railway magnate Plant for the high society, the former luxury hotel is now a museum.
► page 343

Florida Aquarium
This informative facility for old and young is one of the best of its kind. The highlight is an artificial coral reef.
► page 347

Ybor City
In this historic quarter, people think that they are on Cuba; it was built by a cigar manufacturer in the 19th century.
► page 347

Busch Gardens
This combination of a large amusement park and zoo is really worth a visit!
► page 348

Downtown Tampa

Compact, easy of orientation and above all the result of dramatically growth, the city centre focuses on business and is thus as good as dead after hours. But during business hours Franklin Street Mall, a green pedestrian zone between glistening office towers, is by far the liveliest part of the centre. The opulent Tampa Theater (711 Franklin St.) of 1926 is worth seeing. It was once the most modern cinema in the USA and today is certainly one of the most beautiful. On Wednesdays, Saturdays and Sundays backstage tours of this Andalusian-style palace are offered, along with a chance to hear the giant Wurlitzer theatre organ.

City centre transformed

A few minutes' walk further to the west, on the banks of the Hillsborough River, there is a collection of ancient Greek and Roman art that is, for America, simply magnificent. 20th-century American art is also exhibited (600 Ashley Dr. N.; hours: Tue to Sat 10am–5pm, Thu 10am–8pm, Sun 11am–5pm).

✱
Tampa Museum of Art
🕐

University of Tampa · Hyde Park

On the opposite bank of the Hillsborough River the minaret-like towers of the former Tampa Bay Hotel stand out. The railway magnate Henry B. Plant had this ostentatious building constructed in 1891. With 511 rooms it was the accommodation for high society from the cold north-east USA. Today the former luxury hotel is the main building of the renowned University of Tampa. The south wing of this Oriental-style complex still has its original interior and is now the Henry B. Plant Museum, which is dedicated to the life and work of the railway tycoon (401 W. Kennedy Blvd.; hours: Tue–Sun 10am–4pm, Sun 1pm–4pm).

✱ ✱
Former Tampa Bay Hotel
🕐

▶ VISITING TAMPA

INFORMATION
Tampa Bay CVB
401 E. Jackson St., Suite 2100
Tampa, FL 33602
Tel. (813) 223-1111
Fax (813) 229-6616
www.visittampabay.com

CITY TRANSPORT
Buses of the Hillsborough Area Transit (HART) operate in the city. The old-time railway wagons of the TECO Line run between the Cruise Ship Terminal and Ybor City.

AIRPORT
The international airport is located 5mi/8km north-west of downtown on Tampa Bay. Buses and taxis run into the city. Information: tel. (813) 870-8700, www.tampaairport.com

EVENT
Gasparilla Festival
On the first Saturday in February the legendary pirate José Gaspár, who terrorized the settlers on Florida's Gulf Coast in the 18th century, is remembered in a colourful festival.

SHOPPING
Relaxed shopping – without stress and hassle – is possible at Old Hyde Park Village south of downtown around Swan Street and Dakota Street. Several dozen good shops have opened here, selling pretty fashions and other quality products.

The best cigars are available in Ybor City at Tampa Rico Cigar Co. on Ybor Square as well as El Sol Cigars on 7th Avenue.

WHERE TO EAT
▶ Expensive

Baedeker recommendation

① Columbia
Ybor City
2117 E 7th Avenue
Tel. (813) 248-4961
This restaurant, which opened its doors in 1905, serves tasty Spanish-Cuban dishes. The paella a la Valenciana and la completa Cubana (with pork, patatas and black beans) are wonderful. There is also a great Flamenco show almost every evening.

▶ Moderate
② Bern's
Hyde Park District
1208 S. Howard Ave.
Tel. (813) 251-2421
For 40 years some of the best steaks on the Gulf of Mexico have been grilled here in an overpowering, kitschy ambience.

▶ Budget
③ Taj Indian Cuisine
2734 E. Fowler Ave.
Tel (813) 971-8483
The chicken, especially chicken tikka and tandoori chicken, here is delicious.

WHERE TO STAY
▶ Luxury
① Sheraton Riverwalk Hotel
200 N. Ashley Drive
Tel. (813) 223-2222

Tampa Downtown Map

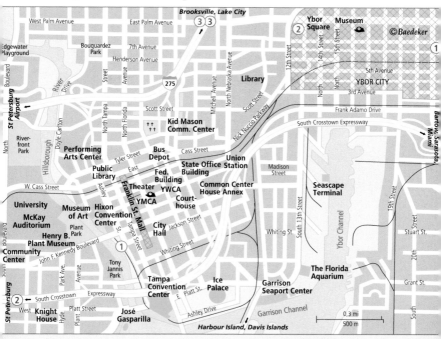

West Palm Avenue   East Palm Avenue

Brooksville, Lake City

Ybor Square   Museum   ©Baedeker

Edgewater Playground

Bouquardez Park

7th Avenue

Henderson Avenue

River Drive

275

Scott Street

Library

YBOR CITY

3rd Avenue

Frank Adamo Drive

South Crosstown Expressway

St Petersburg Airport

Riverfront Park

Performing Arts Center

Kid Mason Comm. Center

Bus Depot   Cass Street

State Office Building

Union Station

Madison Street

Seascape Terminal

W. Cass Street

Public Library

Fed. Building

Common Center House Annex

University

Theater   YWCA

Museum of Art

Hixon Convention Center

Courthouse

McKay Auditorium

Plant Park

City Hall   Jackson Street

Whiting St.

Ybor Channel

Henry B. Plant Museum

John F. Kennedy Boulevard

Whiting Street

Community Center

Tony Jannis Park

Tampa Convention Center

Ice Palace

Garrison Seaport Center

The Florida Aquarium

South Crosstown   Expressway

E. Platt St.

Ashley Drive

Garrison Channel

Grant St.

St Petersburg

West Knight House

Platt Street

José Gasparilla

Harbour Island, Davis Islands

0,3 mi
500 m

Barstow, Sarasota, Miami

Where to stay
- ① Sheraton River Walk
- ② Don Vicente de Ybor
- ③ Gram's Palace

Where to eat
- ① Columbia
- ② Bern's
- ③ Taj Indian Cuisine

Fax (813) 221-5929
www.starwoodhotels.com
282 rooms and suites
Well-run establishment of a luxury hotel chain with beautiful rooms overlooking the Hillsborough River.

► Mid-range
② *Don Vicente de Ybor Historic Inn*
Ybor City
1915 Avenida República de Cuba
Tel. (813) 241-4545
www.donvicenteinn.com

16 rooms
The best accommodation in Ybor City is in colonial style and has roomy suites as well as a cigar and martini bar.

► Budget
③ *Gram's Place*
3109 N. Ola Avenue
Tel. (813) 221-0596
www.grams-inn-tampa.com
8 rooms
Simple accommodation with clean rooms.

View over Hillsborough Bay to Tampa's modern skyline

Hyde Park

From the former Tampa Bay Hotel South Hyde Park Avenue runs to Tampa's most refined historic residential neighbourhood. The Victorian buildings still reflect some of the elegance of the time around 1900. A drive down Bayshore Boulevard presents a wonderful view of the skyline of downtown Tampa. Near Beach Place the three-masted *José Gasparilla* is anchored; in February it is more or less the epicentre of the city's biggest festival.

Old Hyde Park Village ►

Old Hyde Park Village (712 S. Oregon Ave./Swan Ave.) tries to revive the atmosphere of past times. Here there are fashion boutiques, galleries, fine restaurants and nice jazz clubs.

Channelside

Harbourfront on Garrison Channel

The waterside area of downtown Tampa has changed its face completely in the past years. On the north side of the Garrison Channel modern concrete complexes have sprung up, including the Tampa Convention Center, the Ice Palace, the multifunctional Garrison Seaport Center and the Florida Aquarium, which has become a top tourist attraction.

Thousands of plants and animals native to the waters of Florida can be observed here under a remarkable green dome.

The facility is divided into several ecosystems. In Cypress Wetlands there are not only ibis and owls, but also snakes and other reptiles.

The stars in Bays & Beaches are the stingrays. But the absolute highlight is the artificial coral reef with its many colourful fish, which is explained in detail daily at 11am, 1pm and 3pm by a diver. In Off Shore sharks and many other kinds of marine life can be seen (701 Channelside Dr.; hours: daily 9.30am–5pm).

✶ ✶
Florida Aquarium

Ybor City

In the year 1886 the cigar king Don Vincente Martínez Ybor established an eleven-block quarter in northern downtown Tampa. For four decades this was the source of the best hand-made cigars in the USA. The quarter went through all the ups and downs of life and today still has a Latin American atmosphere. The descendants of the Cubans who came to Tampa at that time still sell cigars, but they also run restaurants, music shops and hotels. »La Setima« – the name for 7th Avenue – is reminiscent of the French Quarter in New Orleans: old buildings of wood and brick characterize the street, traffic is watched from wrought-iron balconies, pedestrians stroll along under arcades, the sounds of son and salsa spill out of the dark street cafés. Depression and mass production put an end to hand-rolled cigars, but since the 1990s Ybor City has been experiencing a real renaissance and thanks to its good restaurants and bars has become the popular goal of night owls.

✶ ✶
Historic industrial quarter

Tobacco processing in Ybor City

The daytime attraction is the Ybor City State Museum, which is devoted to the production of cigars in all details. On Fridays and Saturdays there is »living history«, when cigars are rolled in the old way (1819 9th Ave.; hours: daily 9am–5pm).

On this pretty square with various shops and restaurants the Tampa Rico Cigar Company lets visitors watch cigars being rolled by hand. Not far to the north is the legendary Café Creole, which opened in 1888, and the no less historic Cuban Club, which opened in 1917.

Ybor Square

Don't miss a stroll down 7th Avenue, called »La Setima«in Spanish. The Ritz Theater with its magnificent Art Deco lobby opened in 1917; there are various »social clubs« here, too. At one time the various social and ethnic groups in this quarter belonged to societies that represented their interests.

✶
La Setima

North Tampa

Busch Gardens ✹ ✹

Tigers stalk through the »Congo«, orang-utans live in an African village, but who cares about the details? The theme park of the mega-brewery Anheuser-Busch north of Tampa is one of the most popular in Florida and presents itself as a one-of-a-kind combination of zoo, adventure park and amusement park. The fact that Busch Gardens is one of the largest zoos in America and that it has made contributions to the preservation of endangered species usually gets forgotten in the face of the numerous roller coasters and other attractions. But the zoo has had remarkable success at breeding the rare black rhinoceros, koalas and panda bears.

Opening hours:
Daily 10am–6pm, in
the summer to 8pm

The main theme is Africa. Thousands of animals from the »dark continent« live in appropriate quarters. This includes an artificial savannah where zebras, giraffes and gnus feel just as much at home as in their earlier native land.

Busch Gardens is divided into eight areas. Each one presents a different part of Africa, whereby »correctness« is less important than entertainment value. Thus Morocco has not only snake charmers and fire-eaters behind its high fortress-like walls, but also an ice skating revue. In Egypt a copy of the tomb of Pharaoh Tut-Ankh-Amun is open to amateur treasure hunters, and the Montu roller coaster has hair-raising loops for the unsuspecting. In Congo, Timbuktu and Stanleyville there are more stomach-turning rides. In Edge of Afri-

! **Baedeker TIP**

First come ...
Avoid long lines at the roller coasters by arriving at Busch Gardens by 9am. The gates open at 9.30am. This way you can enjoy up to 4 »thrill rides« in the first hour. Later you might have to wait up to three quarters of an hour at each ride.

ca there is a copy of a Massai village and a safari camp. Wildlife Tours with expert guides are also available. Nairobi has a rain forest called Myombe Reserve. The chimpanzees and gorillas who live there apparently enjoy it. The Land of Dragons is aimed at the smallest visitors and has carousels and a tree house. The latest attraction in Busch Gardens is called Sheikra and is presently the steepest roller coaster in the world; it has a loop named after the German fighter pilot Max Immelmann: twice the passengers plunge down practically in free fall only to be shot straight up again.

Adventure Island
Water park ✹

This fun park near Busch Gardens is the best way to recover from adventures in the African savannah. Mega-waterslides with inspiring names like »Tampa Typhoon« and »Gulf Scream« and wave pools promise truly drenching fun (10001 Malcom McKinley Drive; hours: 10am–5pm).

Museum of
Science &
Industry (MOSI) ✹

Anyone who has ever wanted to ride a bike on a high wire or experience a hurricane is in the right place here. This museum in north

Tampa offers hands-on and understandable technology and natural science. Don't miss the detailed exhibition on climate and weather in Florida, which also covers the consequences of global climate change (4801 E. Fowler Ave.; hours: daily 9am–5pm).

This zoo lies about 6mi/10km north of downtown Tampa. Located on the Hillsborough River, it is much quieter than Busch Gardens. Several endangered species can be seen here, like Florida pumas, Persian leopards and Sumatra tigers. In the Manatee & Aquatic Center injured manatees are nursed back to health (1101 W Sligh Ave., hours daily 9.30am–5pm)

★ Lowry Park Zoo

Around Tampa

South of Tampa, at the entrance to Hillsborough Bay, the Tampa Electric Company runs Big Bend Power Station, in whose warm waste water   dozens of manatees spend the winter months. The power company has meanwhile built a Manatee Viewing Center, from where the endearing animals can be watched, and where there is more information on manatees (Big Bend Rd./Dickman Rd.; hours: Nov–mid-April daily 10am–5pm).

Manatees near Big Bend Power Station

On the eastern edge of town (north of the I-4) a cultural centre presents the history and culture of the Seminole Indian tribe. In the Seminole Village with its »chickees«, open huts, Indians show their skilled craftsmanship. There are also breath-taking alligator and snake shows (5221 N. Orient Rd.; hours: April–Oct Mon–Sat 9am–5pm, Sun 10am–4pm, Nov–March Mon–Sat 10am–6pm, Sun 10am–4pm).

Seminole Cultural Center

The nature reserve 20mi/32km north-east of Tampa has the only rapids in Florida outside a water park. However, that is not the only reason to go there. The river landscape is original and lush, with several walkways and trails full of interesting features running through it. Canoes and kayaks to explore the almost Tolkien-like river bends can be rented from the park administration. The rapids are somewhat disappointing since they are only knee-deep.

★ Hillsborough River State Park

A reconstructed stockade fort can be viewed here; the original kept the Indians at bay during the Second Seminole War (15402 US 301 N.; hours: daily 8am–sunset).

◄ Fort Foster

Dade City lies 27mi/44km north-east of Tampa in hill country that is characterized by horse pastures and citrus farms. The main attraction is the **Pioneer Florida Museum**, an outdoor museum on the early settlers in Florida. It has a 19th-century church, an old schoolhouse, a private home furnished in the style of the 1860s, an old railway station with locomotives and railway cars, and various agricultural implements.

Dade City

✳ ✳ Walt Disney World

Region: Central

Elevation: 28m/100ft above sea level
Area code: 407

More than 23 million guests every year! Walt Disney World is »the mother of the mega-theme parks«. And that's only the beginning: only one quarter of the land that was acquired by the Walt Disney Company near Orlando has been developed.

The goal of every child's dreams lies only a half-hour drive southwest of ► Orlando on Lake Buena Vista. Here Walt Disney (► Baedeker Special p. 356) found land in 1963 where he could make his dream of the perfect amusement park come true: a broad expanse of undeveloped land, not far from booming holiday sites on the Atlantic and Gulf Coasts, with good travel connections and a good climate all year round.

In fall of 1971 Magic Kingdom, the first part of Walt Disney World, opened its doors. What started as a giant but manageable amusement park has become a gigantic entertainment machine, which covers well over than 100 sq km/40 sq mi. On the grounds, where the Walt Disney Company is practically king, there are today no less than four theme parks, dozens of »smaller« attractions, TV studios, a sports centre with vacation classes, more than two dozen hotels and resorts as well as a complete village with shopping and nightlife.

More than 30,000 employees see to it that everything runs smoothly every day, and above all that everything is clean, for the empire of the mouse welcomes up to 150,000 guests on peak days!

✳ ✳ Magic Kingdom

The landmark and focal point of Magic Kingdom is the fairy-tale Cinderella's Castle, modelled after the castle of Neuschwanstein in Bavaria. Seven »countries« with about **60 attractions** as well as fast-food restaurants and ice cream stands are grouped around the castle. Main Street USA is the entrance to fun. Horse-drawn carriages and antique omnibuses move up and down this American main street that recreates the atmosphere of the year 1900.

Cross the bridge to Adventureland to go on a Jungle Cruise through ◄ Adventureland the jungles of Central Africa and the Amazon, past the Egyptian pyramids and even to pirates of the Caribbean.

In Frontierland the Big Thunder Mountain Railroad races over ◄ Frontierland mountains and through valleys and dark tunnels. The highlight of the Wild West area is Splash Mountain, where guests ride rafts through bayous and swamps and shoot over a waterfall. Liberty

← *Family fun with Mickey Mouse*

● VISITING WALT DISNEY WORLD

INFORMATION

Walt Disney World
Lake Buena Vista, FL 32830
Tel. (407) 824-4321
www.disney.de
www.disneyworld.disney.go.com/
wdw/index

ARRIVAL

By air
The two closest international airports
are in Orlando and Tampa. Shuttle
buses run regularly to Disney World.
Shuttle buses also run to Disneyworld
from Miami's international airport.

By car
Disney World can best be reached by
car from Orlando via Irlo Bronson
Highway (US 192) as well as Interstate
I-4, which connects Tampa and Orlando. From Miami – Fort Lauderdale
the quickest way is on the toll road
called »Florida's Turnpike« to Orlando.

HOURS

Opening hours vary, but generally all
attractions are accessible between 9am
and 8pm. During the high season as
well as on weekends and holidays
hours may be extended due to the
crowds.
It is wise to be at the gates very early
since queues form quickly. Allow for
queues in the parks, too. At the most
popular rides the wait may be up to
two hours.

COST

Presently the price of a day for each (!)
of the 4 theme parks is US$ 67 (adult)
or US$ 56 (child). Add parking fees,
shuttle bus transfer between the various amusement parks as well as food
and drinks.

Staying several days in Walt Disney
World is a better deal. A 4-day pass
(Four-Day Park Hopper Pass), with
four days of unlimited access to all
four parks, presently costs US$ 202
(adult) or US$ 168 (child). The Five-
Day Park Hopper Plus Pass (US$ 251
per adult, US$ 214 per child) includes
admission to other amusements in the
Orlando area.
Anyone who stays in a Disney hotel
has even more deals available. European tour operators offer package
deals including flights, accommodation and entry to Disney World.

EVENTS

Disney Parade
Every day at 3pm Mickey Mouse,
Goofy and friends hold their big
parade in the Magic Kingdom. From
Main Street to Frontierland they dance
through the streets and wave to their
thousands-strong fan club. At the end
of the parade a colourful show is
staged in front of Cinderella's Castle.
The parade is also held late in the
evening. To end the day there is also a
brilliant fireworks display.

IllumiNations
This truly worthwhile laser and light
show with fireworks can be enjoyed to
the fullest in the EPCOT Centre at the
World Showcase Lagoon.

WHERE TO EAT

► **Expensive**

① **Les Chefs de France**
EPCOT, France Pavilion
The signature of the French chefs Paul
Bocuse, Gaston Lenôtre and Roger
Vergé cannot be missed here. The
restaurant is and remains one of the
best in Walt Disney World.

▶ Moderate
② Coral Reef
EPCOT, The Living Sea
Tastefully prepared fish, lobster and
other seafood, also grilled sausages
made of alligator meat, are served
here. There is also a view of the Living
Seas Aquarium free of charge.

▶ Moderate/Inexpensive
③ House of Blues
Downtown Disney West Side
Tasty Cajun cuisine and spicy
Creole specialties are served here.
Sunday Gospel Brunch is also
popular.

WHERE TO STAY
▶ Luxury
① Walt Disney World's Swan & Dolphin
1500 Epcot Resorts Blvd.
(via Buena Vista Drive)
Tel. (407) 934-4000
2,267 rooms and suites
No less than 17 restaurants, 5 pools,
2 health clubs, tennis and golf are
available at this luxury hotel; it is
also a highlight of modern
architecture.

▶ Mid-range
② Disney's Polynesian Resort
Magic Kingdom Resort Area
Tel. (407) 824-2000
850 rooms and suites
It really looks as if you are in the
South Seas: waterfalls splash, palms
and banana plants sway in the breeze,
orchids show all their glory. It includes two pools, a health club and
various sports programmes.

③ Disney's Port Orleans Resort
2201 Orleans Drive
Lake Buena Vista
Tel. (407) 934-7639
1,008 rooms
The newly renovated accommodation
is modelled on the harbour of New
Orleans around 1900. There are 2
restaurants, several shops and 6 pools.

▶ Budget
④ Disney's Pop Century Resort
1050 Century Drive
Tel. (407) 934-7639
2,880 rooms. Bright decoration and
symbols of pop culture make this
reasonably priced Disney hotel an
attractive option.

Square revives the period of colonial America and the Hall of Presidents introduces all of the presidents of the United States. Right next
door – by coincidence? – is the Haunted Mansion. Ghosts haunt this
run-down house, unearthly musicians play and ghosts even ride
along in the cars.

Here the littlest Disney World visitors will find old friends. Peter Pan   ◀ Fantasyland
and Capt´n Hook shake hands, Snow White jokes with the seven
dwarfs and Dumbo, the flying elephant, trips over his ears. At Mickey's Toontown Fair the world is child-size. Here children meet their
TV heroes, especially Mickey Mouse, Donald Duck and Goofy.

Things are bit more serious in the »land of tomorrow«: with Buzz   ◀ Tomorrowland
Lightyear and high-tech the universe is saved. The Cosmic Coaster, a
racing roller coaster, takes guests into orbit. The evening in the Magic Kingdom ends with the show Wishes, though not every day during
the low season.

Walt Disney World Florida Map

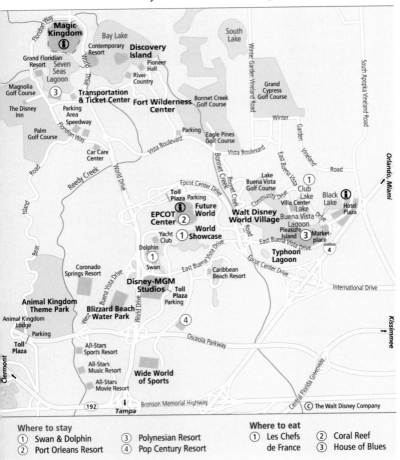

Where to stay
- (1) Swan & Dolphin
- (2) Port Orleans Resort
- (3) Polynesian Resort
- (4) Pop Century Resort

Where to eat
- (1) Les Chefs de France
- (2) Coral Reef
- (3) House of Blues

✷ ✷ EPCOT

The Experimental Prototype Community of Tomorrow is so to speak the scientific counterpart of the Magic Kingdom. It emerged from Walt Disney's dream of a perfect paradise and opened its doors in 1982, the second theme park on the site. Interactive understanding and learning scientific relationships and the latest technologies is fun here. EPCOT has **two parts: Future World and World Showcase.** Spaceship Earth, a giant, gleaming silver globe that looks like a giant golf ball is the trademark of Future World. Around this globe global

US companies – including AT & T, Kodak and General Motors – present the latest information on research and technology. On the Test Track guests ride in an open car at breath-taking speeds around curves and just miss hitting various obstacles. Not for those of a nervous disposition! Mission: Space is the most popular and at the same time most controversial attraction of the entire Walt Disney World. A rocket trip to the moon and to Mars is simulated whereby the guests experience a gravity force of two Gs, something that can harm poor physical constitutions.

Honey, I shrunk the audience is the interactive version of the popular film with (almost) the same name: by means of sophisticated special effects and optical tricks dogs appear as giants on the screen and jump into the audience, as do mice and a rowdy five-year-old.

Living with the Land offers a 15-minute boat ride through various natural areas. The film Making of Me shows the beginning of life. In Body Wars guests take part in saving the immune system in the role of a molecule and travel through the human body.

On an artificial lagoon in the southern part of the park a world exhibition presents eleven countries of the world with their characteristics, which here means no more than that »clichés abound!«. »Germany«, for instance is a naïve ensemble of leather pants, beer mugs and medieval half-timbered houses. France and Italy don't get off any easier. The presentation of Canada is worth seeing: in a round cinema *Oh Canada* presents wonderful pictures from the Pacific over the Rocky Mountains to the lighthouses on the Atlantic.

World Showcase

Mission Space – Disney's newest and most controversial attraction

Walt Disney at work

FATHER OF THE MOUSE

Anyone can turn a fly into an elephant. But the graphic artist Walt Disney did more than that: he turned a mouse into a giant, even an international star who has been fighting evil for more than 70 years and who made his creator a billionaire.

Walter Elias Disney was born in 1901 in Chicago. He started working as a graphic artist at the age of 18. At first he could hardly live on what he made. A job as a cartoonist did not help much either, even though Disney developed a new process: instead of drawing figures with movable parts and photographing them in different positions, he redrew each new position completely. That made the movements more life-like. In 1922 Disney went into business for himself and made commercials with his brother Roy.

The Mouse is Born

Disney's breakthrough came in 1927 when he drew a precocious mouse with giant ears, which he called **Mortimer**. On his wife's suggestion he renamed it, and **Mickey Mouse's** career took off. In 1933 already Walt Disney had made about 5 million dollars with Mickey and his friends. Two years later his first movie-length cartoon, *Snow White*, earned 45 million dollars. Other successes followed, like *Pinocchio* (1938) and *Bambi* (1942). Adventure films like *Treasure Island* and documentaries like *The Living Desert* (1953) made Disney successful in other fields as well. *Walt Disney's Wonderful World of Colour*, produced in 1961, was the first colour television series ever.

New Horizons

Already in **1955 Disney opened his first amusement park** in Anaheim, California. Mickey, Goofy and Donald, larger than life and up close – the idea took off. But soon Disneyland was too small for its creator. Disney sent people out to find the right place to realize his dream. He found it in Florida. Disney's dream was to build a larger amusement park near Orlando, a model city without economic and social problems. He had the land

The world famous mouse in front of the film studios

bought up at rock-bottom prices by front companies. Thus Disney got possession of 43 sq miles (113 sq km) of land.

Creation of a Kingdom

The 400-million-dollar project was supported by the state of Florida. In view of the revenue that Disney promised the region, he did not have to abide by any building regulations and was able to build roads and hotels as he wanted. He did not live to see the **Magic Kingdom open in 1971**, dying in 1966. But his life's work flourished.

Legendary Success

Already in the first 15 years more than 240 million visitors flooded into Disney's new world of wonders. The Disney corporation itself was surprised by the success and expanded continuously to become one of the largest entertainment companies in the world. **Walt Disney Company** (WDC) today includes the American Broadcasting Company (ABC), Walt Disney Studios, three cartoon TV channels and interests in various other television channels, among other things. WDC made headlines when Roy Disney, the nephew of Walt Disney, left the company after a

conflict with the CEO Michael Eisner. But stockholders rallied behind Disney, who was reinstated. Eisner was forced to leave. The firing of several hundred employees when the cartoon branch of the company was closed in the face of digital competition also caused concern.

Enormous Economic Power

Walt Disney's world of wonders – today the entertainment capital of the world – proved to be a powerful catalyst for development for the state of Florida and especially for the Orlando area. Other amusement parks and hotels – whole settlements – sprouted like mushrooms, new highways criss-crossed the landscape, tens of thousands sought and found work here. Disneyworld's success made the population of the Orlando area explode, which is hardly surprising in view of the fact that the Walt Disney Company created over **40,000 jobs in Florida**.

Accusations by ecologists that WDC's land use was irresponsible were met with references to the company's environmental policy. Hardly any petrol is used on the property, energy is won by recycling trash left behind by the visitors and waste water is purified organically.

★ ★ Disney – MGM Studios

Mixture of amusement park and film studios

Opened in 1990, this theme park is an exciting combination of real film settings, amusements and breath-taking rides. Famous film themes were used as a background for the »thrill rides« through well-known film settings, while films and popular game shows are actually made nearby.

The best introduction to the Disney film world is a half-hour Disney – MGM Studios Backlot Tour. Look behind the scenes while films are actually being made, visit the wardrobes and watch make-up artists at work. The highlight of the tour is Catastrophe Canyon: an earthquake makes the walls shake and causes floods, fires and other fearfully lifelike natural catastrophes through special effects. Another highlight is the half-hour Indiana Jones Epic Stunt Spectacular, in which seemingly suicidal stuntmen perform terrifying scenes from the Indiana Jones trilogy.

The Rock'n Roll Coaster accelerates guests in 2.8 seconds from 0 to 60mph (0 to 100kph) and throws them into five curves. The Twilight Zone Tower of Terror is a second-to-none chamber of horrors. With the help of the latest in computer animation effects are created that could make the hair of the toughest guys stand on end. For example: anyone who would like to know what it's like inside a falling elevator can find out here.

★ ★ Animal Kingdom

Animal Kingdom

Truly a kingdom of animals: the open areas are so big that visitors sometimes have to search for the animals. That might confuse the more pampered guests, but on the other hand this area was created to be as much like the natural habitat of these mostly African animals as possible. Animal Kingdomwas opened in 1998 and consists of five areas. The transition from artificial amusement park to a »real« wilderness with live animals is often so smooth that it is easy to imagine an African springbok behind the nearby vending machine.

Tree of Life

The Tree of Life on Discovery Island is the trademark of this part of the park. More than 300 reliefs of animals have been carved into the trunk and branches of the 44m/144ft-high tree. All of the animals that are mentioned in the song *The Circle of Life* – from the film *The Lion King* – can be seen here. Children especially love the 3-D film *It's Tough to be a Bug*, which is shown daily at the roots of the Tree of Life. In the film children meet termites that exude liquids, bad-smelling dung beetles and many other kind of creepy-crawlies.

Camp Minnie-Mickey

But the many well-known Disney figures that can be seen in Camp Minnie-Mickey are cuddly. In the Lion King Theater the thrilling Festival of the Lion King takes place, both on the stage and in the audience.

In **Little Africa** guests can take part in the Kilimanjaro Safari. Ride in an open safari truck through an expertly built artificial savannah. On this Game Drive see all the well-known African animals, giraffes, antelopes, gnus, zebras, rhinos and elephants. The Pangani Forest Exploration Trail, with hippos and – obviously contented – gorillas, is particularly exciting.

Bengal tigers and many other animals populate the **Asia area**. On the Maharajah Trail admire the endangered predatory cats in an area similar to their north Indian habitat. There's fun here too: the Kali River Rapids are a raft ride through a foaming inferno of a river – on a hot day a refreshing experience.

Dinoland USA remains a sensation. In the Fossil Preparation Lab the skeleton of a Tyrannosaurus Rex has been erected. On the Cretaceous Trail plants and animals can

Old-time horse-drawn streetcar in front of Cinderella's Castle

American area

be seen that survived the catastrophe 65 million years ago that killed off the dinosaurs. In Dinosaur go on a virtual trip through time in the Time Rover back to the Cretaceous period, meeting eerie pre-historic creatures on the way. The »Primeval Whirl«, which races around tight curves until everything goes black, is a top-class »thrill ride«.

✱ ✱ Typhoon Lagoon · Blizzard Beach

These two Disney fun pools are – even sceptics agree – the absolute top! Wave pools and water slides in a wonderful South Seas world dominated by the 30m/100ft-high Mount Mayday are the special attractions of Typhoon Lagoon. This resort is more for families.

Top-class water fun

Blizzard Beach, on the other hand, is for the young and fit (and athletic adults!). The truly breath-taking water slides have all sorts of twists and turns. The absolute highlight is the Summit Plummet: those who dare slide down from a height of 40m/130ft at break-neck speeds and reach the pool at the bottom at a speed of 55mph/90kmh.

PHOTO CREDITS

LIST OF MAPS AND ILLUSTRATIONS

PUBLISHER'S INFORMATION

Illustrations etc: 191 illustrations, 32 maps and diagrams, one large map
Text: Inge Scherm, with contributions by Annette Bickel, Helmut Linde, Andrea Mecke, Thomas Mittmann, J. u. P. Seeberger, Lydia Störmer, Reinhard Zakrzewski.
Text updates:
Ole Helmhausen
Editing: Baedeker editorial team (John Sykes)
Translation: Barbara Schmidt-Runkel
Cartography: Christoph Gallus, Hohberg; MAIRDUMONT/Falk Verlag, Ostfildern (map)
3D illustrations: jangled nerves, Stuttgart
Design: independent Medien-Design, Munich; Kathrin Schemel

Editor-in-chief: Rainer Eisenschmid, Baedeker Ostfildern

1st edition 2009
Based on Baedeker Allianz Reiseführer »Florida«, 8. Auflage 2008

Copyright: Karl Baedeker Verlag, Ostfildern
Publication rights: MAIRDUMONT GmbH & Co; Ostfildern

Printed in China

DEAR READER,

We would like to thank you for choosing this Baedeker travel guide. It will be a reliable companion on your travels and will not disappoint you.
This book describes the major sights, of course, but it also recommends the best beaches, as well as hotels in the luxury and budget categories, and includes tips about where to eat or go shopping and much more, helping to make your trip an enjoyable experience. Our authors ensure the quality of this information by making regular journeys to Florida and putting all their know-how into this book.

Nevertheless, experience shows us that it is impossible to rule out errors and changes made after the book goes to press, for which Baedeker accepts no liability. Please send us your criticisms, corrections and suggestions for improvement: we appreciate your contribution. Contact us by post or e-mail, or phone us:

▶ **Verlag Karl Baedeker GmbH**
Editorial department
Postfach 3162
73751 Ostfildern
Germany
Tel. 49-711-4502-262, fax -343
www.baedeker.com
www.baedeker.co.uk
E-Mail: baedeker@mairdumont.com

Baedeker Travel Guides in English at a glance:

▶ Andalusia
▶ Bali
▶ Barcelona
▶ Berlin
▶ Brazil
▶ Budapest
▶ Dubai · Emirates
▶ Egypt
▶ Florida
▶ Ireland
▶ Italy
▶ London

▶ Mexico
▶ New York
▶ Paris
▶ Portugal
▶ Prague
▶ Rome
▶ South Africa
▶ Spain
▶ Thailand
▶ Tuscany
▶ Venice
▶ Vienna